Roman Roads

Frontispiece   Aerial view of Watling Street west of Pennocrucrum, taken by Arnold Baker

Roman Roads

RAYMOND CHEVALLIER

Director of School of Latin Studies, University of Tours

Translated by N. H. Field

University of California Press

Berkeley and Los Angeles 1976

First published in this edition 1976

Raymond Chevallier

Translation © B. T. Batsford Ltd 1976

University of California Press
Berkeley and Los Angeles, California

ISBN 0-520-02834-1

Library of Congress Catalog Card Number 74-82845

Printed in Great Britain

Foreword by
Professor A. L. F. Rivet

It is a great pleasure to be invited to introduce a book by my friend Raymond Chevallier to the English reader. M. Chevallier is already known to a widening circle of British archaeologists as the enterprising editor of the periodical *Caesarodunum*, as the indefatigable organiser of international colloquia on all aspects of the Romano-Celtic world, and, perhaps above all, as the compiler of invaluable bibliographies of Roman Gaul. As the reader will quickly discover, the extensive bibliography is not the least useful part of the present work.

Julius Caesar remarked that in his time the manners and customs of the inhabitants of Britain (at least, of the south-eastern part of it) were in general similar to those of the Gauls. This could hardly be said to-day of British and French archaeologists, for the study and practice of archaeology have developed along rather different lines in the two countries, and especially in respect of things Roman. Some of the reasons for this may be found in our different cultural traditions and specifically in different degrees of continuity with the Roman period. French is a Romance language, English is not. France has a much greater wealth of upstanding Roman monuments than Britain and, unlike Hadrian's Wall, they are almost all of civil, not military, origin and so less likely to be regarded by the ordinary Frenchman as the curious symbols of a remote and alien domination. A hundred French cities preserve in their very names the memory of the tribal states which made up Roman Gaul. Besides this, there is a much greater body of contemporary written material, both literary and epigraphic, relating to Gaul than there is relating to Britain. As a result, it can almost be said that while the British archaeologist digs to create his Roman history, the French archaeologist digs to illustrate it.

And herein lies the particular value of this work to the British reader. It is essentially a French book, written from the French point of view, and the publishers have wisely refrained from trying to anglicise it in any significant way except in the language. It does not seek to instruct the British archaeologist in the identification of Roman roads in Britain – though even here he may find food for thought in some of the methods which M. Chevallier advocates for France. Rather it is concerned to discuss Roman roads in their wider imperial setting and in all their aspects – military,

53942

commercial and administrative – and in so doing brings to notice a vast wealth of comparative material not only from Gaul but from the whole of the Roman Empire. Accordingly, while there is much here that is familiar to the British archaeologist – the use of maps and place-names, for example, and parish or commune boundaries, of air photographs and of the spade – the product of these techniques is all related to its proper historical background and a new picture emerges not only of the roads of Gaul but of those of Britain too. In both cases they are presented not as the subject of a parochial exercise in archaeological expertise but as parts of the vital framework of the great Empire of which both countries once formed part and the book is thus one to be read not merely by archaeologists but by all who take an interest in Roman imperial history.

University of Keele   A. L. F. RIVET

Contents

The Illustrations

Preface to the English edition

As I finish reading the English version of my book on Roman roads I am most anxious to express my gratitude to the author of the foreword, the translator and the publishers. I am happy to say that the work has had a very favourable reception[1], apart from a couple of critics. One is young, as yet without an international reputation, and appears to be looking for an argument with me: as far as I am concerned, a manual (Handbuch) is not a Forschungsbericht, a form of publication anyway which I have contributed to the Mélanges Vogt. In any case it is nonsensical to suggest that the present manual (which has never claimed, be it noted, to be competing with the irreplaceable – and unobtainable – volume by Grenier) is a work with a message. We do not need to think deeply about history to realise that all roads, Roman or not, have fulfilled, either successively or simultaneously, strategic or economic roles: while the *via Aemilia* probably answered 'socio-economic' problems, it also served as a strategic road against the Ligures of the Apennines.

Furthermore, in my view it is valid to compare streets in towns with roads in the countryside, if only because neglecting the continuity of usage linking both groups is the best way of not understanding the influence of topography on settlement

---

[1] The book has been awarded the Prix Broquette-Gonin by the French Academy.

x

and the salient features of the landscape, too often unrecognised until the very recent problems spotlighted by the Congress on Greater Greece.

In general, my critics have appreciated

the range of information;

the use of illustrative material that has been taken not just from archaeological works, but also from literary sources, including some technical details (though the latter admittedly are not numerous enough, even allowing for the need to select);

the importance of the bibliography (although one critic considers it too long) and its classification, always allowing that some titles might figure under different headings. But it is no good blaming me for not listing all the entries in the Real-Encyclopadie that have any connection with the subject.

Is this the place to justify shortcomings? Given the fact that in describing the road network of the Empire the accent would be on Gaul and Italy, I was well aware that I would displease the specialist interested in Andorra or Lichtenstein. But was the purpose of filling pages and pages with lists of stations to be found in the various editions of the itineraries?

In all event I thank my teachers, friends and colleagues, particularly Monsieur Hano, who have been kind enough to point out a number of errors. These have been corrected in the present edition, which also includes additions to the index.

RAYMOND CHEVALLIER

Introduction

HOW ROADS BEGAN

The earliest roads were the work of the elements and wild beasts, mere huntsmen's trails, as Fustier has recalled in a recent book. The hunter is well aware of the fairly regular movements of game animals, instinctively drawn towards country where they may find their prey or where there is pasture or water. In uplands such tracks will fit in as a normal course with the rise and fall of the ground. It is an interesting experiment to study how footpaths, with their smooth curves, always aim at avoiding natural obstacles. We should take a closer look at ancient ways along which transhumance occurred.

It is in this light that Dion has given a masterly introduction to the study of the geography of traffic in France[1]. If the use of the horse and the wheeled vehicle seems right enough on the steppes, such was not the case in Gaul until the forest cover had been penetrated. In the forest one has to walk in single file. In this way arose the ridge-way, little affected by erosion, and the 'drailles' of the South of France may have been brought about by animal migration. Changes in climatic conditions play an important part here: we know that the horse was first driven towards the grass-lands of Central Europe by the extension of forests at the end of the Palaeolithic. The horse was seen again in the West as a domesticated animal after the arrival of the ox at a time when forest clearance was taking place at the hands of the earliest farmers. 'The history of human movement is closely connected with the develop-ment of agriculture, and we may usefully note that there has been a contrast in France since the Bronze Age between those regions already converted into open country and provided with a stock of sheep and horses and with an array of wheeled vehicles and other regions which by contrast were strongholds of the forest belt.' In the first group Dion gives as an example Champagne, where La Tène burials show that swift, light war chariots with two wheels were in use. The broad plains of North-Western Europe, together with gaps and valleys, have usually encouraged human movement. On the other hand, claylands have been a handicap.

What archaeological evidence is at our disposal? The wheel seems to have been known in Mesopotamia as early as 3000 BC. There are clay models of four-wheeled waggons in the Danube valley about 2000 BC and wheels of solid wood, belonging to the same period, have been found in the Low Countries. This progress west-wards of the wheel is certainly connected with the movement of prehistoric peoples. In this way the two-wheeled war chariot was introduced into Western Europe (it is mentioned in Caesar's account of the Gallic Wars[2] and was still in service in Britain during the first century AD, as Tacitus makes clear in his *Agricola*[3]). From the end of the Bronze Age, there were wheels with felloe and spokes made of metal. The technique was still being perfected in the Early Iron Age. It has been possible for Joffroy to put together the parade chariot of the princess of Vix thanks to the careful recording of the position of all the metallic parts, followed by com-parison with similar finds elsewhere (the chariots from Ohnenheim, Dejbjerg and Bell im Hunsrück), and the support of the Nancy laboratory (A. France-Lanord). We may refer to the long description given by the author of *The Treasure of Vix*[4]: wheels with iron tyres and spokes jointed into the felloe and bosses covered with overlapping bronze plates, together with a steerable limber and a chariot frame that could be taken to pieces. Other evidence could also be quoted: the early chariot from La Côte-Saint-André[5], the Gallo-Roman chariot (second or third century AD) from Fa (Aude), the bronze-cast wheels of which are on show in the Musée Saint-Raymond at Toulouse, as well as a piece of decorative gear from the same source.

What kinds of road may be associated with these vehicles? It is difficult to say, but there were expedients certain to have been used: on swampy ground, corduroy roads and, in mountainous country, rutted tracks.

ROADS IN EARLY HISTORY AND LEGEND

Happenings in myth and legend may well recall actual events of long ago. Just as the *Odyssey* has given epic form to early Mycenean voyages, so the travels of the Argonauts and the myth of the Hyperboreans merely seem to mask the sea-routes along which Mediterranean bronze was exchanged for Baltic amber. In the same way, the myths that have as their theme the journeys made by Dionysos allow us to follow the movement of Greek wine on its way to the Barbarians, for one of the aims of colonisation was always to produce wine in the immediate neighbourhood of those peoples who had been buying it at a high price.

The Myceneans had already fallen under the spell of the Mediterranean Far West, as represented by Tartessos, if we are to believe Ulysses' visit to Calypso. These contacts between both ends of the Mediterranean were even more ancient than this, judging by the legend of Heracles going to seize Geryon's cattle[6]. This story helped Greek merchants to stand up to Phoenician claims of complete con-trol over the route to the Spanish orefields and the sea-ways to amber and gold. Pytheas was to undertake his exploration in the wake of the Hero. In his *Promenades du pays de la Dame de Vix*, Carcopino has suggested how the spread of the same folk tale brought the Hero as far as Alesia.

Likewise, the return of the Argonauts, best known through the *Argonautica* of Apollonius Rhodius[7], as they passed from the Danube across to the Adriatic, then up the Po and the Ticino and over the Alps, to come down the Reuss Valley, across Lake Lucerne, then along the Aar and the Rhine, from which point the goddess Hera forced them to return towards the Aar, Lake Neuchâtel, Lake Geneva and the Rhône, provides an example in legend of the use of the trunk route along the Danube and the Sava, linking the Black Sea and the Adriatic by easy overland portage. Dion has emphasised a statement by Strabo giving credence to this journey: 'Everyone agrees that the expedition of the Argonauts and their halts on particular islands are facts of which the authenticity cannot be denied. Until the Roman period, the river Ister or Danube was very little known and there were no clear ideas about its upper course. The river and its tributaries were confused with the trade-routes opened up along their valleys.' This explains why we find in Herodotus the notion of a Danube splitting Europe in two, along a line extended by the Po, the Durance and the route skirting the foothills of the Pyrenees. Dion has shown[8] that the story of Heracles illustrated this second part of the great highway across Europe. Jason, we may remember, did not manage to go beyond the Swiss plateau, whereas he had been thinking of sailing round Western Europe by emerging from the mouth of the Rhine and then passing through the Strait of Cadiz. To explain this anomaly, Jullian, in an inspired moment, has suggested: 'Let us imagine that La Tène was a great Celtic market-centre and further that the Greeks had either the right or the opportunity of going through it, but were forbidden to go beyond, then the fact that the Argonauts had to halt finds a satisfactory explanation and all that Juno did was to remind them of the regulations imposed by the local inhabitants.'

Thus it was that along these routes, and especially where fairs were held[9], the crafty Mediterranean traders made sure they were preceded by Greek Heroes, who were shown as being, on the one hand, tough towards the wicked – whether these were brigands or simply hostile to buying and selling[10] – and, on the other hand, well disposed towards those who welcomed them as guests. These Heroes, whose exploits illustrated the great trade routes, were to some extent guarantors under whose authority future dealings were to take place. It was thanks to their support that it was possible to establish openly vital claims to spheres of influence in the face of later competitors.

A number of other legends appear to deserve an explanation of this kind, for example, the story of Diomedes in Italy that throws light on the roads crossing the Apennines.

Some texts of classical date, which belong no longer to myth, but to history, and which hint at an ancient system of genuine trade routes, together with archaeological evidence, allow us to trace some of these highways, which may have specialised in the movement of one particular product, tin or amber. Thus Herodotus (v, 9–10)[11] draws attention to a strange folk, 'nomadic traders', who used to hawk their wares from waggons, along the Danube as far as the borders of the Veneti, and were known to the Ligures in the hinterland of Marseilles.

This very route is mentioned in a text of Pseudo-Aristotle (*De mirabilibus auscultis,* 85): 'They say that from Italy as far as Celtica, in the territory of the Celtoligures and the Iberians, there is a road bearing the name of the Heraclean Way. Should a Greek or a local man venture along it, the inhabitants make sure that no harm befalls him, as they would bear the penalty.'

The profits drawn from tolls and portage do explain why those who dwelt by roads should have become expert, during the later prehistoric period, in maintaining and safeguarding some routes, particularly where these passed through ports, along rivers and over mountains, as, for example, the Celts in the case of the Alpine passes[12]. This role as guide, well attested in historical times[13], has long been considered by mountain folk to be their prerogative[14]. This was pointed out in the sixteenth to eighteenth centuries by travellers crossing the Alps or the Apennines.

It is worth quoting the famous passage from Diodorus, referring to the tin routes (v, 22, written between 60 and 30 BC, but using much earlier sources, such as Timeas, third century BC, and Posidonius, 100 BC): 'The traders who buy tin [in Britain] transport it over to Gaul, which they then cross on foot in 30 days, with their load on pack horses, to reach the mouth of the Rhône.' Another passage confirms this statement: 'A large amount of tin coming from the British island finds its way over to the shore of Gaul opposite. Through Celtica, the traders take it by pack-horse to the people of Marseilles and the town called Narbonne.' Dion[15] has shown that this route goes along the estuary of the Gironde and the valley of the Garonne by way of Bordeaux, Toulouse and Narbonne.

But several highways were being used at the same time or one after another. As the numerous middlemen were unaware of the extremities of the chain, discussion is by no means finished on the possible courses, particularly since the journeys were often a combination of transport by land and by water, going up the valleys of the navigable rivers as far as the gaps, where portage became necessary:

> the Seine valley – Vix – the Burgundy gap, the Saône–Rhône or the Swiss plateau and the Alpine passes;
> the Loire valley – portage possible from several places (Roanne) – the Rhône valley;
> the Garonne valley (Carcassonne or Naurouze gap).

What is certain is that the Mediterranean penetrated a long way, right into Germany where Tacitus[16] came upon the tracks of Ulysses. So, from that time on, there had been a spread of cultural influence: the discovery of the Hirschlanden warrior, the most northerly *kuroi* to be sculptured by a native, and which has its counterpart in the Entremont statues, throws light, according to Benoît[17], on the legend mentioned by Tacitus that Northern Celtica had been hellenised. Ulysses had been attributed with the foundation of the naval station at Asciburgium, identified as Eschenburg, near Duisburg, on the Rhine, a depôt on the amber and tin trade routes. At the time of the historian, there would still have been in existence monuments bearing Greek inscriptions at the cross-roads between Germany and Rhaetia. Since the dawn of history, the discovery of relief sculpture has provided vital clues in tracing the great highways of trade. In the same way, the find spots of products from Greece and Etruria and of coins and pottery from Marseilles pinpoint the roads along the valley of the Rhône and along the Pre-Alps (the upland route parallel with, and east of, the Rhône).

The situation was the same throughout the Roman West on the eve of the Roman conquest. Everywhere, there were tracks in use by traders, who almost always preceded the soldiery. On the coinage of the Arverni, the amphora symbolises the economic stranglehold of Italic merchants on a Celtica that was still free; there are amphorae all along the road bringing wine from Marseilles.

That such land tracks existed and were used by Hannibal[18] is supported by the migration made by the Helvetii in waggons and by the swiftness of Caesar's movements in Gaul. The Roman general also mentions engineering works, such as the bridges over the Loire[19].

It is clearly difficult to date these roads. Distribution maps can help in this direction by showing the archaeological material found in association with these routes, particularly at focal points such as fords and passes. It is helpful, too, to note links with the *oppida*[20], as for example in the case of the *oppidum* of the Caisses de Mouriès (fourth to third centuries BC), lying at the entrance of the valley of the Vallongue. This valley connected the Crau lowland with the fords over the Durance and was a prehistoric track used in the seasonal movement of herds and improved in the Roman period. Cassini's map, on which the extent of forest cover is clearly displayed, brings out a chain of clearings linked by age-old paths. If we turn to the case of Vermand, the *oppidum* that was replaced by Saint-Quentin, we find that each was the centre of a different road network, suggestive of development at successive times, probably within the Roman period. Agrippa may have been responsible during his residence in Gaul, first 39–37 then 19 BC. The time had come when a Roman town managed to attract to itself a pre-existing network of native roads, some of which were already in service close to the new centre.

Evidence from literature and inscriptions

1 LATIN WORDS FOR ROADS AND STREETS

A look at the ancient language at this point is extremely useful, since it throws light on the economy and in a more general way, on the civilisation of Rome. Besides, this will enable us to understand some of the very revealing place names, whose importance will be emphasised later.

André[1] has shown how the Indo-European name for road or track (its derivative in Latin, *pons*, developed a special sense) was replaced by groups of words closely connected in meaning with the ground surface and with everyday living, words to be expected from a nation of peasant farmers. Thus we find: *via,* a carriage road, allowing two vehicles to pass (from *vehere*); *semita,* a small path, one foot wide, dedicated to the goddesses, the Semitae, a way between two garden-beds; *vicus,* first a country township, then a city street; *callis,* a track used for seasonal trans-humance (whence the Spanish 'calle'); *trames,* a mountain path at right angles to the line of the crest. Some words have evolved from the concrete to the abstract or vice versa: *iter,* a route, a connecting road, a right of way, a footpath (two feet wide, for travellers on foot, horsemen or litters); *actus* (from *agere,* to drive cattle) a right to drive animals, then a track for animals, later for vehicles, a one-lane road of four feet; *limes,* a road of bare soil (cf. *limus,* mud ?), often acting as a boundary, a byroad, a subdivision for centuriation, then a road outside the ramparts, finally in the special military sense of a fortified frontier-work. The following words may also be mentioned: *agger,* a causeway forming a road[2]; *compendiaria,* a short cut; *flexus,* a fork or a turning.

With the development of town life there appear words that are strictly urban:

vicus takes the meaning of district, then street, while *semita,* originally footpath, in towns becomes pavement or sidewalk (*margo* and *crepido* are also found). In addition to *via,* for the street is simply the prolongation of the highway (for example, the city section of the *Flaminia* is called *via Lata*), we find the following: *ambulatio,* a public walk open to the sky (whereas the *porticus* had a roof)

angiportus, a lane or alley between houses (according to ancient Roman law the owner had to be able to go right round his dwelling)
area, a threshing-floor, then an open space
clivus, an ascending or descending street
forum, a market place, originally the enclosure within the Indo-European house
fundula, a cul-de-sac
pervium, a town thoroughfare
platea, an approach road, then a square
scalae, steps or stairs.

Except for *angiportus* and *fundula,* these are all former rural words with changed meanings. The evolution of the words *actus* (cf. above) and *limes* (which has a variety of adjectives) reflect the way in which local services and dues were given legal form.

Via, having entered general use, finds competition in the third century from *strata* (*via* is meant), indicating first of all an embanked road, so giving us 'strada', 'strasse', 'street'.

In some districts, *via* is replaced by *rupta* (*via*), the beaten track, the root of the French 'route'.

In Vulgar Latin, *furca* and *quadrifurcus* are found instead of *bivium* and *quadrivium*.

Ruga ('rue') is used figuratively in early Romance in place of *vicus,* whilst a Celtic word forms the root of the French 'chemin', the Italian 'cammino', and the Spanish 'camino'.

It would be interesting to discover from official documents drawn up in Greek exactly how these words were translated from Latin. These equivalents would throw light on the way in which semantic changes occurred by means of analogy.

2 THE ROAD IN LATIN LITERATURE

One would expect to find, especially in the Histories, detailed information on the construction and use of roads, which were the basis of Roman power. But this is far from the case, since history was for the Romans above all the study of politics and of human behaviour.

The following is the result of a close examination of what is left of Livy's works[3].

Only seven times is there mention of the building of roads by civil magistrates:

IX, 29: the censor Appius Claudius, responsible for the Appian Way.

IX, 43: the censors Bubulcus and M. Valerius Maximus, builders of local roads (*viae per agros*) at State expense.

X, 23: the *aediles curules,* with the money obtained from confiscating the wealth of usurers, had the road from the Capena Gate to the Temple of Mars resurfaced with paving-stones.

X, 47: use by the *aediles* of fines levied on farmers grazing animals on public pasture in order to pave the *via Lavicana* from the Temple of Mars as far as Bovillae.

XXXVIII, 28: the repaving of a Roman street leading from the Capena Gate to the Gate of Mars undertaken by private enterprise.

XXXIX, 44: the censor Flaccus had a highway built, in the interests of the people, leading to the waters of Neptune and had a road tunnelled through the mountain of Formies.

XLI, 32: the censors were the first to put out for tender paving the city streets, gravelling and embanking the highways, and building bridges at a number of points . . .; they had the way up to the Capitol paved.

One passage only mentions the building of roads by the army:

XXXIX, 2: After having pacified Liguria, Aemilius had his army build a road from Piacenza to Rimini to join the via Flaminia . . . After restoring peace to his province, the consul Flaminius would not allow his soldiers to remain inactive and had them build a road from Bologna to Arretium.

Some references are incidental:

2nd, 3rd and 8th milestones of the *via Gabina* (II, 11; III, 6; V, 49). 3rd mile of the *via Salaria* close to the Arno bridge (VII, 9), 8th milestone of the *via Appia* (VII, 39), statue of Mars on the same road (XXII, 1, in connection with a portent), the *via Nomentana* formerly named *Ficulensis* (III, 52, at the time of the mutiny on the Sacred Mountain).

What is shown in particular is the manner in which the army made use of the roads:

IV, 41: a consul returning from campaign along the *via Lavicana,* close to Fanum Quietis. Horses and waggons are sent there from the city to pick up the troops exhausted by battle and a night's marching.

XXII, 11: the dictator going off along the *via Flaminia* to meet the consul and the army.

XXII, 55: after Cannae, Q. Fabius Maximus has light cavalry dispatched along the *via Appia* and the *via Latina* to question the fugitives.

XXVI, 8: a more enlightening text: the proconsul Q. Fulvius proceeded along the *via Appia,* sending messengers ahead to all the towns on that road, such as Setia, Cora and Lanuvium, so that there should be food ready in those towns, brought in from the surrounding countryside.

XXXIX, 2: the pursuit of the Ligures in the Apennines over difficult tracks.

Roman roads were sometimes used by the enemy:

II, 39: C. Marcius on the *via Latina*.

IX, 43: the Samnites cut the roads and occupy the passes.

X, 36: the Samnites try to seize Interamna on the same road.

XXVI, 8: Hannibal goes along it.

Except for the previous references, the streets of Rome are seldom mentioned:

a statue of Clelia on horseback at the top of the Sacred Way (II, 13);
people killed by lightning in the *via Fornicata* (XXII, 36);
demolition by order of the censors of houses projecting onto the public highway (XXXIX, 44).

The geographers (Strabo, Pliny the Elder, Pausanias) provide more information but a great deal again can be found in the vast number of written sources. As regards Syria, for example, the authors used by Father Poidebard are Josephus, Ammianus Marcellinus[4], Plutarch, Dio Cassius and Procopius, without counting the Road Itineraries. *

TRAVELS OF A RICH CITIZEN – PLINY THE YOUNGER

As an example of the movements of a wealthy Roman, we may consider those of Pliny the Younger, whose *Letters* provide us with some details.

His main reason for travelling was to visit his estates, for 'there is enchantment in a change of air and landscape and even in merely journeying around one's properties' (III, 19, 4, cf. I, 3, 2; IX, 15, 3: 'I mount my horse and I play my part as landlord by riding around'; IV, 14, 8: 'I travel about my holdings and listen to many a countryman's tale of woe').

More often all he is seeking is the physical exercise and the uplift from seeing new places (IV, 14; VII, 4–8; IX, 36: 'I get into my carriage.' He has the same interest when passing along the garden walks in his villas as when out riding, cf. V, 6, 17. 'My mind maintains its alertness, refreshed by the very change.'). In this respect he followed the example of his uncle, Pliny the Elder, who used to work with his secretary on his travels, and even in Rome, borne along in his litter (III, 5).

The reasons for moving around might be trivial – sight-seeing, a delight in the oddities of nature, 'which set us going on our travels, down the road and across the sea, yet leave us unmoved if they lie within sight.' (VIII, 8, 20). Or the reasons may be serious: 'I had been away in Tuscany to preside over the first stages in the construction of a public monument being built at my expense, having obtained leave of absence as Prefect at the Treasury', while it is his important mission to Bithynia, on which Book X of the *Letters* gives us such useful details (journeys into the Province, official reception of magistrates, embassies, travel permits, messengers).

In a letter about the illness of the freedman Zosmius (V, 19), whom Pliny sent first to Egypt, then to Fréjus, because he was spitting blood, we learn also that people used to travel for their health.

It has been possible to find only three other quotations about travelling conditions: the employment of a closed carriage one day when Pliny was suffering from eye-strain (VII, 21) the sandy build-up of the track which, forking off from the *via Laurentina* or the *via Ostiensis,* led to his villa of the Laurentes (II, 17: 'Horse-carriages move along it slowly and with some difficulty, but it is a short road and a good one for a horseman'). Finally a worrying item of news, which shows that brigandry had remained endemic in Italy, namely the disappearance of a centurion in the course of a journey (VI, 25).

The *Lives of the Twelve Caesars* by Suetonius acquaints us with the manner in which the Emperors travelled and their reasons for so doing. We pick out at random:

Caesar, XXXIV: from Corfinium to Brindisi, passing down the Adriatic coast, then off to Spain. LVIII: the crossing from Brindisi to Dyrrachium in winter.

Augustus, who preferred to travel by water, did not hesitate to face storms (LXXXII), but he travelled to Egypt following the coast of Syria and Asia (XVII). In his later years, he used a litter for travelling, almost always at night, at a slow speed and in short stages, taking two days to journey to Praeneste or Tibur.

Tiberius, who, as a young man, travelled extensively (cf. XI: sea-voyage as far as the Rhône, XIV: crossing of Macedonia for an expedition into Syria), did not move far in his old age (XXXVIII, XL, LXXII, returning from Capri to the outskirts of Rome in a trireme and on another occasion approaching the city along the *via Appia*). He was not, however, free from sudden impulses, and in case he wished to make journeys into the provinces, made sure that necessary supplies were available in the *municipia* and the *colonia*. (XXXVIII)[5].

Caligula, when leaving on an expedition, hesitated between two extremes, either so swift a travel rate that the praetorian cohorts were obliged, in order to keep up with him, to put their standards on pack animals, or so slow a speed that he was able to be borne along in a litter by eight bearers, while ensuring that ahead of him the local *plebs* swept and watered the road to keep down the dust (XLIII). He too went in for sight-seeing and visited the river Clitumnus and its sacred grove at Mevania (ibid.).

Claudius, on his way from Ostia to Britain, was twice almost shipwrecked because of storms. So he travelled overland from Marseilles to Boulogne (XVII). A keen gambler, he kept up his dicing in a carriage specially arranged for the purpose (XXXIII).

Vitellius would display his gluttony in wayside taverns 'seizing almost from the very fire dishes that were still steaming or leftovers from the day before and half-eaten food'. The same *Life* (XIV) informs us that the Emperor was not exempt from road tolls.

Vespasian (XXI) went about in a litter.

Titus (V) made his way to Paphos to consult the oracle of Venus.

Domitian (XIX) during campaigns or when travelling seldom rode a horse but normally used a litter.

These snippets of information (there are many others in the *Scriptores Historiae Augustae*) lack some of the details we should like today. However, Suetonius gives us some interesting information about imperial policy for roads, which were mainly constructed for the purpose of prestige. Such a policy had already been thought up by one C. Gracchus, who, according to Appian, 'had great roads built the length and breadth of Italy and set to work on his behalf a horde of workmen of every kind, ready to do all he wanted'[6]. We may quote from Suetonius:

> Caesar's plans (XLIV): the construction of a road from the Adriatic Sea to the Tiber over the ridge of Apennines, the digging of a canal across the Isthmus of Corinth (an idea taken up by Nero, XIX), the enthusiastic erection of a bridge over the Rhine (XXV).
> the more realistic and successful efforts of Augustus:
> XXX: repairs at his own expense to the *via Flaminia* as far as Arminum, the other roads being 'shared amongst the generals honoured by a triumph, who had to find the money for this out of their battle-spoils'.
> XXXII: the suppression of brigandry by setting up military posts along the roads, for 'in the country districts travellers were being kidnapped and were being held within the *ergastula* of the villa-owners themselves'.
> XXXVII: a department was created to look after public works, highways, water-supplies and the river Tiber.

These measures were repeated by Tiberius:

> VIII: Suetonius comes back to the subject of lawlessness on the roads: 'Workshop owners were suspected of holding on to travellers as slaves after having received them as guests';
> XXXI: the Emperor made an unsuccessful request to the citizens of Treba that they should authorise for the upkeep of a road a sum of money bequeathed to them for the construction of a theatre;
> XXXVII: he increased the number of military posts throughout Italy, a move justified when the inhabitants of Pollentia halted a supply column in the charge of a senior centurion.

Caligula (XIX) 'caused to be built between Baiae and the Pozzuoii jetty a bridge that was made up of barges covered with soil so that the whole thing looked like the *via Appia*. According to most reports, Caligula's idea was that such a bridge would rank with the one built by Xerxes, but others held that he was trying to terrify the Germans and Britons, then making warlike threats, with the news of a vast engineering feat.'

Claudius (XXV) issued a decree forbidding travellers to go through Italian towns other than on foot, in a sedan chair or in a litter.

The *adventus* evolved considerably in the Early Empire. When Caligula came back from Germany, the praetorian cohorts marched ahead of him and the people of Rome ventured out as far as the twentieth milestone (cf. the triumphal entries made by emperors on horseback or in a chariot: Otho, X, and Vitellius, X).

Likewise the *Historia Augusta* and inscriptions yield information on Hadrian's journeys.

THE SUBJECT OF TRAVEL IN THE 'METAMORPHOSES' BY APULEIUS

This work suggests a very mobile society. Who was travelling and why?

> sightseeing: 'I was still in the charge of my guardian, when, having come from Miletus to attend the Olympic Games, I made up my mind to look round that part of the illustrious province in which we lived' (II, 21);
> religious purposes: Lucius went to Rome for initiation (XI); the priests of the Syrian goddess were begging their way from town to town (VIII, 24);
> business reasons: 'I was proceeding to Thessalia on business' (I, 2); 'I trade in honey, cheese and other foodstuffs of that kind used by innkeepers and I go all over Thessalia' (I, 5).

Before leaving on a journey, as people were superstitious – 'I had started off left foot first and so I was foiled of my expected profit' (I, 5) – the advice of the gods was sought:

> 'A Chaldean states which day is best chosen for travelling by road or propitious for putting to sea' (II, 12)[7];
> 'A business man consults a fortune-teller to know the best day for a journey' (II, 13);
> 'quack priests made up a single augury which could be applied in a number of cases: "If oxen are yoked and straightaway plough their furrow, that is a sign that their efforts will yield a rich harvest". Was there someone with a journey in mind who wished to receive the omens vouchsafed by the goddess? Then the most docile animals in the world, already yoked, were ready to hand for him and what the soil would yield guaranteed a successful outcome' (IX, 8).

How did people travel? Moving around was expensive: when Lucius went to Rome, his outlay 'melted away his humble inheritance' (XI, 28). People travelled on foot, on horseback or on a mule, in two- or four-wheeled vehicles (*carpentum, raeda*), the rich having a whole escort: 'Thiasus showed disdain for his luxury carriages and used to turn his nose up at their rich furnishings. The useless vehicles were pulled along in the rear of his retinue, with their curtains indifferently up or down, while he displayed the same little consideration for his Thessalian steeds and for his Gallic horseteams, creatures of noble breed and well prized' (he preferred his mule named Lucius) (X, 18).

On the road, the going was rough and there were many obstacles:
'Did we have to cross the river flowing beside the road?' (VII, 18). The track is sometimes 'heavily rutted, now a morass of stagnant water, now covered by a layer of slippery mud'. This must often have been the case in winter[8]. Elsewhere there was 'a lane that was a mass of stones and obstructed by tree-stumps of every kind' (IX, 9)[9].

At the staging-point, hospitality was exchanged at the inn (I, 4), and story-telling was common (IX, 4), but comfort was limited: 'My couch, besides being rather short, had a leg missing and was worm-eaten' (I, 11)[10].

Self-respecting travellers putting up in towns went to houses for which they had letters of introduction (I, 21), for example the military courier who went to a decurion's house (x, 1).

At the end of the day, the weary traveller made a few purchases at market and in particular went to recover at the baths (I, 5; I, 24), before giving his hosts 'news of his native country, its leading men, its governor' (I, 26), which was then a common way of learning about current events.

Road travelling was indeed arduous.

It was little use whiling away the length of a journey by exchanging stories, whether they were true or imaginary: 'He held us so spellbound with an entertaining tale that I came to the end of that long and difficult climb without discomfort and without boredom' (I, 3, 20). Many dangers lay in wait for the traveller both on the road and at the posting-station.

There was the misadventure of the trader who travelled through Macedonia on business. After nine months of hard work, he came back with plenty of cash, only to be attacked by brigands, then looked after by an old woman who was running an inn (I, 6f.).

Then we have the case of the gardener who was going to the neighbouring town and met a soldier (IX, 39) travelling to Rome by order of his senior officer with a letter for the Emperor (x, 13). The legionary 'asked him in a haughty and arrogant manner where he was taking that unburdened ass', then managed to seize the animal (x, 1) and loaded it with his gear, helmet, shield and javelin.

Other awkward encounters took place with dogs and wolves: 'When the farmers on a country estate near which we were passing[11] saw us in such numbers, they thought we were brigands . . . They sent after us huge dogs' (VIII, 17, to be compared with IX, 36, where we learn of 'farm dogs, enormous, savage creatures, accustomed to feeding on corpses left in the fields and trained in addition to bite without any distinction all passing wayfarers'); 'packs of huge wolves had reached the point of besieging the roads and attacking travellers in the same way as bandits . . . Travellers must walk in groups and keep close together' (VIII, 15).

Sometimes there were meetings with police patrols: 'and behind us comes a squad of armed horsemen' (IX, 9). More often the meeting could be with robbers: 'Don't you realise that the roads are swarming with brigands, starting on your way at this time of night?' (I, 15)[12].

Long journeys included sea-crossings: 'My brother, tell me how your journey has gone, by land and sea, since you left the isle of Euboea' (II, 13) and 'Travelling partly by land, partly by sea, we finally reached Corinth' (x, 19).

Such crossings were hazardous and the writer pointed out 'the thousand and one difficulties of the trip and the terrors of the sea' (VII, 6) even when it was only a matter of coastal traffic: 'The passengers, seeing that the night was well advanced, had retired to bed to avoid the rough sea in a small inn near to the coast and the ship' (VII, 7).

Regarding the cult of the *mare clausum* and the *navigium Isidis* we may simply refer to Rougé's commentary: *Recherches sur l'organisation du commerce maritime en Méditerranée sous l'Empire romain*[13].

In spite of all the handicaps so depicted, the *Metamorphoses* show that people enjoyed travelling, because mobility was a keynote of society, and also because the author, inquisitive to see everything, liked new surroundings.

We may conclude the theme of travel as an aid in character-training, with this reference to the beginning of the *Odyssey*: 'Wishing to present to us a man of match-less wisdom, Homer wrote of him that he had acquired the highest virtue by visiting many cities and making friends amongst many nations' (IX, 13)[14].

THE SYMBOLISM OF TRAVEL

It is impossible to study the subject of travel in the literature of Antiquity without recalling the symbolic meaning attached to it, since at least as far back as Parmenides' poem, which was wholly based on the figurative image of the Road and the Gate.

The Roman liked travelling on business or for amusement. One of Seneca's letters (III, 28) rests on this assumption and might be given the title: 'Journey into the Land of the Soul': 'You are surprised that you have made such a long journey and by such a variety of routes, yet you have not dispelled the gloomy heaviness within your heart? You need a change of soul, not of clime . . . It serves no purpose to be unsettled in this way. You ask why you find no relief in running off. It is because you are still with yourself.'

But the commonest form of symbolism was the allegory of the Last Journey: as early as the Etruscans, the passage into the next life was thought of and represented as a journey, by land or by sea. Some Roman mosaic floors illustrate this crossing over to the Isles of the Blessed. For some sects, the journey took place through the air, as in the case of the Pythagoreans, who believed in the identity of the soul and the stars. This explains one important aspect of the symbolism associated with funerary monuments: the deceased is seated in a vehicle (we must not forget, after all, the importance attributed to the horse as a conductor of souls) and is going past a milestone on which the figure was that of the number of years he had lived.

This symbol was also used by the Christian apologists, like Tertullian (*De resurrectione carnis*, 43), for whom the body is compared to a traveller who finally comes back to his own country.

APPENDIX I

A famous text: Horace's journey to Brindisi[15]

When I left mighty Rome, I found bed and board in a modest inn at Aricia[16]. My companion was the rhetorician Heliodorus[17], far and away the most learned of the Greeks. Next we reached the Forum of Appius[18], swarming with sailors and knavish tavern-keepers. We felt lazy enough to cut this stretch in two, whereas travellers who gird up their loins take it in one go: the Appian Way[19] is less tiring to those who are not in a hurry. There, by reason of the water, which was frightful, my stomach and I were on hostile terms and I waited with some impatience for my companions, who were dining.

Already the shadows of night were beginning to creep over the earth and stars were pinpointing the heavens[20]. Then slaves bellowed at boatmen and boatmen at slaves: 'Heave to, here', 'You've got three hundred in'! 'Stop! that's enough.' After the fares had been collected and the mule harnessed, a whole hour went by. The cursed mosquitoes, the frogs of the marshland drove off sleep. Whereupon, after their fill of poor wine, a boatman and a passenger[21] vied in singing of the girl each of them had left behind. At length, the weary passenger fell asleep and the lazy boatman unharnessed his mule and let it out to graze, tying its leading rein to a stone. Then he too started to snore away on his back. And it was already daylight when we found that the boat was not yet under way. So one of us, hot-headed fellow, jumped ashore and, with a stick cut from a willow, belaboured head and back of both mule and boatman. At last, upon the fourth hour[22], no earlier, we came ashore. We washed face and hands in thy waters, O Feronia[23]! Then, after, having had breakfast, we struggled along for three miles to reach the foot of Anxur[24], perched on its white rocks gleaming from afar.

Here the gallant Maecenas and Cocceius were to meet us, both sent as envoys to deal with important matters and both accustomed to bringing together divided friends. Here, too, I made use of a black ointment on my sore eyes. Meantime up came Maecenas and Cocceius[25], together with Fonteius Capito, a man of matchless perfection, so that Antony can have no closer friend[26]. We were not sorry to leave Fundi[27] and its praetor Aufidius Luscus, laughing at the knick-knacks with which that old clerk bedecked himself in his crazy vanity, laughing too at his bordered robe and his broad stripe and his pan of charcoal. Then, weary indeed, we made a long halt in the town of the Mamurrae[28], where Murena[29] provided us with lodging and Capito with board.

Dawn the next day was most delightful: for at Sinuessa[30] we were joined by Plotius, Varius and Virgil. Earth has never borne purer souls, there is no man more attached to them than I. Oh! the embraces and the joy! So long as I have my senses, nothing will compare for me to the delight of friendship.

The little post-house close to the Campanian bridge[31] offered us the shelter of its roof, while the state purveyors dutifully provided wood and salt. Next, at the appointed time, our mules laid aside their panniers at Capua. Maecenas went off for exercise, while Virgil and I retired to sleep, for sport is the enemy of weary eyes and sore stomachs.

Our next stop was at the richly furnished villa of Cocceius, situated above the inns of Caudium. Now come to my aid, Muse; come and help me to recall briefly the contest of wits between the clown Sarmentus and Messius Cicirrus[32] and to give the ancestry of these two adversaries. Messius has a well-known family in Osca; the former mistress of Sarmentus is still alive[33]. With such forebears they came to do battle. First of all Sarmentus: 'You, I must say, are like a wild horse[34].' We laughed. Messius for his part said: 'Agreed' and tossed his head. 'Oh!', said the other man, 'if your forehead had not had its horn removed, what would you not be doing, since you are making such threats, even without it?' The truth is that on the left side of his face a scar had made a nasty gash disfiguring Messius' tousled brow[35]. After many a quip on his Campanian disease and his face, Sarmentus begged him to dance the Cyclops shepherd's dance, saying he would not need a frightful mask nor the buskins of tragedy. Cicirrus was not behind in this: he asked Sermentus if, when he had acquitted himself of his vow, he had given his chain as an offering to the Lares? Simply because he was now a scribe, the rights of his mistress had in no wise been taken away[36]; and, finally, why had he ever run off, since all he required was a pound of corn, skinny, puny creature that he was?

A merry company did we make over that meal[37]. Thence we made our way straight to Beneventum[38], where, in his eagerness to please, our host, was nearly burned up[39] while turning some lean thrushes over the fire. For Vulcan slipped out and the wandering flame spread through the old kitchen, rising to lick the very roof. Then you would have seen the starving guests and the trembling slaves grabbing the meal, and afterwards doing their best to put out the blaze.

Thenceforward Apulia[40] was beginning to reveal its mountains, which I know so well, scorched by the Altino[41] and over which we would never have been able to scramble, had we not found a welcome at a country house in the neighbourhood of Trivicum[42], not without smoke that drew tears[43], for in the hearth were burning damp branches, leaves and all. There, in my complete stupidity, I waited until the middle of the night for a lying wench; however, sleep overcame me, impassioned as I still was; and, while I lay on my back, lustful dreams soiled me.

From that point we were taken 24 miles in Gallic carriages, to halt in a small town whose name cannot be put into verse, though it is easy enough to give some clues[44]: the commonest of things, water, is sold there[45], but the local bread is quite magnificent, so much so that the wise traveller takes a quantity with him as he goes on his way, for at Carnusium[46] the bread is as hard as stone[47], while there is not a jugful of water to be had in this town founded in bygone days by brave Diomedes[48]. Here Varius sorrowfully took leave of his weeping friends.

Next we came to Rubi[49], very weary indeed, for we had gone a very long stage, with conditions made worse furthermore by the rain. The following day, the weather improved, but the track was even viler, until we reached the walls of the little fishing-port of Barium. Then Gnathia, a town built despite the water-nymphs[50], gave us occasion to laugh and make pleasantry: for there people would have it that incense placed on the temple threshold melts without the need of fire. The Jew Apella[51] may believe it; I do not, for I have learnt that the gods spend their time eternally at repose and that, if there are extraordinary phenomena produced by nature, it is not they who, to relieve their boredom, send these things down from their heavenly abode on high[52].

Brundisium[53] is the end of this long tale and this long journey.

(Horace, *Satires*, I, V)

APPENDIX 2

The mountain-passes across the Alps, according to Strabo, the Greek geographer of the Augustan Age

(IV, I, 6.) Sextius [conqueror of the Salyes in 123–22 BC] drove the barbarians from the whole coastline leading from Massalia into Italy . . . He forced them to withdraw a distance of 12 stadia [2·22km] from the sea, along where the coast offers good harbours, and up to 8 stadia [1·48km] at points where it is rocky, but he presented the people of Massalia with the land thus freed.

(IV, I, 2.) The road [from Iberia to Italy] has one alternative leading directly to the Alps and a shorter one through the land of the Voconces. The coastal route, at first in the territory of Massalia, then in that of the Ligusti, is longer, but the passes that it takes to enter Italy are easier since the mountains are already lower in that area.

(IV, 6, 2.) The whole coastline, from the port of Monoecus down to the Tyrrhenian Sea, is exposed to storms and short of harbours, except for shallow moorings and anchorages. Owing to the exceptionally sheer face that the mountains present to the sea, there is only a narrow strip for coastal movement.

(IV, 6, 3.) The Salyes were the first of the Transalpine Celts to come under the domination of the Romans, who fought a long war against both this tribe and the Ligyes, for these two peoples barred the way that led to Iberia along the coast. They were indeed so successful with their brigandry on land and sea that this road was scarcely passable even to large armies. Finally, after 80 years of warfare, the Romans established with difficulty free transit over a width of 12 stadia for travellers on official business[54].

(IV, 6, 6.) Formerly Italy was dominated by a number of small tribes, poverty-stricken and thievish in their ways. Today they have been either wiped out or so completely mastered that the passes leading through their territory, which were formerly few in number and difficult to cross, have now been multiplied and the inhabitants can be regarded as trustworthy, while the roads, thanks to engineering works, are as passable as maybe. Indeed, Caesar Augustus finally suppressed brigandry through road-building . . . In some places, the road is so narrow that it causes giddiness [description of avalanches follows] . . .

(IV, 6, 7.) For the traveller coming from Italy, the road first follows the valley of the Salassi. Then it divides into two [at Aosta], one branch going over the Poeninus as it is called, impassable for vehicles nearer the Alpine crest, the other [the Petit-St-Bernard] crossing more to the west through the territory of the Ceutrones . . .

The Salassi used to wreak havoc with their brigandry on travellers going through their land in order to cross the mountains. Thus, when Decimus Brutus fled from Modena, they made him pay one drachma per head on behalf of himself and his men, and, when Messala had his winter quarters close by [in 34 BC], he had to pay cash for firewood and for the elm-wood needed to make javelins and practice weapons. These folk even went so far one day as to steal money belonging to Caesar Augustus and roll boulders down onto columns of soldiers, with the excuse that they were constructing a road or building bridges over the torrents. However, to end the matter, Augustus subjugated them completely and had them all sold off as warbooty. He then sent in 3,000 Romans who founded the town of Augusta . . . and today there is peace in all the surrounding district as far as the top of the Alpine passes.

(IV, 6, 9.) Tiberius and his brother Drusus took one summer [15 BC] to put an end to the frenzied raids of tribes from beyond the Adriatic.

(IV, 6, 10.) In the exchange of goods between Aquileia and the town called Nauportum the mountain massif of the Carni is crossed in covered waggons. From that point transport is by water.

(IV, 6, 11.) One of the passes which allows movement from Italy into Trans-alpine and Northern Celtica is the one leading to Lugdunum through the land of Salassi. Two routes are possible, one passable for vehicles over most of its length, the other going by the Poeninus, steep and narrow, but short (the Little and the Great St Bernard). Lugdunum lies in the centre of Celtica, of which it forms in a way the citadel, since it lies at the confluence of the rivers and is conveniently placed for the different parts of the country. Agrippa, therefore, made it the point of departure from the main roads: the first crossing the Cévennes Mountains and ending in the land of the Santones in Aquitania, then the one down the Rhine and the one to the Ocean, which is the third and which leads to the Bellovaci and the Ambiani, finally the one going into Narbonensis and to the coast of Massalia, the fourth. But one can also, by leaving on the left Lugdunum and the lands upstream from that town, fork off into the Poeninus itself, cross the Rhône or Lake Lemannus in order to reach the plains of the Helvetii and thence, by a pass which goes over the Jura mountain, reach the land of the Sequani and the Lingones, where the road divides into two, one fork leading to the Rhine, the other to the Ocean.

(IV, 6, 12.) Polybius names only four ways through: the first through the territory of the Ligieni, quite close to the Tyrrhenian Sea, then the one traversing the land of the Taurini and used by Hannibal, next the one taking in the territory of the Salassi, finally the fourth through that of the Rhaetii, all four being steep.

(Strabo, Geography IV)

3 THE ROAD BOOKS

THE *Peutinger Table* AND THE QUEST FOR THE OLD ROADS

The *Peutinger Table,* a medieval copy of an ancient map, found at Worms at the end of the fifteenth century, and given in 1508 to Conrad Peutinger of Augsburg, after whom it is named, is today conserved in the Library of Vienna, Austria. At first sight it is something of a disappointment. It would appear to be a late compila-tion[55], with endless discussion on its ancestry. There has been an attempt to connect it, in a pedigree linking all the Roman road books, with an official document of the first half of the third century, contemporary with the *Forma Urbis* in the Capitol, which itself is derived from the map drawn up under the direction of Agrippa and painted after his death under the Portico of Polla in Rome for propaganda purposes[56].

What is immediately noticeable is the geographical distortion affecting the appearance of the rivers and mountains. It is not enough for people to attribute this to the shape of the material on which the map was drawn. It is claimed that the elongation of the map was caused by the long narrow shape of the parchment roll (6.80 by 0.34 m), a format similar furthermore to that of the version in the Portico. The fact is, the road routes themselves are looked upon as being more or less rectilinear and are drawn independently of each other. There is no guide to the orientation of the roads nor to the significance of their bends and twists, so the road stations are not sited in their correct relative positions.

Here we must realise once more that the Romans, whose utilitarian outlook is well known, were unconcerned with the scientific representation of land-shapes[57] and simply required their maps to give practical information: road distances, the best way of moving from one place to another, amenities (posting-stations, baths – hence the frequency of the symbol indicating bath establishments: namely four buildings in the form of a square, alongside the little illustrations of cities: two towers with pointed roofs).

When he has come to terms with these arrangements, the investigator will more willingly accept the *Table* as it is, without thinking that he is justified from a first view of the map in carving up the information.

For, strangely enough, despite its appearance of having been compiled at a late date, the *Table* enjoys such a reputation that for a province to see one or other of its ancient roads depicted on it is like laying claim to nobility. Hence the many efforts of wasted erudition (we could call them cooked-up, pseudo-philology), aimed at making the *Table* agree with road details garnered elsewhere that fitted more particularly with fanciful etymologies, inspired, one can only say, by local patriotism.

It is certainly possible to accept in the last resort errors in manuscript (examples of figures written one above the other; edges of map portions which have been damaged or where there are omissions at the joins; confusion between different *sigla*: V having become II through separation of the verticals or, conversely, II transformed into V by bringing together the two strokes, confusion between X and V; omission or duplication of a figure, with mistakes having been possibly super-imposed). Present-day publishers and especially scholars have been too inclined to make corrections, by assuming that lines have been omitted or displaced and that figures have shifted, so that one conjectural mistake has brought about another[58].

We find one of the most healthy reactions to this attitude expressed by Colonel J. Baradez, whose knowledge of topography and capacity as a field-worker can hardly be in question[59]. He has written somewhat paradoxically: 'Even the dia-

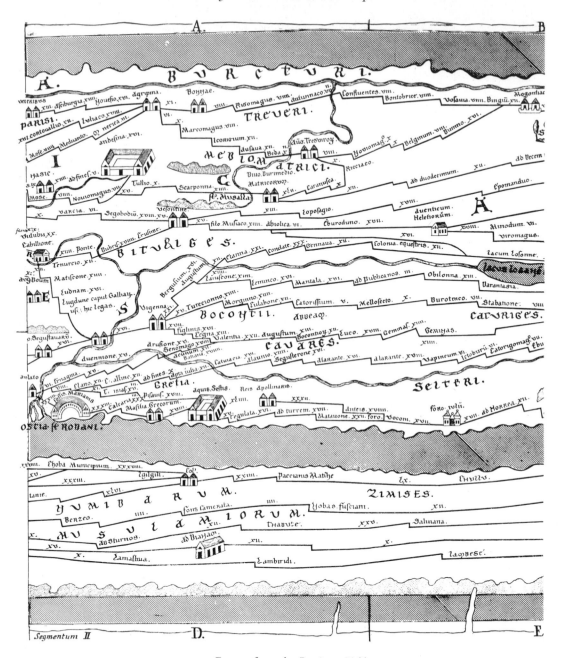

1   Extract from the *Peutinger Table*

grammatic style of presentation in the *Table*, linear as it is, gives me entire satisfaction as a former air force navigator with exacting requirements in the standards of maps.' It must be evident to anyone having an overall view of the whole of a country's road network that the Itineraries 'did not aim at showing in what way one travelled from this point to that, but rather that they chose from amongst the many stretches of road those which, at a particular time and for a particular purpose, allowed movement through particular regions'. Let us not forget that there always have been between two points supplementary routes (as for example, the doubling of tracks close to difficult sections: a steep hill or a ford, sometimes with traffic in one direction only)[60]. Thus the road guides indicate only one of the possible methods of reaching Y from X, since an itinerary may be reckoned to have included different sections of several roads. The difficulties often encountered in working out distances may be explained by the fact that we are dealing with texts compiled at different dates and also because in the course of time changes of line took place. A road may be compared to a vibrating cord, which is taut when the traffic is heavy (with straightening due to short cuts), but is loose and sinuous at slack periods. To become aware of the secret rhythm in the inner life of the countryside, it is enough to take notice of the present-day down-grading of many minor roads. 'The *Peutinger Table*, therefore, describes particular routes involving one after another a series of stretches from the existing network of roads and of connections between these roads. It does not depict any single road. It does not depict either all the roads' (J. Baradez).

The normal scale of the archaeological maps that have been published (1/500,000 or even 1/1,000,000) is anyway deceptive. It is not enough to state that a road goes through two points A and B and then to join them up to obtain an exact line on the ground. Drawing a map of the Roman roads of an area has too often been simply a matter of linking the cantonal capitals, which results in beautiful star patterns. Hence the reputation of Roman roads for being straight, which is correct only in flat country and in the case of the great strategic trunk routes. Elsewhere the straight line very often breaks down. Much fruitless discussion about the distances shown on the *Table* – and these are missing for many cross-routes – arises therefore from a misunderstanding of the actual course of the road on the ground. Let us not forget either that some sections of the Itineraries may correspond to movement by water and that the intervals between stations are given to the nearest mile, so that an error of up to half a mile is possible. It may be that the map is showing the milestone and not the actual distances: Goodchild[61] is of the opinion that lists of milestones were used in compiling the road routes.

As regards the identification of the stations[62], one of Colonel Baradez's revealing suggestions is that the *Table* 'does not always indicate the stations or the population centres that are passed through, these lying frequently off the road, but rather the crossroads and forks[63] where uncertainty or an error in direction were to be feared'. It is from these cross-roads, which the *Table* brings out well, and not from the point of arrival or departure as such, that some distances should be calculated.

There is confirmation of this idea in that the symbols do not always correspond to important places: the network that is depicted does not show the complete network of the Roman roads in the Empire, but those used by the Imperial Post[64]. Audin has noted that the Itineraries are set out so as to avoid difficult slopes, that is, as an aid to heavy transport.

Finally, the *Table* must not be studied on its own, but in conjunction with other road lists, of varying date and purpose, particularly the Antonine Itinerary, a more accurate compilation, it seems. Most important, all possible resources must be brought to bear on the problem: literary texts, inscriptions, archaeological discoveries, place names and – this is something that must be emphasised – examination of the terrain, as it was in the past and as it is today (maps and air photographs), not forgetting fieldwork.

A recent publication, which looks at the *Peutinger Table* against the wider background of the mapwork of antiquity[65], has given a detailed report on the 555 symbolic illustrations of the road amenities. These are:

in particular, a double tower of which only the front is visible (429, with 79 variants and 4 main types); sometimes a half-circle seems to suggest a surrounding ditch;

a building in the form of a temple, of which only the front and one of the sides can be seen (44). Must we take it that this representation indicates the existence of a real temple?

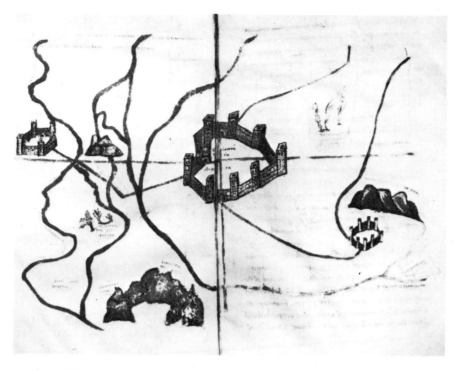

2   Examples of illustrations from the *Peutinger Table* (in order from left to right and top to bottom)
(a) 2 towers linked by a central block (b) independent towers lacking a superstructure (c) twin towers
(d) three towers (e) temple-like buildings (f) bath buildings (g) horrea (h) town of Aquileia (i) town
of Ravenna (j) Rome and St Peter (k) port of Claudius at Ostia (l) pharos (Bosphorus Alexandria)

'spas', bath establishment (and pump-room?) of square plan, of which we have
a bird's-eye view (52) and comprising a central open courtyard with buildings
along the four sides;

a composite building, also seen from above (10), made up of two or more parallel
units, sometimes of differing length, symbolising *horrea*;

city-walls of circular shape, seen in perspective (6);

three larger illustrations, personifying the metropolises of Rome, Constantinople
and Antioch;

two ports, shown as semi-circles (Ostia, Fossae Marianae);

lighthouses (Ostia, Alexandria);

various: altars (at the ends of the known world), a tunnel between Naples and
Pozzuoli (Crypta Neapolitana). We also notice a few landscape details (mountains,
trees).

Some of the little pictures are clearly additions, made in the course of later editing:
at one time, there seems to have been a shift in emphasis towards the East.

The authors think that this can help with the dating. There appear to have been
two phases earlier than the copy as we see it:

one belongs to the beginning of the third century and was edited in the West:

the details are shown on a larger scale because they were closer to the penman[66]; the other is dated to the end of the fourth century or the beginning of the fifth, to which period can be assigned the six walled towns, the illustrations of Constantinople and of Antioch, as well as of the church of St Peter, and a few Christian entries. The laws of the *Theodosian Code* bear witness to the great interest then taken by the Emperors in the *cursus publicus*. This second stage of the map probably dates from Theodosius II, who is thought to have carried out terrestrial measurement. The good relations that the Eastern Roman Empire enjoyed at the beginning of the fifth century with Persia appears to explain the inclusion of certain illustrations depicting stations in the East. The map certainly reflects the extent of geographical knowledge and the administrative organisation of the Empire.

There do not seem to have been any medieval alterations: for in that case, one would notice typical additions such as monsters, more mistakes in the names and more fanciful treatment of the illustrations. A few details have been changed in respect of the three great cities of Rome, Constantinople and Antioch, the symbols for which remind us of thirteenth-century miniatures (the Colmar monk ?).

A ROAD BOOK: THE *Itinerarium Antonini Augusti*

For each route quoted, this road book gives a list of *mansiones* with their distances[67].

The word 'Antonine' seems to refer to Caracalla (212–17), a date confirmed by ground evidence from the roads of Britain and the legionary fortresses. But the whole work probably dates from the end of the century, judging by the mention of titular offices of the time of Diocletian and Maximian (284–305). Some scholars claim to have found in the *Itinerary* references to the raids of 256 and 275 in Gaul[68]. The text also includes later additions. In this respect we could make the same comments as were made for the *Peutinger Table*. Of course, there are many mistakes, especially in the figures (and the successive use of entries in miles and leagues has not yet exhausted the ingenuity of commentators), but those who use the text with care continue to confirm the data in the *Itinerary*. Before correcting the text because we can see nothing but inaccuracies, contradictions, repetitions, and gaps, we should start by considering it in its original state by placing it alongside the information from the other road sources. It must not be forgotten that light will dawn most often following a comparison with maps old and new, with air cover and with the ground itself[69].

According to Kubitschek, the *Itinerary* is based on a wall-map of the time of Caracalla and so would seem to be a clumsy compilation drawn up in the first years of the reign of Diocletian, between 280 and 290, when he was reorganising the *annona*.

Van Berchem's view[70] is that the *Antonine Itinerary*, which is apparently more concerned with listing the greatest possible number of places than with satisfying the real needs of travellers, is in truth a list of *mansiones* connected with the

ITER AB AQVILEIA BONONIAM M. P. CCXVI Sic

CONCORDIA	M. P. XXXI	MVTINA	M. P. XXV
ALTINO	M. P. XXI	BONONIA	M. P. XXV
PATAVIS	M. P. XXXII	A VERCELLIS	LAVDE M. P. LXX Sic
ATESTE	M. P. XXV	LAVMELLO	M. P. XXV
ANNEIANO	M. P. XX	TICINO	M. P. XXII
VICO VARIANO	M. P. XVIII	LAVDE	M. P. XXIII
VICO SERNINO	M. P. XX	A CREMONA BONONIA M. P. CXII Sic	
MVTINA	M. P. XXIII	BRIXELLO	M. P. XXX
BONONIA	M. P. XVIII	REGIO	M. P. XL
A VERONA BONONIA	M. P. CVSic	MVTINA	M. P. XXVII
HOSTILIA	M. P. XXX	BONONIA	M. P. XXV
COLICARIA	M. P. XXV		

ITER A FAVENTIA LVCAM M. P. CXX Sic

IN CASTELLO	M. P. XXV	PISTORIS	M. P. XXV
ANNEIANO	M. P. XXV	LVCA	M. P. XXV
FLORENTIA	M. P. XX		

ITER A PARMA LVCAM M. P. C
VIA CLODIA
ITER A LVCA ROMAM PER CLODIAM M. P. CCXXXVIII Sic

PISTORIS	M. P. XXV	VVLSINIS	M. P. XXX
FLORENTIA	M. P. XXV	FORVM CASSI	M. P. XXVIII
AD FINES SIVE CASAS		SVTRIO	M. P. XI
CAESARIANAS	M. P. XXV	BACCANAS	M. P. XII
ARRETIO	M. P. XXV	ROMA	M. P. XXI
AS STATVAS	M. P. XXV		
CLVSIO	M. P. XII		

ITER A ROMA FORO CLODI M. P. XXXII
ITER AB ARIMINO DERTONAM M. P. CCXXIX Sic

CVRVA CAESENA	M. P. XX	TANNETO	M. P. X
FORO LIVI	M. P. XIII	PARMA	M. P. IX
FAVENTIA	M. P. X	FIDENTIA	M. P. XV
FORO CORNELI	M. P. X	FLORENTIA	M. P. X
CLATERNA	M. P. XIII	PLACENTIA	M. P. XV
BONONIA	M. P. X	COMILLOMAGO	M. P. XXV
MVTINA	M. P. XXV	IRIA	M. P. XVI
REGIO	M. P. XVIII	DERTONA	M. P. X

3 Lists of stations taken from the *Antonine Itinerary*

levying of the *annona*. Among the important roads that he quotes (some often involving detours, others being repeated or confused) there is a very long one going from Rome to Egypt down the Danube and across Asia Minor, reminiscent of a military expedition, in this case the journey to the East made by Caracalla (214–15). The route in question would correspond, furthermore, not to the itinerary actually followed, but to the one that had been prepared. Such movements had indeed to be made ready well in advance and edicts sent to the provincial

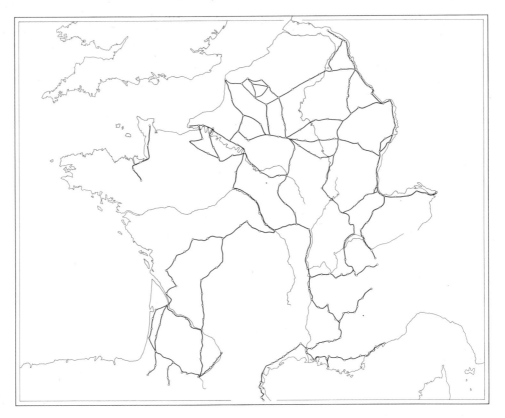

4   Main roads in Gaul, according to the *Antonine Itinerary* (after E. Desjardins, *Géographie de la Gaule*, vol. iv, pl. ii.)

governors would fix the successive road stages, indicate the stay at each station and list orders for the repair of roads (cf. the discovery of milestones along this route) and for the victualling at the *mansiones* of the Imperial court and the troops. We are aware of this through the *Life* of Septimius Severus in the *Historia Augusta* (45–47), which can be set against a text of Dio Cassius (LXXVII, 9): 'We were obliged, whenever he left Rome, to make ready for the Emperor, at our own expense, accommodation of all kinds and sumptuous resting-places mid-way, even on short journeys, at places where he never stopped and even at some which he was not going to see. In addition, we used to build amphitheatres and circuses wherever he was spending or hoped to spend the winter, without receiving from him any compensation.'

The *Itinerary from Rome to Egypt* on this argument was part of an edict issued by Caracalla on the eve of his campaign and the *Antonine Itinerary* a collection of such edicts, of varying date and importance[71], but all governed by events. According to the names borne by some towns, the compilation was probably made around 280 to 290, that is, during the years when Diocletian reorganised the *annona*. Advantage was taken of the experience gained in raising this tax and, by making use of the files in the office of the praetor, itineraries were grouped together, that is, lists of *mansiones* that had been made ready. They were probably classified in a certain order of merit and to round matters off, for those provinces which until then had not been involved in troop movements, new lists would have been prepared of *mansiones* already in service or that needed to be built. Finally, to give the collection a title, it received the heading of a famous edict of Caracalla. Such is the most recent and most attractive theory of the origin of the *Itinerary*.

Itinerarium Burdigalense sive Hierosolymitanum
(ITINERARY FROM BORDEAUX TO JERUSALEM OR HIEROSOLYMITAN)

This record of a pilgrimage[72] to the Holy Places occurred during the consulate of Dalmatius and Zenophilus (333) and mentions the stations that were passed through, no doubt according to a map or an itinerary. The section in Gaul comprises 371 miles, 30 changes or posting-stations, 11 *mansiones* or staging-points: Bordeaux, Bazas, Auch, Toulouse, Narbonne, Via Domitia, Arles, Valence, Aosta, Die, Luc-en-Diois, Mont-Saléon, Gap, Suse . . .

Jullian[73] has pointed out that the road going through Aquitaine abandons the old way along the valley in order to pass along the heights, free from the danger of floods and encounters, and corresponds to the 'chemin Gallien', which possibly dates back to the Emperor of the same name (254–68).

The *Hierosolymitan Itinerary* gives a detailed account of the crossing of the Alps and so allows correction of both the *Peutinger Table* and the *Antonine Itinerary*.

There has been discussion why the route makes detours in places and perhaps this was to allow visits to local chapels containing holy relics. The places involved might not be mere relaying-inns, but the homes, either contemporary or earlier, of fellow-believers.

THE *Peregrinatio Aetheriae* AND THE FIRST ACCOUNTS OF PILGRIMAGES

The *Journey of Aetheria* is the account, discovered in 1884 at an Arezzo convent, of a pilgrimage to the Holy Places, undertaken around the year AD 400, by a woman of rank, probably a nun. She writes to her 'sisters' in a simple, affectionate and lively manner, but lacks both literary knowledge and artistic sense. The surviving fragment is concerned with Sinai, Jerusalem, Mount Nebo, Mesopotamia, Antioch, Cilicia, Cappadocia, Galatia, Bithynia and Constantinople, where the authoress did her writing, displaying interest in the places mentioned in the Scriptures and in legend. She thereby gives us much topographical information, as well as the account of long marches across the desert, encounters with hermits, conversations with bishops, impressive ceremonies.

The above two texts may be considered to be the beginning of a long series[74] that we shall meet again in dealing with medieval sources.

4 GEOGRAPHICAL WORKS

PTOLEMY'S *Geography*

Claudius Ptolemeius was a mathematician and astronomer of Alexandria (first half of second century AD) who drew up general maps covering the most important towns, rivers and mountains and their astronomical coordinates.

A *Geography* bearing his name has come down to us, a Byzantine compilation of the tenth or eleventh centuries, including material derived from Ptolemy and other geographers, together with maps which are probably of later date.

The most ancient copies are those of Vatopedi (the monastery of Mount Athos), n. 754, belonging to the end of the twelfth century or the beginning of the thirteenth; and the later *Vaticanus Urbinas Graecus* 82.

On the medieval maps revealed by these documents, the names of the towns are enclosed within an irregular quadrilateral having embattled walls, sometimes with towers, a genuine symbol illustrating ramparts and going back to the Roman period. The size of these symbols varies and corresponds to the classification of towns made by Ptolemy according to how far he was certain of their geographical position.

The maps that accompany modern editions show us, not the roads (Ptolemy's view is that these are the province of the geographer proper), but some topographical information, the political and administrative divisions and a detailed list of town names. The maps have been drawn by Mercator, the Dutch geographer, mathematician and engraver (1512–94), and are based on lost versions going back maybe to the Greek Agathodaimon (fifth century).

Ptolemy himself used road books and descriptions of itineraries: it is perfectly possible to argue from his information where data occur in a significant line, but the geographer has missed out details that would enable the interrelationship of itineraries to be established.

THE *Ravenna Cosmography*

This compilation, made by a monk in the eleventh century – he called the *via Aemilia* 'Imperialis Estrata' – summarises documents that certain place names suggest date back to the fifth century. The fifth century copy was itself lifted from a road-map, a more complete one than the *Peutinger Table*[75], but these documents are very corrupt (some names have been arbitrarily cut out) although no earlier than the Late Empire. Besides the lists of stations – shortened at some point in the transcription – the *Cosmography* provides river names[76] and a few landscape details. The information from the road-map appears in two forms: names of the stations listed one after another in the same order as for the itineraries, which are carefully identified; and names inserted into the lists of towns, amongst those coming from other sources. Could one of these sources have been signposts erected where travellers left towns and listing all the towns ahead, just as today, on the way out of a built-up area, destination boards display a number of place names en bloc without showing that it will be necessary to take different forks in order to reach them? Set against the *Table* and the *Antonine Itinerary,* the *Cosmography* enables us to complete some of the identifications.

5 MILESTONES

The word for milestone, *milliarium,* came from *mille*[77], a thousand, the unit of distance being a thousand Roman paces, 1,481·5 metres or 1,611 English yards. The Roman pace or double-step (*passus*; *gradus* = step) was equal to 1·48m, that is almost 5ft, but in the beginning there was apparently an attempt to establish the equivalents of Greek measures: the mile corresponded to ten Greek stadia, which may have been the case of the *via Appia,* then to eight stadia[78] for the Greek settlements in Southern Italy, which may have affected the *via Domitia.*

We shall consider later the problems raised by the Gallic and Roman leagues and how it is possible to calculate the position of vanished milestones, with the additional help of place names. It is sufficient here to notice that in medieval documents milestones may be quoted as marking the boundaries of estates or of administrative areas. Lebel has shown that along Agrippa's road from Lyons to Langres there are striking coincidences between the siting of milestones and lanes forming the boundaries of registered land. As far as possible, milestones were placed in prominent positions, such as hill-tops and bridges, which have for long served as boundary marks.

It is common knowledge that the stones take the shape of cylindrical or oval-sectioned columns, occasionally parallelepipeds, and are made of limestone, sandstone, granite or basalt. They stand on a square projecting base to allow a firm setting. The height varies from 2 to 4m and the diameter from 0·5 to 0·8m, the smaller diameters seeming to be earlier.

Some milestones, erected against a rock or a building, have their rear face shaped.

Milestones were illustrated in antiquity – for example, there are three Gallic relief sculptures showing a vehicle passing in front of a milestone[79] – and in addition they are mentioned in literature[80]. A typological comparison could be made between Roman milestones and those of recent origin.

There were also *lapides tabularii,* stadia stones[81], the equivalent of modern French 100m stones, which used to bear letters in place of figures. A connection with the word meaning messenger (*tabellarius*) has led to these being interpreted as mounting stones for horsemen[82].

The number of milestones inscribed in Latin amounts to some 4,000, with as many in Greek, and more than 2,300 of these are in Africa, 600 in Italy, the same number in Gaul and Germany, about 100 in the Balkans and 95 in Britain[83]. Confronted by this mass of valuable evidence the publication of which is either inadequate or dispersed (until now the reports have been scattered through the different volumes of the CIL under the heading '*via publicae*') the Institute of Ancient History and Epigraphy in the University of Berne, in cooperation with the Academy of Sciences in Berlin, has undertaken the publication of sections of Volume XVII of the CIL, which will bring together all the milestones. Furthermore new discoveries have added something like 30 per cent to the corpus and many studies made in the past prove inaccurate when the stones are re-examined. A card index has been prepared, using various types of on-the-spot survey, always a tricky matter with curved surfaces: photographs, moulds in special papier mâché or in latex, hand tracings. Progress is being made with distribution maps to bring out dating differences, which will provide historical information of the greatest importance on the phases of road construction, from 252 BC, the date of the earliest known milestone[84].

5   A milestone from northern Italy
CIL III, 5708 = ILS, 464, S. Lorenzo di Sabato
(photo: R. Chevallier)

At the same time, a series of summaries is being edited, under the title of *Itinera romana,* the first of which deals with Swiss milestones, the second with the road over the Alpis Poenina. By 1968 inventories had been completed for Lusitania, Gallia

Narbonensis, the Three Gauls, and the Germanies and Norica, as well as for part of northern and central Italy, Britain and Pannonia.

The inscriptions on the milestones may have been engraved directly onto the rounded part of the column or else within a specially flattened space, which is depressed or raised. Some stones are not inscribed, these being earlier or examples which there had been no time to engrave (many kilometre-stones along French roads have been waiting to be inscribed for years). It is also very likely that some wording was painted on, especially since many signposts were of wood, while besides the official stones there were private ones.

The normal inscription includes the name of the builder or restorer of the road, the two operations being sometimes purposely confused. This name is in the nominative case, where the person responsible himself carried out the work or in the dative case more and more, when there is a dedication by the *civites,* or in the ablative for the date, the name of the executor of the work being added, possibly an imperial legate (*per talem* or *curante* so-and-so).

There are regional distinctions. The dependent genitive is a late feature. The wording of the titles usually provides an accurate date, with restoration being possible where inscriptions are incomplete or difficult to decipher[85]. In many cases all we have are fragments and old drawings.

The dating evidence is a little less certain when we examine the positioning of the inscription, the size of the space on which it is engraved, the shape of the lettering and the forms of address used. In the later milestones where the Emperor's titles are shortened, there is a dedication in the dative (and not a date in the ablative). It ought to be possible to identify different workshops according to the quarries that were worked.

The stones display the distance between the spot at which they were set up (which is never mentioned) and the point of departure or arrival as it may be, the latter being possibly the centre of the town (in Rome, the 'golden milestone'), the *forum* or, most often, a gate[86]. The *statio* may also have been at the city limits or at a place where a branch road left the main highway.

The place to or from which the distance is measured is often a town, as in the case of the Lutetia milestone, which was found alongside a road leaving Paris, perhaps the one to Sens, and which, in its inscription of the time of Maximus Daia (305–9), mentions the *civitas Parisiorum,* the first appearance of the name of Paris. Distance might also be measured from the boundary of a *civitas* (with the wording *ad fines*[87]) or from a geographical feature like a river or a pass.

The distances shown are sometimes multiple, expressed in miles (*MP*) or leagues (*L*)[88]. Calculation makes it clear that the latter unit had two values, representing either the 'Gallic league' (with values of 2,338–2,400–2,410–2,430 and 2,475m) or the 'Roman league (2,208 to 2,220m). It is understandable to find in Gaul a local unit of measurement[89] used in unromanised districts and such use of the league along local roads, possibly involving native entrepreneurs, could be associated with the revival, in the time of Trajan and above all the Gallic emperors[90], of native customs as well as local cults and pottery types. The league of 2,222m is equivalent to $1\frac{1}{2}$ Roman miles

(3,000 single paces)[91]. It was made official by Caracalla. There were also a few other local units of distance, an African mile of 1,625m in the neighbourhood of Gabès and a *milia* in Spain of varying length.

A selection of inscriptions from milestones is now given by way of example:

The Sacquenay stone 43 BC (CIL, XIII, 9044)

> Tiberius Claudius Drusi filius Caesar Augustus Germanicus, Pontifex Maximus, Tribuniciae Potestatis III, Imperator III, Pater Patriae, Consul III, Consul designatus IV, Andemantunno [Langres] millia passuum XXII (= 32·560km, the correct distance).

A milestone found 20km from the Porta Nigra at Trèves (CIL, XIII, 9129, dated to 212:

> [Imp(*eratori*) Caes(*ari*) M(*arco*) Aurelio S]evero [Antonino P]io Felici [Aug(*usto*) Ar]abico, Adiabenico, Parthico max(*imo*), Brit(*annico*) max(*imo*), pontifi(*ici*) max(*imo*), trib(*unicia*) pot(*estate*) XV, imp(*eratori*) II, co(*n*)s(*uli*) III, p(*atri*) p(*atriae*). Ab Augusta Trev(*erorum*) leug(*as*) novem.

A stone from Sirmium (date 354–55), ILS, 732 (CIL, III, 3705):

> m.p.V. / – Imp. Caes. Fla. Iul. / Constantius pius fel. / Aug. victor maximus / trimfator aeternus, / divi Constantini optimi / maximique principis [filius *understood*], divo/rum Maximiani et / Constanti nepos, divi / Claudi pronepos, ponti/fex maximus, Germanicus / Alamamnicus [*sic*] maximus, / Germ. max., Gothicus / maximus, Adiabin. [*sic*] max., / tribuniciae potestatis / XXXII, imp. XXX, consuli VII, / p.p., proconsuli, viis muni/tis, pontibus refecti [*sic*], / recuperata re publica, / quinarios lapides per Il/lyricum fecit, / ab Atrante ad flumen / Savum milia passus / CCCXLVI

> The Emperor Caesar Flavius Julius Constantius, holy, fortunate, Augustus, very great victor, eternal triumpher, son of the divine Constantine, very great and noble first citizen, grandson of the divine Maximian and Constantius, great-grandson of the divine Claudius [II Gothicus], very great pontiff, Germanicus, very great Alamannicus, very great Germanicus, very great Gothicus, very great Adiabenicus, in his 32nd tribunician power, greeted 30 times as emperor, consul 7 times, father of his country, proconsul, after having built the roads, remade the bridges, restored the common weal, he has set up across Illyria milestones every 5 miles from the river Atras to the river Sava 364 miles.

Some of the details make this an interesting inscription: the complete list of all the Emperor's titles, the embellishments of the traditional form of address and the craftsman's errors, hardly a surprise at that late date and in so remote a province.

The formulae used vary and may be more or less suitable for inscription:

refecit (*et restituit*);
viam faciendam curavit;
viam ante hac lapide albo inutiliter stratam et corruptam silice novo quo firmior

commeantibus esset, per milia passuum X sua pecunia fecit (ILS, 5822, year 216)
viam Juliam Aug(*ustam*) a flumine Trebia quae vetustate interciderat sua pecunia restituit (ILS, 5823, year 125);
silice sua pecunia stravit;
viam Aemiliam vetustate dilapsam operib(*us*) ampliatis restituendam cur(*avit*) (ILS, 5824, year 143). Elsewhere one reads: viam diutina incuria prorsus corruptam, (ILS, 5876) or *amissam* (ILS, 5875);
viam munit per millia passuum X (ILS, 5829);
redactam in formam provinciae Arabia viam novam a finibus Syriae usque ad mare Rubrum aperuit et stravit per C. Claudium Severum leg.Au[g. pr.pr.] (ILS, 5834, year 111);
miliaria vetustate dilapsa [*or* conlapsa] restituit (ILS, 5849);
miliaria novae praetenturae poni iusserunt (ILS 5850);
mil(*iaria*) commeantibus innovavit (ILS, 5853);
miliaria orbis sui restituit (ILS, 5855);
viam stratam novam instituerunt (ILS, 5861);
substructionem contra labem montis fecit (ILS, 5856);
vias exaustas restituit ac novis munitionibus dilatavit (ILS, 5862).

Some inscriptions from other sources, like bases or *cippi,* nevertheless come close to milestones and signposts in their wording:

viam prolapsam nova substructione restituit (on a base, ILS, 5827);
viam diu neglectam . . . usui publico reddidit (ILS, 5888, in a vault).

We may refer to a stone from the road from Capua to Reggio, known as the milestone of Popilius Laenas, consul in 132 BC, but attributed by Bracco to the consul of 153, T. Annius Luscus[92]. It is in fact a limestone tablet, bearing what amounts to an *elogium,* in language that is still archaic:

viam fecei ab Regio ad Capuam et in ea via ponteis omneis, miliarios, tabelariosque poseivei. Hince sunt Nouceriam meilia LI Capuam XXCIII Muranum LXXIV Consentiam CXXIII Valentiam CLXXX ad Fretum ad Statuam CLXXXI Regium CCXXXVII. Summa af Capua Regium meilia CCCXXI. Et eidem praetor in Sicilia fugiteivos Italicorum conquaeisivei, redideique homines DCCCCXVII. Eidemque primus fecei ut de agro poblico aratoribus cederent paastores. Forum aedisque poplicas heic fecei.

The man responsible for the work takes pride in having laid out the road, built a forum and handed back the pastures of the *ager publicus* to the tillers of the soil. The terminology used is an excellent illustration of the economic importance of the main highways, acting as tangible axes in the settlement and development of the land.

It is also worth referring to CIL, XII, 1524, which commemorates the opening of a road by the praetorial prefect for the Gauls, Dardanus, who was a correspondent of St Augustine, in whose honour the name of Theopolis was given to the Chardavon basin in the Basses-Alpes.

Other inscriptions provide us with valuable information on the roads, the engineering works and the buildings alongside. The following are some typical examples, chosen from the *Inscriptiones Latinae Selectae* by Dessau.

Among engineering works, bridges take first place:

ad mil(*iarium*) XXXV (*de la via Caecilia*) pontem;
viam et pontes pecunia sua (5866);
pontes fecit veteres restituit (5887);
viam imbribus et vetustate conlapsam cum pontibus restituit (5869);
pontem peilas faciundum coiravere (5896);
pontem faciendum locarunt eidemque probarunt (5897);
pontem lapideum de suo f(*aciendum*) c(*uravit*) (5898);
pontem fluvi a solo restituerunt et transitum reddiderunt (5899);
pontem ligneum qui per multo tempore vetustate conlapsus adque destitutus fuerat, per quo nullus hominum iter facere potuerat, providit, fecit, dedicavitque (5902);
pontem vetustate corruptum in usum cursus publici restitui aptarique iusserunt (5903).

Other inscriptions mention schemes protecting roads against flood damage, a matter of vital concern and rightly so, to the Roman engineers.

viam inundatione aque (*sic*) interruptam restituit (5859);
viam Anniam longa incuria neglectam influentibus palustrib(*us*) aquis ververatam sic et commeant(*ibus*) inviam . . . restituit (5860);
vias per fines Ceutronum vi torrentium eversas, exclusis fluminibus et in naturalem alveum reductis molibus pluribus locis positis (5868);
viam torrentib(*us*) exhaustas restituit ac novis munitionibus dilatavit (5871, cf. also 5887).

Similar to these raised causeways are the built-up embankments:

substructionem contra labem montis fecit (5856);
murum ad defension(*em*) viae vetustate conlabsum restituerunt (5858).

Many inscriptions are found carved on rock-faces left after engineering work:

montibus excisis anconibus sublatis viam fecit (5863);
viam fluminis vi abruptam interciso monte restituerunt (5864);
montibus inminentibus Lyco flumini caesis viam delatavit (5865);
montem cecidit et viam et sessionem d(*e*) s(*ua*) p(*ecunia*) f(*ecit*) (5883);
hoc iter ubi homines et animalia cum periculo commeabant apertum est (5885);
titulum immanem, montem Alpinum ingentem litteris inscripsit (5886).

A series of inscriptions recalls the building of *stationes, stabula* or *horrea*. The following are examples:

stationem a solo fecerunt (5905);
stabulum ne animalia cursus publici longi itineris labore diutius deperirent, providit, constituit, aedificavit adque dedicavit (5906);

locum ruinis obsitum, qui antea squalore et sordibus foedebatur, ad necessarium usum et ad peregrinorum hospitalitatem in meliorem (*aditum*) et aspectum propria pecunia reformavit (5907);

horrea ad securitatem populi Romani pariter ac provincialium constructa omni maturitate dedicavit (5910);

horrea fortia et felicia (5912);

horrea compendiaria armaria (5914).

But also at the roadside were to be found:

altars: Triviis Quadriviis [goddesses at crossroads with three or four forks] ceterisque dibus aram (5886);

temples and bath-houses: templa et balneas pecunia sua restituit (5868).

Some inscriptions, not the least interesting, mention the authorities who were responsible for the construction work, gifts by public or private bodies and other details of financing:

curante . . . legato pro praetore (5828);

per talem legatum Augusti pro praetore (5834);

per legionem III Augustam (5835): paving of the road from Carthage to Theveste in 123 BC);

per legionem III Gallicam (5865);

Curante . . . legato Augustorum (5847);

per talem proc(uratorem) suum (5851);

Centurio legionis qui operi institit (5864A);

curator viarum sternendarum viam sua pecunia fecit (5881);

curator viarum et pontium Umbriae et Picini (5891);

curante quaestore (5886);

hanc viam derectam per centurionem post sententiam dictam ab legato . . . restituit . . . primipilaris (5888);

award of contract and 'manceps' (5799);

work done by roadside dwellers: via nova strata per possessores territori Cirtensium (5873);

HS . . . quae possessores agrorum contulerunt;

or among private individuals, a mother in honour of her son:

ob honorem eius in via ducente Herdoniastria milia passuum ex d(*ecreto*) d(*ecurionum*) intra lustrum honoris eius repraesentata pecunia stravit (5878);

use of taxes or sums of money:

via munita de vectigali rotari (5874);

reddito ordinario vectigali (5876);

sums given ex decreto decurionum (5882, cf. 5878).

Sometimes there was an address of welcome to travellers: 'May he be invigorated in mind and body who, across thee, O most venerable Mustis, makes a pleasant journey, through thy ever-varied landscape![93].'

The distribution and dating of milestones clearly throw much light on general history, for their inscriptions, which it is interesting to compare with the legends on coins, are very informative on Imperial policy and still more so on the political atmosphere of the times[94]. We must bear in mind that some were recarved, reworked or replastered. In the first place an inscribed stone bears witness to the devotion and loyalty of the local people before it commemorates road-building or repair, unless this is specially mentioned. This explains the clusters of milestones, constantly added to and serving a double purpose, especially at land boundaries.

Another aspect of milestones has received too little attention: the dates when the quarries were in use. Thus the milestone from Solaise, to the south-east of Lyons (AD 43), marks the beginning of the exploitation of the 'choin' stone from Fay, a quarry lying close to the Rhône, some 60km upstream, whereas, until then, use had been made in Lyons of Seyssel stone (the material for the Augustan tombs at Choulans). But the fire at Lyons showed that this fine limestone, very suitable for the mouldings on columns, was unsuitable for structural purposes. The Fay stone was more durable and had the advantage of being closer to Lugdunum.

A host of information may be forthcoming from a newly discovered milestone. For example, the Constantine milestone from Mont Gaussier[95] establishes the line of the road from Aix to the Rhône through Glanum, confirms that that city was destroyed earlier than the fourth century and that it was transferred to the site at St Rémy, supports the siting of Tericiae at Mouriès, and finally adds useful dating to the *Peutinger Table.*

Sometimes milestones have remained in situ, marking symbolically the scene of open-air courts or used as property boundaries, hence place names such as 'Three Lords' stone' or 'Three Bishops' stone', and 'Toll stone', and hence, too, the frequent connection with commune boundaries. Between Chavanne-l'Etang and Montrevieux (Haut-Rhin) a milestone marked the frontier between France and Germany during the last war. The 'High-Stone' at Fontaines-sur-Marne stands where the Haute-Marne meets the Meuse department.

Some milestones have been turned to Christian use and topped with a cross (although the siting may vary), because they used to attract local respect, a remote survival of the cult of the god Terminus[96]. There was, for example, the local name for the Sacquenay stone, 'The Beautiful Stone', the moving of which caused great concern amongst the people of the neighbourhood.

Occasionally there is confusion with megaliths (probably themselves used as boundary stones), while local folk-lore may arise, as in the case of the 'Peiro dei Novi', the stone of the betrothed[97]: 'The people of Jonquières, who did not have a notary in their village, used to go as far as that boundary stone to sign their marriage contracts in front of the notary from Redessan [Gard], who, for his part, had no right to go beyond it.'

The majority of milestones have come to light, not in their original location, but in some reuse, for example in churches as columns (there are cases where conversely columns have been employed as milestones) or as holy-water stoups. They have been found, again, as thrashing-stones at the village wash-place, as heavy rollers, as hones for woodcutters' axes, as road ballast, as headers in walls, and often hollowed out to serve as drinking-troughs or sarcophagi (milestones from Paris and Tours) – the converse may apply.

When a milestone has been moved, it is difficult to be sure of its original siting[98], since the distances can be given only approximate equivalents in metric terms. No fractions were given and, while we find the wording *m[ilia] p[lus] m[inus]*, is the higher or the lower figure meant? Were the distances calculated as the crow flies or did they take into reckoning ultimate detours? Sometimes there were mistakes in carving (addition or omission of an X, confusion between V and X or II, figures reversed, carelessness over ligatures). It follows that metric data simply offer a range of probability.

In order to check the calculations that we make with road itineraries, we must work from both directions. There may be a point at which milestones are crowded or where there is a change in the system of road measurement and this may assist in locating the boundary between one *civitas* and another. In the same manner today, a change in the road surface often betrays the fact that we are passing from one administrative district to another.

6 OTHER EPIGRAPHIC EVIDENCE

THE VICARELLO GOBLETS[99]

These four silver goblets, now at the National Museum of the Thermae in Rome, were discovered amongst votive offerings at Aquae Apollinares (Lake Bracciano). They are shaped like pillars with the names of *mansiones* and their distances apart arranged on them in vertical lists. Their heights vary from 9·5 to 15·3cm and the technique is uneven. The goblets may be patterns from one workshop. They seem to belong to the same period, but the fashion that inspired them probably lasted some time.

Two facts suggest that this information was not a guide to help pilgrims. First, there is no reference to Apollo or to the Nymphs, and second, the route taken to Rome does not divert (the *Flaminia,* which does not pass by Lake Bracciano). Perhaps the owner, from Cadiz, made a gift of them to Apollo the Healer when visiting Rome. The lists may reflect the interest that was aroused by construction or repair of the road from Rome to Cadiz and appear to correspond to routes described by the Augustan geographer, Strabo.

Dion, in a lecture at the Collège de France[100], has clearly shown how the self-interest and ambitions that took Mediterranean peoples from the earliest times as far as the Atlantic coastline (the Greek Hercules being in rivalry with the Phoenician Melqart) might in a general way be summed up in a passage from the *Res Gestae* of Augustus (26): 'I have pacified the whole Atlantic coast from Cadiz to the estuary of the Elbe.' Naming Cadiz in connection with operations that were conducted on the western and northern limits of the known world, says Dion,

'. . . was one way of creating the highest public respect for such oceanic feats. For Cadiz was, in the eyes of the Ancients, one of the places in the world where there was the clearest revelation not only of the imperial mission handed down by the gods to the Roman people, but also of that bond of tradition linking that mission with the deeds of Alexander. [The latter] sought to wrest from Phoenician domination the famous columns that he thought his ancestor Hercules had set up at Cadiz.'

There is confirmation for this point of view in the milestones that lie along the road to Spain, the *via Augusta,* marking the way to a renowned destination: *ad Oceanum*[101].

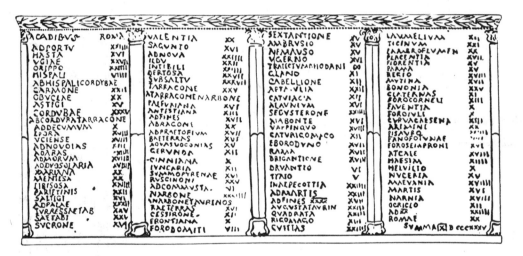

6   Inscription from one of the Vicarello goblets (after E. Desjardins, op. cit.)

As it happens, the Vicarello goblets closely resemble milestones and recall the *cippa* illustrated on the reverse of the denarii issued by L. Vinicius to commemorate the reconstruction of the *via Flaminia.* These coins could be showing reproductions of the 'golden milestone' (actually of marble with gilt-bronze letters) erected in the Forum at Rome in 20 BC by Augustus as *curator viarum.* There may have been a column of the same type at Cadiz (cf. the pillars surmounted by Corinthian capitals which separate the lists of *mansiones* on the goblets[102]) just as there were at the end of the *Popillia* (Rhegium) and the *Appia.*

We might even consider that the 'Cadiz milestone' was kept up to date. This would explain the different readings on the four goblets. These readings must derive from different prototypes. Is it possible to establish their relative dating? There are variations in the place names and the spelling in places is debased; for already, by the time of the Republic, vulgar forms existed by analogy permanently in the ablative case, alongside the official spellings in the accusative, theoretically the older. But external criteria (the smaller size, hastier design, and cursive lettering) allow us to give separate consideration to the fourth goblet, which may thereby be dated to the end of Augustus' reign.

But in particular it reveals alterations in the road route:

between Cessero (St Thibéry) and Forum Domiti (Montbazin) we notice a *mansio Frontiana* (*villa* understood), which has become the seat of one of the relay stations of the *cursus publicus*. This is no longer the case in the *Antonine Itinerary*;

goblets I and III show that the Rhône was crossed at Arles and II leapfrogs the problem. But IV names a new station, Traiectus Rhodani, which replaces the native name of Tarascon and fits in with a direct road between Aix and Nîmes which (cf. the milestones) bypasses Arles. One can easily imagine the competition there must have been between towns like Arles, using the Rhône waterway, and Nîmes and Narbonne, favourably placed for navigation on the lagoons[103]. In the Late Empire, Arles, having become one of the capitals of the West, was to win its place back on the itineraries;

whereas the first goblet has left out by mistake *ad Fines*, between Cabellio and Apta, as can be worked out from the mileage figures, there was no sign of *ad Fines* on the fourth. Perhaps this is a reflection of Augustan policy which aimed at bringing native cities to an end. The station reappears, marking the boundary between the Vienne basin and the Second Narbonensis, both in the *Antonine Itinerary* and on the *Peutinger Table*. It is known that in the Late Empire there was once again respect for native traditions;

for the crossing of the Alps, whereas the first three goblets mention native Celtic names, lying along the old road followed by Hercules, Hannibal and Caesar (Segusio, Gaesao), the fourth goblet shows new place names worded with the Empire and Rome in mind:

the mention of the *Taurini* is replaced by that of the *colonia Julia Augusta Taurinorum*, founded by Augustus[104];

there now appears *ad Fines Quadragesimae Galliarum*: the *portorium* was first levied under Augustus or Tiberius (cf. infra);

in Alpe Cottia is later than 8 BC (when Cottius came into office);

ad Martis (*templum* understood) must point to a temple built to commemorate the pacifying of the Alpine tribes (cf. the trophy at La Turbie);

Gaesao is replaced by *Tyrium* (today Turres, the name of both the village and the stream, unless we have to have a connection with the Doire).

Now we are aware through Ammianus Marcellinus (XV, 10, 2) that Cottius was responsible for building the road over the pass at Mont Genèvre. It could well be that the fourth goblet celebrates that event[105]. It would then date from the end of the reign of Augustus or from the beginning of that of Tiberius, with the other three going back to the early days of the Principate (II and III being the oldest and I intermediate in date but closer to the earlier group).

One of the major contributions made by the Vicarello goblets is to lay bare the political aims behind the establishment of long-distance routes. They need to be compared with the enamelled *paterae* from Britain, which are likewise road lists in a portable form.

THE AMIENS *Patera*[106]

In a Roman villa of imperial date, excavated at the time when Amiens was rebuilt, there came to light a bronze *patera* decorated with champlevé enamelling, a counterpart of the Rudge cup[107], which has been known since the eighteenth century, except that the latter has no handle. There are other examples of this series of enamelled bronzes produced in the workshops of Brittany and Belgium.

The Amiens cup is 10cm in diameter and 5·6cm high. It carries an inscription in red on a background that is alternately blue and green according to the succession of the proper names. Below, on the girth of the vessel, a red line in crenellated form gives a diagrammatic representation of a wall with seven towers. Crescents or peltae decorate the gaps that make up the crenellations. These groups of peltae may have been intended as charms against disease; they are of Celtic origin and can be traced again in the double wavy lines on the handle. But could they be picturing the defenders' shields as they stand on the *limes*? The lower part of the wall does appear as a checker-board of blue and green rectangles, clearly decorative, but not unlike courses of masonry.

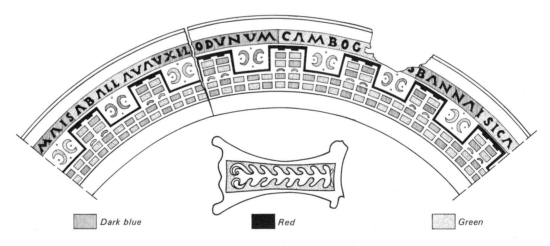

|▦| Dark blue |▮| Red |▧| Green

7   Inscription and motif from the Amiens patera (after J. Heurgon, *Monuments Piot*, p. 98)

This motif of the crenellated wall may be found on a number of mosaics (for example, one from Avignon, in the Musée Calvet), since the taste for frames and panels inset with decoration was widespread in the Empire during the second century, but the ornament on the Amiens cup also calls to mind certain continental wares.

An argument can be made for a date in the Antonine period, some time having had to elapse before the theme of Hadrian's wall could have found its way into art.

The inscription, unpunctuated, in letters 0·05cm high reads as follows:
MAISABALLAVAVXEL(L)ODVNVMCAMBOGLA(NI)SBANNAESICA
and is paralleled by the one on the Rudge cup, as follows:
AMAISABALLAVAVXEL(L)OD(VN)VMCAMBOGLAN(NI)SBANNA
and in return allows the latter to be checked.

The inscriptions are concerned with stations along the western part of the wall:

Maia, great camp, terminal station (the place name comes from *major,* rather than
from *Maia* or *Matres*);
Aballava, which is derived from the Celtic word for apple tree, cf. Avallon;
Uxellodunum, 'high town', the place name fitting the site;
Camboglanna, in Celtic 'curving river bank', at a river-bend;
Banna, forward-post on the *limes*;
Esica, in which we find the word for the Celtic god Esus or river names (Aesis,
Esino).

The garrisons of these stations are likewise well-known from inscriptions, but their
names, as revealed by the *Notitia Dignitatum* or the *Ravenna Cosmography,* are often
in debased form.

There are omissions from both the cups in question, with the one from Amiens
giving one extra name. How can we explain this selection? It does not seem that here
we should be satisfied to offer chance as a reason. The craftsman may very well have
made use of a document showing road routes. In the *Ravenna Cosmography,* where
the list proceeds in the opposite direction and seems to come down from the same
original source (perhaps via a Greek transcription, for some names have Greek
endings) the lists radiate from certain places. The fact that less important stations are
left out may be explained by a principle of geographical description laid down by
Pliny the Elder: not to mention the same towns twice. This may have led, when
dealing with the Wall, to the omission of the names of those forts already listed at the
ends of roads. So the compiler of the *Ravenna* does not mention Camboglanna for
the Wall, because the station has already been given for the Stanegate, which
here is taking the same line as the *limes*.

The chronology must also be taken into consideration. The latest explanation
appears to involve a slight change in the exact paths followed by the roads. Traffic
along the Wall between Luguvallium and Cilurnum for a long time kept to a road
built by Agricola, the 'Stanegate', which diverges from the *limes* along one sector.
Then a new military way was laid out (140) in close alignment with the Wall. It is
this road that is described by the source common to both our *paterae* and the *Cosmography*. In this case the Amiens cup appears to take us back to the state of affairs
on the *limes* at the beginning of the third century. The choice of the stations might be
connected with an abandonment of part of the Wall for a line of defence running
obliquely along the strategic road from Old Carlisle to Maryport.

The origin might be a road guide bringing together several separate itineraries.
In honour of the building of the *via militaris* in 140, there could have been a reor-

ganisation of the *cursus* and new road routes may have been arranged. Perhaps this involved the erection of some kind of local 'Tongres milestone'. A smart craftsman then seized upon this opportunity to make souvenirs at his workshop. We may recall what has already been said about the Vicarello goblets. The enamelled bronze cups comprised war mementoes for the veterans of the *limes*[108], in the same way as the famous leather buckler from Duro-Europos (third century) brought its owner back memories of long marches. The fragmentary Hidburgh cup discovered in Spain between Leon and Zamora had perhaps been carried home by a soldier belonging to the Cohors I Asturum garrisoned in Britain from the time of Hadrian. Amiens, which has yielded an epitaph of a leading centurion in the *Legio VI Victrix*[109], was a staging-post for the troops who were leaving for Britain and a place of retirement for the veterans.

'ROAD SIGNS'

These were more informative inscriptions than those found on milestones and were located in or close to towns and at important cross-roads. Understandably, painted wooden signposts have disappeared, but the 'golden milestone' in the Roman Forum, already mentioned, had counterparts elsewhere, of which portions remain:

The four tablets from Astorga in Spain, pottery plaques measuring 9cm by 12cm, which could be suspended through a hole in the dovetail-shaped scroll. On them, incised in cursive script before firing, were lists of road stations in north-west Spain, with the distances between them and the signature of a municipal *duumvir*. These town documents must have been displayed in a public building, either a curia or an office of the *cursus*[110]. They appear to date from the second century AD.

The Tongres milestone[111], found in 1817 outside the St-Trond gate and now kept in the Musée du Cinquantenaire at Brussels. The inscription was cut about AD 200 in capitals, with close attention to grammatical accuracy (places of departure in the ablative, staging-points in the nominative, distances in Gallic leagues) on an octagonal column that was broken at the time of the invasion of 256 and reused in the Late Roman town walls. The three faces of which parts survive bore respectively the route from Cologne to Worms, from Cologne (?) to Rheims, Soissons and Amiens, from Cassel to Arras and from Bavai to St-Quentin (?). As always, comparison must be made with the *Peutinger Table* and the *Antonine Itinerary*.

The Autun milestone[112], dating to the early third century, was made up of marble plaques, probably fixed to some pillar of polygonal shape and displaying lists of stations that opened wide horizons to travellers, including the road to Rome and the road to the Rhine. There are also details of the great highway from the Saône to the Rhine and of a local road from Auxerre to Entrains.
A similar fragment was found near to Junglister in Luxembourg. It listed the stations from Mainz to Trier along a branch road leading south-westwards from

the route down the Rhine, together with the stations along the latter road.

There has been much argument[113] over the authenticity of the road sign from Macquenoise (close to Chimay in Belgian Hainault), also known as the road-map of Momignies. This is a polished slab of red stoneware (measuring 52cm by 36 by 6), deeply inscribed before firing. On its upper part, which is topped by a pediment, there are relief sculptures of three small temples, also with triangular pediments. Below, a straight line runs across the slab, representing the road from Bavai (Bagacum) to Marseilles (Massilia) and a branch road. The intermediate stations are indicated by gabled temples or aedicula, perhaps symbols for a sanctuary. On the lower part of the slab are listed in four columns the 26 stations of that road.

Glass was manufactured in the locality from the earliest times, while contacts were kept up with Provence, which provided soda. The plaque was probably vitrified in an accidental fire.

Some experts date the plaque to the sixteenth century and connect it with *La Guide des Chemins de France* (1553)[114]. Lebel has pointed out several awkward details in the epigraphy that are inconsistent with ancient custom (modern punctuation) and has noted that there is no hole for suspension. He thinks that the whole thing is a clumsy combination of the *Peutinger Table* and the *Antonine Itinerary* and the place names appear to follow those given by Desjardins. His conclusion is that it is a hoax and he even outlines how the forger set about his task.

Vannerus, the Belgian expert, also considers that this is not a genuine antiquity. This last stone may be compared with a modern structure, a seven-faced column dating from 1716, which stood at Bavai to mark the point of departure of the seven Brunhilda highways, and seems to have replaced an older monument sited on ruins that were the source of much medieval speculation.

Cremona has yielded fragments of a plan of Roman roads[115].

A Gallo-Roman lintel from Antibes, a station on the *via Aurelia*, bears an inscription of uncertain interpretation: *Come hither, O traveller! Enter, if you will: here you will find a tablet of bronze that will give all the information you need.* Is this an inn sign, a list of city regulations or a road-map[116]?

ROAD ITINERARIES AND THE LATER DEVELOPMENT OF LATIN[117]

The milestone of Popilius Laenas (132 BC) had laid down the official code: point of departure in the ablative, destination and road stations in the accusative. But, amongst the road signs like the milestones of the third century AD, there was freedom of choice in the use of cases: nominative (Autun and Tongres milestones), accusative, genitive, locative, ablative singular or plural, with non-Latin place names often remaining indeclinable.

In the masculine and neuter accusative, the vowel U, now in final position, was opening out into O, hence the confusion between accusative and ablative, with the names of places apparently becoming established in the latter case. A reaction occurred against this slackness in the spoken language, particularly when a literary style of Latin developed amongst the Scipios and their following.

A number of reasons can be found for the changes, as, for example, the effect of analogy. Since the majority of place names in the singular tended to be confused, as regards spelling, with ablatives, people may, more or less consciously, have given nouns an ablative ending, especially since confusion could have arisen between the local meaning and the function of the locative case. We should also take into account regional peculiarities.

What is quite certain is that the restoration of grammatical spelling was artificial, whether it came from geographers like Mela or Pliny the Elder or from official inscriptions[118].

Everyday spelling and pronunciation developed side by side and found common ground in cursive form on documents.

Some inscriptions from the second century show that there was a reaction towards purer language and lead us to think that the Imperial government made an effort to fix the use of place names in the nominative, the case in which a noun is thought of when it is out of context, as for example in lists. But if there was a reaction, it did not last long.

Which all brings us to conclude that it is wise not to draw conclusions about dating from the study of the grammar used in inscriptions.

7 MEDIEVAL AND RECENT SOURCES

SAINTS' LIVES AND PILGRIMAGE ROUTES

Even if there were roads developed in the Middle Ages[119], those of Roman times very often survived and were admired by medieval people for their solid build, straightness and sheer length.

They form the itineraries that are described not only in the lives of the saints (in particular, St Martin's, known through Sulpicius Severus), but also in the stories of the journeys made by the relics of saints, including their severed heads. The places where miracles happened are often carefully identified in relation to pagan sanctuaries that had become Christian. Churches that had as their patrons the earliest saints (St Peter, St Martin, St Stephen and St Lawrence)[120] or the Virgin Mary stood along the Roman roads, represented especially as isolated chapels in open country and as crosses which either replaced milestones or were erected upon them (for example, beside the 'Grande Romanie'). Place names alone which survived structures that have vanished can be useful evidence. Here are two examples.

The first concerns a road that may, anyway, be pre-Roman in origin[121]. The Passion of St Gervais seems to be a distant reminder of one of the tin routes, which in Hallstatt times linked the Channel and Atlantic coasts to the Mediterranean across the Alps and the Jura without taking the Rhône valley, open to international trade only in the third century BC. This route, neglected by the Roman government, came into reuse in the later days of the Empire, when Celtic traditions revived in many spheres of activity.

Amongst the Lingones, the legend of the martyrdom of St Florens can be connected with a river. The saint was decapitated on the bridge at Til-Châtel and the current carried his head down to the Ile-Barbe at Lyons, where it was recovered. It is more likely that the relic was taken there by water. Now, in the fourth century AD, the poet Claudian wrote of wheat being taken by water from the territory of the Lingones to Rome (*De laudibus Stilichonis,* III, 82): 'What an example it is that the fertile plains of the Great Bear, the harvests soaked with the sweat of the tribes- man of the Lingones should ere this day have sailed for the Tiber!' and this may be compared with lines 404–5 of *In Eutropium*: '(The harvests that the South refused us have been made up by those from the North'. Fleets that had come down the Rhône were entering the mouths of the Tiber and the fertile banks of the Saône have replaced those of the Cinyphus.' If this wheat did come from the area around Langres, it must have been brought down the Roman road as far as Til-Châtel, then taken by boat from there as far as the Saône, then on to the Rhône. These words reveal a Roman trade route linking Langres to the Rhône valley with the aid of transshipment and originally used perhaps for the movement of tin. It is worth noting that this itinerary must have been followed in the opposite direction by Christian missionaries: the *civitas* of the Lingones, after an early conversion by St Benignus, could then have had bestowed on it martyrs' relics from Lyons and these would have come up the Saône[122].

The pilgrimages are likewise connected with the old roads, although we have to allow for a number of detours. These may have been caused by the breakdown of certain stretches of highway, owing to the foundation of an abbey or a hospital, the creation of new towns, the revival in importance of others (like Le Puy) so capturing local traffic, and finally the activities of bandits forcing travellers to take a way round.

Medieval imagination has embroidered many a story about old roads, attributing their construction to historical figures who have become legendary: Charlemagne, Brunhilda, whence place names of the type: chemin Chasles, chemin de Brunehaut – sometimes even with an attribution to the devil.

The growth of a legend into an epic was tied up with the habit of travelling that characterised the restless society of the Middle Ages[123], constantly setting off on pilgrimage or crusade. Bédier[124] has shown that poems about saints and heroes enter- tained travellers taking their repose in wayside inns. Wandering minstrels have in this way handed down many allusions to places. For example, the *Charroi de Nîmes* illustrates the 'Régordane' going from Clermont-Ferrand to Brioude, Le Puy, Alès, and Nîmes.

Of course, caution is necessary. All these roads are not Roman and place-names like 'Camin' Roumiou, chemin roumieu' mean 'road of the Roumious', road of the Roman pilgrims, on their way to Rome, then simply pilgrims.

Rome was overshadowed by the double popularity of Jerusalem and Compostella, by the holy places associated with St Martin, the healing saints and St Michael and

by others such as Chartres, Utelle and Le Puy. The pilgrimage roads were lined by
cairns and crosses, chapels and oratories, each with its patron saint, and by almshouses
(Great St Bernard, Port d'Aspe, Roncevaux, Aubrac). The orders of hospitallers
developed in the twelfth century. It is noticeable that the establishments set up by
the religious or military orders, like the Hospitallers of St John of Jerusalem[125],
almost always were sited close to the busiest roads.

A useful example of a medieval source is the *Guide du Pèlerin de Saint-Jacques*[126],
an account of an actual pilgrimage, bringing in geography, social customs and
folklore and giving valuable details about men and places. A recent book[127],
dealing with the 'camino francès', shows how road routes developed and how they
became stabilised in the eleventh and twelfth centuries; it further describes their
connections with Roman roads and where there were alternatives and road junctions.

The 'chemins de Saint-Jacques', the roads of St James, which were more numerous
in France than in Spain, especially close to, and north of, the Pyrenees, followed
courses that changed noticeably with time over some stretches and more particularly
in France. They took advantage of the patron saint to conceal a whole group of
routes, which in practice and purpose were far more complicated than a network
used by pilgrims. It was not only that the 'jacquets' could at will move from one road
onto another, but they were certainly not the only users. By keeping up the service
performed by Roman roads over long distances in the Middle Ages and since,
these routes helped many other travellers, not the least merchants. Pilgrimage
stimulated trade all the way to Galicia.

Bottineau has described a pilgrim's life, and the dangers of journeying by road,
which were mitigated by the protection of the law and the offers of hospitality,
thanks to the initiative from Cluny. The French indeed had a great part in the growth
of population along the pilgrim routes in Spain, this being a special feature of the
overall view that we might obtain from a human geography of the 'camino';
the 'camino' indeed was the great trade route in the north of Spain. Foreigners
settled along its course, often with their private rites and their brotherhoods,
and welcomed pilgrims of their own nationality, profiting by passing trade with
other foreigners and enjoying a privileged legal position. Yet they felt comparatively
isolated and were surrounded by hostile feeling. So in that country that provided
them with a living they tried to create a clear-cut right for themselves, giving
precedence over the natives, who disapproved of them. The existence of this right
was suggested by the epics when they sung of Charlemagne's exploit in delivering
the tomb at Santiago. In this way the presence of the 'Francs' was justified by an
heroic legend[128]. By being coupled with the story of Charlemagne, the Santiago
legend managed to flourish once more during the Middle Ages. Bédier came to the
conclusion that the *Chanson de Roland* arose in the eleventh century because the poem
had close connections with stations along the roads taking pilgrims via Roncevaux
towards St James. For its inspiration was the same as that aroused in the Holy War
which had raged in the Peninsula from the eleventh century onward. The story of
Roncevaux probably came into being as a local legend at Roncevaux itself and in the
churches along the roads leading that way; it had perhaps persisted unnoticed in

these churches from an early date and took poetic shape only in the eleventh century. But if it is easy to imagine the exchange of epic literature between France and Spain taking place along the pilgrim routes and if it is right that Roncevaux took advantage of the cult of Roland, we cannot find in the *Chanson* any sign of special veneration at Santiago or of the pilgrimage to Compostella. Besides, there has been recently discovered a version of the event at Roncevaux earlier than the Oxford manuscript copy of the *Chanson*. It has been wrong to associate Charlemagne's fame with that of St James.

We could make a similar analysis of the Alpine passes[129]. The French romances belonging to the Carolingian cycle were popularised in Italy from the first half of the twelfth century by both the pilgrims and the minstrels who entertained them at road halts. In return, they brought back from the peninsula a reasonably accurate notion of its geography, together with legends about places[130], which they introduced into their stories. Like the 'camino francès' in Spain, road routes called 'strata publica peregrinorum, via Romea, strata francigena, via francesca' often conceal Roman roads. A Franco-Italian poem of the thirteenth century established Roland's birthplace at Imola, giving as his parents Bertha, Charlemagne's sister and the knight Milo, who were both fleeing from the wrath of the Emperor along old highways. The exploit of the 'Ogier Knights' took place on the 'Francisca' road, with its series of 15 or so road stages from the Great St Bernard to Rome. At Sutri, a main halt on the *via Cassia,* people used to point out the 'Grotta d'Orlando' and the ruins of Charlemagne's palace. The legend even reached Brindisi where the mosaic pavement in the cathedral depicted scenes from the *Chanson de Roland*. Ruins of significance have inspired the story of an expedition by the Emperor and tales of churches and abbeys founded by his nephew and himself.

There are many accounts of pilgrimages. All can add something to our knowledge[131].

GUIDE-BOOKS AND TRAVELLERS' TALES

The *Guide des chemins de France* by Charles Estienne is more or less a summary of the road network of France at the time of Henri II. The unsigned edition of 1552 enjoyed great success (28 editions up to 1668).

The very lay-out of the book makes us think of the old road lists. The reader is told that the intention is 'to satisfy what I have known for long thou desirest concerning antiquities (which more appear by this means than any other form of writing) . . . by following what the Emperor Antoninus has left us in writing in his "Itinerary" of the Provinces or else the maps drawn up by good King Ptolemy'[132].

The sources used by Estienne are the same as those used by the early geographers: written information, as well as details from traders, pedlars and pilgrims (which explains the uncertain spelling of place names, with their echoes of local pronunciation and strange etymologies).

The way in which the information is presented also throws light on the format of the old road lists. They are grouped to cover large areas and the lists of road stations radiate from certain towns, which are taken as focal points. The preface makes it clear that the guide 'does not lay down a road' (cf. what has been said earlier about the choice of routes on the *Peutinger Table*), but invites views.

The *Guide* is a compendium of useful details for travellers going by road:

lists of towns passed through and of places where one can eat and sleep (with hints to the gastronome)[133];
mention of posting-stations (p.), days' journeys (j.), leagues (l.);
cross-roads (and crosses), forks, climbs, descents, difficult sections in bad weather (marshland) or in other ways (woods and threats from bandits), state of the roads, viewpoints;
river-crossings (bridges, ferries, managed fords).

164

A Turin, ville capitale de Piedmont.

Sainct Iean de Morienne, *cy deſſus.*		
Sainct Iulian	i	P.
Sainct André v. ch.	iii	P. R.
Bregarre	i	P.
Bourget, *a main gauche*	i	P.
Braſme	i	P.
Sollieres	i	P.
Treſmignon	i	P.
Laſnebourg	ii	P. g.
Le mont Senys		
Monte roide.		
La Ramaſſe	i	P.
Noſtre Dame des Neiges, a gauche.		
La Chappelle des tranſiz	i	P. d.
Au milieu de la place ſur le mont.		
La Tauernette	i	P. R.
L'hoſpital	i	P.
La Ferriere b.	i	P.
La Noualeſe v.	ii	P. g.
Suze v.	i	P.
Borſeling	i	P.
Sainct George v.	d	P. R.
Sainct Ambroiſe v.	ii	P.
Sainct Michel	ii	P.
Viglanne v.	i	P. g.

165

Reſmiers, *Hoſpital ſainct Antoine* v.		i	P.
Riuole v. ch.		ii	P.
Turin v. ch. vn.		ii	P. R.

Ville capitale , Parlement , & Archeueſché, dicte Taurinum, *a cauſe du mont* Taurus, *qui eſt l'Alpe de ceſt endroit.*

Le Daulphiné, & ſes dependences.

Le Daulphiné cōmence a la Guillotiere, faulxbourgs de Lyon, bornant la riuiere du Roſne en amont, le long duquel eſt ſeparé de la Breſſe, pres Quirieulx: adhere au Marquiſat de Saluces & a la Prouēce, vers Cyſſeron, au conté de Veniſe a Montelimart, au Piedmōt, a ſainct Ambrois, a la Sauoye, a Pierre Chaſtel, & au pont Beauuoiſin. Ce pays eſt ſitué, partie en mōtaigne, partie en plaine , mais ne ſont les montaignes de Daulphiné tant infertiles, que celles de Sauoye, en teſmoignage de la montaigne de Chalemont, dont viennēt les bons vins du coſté de la montaigne de Vauloire & Vauloiron, la Vache, & de Nybe, & encor de la Vaulpute, qui ſont endroits fertiles en toutes choſes que lon ſcauroit ſoubhaiter.

l.ſii.

8   Extract from *La Guide des Chemins de France* by Charles Estienne (after J. Bonnerot, *La Guide des Chemins de France*, 1553, par Charles Estienne, vol. ii, Paris, H. Champion, 1936)

It also takes into account details touching on politics (local boundaries), economics (fairs and markets, tolls, messengers, relays, fares), tourism (sights to see, historic places, pilgrimages, landscapes), history (battles, disasters, legends, folk origins and settlements, visits by famous people) and archaeology (identification of sites and description of ancient remains: defences, tombs, springs, aqueducts, amphitheatres, columns, harbours, inscriptions).

Towns that are quoted as possessing commanderies, leper hospitals and Roman roads include: Aiguebelette in the Alps, Argenton, Auxerre, Bourges, Chartres, Châtillon-sur-Seine, Dreux, Dun-sur-Auron, La-Ferté-St-Aubin, Houdan, Ingrandes, Levroux, Lorris, Lyons, Metz, Montfort l'Amaury, Montreuil-Boulogne, Orléans, the Puy-de-Dôme, St-Marcel-d'Estréaux, Saintes, Toul and Tournus.

It is important to understand that the *Guide* was not drawn up by starting with the examination of a map. As in the case of Pliny, with his geographical lists, references have been mixed, which explains why there are facts transposed or omitted. Confusion has also arisen between place names of different types (towns, districts, rivers). In fact, it was the *Guide* that provided a basis for map-making (cf. infra for the example of Ptolemy). The first maps (Oronce Finé, 1536) were local ones; progress was made by assembling these in groups. It was only in 1646 that Boisseau completed the map work for the *Guide,* the earliest road-map proper having been completed by Tavernier (1632, to show mail services).

There is an unending list of guide books. If one wishes, links can be traced between them and a study made of their improvement with time[134]. From them it is possible to glean much valuable information about the old road lists and ancient sites.

As an example of the material available for research into early roads through travel accounts of more recent date, we may take Montaigne's *Journal de voyage*[135]:

Travelling conditions, which had at that time hardly changed since the earliest days, were difficult and it is understandable that there are many passages that may preserve for us information about roads often of great value in interpreting the ancient itineraries. General details may come to light concerning not only the various alternatives, but also the survival of the ancient names for the roads, the spacing of the stations and the operation of the relay system.

From Fossombrone to Rome (p. 267) the *via Flaminia* had kept its name. Many important connections were made partly by land and partly by water (p. 262) 'From Loreto one can go along the coast, in a week's short stages, as far as Naples. One has to go to Pescara and the city of Chieti, whence a mail-coach leaves every Sunday for Naples.' Montaigne had hoped to reach the latter town. It is a pity he did not manage to carry out his plan.

The situation in Liguria did not seem to have changed since Roman times, or rather it had reverted to a pre-Augustan state of affairs. We may judge from the following (p. 428):

There were 'two roads from Sarrezana, close to Luni, leading to Genoa . . .' (where Montaigne did not go, since 'the roads from Genoa to Milan are infested with thieves') '. . . one takes three days' journeying from Sarrezana and has 40 miles of dreadful track, very hilly, with boulders, precipices, and foul inns and very few travellers. The other road passes through Lerici, three miles distant from Sarrezana. There you embark and in 12 hours you are in Genoa.'

It is known that the Roman conquest, in Liguria just as much as in Provence, was not very successful with its occupation of the coastal belt, through which ran the road to the province of Spain: 'The whole coastline', wrote the geographer Strabo (IV, 6, 2), 'is dominated by unusually high mountainous escarpments, leaving between them and the sea only a narrow way . . . After eighty years of warfare, the Romans managed to ensure with great difficulty that there should be free passage over a width of 12 stadia for travellers on official business.' This text, though dealing with the Provencal coast, holds true for that of Liguria. All this explains the extreme importance, in the maintenance of Roman travel connections, of the ports of Pisa, Luna, Genoa, Marseilles and the early advance in the plain of the river Po, which, strangely enough, ensured the safest communication with Spain, thanks to the easy climb over the Mont-Genèvre pass. Even in Montaigne's time the Ligurian pirates were still to be feared!

His diary contains indeed many details about the distances of one road station from another (for example, p. 430: Fornovo was two stages from Parma), about road measurements (at Sienna, p. 193, the length of the mile was different), about the organisation of the relays (the hiring of horses, which worked well on the whole, cf. p. 198, and could not have changed since the Roman *cursus publicus*) and about the costs of tolls and taxes (p. 430, the Apennine mountain-folk taxed travellers[136] and in northern Italy, tolls were levied at strongholds that lay athwart the roads: Montaigne noticed 'several enclosures that obstruct and close'). This would explain certain peculiar features notices along Roman roads, both in Italy and in France, bends that are not easily explained on flat ground, with the curve being completed on the opposite side by field-boundaries, hedges or lanes, so that the oval thus formed encloses the site of the *burgus* formerly watching over the road. The course of the highway before its diversion can sometimes be made out as the major axis of the ellipse, if the ground is not built upon[137].

Water tolls were paid during the crossing and not on landing (to avoid arguments!): it was a Roman and an Italian custom.

Another ancient tradition can be quoted, where hosts led the way over dangerous stretches (p. 185, in the Apennines). This practice was recorded in early times for the Alps[138].

Now some remarks about road conditions. The Alps were crossed with ease, in fact everywhere in a very picturesque manner: the climb up to the Mont Cenis pass was made in a sedan chair, the descent on a sledge (p. 445): 'I went up the Mont Cenis pass partly on horseback, partly in a chair carried by four men, with four others acting as relief bearers. I was borne on their shoulders. The ascent lasts two hours, it is stony and awkward for horses unaccustomed to it, but otherwise free from danger and difficulty.'

The fact that the Alpine chain could be crossed so easily amazed the Ancients: 'There are many more passes . . . today', wrote Strabo[139], 'and, thanks to engineering works, they are as practicable as may be. Indeed, Caesar Augustus completed the wiping out of the bandits by means of road construction' . . . and a little later[140]: 'One of the passes which allow movement from Italy into transalpine and northern Celtica leads to Lugdunum by the land of the Salassi. It gives two choices of route, one being possible for vehicles over the greater part of its course' (the Little St Bernard).

On the other hand, Montaigne found that crossing the Apennines was troublesome (except along the Magra road which proved easy) (p. 184): they were 'more difficult mountains than on any other part of this journey'. The course of the autostrada del sole must not make us lose sight of the problems facing the remaining road links, with their steep slopes and with the 'frane' (precipices) a constant obstacle to maintenance. Hannibal is known to have had more trouble crossing the Apennines than the Alps[141].

Montaigne made careful note of the difficulties of travelling by road, chiefly caused by rivers or marshy country:

(p. 182) close to Ferrara: 'it is awkward going for foot-passengers in miry weather . . . as the roads have ditches on both sides, there is no means of walking clear of the mud';
(p. 193) the pot-holes of the Paglia: 'We crossed and recrossed a hundred times over a torrent rushing all the way down' the road;
(p. 400) at San Chirico 'the beast of burden which was carrying our baggage having fallen into a little stream that we were fording, all my clothing and the books in particular were spoilt'.

In the eighteenth century, Charles de Brosses was to relate a similar mishap in northern Italy.

Finally, a number of observations about crossing rivers: bridges, fords and ferries.

There were few bridges; they were kept in repair only at the frontiers of the various states (p. 196, for the Church) in order to maintain prestige. It is quite certain that the majority of the stone bridges that we find mentioned dated from the Roman period. A number of the routes followed included sections travelled by water, especially in northern Italy, and this had already been the case in the *Antonine Itinerary*[142].

(p. 166) at Rovereto: 'They put their travel-chests on these *zatte* that in Germany are called floats, in order to bring them down to Verona along the said river Adige.'
(p. 172) at Casa Fucina: 'an inn where one embarks in order to make one's way to Venice'.
(p. 174) Horses tow the boat.
(p. 176) Battaglia: 'a canal, which, although it is not very deep, is used nevertheless by some strange boats'.
(p. 179) On the Adige: 'a floating bridge constructed on two small boats and capable of carrying fifteen to twenty horses, moving along a rope secured across the water 500 paces away, and to hold this rope up, a number of small boats moored between two more, which with the aid of stakes keep the rope out of the water'.
(p. 240) 'They get three or four pairs of buffalo to tow their boats up the river Tiber.'[143]

(p. 436) 'We crossed the Po on a floating bridge resting on two boats and possessed of a little cabin. It is steered across with the aid of a long rope supported at several points on small vessels moored against each other in the river.'[144]

(p. 440) The Naviglio: 'the canal is narrow, but so deep that it brings up quite large boats to Milan.' The Ticino was crossed by boat: 'at Chivassa travellers moved across several rivers and streams, sometimes by boat, sometimes on foot'.

Fords are mentioned on many occasions.

There are several details dealing with the build of the road, often going back to the Roman period. In northern Italy, there is frequent mention of embankments (hence the place name 'Levata') alongside waterways, cf. pp. 172, 177, 178: 'a canal with two roads raised on each side'.

This landscape had changed little since ancient times, for drainage and irrigation works had been carried out within the areas marked out for centuriation by those responsible for highways; water-courses have turned out to be the boundaries of subdivided centuries. The old road in such cases had a ditch alongside, often filled up later. The role of *cardo maximus* was frequently played by a road running parallel with an artificial waterway or a stream that had been straightened. Montaigne noticed the paving of Roman roads:

p. 198 (close to Rome): 'Some causewayed roads with very fine paving seemingly ancient'; he observed engineering works:

p. 267: the *via Flaminia* was cut into living rock and possessed firm foundations: 'In that vicinity there is much to be seen of construction in masonry, built up from the bed of the stream, well below the road; immense crags that have been carved and smoothed; and all the way along, traces of their heavy pacing now mostly buried.'

p. 420: an example of double superimposed 'bridges', like the Pont-du-Gard.

A few more passages may be quoted about the old roads of Italy. 'The road from Ostia to Rome, which is the *via Ostiensis,* still gives many reminders of its former grandeur, causeways, ruins of aqueducts, almost the whole route strewn with building remains, and more than two-thirds of the said road still paved with that black quarrystone, with which they surfaced their highways . . . (p. 229) Amongst other ruins, we came across about half-way on our right hand the very fine tomb of a Roman praetor, on which the inscription can still be read in its entirety.'

In the opposite direction, Montaigne went to Tivoli (p. 243): 'At the Lucan bridge, which still bears its ancient name, there are some old inscriptions, with the chief one very readable. There are also two or three Roman tombs along that road; there are no other traces of antiquities, and very little of the old paving; this is the via Tiburtina.' The 'Ponte Lucano' which crosses the Aniene not far from Bagni di Tivoli, owes its name to Lucanus Plautius. Quite close by stands the circular tomb of the Plautii, dating to the early Empire and bearing the priases of the members of that family. It was these inscriptions that Montaigne saw.

Let us follow Montaigne on his travels through central Italy. He noticed (p. 250) in the Tiber 'great masses of stone, the remains of the bridge that Augustus had built there to link the territory of the Sabines with that of the Falisci'. We can identify this with the *Ponte Felice,* near Borghetto, on the *via Flaminia*; it was indeed constructed by Augustus, but rebuilt by Sixtus v (1589, shortly after Montaigne's visit).

Concerning the Furlo pass, cf. infra p. 105.

A bibliography of travellers' tales can be found in the following sources: the *Bibliothèque universelle des voyages* by Boucher de la Richarderie (1808); d'Ancona's commentary on the *Journal de Voyage de Montaigne*; the catalogue of the Fossati-Bellani collection in the Ambrosiana of Milan; the catalogue under preparation of the Tursi collection of the Marciana in Venice; the files of the Hertziana Library in Rome and the German Institute in Florence (much surprising information will come to light by consulting cards under headings in the different languages: journal, diary, reisen . . . and different countries, not forgetting anonymous writers – there were many in the seventeenth and eighteenth centuries – and by consulting original manuscripts).

A compilation with a good bibliography has been made by Schudt: *Italienreisen im 17. un 18. Jahrhunderten*, Vienna, 1959; and there are a couple of good monographs:

for Egypt: J.-M. Carré, *Voyageurs français en Egypte,* Cairo, 1932;
for Sicily: H. Tuzet, *La Sicile au XVIIIe siècle vue par les voyageurs étrangers,* Strasburg, 1955 and *Voyageurs français en Sicile au temps du romantisme,* Paris, 1946, but this work has only a literary purpose.

OTHER WRITTEN SOURCES

From the eleventh century onward, with the extension of manorial tenure, those lords holding well-sited castles were able to claim the right to exact tolls or to provide guides or escorts. Land schedules may give the list of places where the toll sections began, that is to say the keypoints lying alongside the 'great toll roads'[145], which werc 10ft wide.

Speaking generally, all archives whether religious or otherwise (charters, diplomas, wills, travellers' accounts, reports of military expeditions, monetary statements) may furnish valuable information about topography, especially where there are roads crossing or skirting estates (*via romana, strata publica, via, iter*)[146]. To these we should add the results of official enquiries[147].

A trial investigation among the archives of the French government departments dealing with Roads and Bridges, Waterways and Forests, and Public Works has shown what possibilities there are in quantity surveys and specifications arising from civil engineering and maintenance. Already, when Sully was in charge, the Treasury was required to give reports to the King's Council on the overall condition of the roads, together with estimates of the repairs considered necessary. The eighteenth century, a time of great road development, provides many such documents. A number of technical notes about the materials needed to metal highways mention how reuse was made of 'paving' from old roads, which were treated as quarries. These activities, which have left clear evidence on the surface, went on to help the early railways pay their way: several Roman roads in Berry were used as sources of ballast. Sometimes the destruction was only partial: one nineteenth-century document dealing with the straightening of an Imperial highway in Provence authorises the sale of half the Roman road, which was more than 8m wide. Only 3m were retained, leaving the rest to fall into the hands of the owners of adjoining land.

All the Roman provinces took part in this type of reuse. In his *Lettres familières écrites d'Italie*, Charles de Brosses noted: 'The very poorest people in the district have scaled the *via Appia* as though it were a carp.'

Early maps are important, but difficult to use before the seventeenth and eighteenth centuries[148]. We shall deal below with the contribution to be made to our studies by maps.

2

The archaeology
of Roman roads

I CLASSES OF ROAD

Our starting point must be a significant note on the classification of roads made by Siculus Flaccus, a surveyor of the first century AD[1]: 'Public highways, constructed at State expense, bear the names of their builders and they are under the charge of administrators (*curatores viarum*), who have the work done by contractors; for some of these roads, the landowners in the area are required, too, from time to time, to pay a fixed sum.'

In addition to the *viae publicae,* usually mentioned in the itineraries, and which, being named after the magistrates building them, were also called *praetoriae* or *consulares,* we find reference to *viae militares*[2], which were roads possessing strategic importance, at any rate at a particular time, rather than roads specially designed for troops and financed from military funds. These *viae* were always *publicae,* but the converse is not the case. Inscriptions tell us what the surveyor wanted us to know about the sources of funds for the *viae publicae*: contractors were paid by the *curatores viarum* with monies from the *aerarium,* to which were added subsidies from the imperial *fiscus* and contributions from the inhabitants of each *civitas* and those living beside the road, with the governor of the province officially checking the execution of the contract. Siculus Flaccus went on:

There are in addition local roads [vicinal, from *vicus,* a township, the chief town in a *pagus*] which, after branching off from the main highway, go off across the country and, often, lead to other public ways. They are built and maintained by the *pagi,* that is to say by the *magistri* of the *pagi,* who usually see that landowners provide the work force, or rather hand to each landowner the job of looking after the stretch of road going over his land. At the ends of such sections, inscriptions may be seen of the name of the territory and of the owner in question, together with details of the piece of road that he has to keep serviceable. There is free movement along all these public ways . . .

Finally there are ways leading across private estates that do not afford passage

to everyone, but only to those who need to reach their fields. These ways lead off
local roads. Sometimes, too, they fork off from roads belonging jointly to two
landowners, who have come to an agreement to take charge of them at the edges
of their estates and to share their upkeep.

Finally, the public highways, the local roads and amongst the private ways,
those jointly belonging to two landowners, all coincide with boundaries. However, these roads were not laid out to act as boundaries but to open up
communications.

The local roads (*actus*) must have made up the greater part of the network. The private roads (*privatae, itinera*) were linked to the great estates. We find them mentioned
on inscriptions (*privatum iter*).

A sentence from Pliny the Elder confirms that roads acted as boundaries, a function
that was long-lasting. 'In Campania, the *Leboriae* is bounded on each side by a
consular road: one road goes from Pozzuoli to Capua, the other from Cumae to
Capua[3].'

The Roman classification may be compared with the French system of motorways, and national, departmental and local roads. These are grouped broadly to
serve as main links between important towns, then for community purposes,
between communes, and finally, for everyday use, from hamlets to communes. It
will be a useful exercise to note how one category passes into another.

The width of Roman roads varied with their class, although this is not an infallible
guide:

> from the law of the Twelve Tables, fifth century BC[4]: 'Military roads must be
> 8ft (0·295m) wide on straight sections and 16 on bends[5]';
> from the so-called Augustan law[6]: 'The major axes of centuriated land, the
> *decumanus* and the *cardo maximus* [cf. below] must be respectively 40 and 20ft, the
> other *decumani* and *cardines* 8ft. The same writer Hyginus gives elsewhere different
> figures[7]: 30, 15, or 12ft for the axes and 8 for the other ways.

This information may be compared with that given by Pliny the Elder[8]: 'Vineyards
must be bounded by a *decumanus* 18ft wide so as to allow two waggons to pass each
other. *Cardines* 10ft wide must be laid out through the middle of the *iugera*, or, if
the vineyards is extensive, these cardines will have the same width as the decumani.'

This freedom of movement, mentioned by Siculus Flaccus, will be considered
again with regard to centuriation and the regulation *Iter Populo debetur*.

Further classification of the roads will arise when the methods of construction are
studied.

2 TOWN STREETS
THE EXAMPLE OF ROME

In his fine work on the Tiber (*Le Tibre, fleuve de Rome dans l'Antiquité*[9]), Le Gall has
emphasised the importance of the site of Rome, which lay at the lowest bridging
point of the river, where the *via Salaria* crossed a road running from Etruria down
to Campania. The first of these roads was in fact formed of two parts: initially, from

the salt marshes north of the mouth of the Tiber as far as Rome, it was the *Campana*. This was a very ancient way, as is shown by the existence of the sacred grove of the Arvales at the fifth milestone where it emerged from Roman territory. Its course was probably improved about 350 BC at the time when Ostia was founded. The road crossed the Tiber by the Sulpicius bridge and continued towards Sabine territory as the *via Salaria*. On it, the town of Fidenae, which was in the hands of Veii, controlled the salt trade, so vital to the people of the mountains[10]. This direct route from the Apennines to the sea is a reminder of one of the great economic realities of Italy, as of Provence: the phenomenon of transhumance, the role of which in Roman history has been well described by Grenier[11].

On the whole, the Roman network of roads radiated from the centre towards the neighbouring towns, which gave their names to the roads (Ostiensis, Tiburtina) and it was along these that the city grew. The gateways in the city walls often have the same name as the roads leading through them: *porta Appia, Aurelia, Flaminia, Latina, Nomentana, Ostiensis, Portuensis, Praenestina, Salaria, Tiburtina*[12].

In the outskirts, we find alongside the *viae* tombs[13] and cemeteries (the tombs of the Scipios and of Caecilia Metella on the *Appia,* and of Bibulus on the *Flaminia*), catacombs (that of Domitilla on the *Ardeatina*), temples (temple of Mars on the *Appia*), altars and sacred groves. The aqueducts crossed over the roads on an ornate series of arches: the one serving the *aqua Virgo* over the *Flaminia* celebrated Claudius' British triumph; the so-called Drusus arch over the *Appia* was used for the *aqua Antoniana*. The arches of the *aqua Claudia et Aniene,* which bestride the *via Praenestina,* later became a monumental gate (*porta Maggiore*).

Within the city, which grew without let or hindrance on hilly terrain, the streets followed courses that were far from straight, very narrow (4·5 to 5m, with 6m the maximum), often on a slope. There are several *scalae,* some of them shown on the *Forma Urbis,* like the *Scalae Caci* leading from the Palatine to the Great Circus or the *Scalae Gemoniae,* the 'staircase of groans', at the side of the *arx*, where the bodies of executed criminals were exposed to view. The streets were lined by high buildings and the traffic problems are evoked in a colourful passage from Juvenal:

One needs to have a lot of money to sleep in this town . . . The vehicles moving down the narrow, winding streets, the quarrelsome crowd refusing to move on, all would rob even sea-calves of sleep. The rich man, when called away on business, will have himself borne through the crowd, which opens to make way for him; he will make swift progress over everyone's head in his vast Liburnian litter. As he goes, he will read, write, sleep within, for with windows closed, one can sleep the sleep of the just. And for all that he will arrive before us. In my case, the human tide in front of me prevents me from hurrying: the hastening throng behind me is thrusting into my back. Someone shoves an elbow into me; another man gives me a nasty jolt with a long beam. Here's a fellow also set on giving my head a whack with his joist and yet another with a mighty cask. My legs are all over mud. Down comes a large boot on my foot, leaving a military stud stuck in my toe. Can you see the crush of people and the smoke where the sportula is

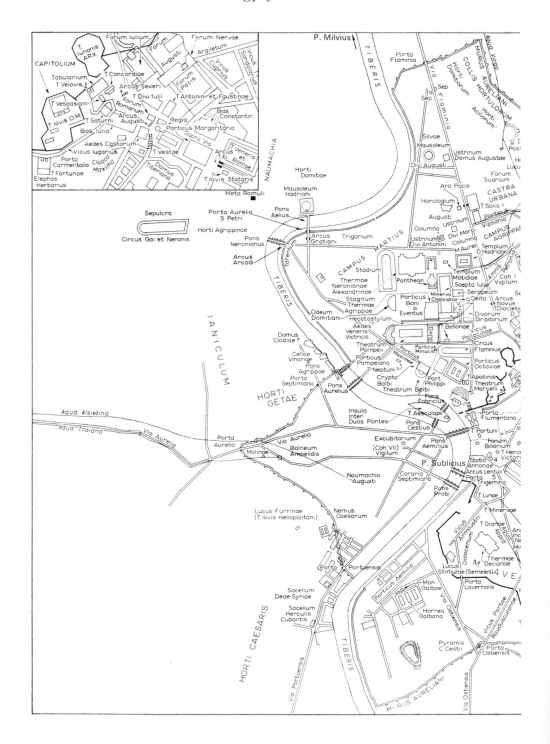

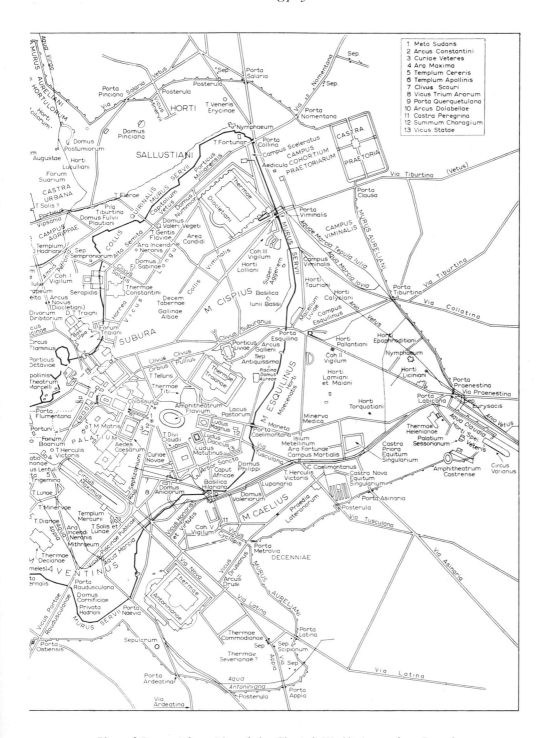

9 Plan of Rome (after *Atlas of the Classical World*, Amsterdam–Brussels, Elsevier, 1959, p. 145)

being handed out? See, my tunic's torn and it has only just been mended. A waggon is coming forward with a great baulk of timber swaying about on it; a second is loaded with a pine trunk. These are threatening the crowd as they swing in the air. What if the axle bearing Ligurian marbles happens to break and, losing its balance the whole mass tips over onto the passers-by? How much then would be left of the bodies? . . . Just consider now the dangers of another kind to which one is exposed at night, the great height from the ground of the roofs perched up in the air, sending down a tile to give you a crack on the head . . . There are also some folk who are sent to sleep by the noise of a rousing quarrel . . . A host of other mishaps may be feared. There won't be a shortage of people to strip you, once the houses are closed up . . . The odd cut-throat may approach unexpectedly, waving his knife around[14].

These famous lines are echoed by another quotation, not so well known, from Martial:

In town . . . it is quite impossible for a poor wretch . . . to get any rest. We are refused the right to live, in the morning by schoolmasters, at night by bakers and all day long by tinkers hammering away; over here, the money-changer with no customers is jangling his stock of Neronian denarii up and down on his hollow-topped table, and there, the Spanish gold-beater is striking his worn stone with his polished mallet; and there's no rest from the crowd truly possessed by Bellona, first the shipwrecked sailor with his bandaged body and his gossip, then the Jewish child trained by his mother to go begging and the rheumy-eyed hawker with his sulphur matches . . . We are woken by the laughter of the passing crowd, and Rome is at our very bedside[15].

In only two instances were the city throughfares merely given the names of *via*:

the *Sacra Via,* which began close to the Colosseum, then crossed the *Velia,* the *Fornix Fabianus,* and the arch of Augustus to be continued as the *Clivus Capitolinus.* Its course was doubled in width after the temple of Caesar was built. Along it passed the religious processions which used to go up to the Temple of Jupiter on the Capitol. Piganiol thinks it was the *decumanus* of the Etruscan *Roma quadrata.* It is impossible to speak of the Sacred Way without calling to mind the pomp and circumstance of the Roman triumphs which were the means by which the sovereign people in one of the most impressive spectacles of ancient Rome gave itself a display of its own greatness. There, one could see, in addition to war booty, the trophies seized by the enemy from neighbouring nations, captive chiefs and their families and tableaux of mountains, rivers and battles. It was as if the spoil of a whole province was being dragged into captivity[16];

the *Nova Via,* on the north slope of the Palatine Hill (to the east, it was called *summa,* to the north-west, *infima*). Another *via Nova,* close to the baths of Caracalla, lay parallel to the first section of the *Appia,* while the *via Lata,* which indicated a flat district to the east of the *via Flaminia* originally called the *via Lata,* gave its name to the seventh precinct of Rome.

Semita (*alta semita*, today 'viale di xx settembre') stood for a minor street, *angiportus* a lane or a dead-end street and *clivus* a street on a slope, as for example:

the *clivus Argentarius*, linking the Forum (passing between the Temple of Concordia and the Arch of Septimius Severus, with a section still visible between the *arx* and the *Forum Julium*) with the Field of Mars and the *Flaminia*;

the *clivus Capitolinus*, the only street which went up to the Capitol in ancient times, starting from the Arch of Tiberius. The part still to be seen dates from the end of the Empire;

the *clivus Palatinus*, leading off the *Sacra Via* to the north of the Arch of Titus;

the *clivus Scauri*, rising from the valley between the Palatine and Caelius Hills;

the *clivus Suburanus*, climbing up, behind the Imperial *fora*, between the Oppius and Cispius Hills in the direction of the *porta Esquilina* through the Servian wall-curcuit (the Argiletum, the district lying between the Roman Forum and Subura next becomes the street emerging between the Curia and the Aemilia Basilica);

the *clivus Victoriae*, on the north side of the Palatine.

A city street was normally called *vicus*, such as:

the *vicus Capitis Africae*

the *vicus Iugarius*, part of a business street leading from the Tiber to Sabina and, inside Rome, linking the Forum (with an arch at its entrance) to the *porta Carmentalis* in the Servian walls. Was this the 'street of the yoke-makers'?

the *vicus Tuscus*, also going from the Forum to the Tiber (*Forum Boarium* and *Circus Maximus*), the 'Etruscan street' where traders and artisans of Etrurian origin had been settled since pre-Republican times. It had a bad reputation because of the slave market that was held there.

The *vici* were named after details of the local topography, buildings, or statues standing alongside them (*vicus longus, Apollinis, delphini*), trades (*argentarius*), gens names or *cognomina* (Aurelius, Gemini).

The date of the first paving in the town was as late as 238 BC (*clivus Publicius*); in 174 BC its use was made more general by the censors (with sidewalks or *margines*). It was skilfully laid, employing an overlapping technique.

We have noted incidentally the part played by arches in the townscape. Just as they were erected to mark the points at which major roads reached the city (*Appia, Flaminia*, cf. the arches at Rimini, Susa, and in Gaul, at Orange and Glavum), so, inside the town they formed a monumental background to a street (the arch of Titus at the top of the *via Sacra*) and in the town setting had the same role as the trophies that lay at intervals along the main roads in the open country.

Alongside the Roman streets, in addition to houses, there were temples, fountains, altars (for example, the *compitum Acili* where the *vicus Cuprius* crossed a road running towards the *Carinae*) and statues.

We may note here that the 'golden milestone', erected by Augustus in 20 BC *in capite fori romani*[17], *sub aede Saturni*, consisted of a marble column with gilt-bronze plates affixed to it, displaying the distance of the great towns in the Empire (we may compare French road measurements taken from Notre-Dame in Paris). This should not be confused with the *umbilicus Romae*, a neighbouring monument dating from the Later Empire.

Imperial streets were wider, especially those laid out after the fire in Rome at the time of Nero. It is worth while recalling what Tacitus said in the *Annales*:

> Roman building-land on which Nero's palace had not encroached, was not, as happened after the fire caused by the Gauls, used haphazardly for housing: new construction had to observe a building line, streets were widened, the height of houses was reduced, open yards were provided and porticoes erected to protect the fronts of blocks . . . These measures, which were popular because they were useful, also enhanced the beauty of the new town. Some people thought, however, that the former lay-out of Rome had been much better for the health, since the narrowness of the lanes and the height of the houses prevented exposure to the burning heat of the sun, whereas today, those wide spaces, offering no shade, are scorched in far more unbearable heat[18].

Balland has considered these words and thinks that they refer to a programme involving reconstruction and control rather than new development[19]. Nevertheless in one part of the *Nova Urbs* (translated from the Greek 'neapolis', meaning 'new city') the principles of classical town planning were introduced: the eastern part of the *Sacra Via,* lined by arcades, as well as the *clivus Palatinus.* The *Domus Aurea* was entered through enormous porticoes of monumental proportions. In particular, anxious that his new creation should follow in the Hellenistic tradition, Nero hoped to expand Rome towards the sea by constructing new harbour installations. The last words of the quotation from Tacitus may well reflect detailed talks that would have been based on the theories put forward by Hippodamos of Miletus. In practice, the term *Nova Urbs* – originally to be the title of a plan of major development before the fire of 64 – became, through the force of circumstances, the scheme for reconstructing the districts in the old town. Nero did not have either the technical or the financial means to compete with the large-scale works in Alexandria by carrying out plans that had been beyond Caesar's power: that is, to transform Rome into a Neropolis, which by following the example of the great classical cities of the Hellenistic period[20], would be a reminder of the glories of Alexandria. But the Emperor was quite well aware that this project created practical and aesthetic problems in the economic field and in town planning. The new type of rationally designed domestic architecture was to become the rule in the second century.

Under the Republic, street construction in Rome was the responsibility of the censors; resurfacing, paving, cleansing, as the *lex Julia municipalis* tells us, were the duties of the *aediles* (one for each of the four districts), the *duumviri viis in urbe purgandis* (under Augustus *IV viri viarum curandarum*) and the *duumviri viis extra propiusve urbem Roman passus mille purgandis,* who disappeared when Augustus introduced the *curatores* in charge of streets outside the city limits. Some very unusual magistratures were also created: a *curator viis sternundis* (a consul in 92 BC), though we do not know if his sphere of action was Rome or Italy; a *curator viarum e lege Visellia* (a tribune in 71 BC); and a *curator viarum* (Fabricius, ten years later).

Under the Antonines, inscriptions mention a *procurator silicum*[21], and a *procurator regionum urbis adjuncto sibi officio viarum sternendarum urbis partibus duabus*[22].

These magistrates had the task of seeing that public property was respected and that there was no movement of heavy waggons from sunrise until two hours before sunset, except in cases of material intended for public works such as building and demolition, a concession that did not apply on holidays (according to the *lex Julia municipalis*[23]). The ban was renewed later[24].

The way in which private owners encroached on public property created concern that was again manifest in the Late Empire[25]. Thus, in Constantinople, on 11 October 398, Arcadius and Honorius ordered the city prefect to pull down lean-to buildings that were reducing the width of approach roads[26]; again, on 1 November 439, Theodosius II and Valentinian III instructed the prefect to lay charges against those who were including lanes wholly or in part within their property[27].

By contrast with the old towns, cities that were newly built *ex nihilo*, and in particular the *colonia,* had the advantage of a genuinely classical lay-out, following the orthogonal model of Hippodamos. In the *De Lege Agraria*[28], Cicero contrasts Rome and its irregular plan, resulting from its uneven site, with a wealthy lowland city and its well-planned grid of spacious avenues.

It is known that the foundation ceremony, while well recorded in Roman times, went back to an Etruscan origin[29]. Making use of offsets to astronomical bearings, the augur traced out the axes of the city, the *cardo* and the *decumanus maximus,* with the aid of the *groma*. There is information on this technique from surveyors who were describing how land was centuriated. The next stage was a ritual furrow: the *sulcus primigenius* marked the line of the rampart. This event is pictured on a relief sculpture from Aquileia and on coins commemorating the foundation of new colonies, in addition to being summarised by several writers. Servius[30] tells us that an Etruscan town could not be considered properly founded (*justa*) unless it had three temples (dedicated to Jupiter, Juno and Minerva), three gates and three streets. How can this definition be reconciled with an orthogonal plan, which should apparently include four gates, one at each end of both axes? In practice, the circuits of Etruscan towns were adapted to the terrain and none of these cities seemed to have had a regular plan. A passage from a work by Festus (AD 339), which points out that the seat of the major gods, on the Acropolis, lay to the north, from where they could watch and protect the city, puts us on the track of a solution: since the way to the north was excluded, only three gates and three streets in fact remained – so the gods enjoyed a panoramic view of the town.

It does appear that the first Etruscan cities were irregular, with the criss-cross plan coming into use only when colonies were founded, closely linked with Greek ones. Etruria was in constant touch with Ionia, the homeland of Hippodamos of Miletus, who codified these theories of city-planning in the first half of the fifth century BC. The dating on both sides seems to coincide. At Marzabotto, founded at the end of the sixth century BC on a plateau overlooking the Reno, the *insulae* are bounded by streets of ample dimensions, with widths of 15m for the major axes and 5m for the minor.

We meet this town pattern again in the normal lay-out of Roman camps, whose four gateways, oriented in Republican times on the cardinal points, were linked by two great streets intersecting at right angles two-thirds of the way along the major axis: the 50ft-wide *decumanus maximus* ran from the *porta praetoria* to the *porta decumana,* while the *via principalis,* 100ft wide, extended from the *porta principalis dextra* to the *porta principalis sinistra.* We know this arrangement from Polybius.

Under the Empire, Hyginus, in his *Liber de munitionibus castrorum,* confirmed by the results of excavations, gives the details of a rectangular camp, in which the main axis, the *decumanus,* 60ft wide, is cut by the *via principalis* (60ft) and the *via quintana* (40 or 50).

PROVINCIAL TOWNS

As examples of provincial towns we shall consider, first, an Italian town of ancient origin but regular plan, Pompeii, and, second, a town of colonial type in Gaul – Autun.

Pompeii lay on the site of a township that was native at first, then Greek, Etruscan, Greek again, then Samnite and finally a Roman colony in 80 BC. On the whole, its plan is regular and the anomalies can be explained by the existence of earlier nuclei. The main axes are two *decumani* running east–west, the *via di Nola* and the *strada dell' Abbondanza* with two *cardines* running north–south, the *via di Stabia,* linking the *porta Vesuvio* with the *porta di Stabia,* and the street joining the *porta di Nocera* and the *porta di Nola.* The *decumanus maximus* (*strada dell'Abbondanza*) is 8·5m wide, with pavements of about 4m; for the *via di Nola* the figures are 8m and 3·5m; the *cardo maximus* (*via di Stabia*) is nearly 7·5m wide, the pavements about 4m. The other streets vary from 3 to 5m. They are all paved.

Doorways of both houses and shops opened on to the pavements (*margines, crepidines*), on which there must have been placed benches and stalls to take advantage of the daylight. At intervals, large slabs of stone allowed the streets to be crossed after heavy Mediterranean showers. Owners were enjoined to keep the road clean in front of their dwellings, under the watchful eye of the aediles. Walls were covered with graffiti, inscriptions and caricatures. To these we must add a variety of pictures of deities and signs of all kinds. It is possible to conjure up, in these quiet streets where today in summer the tourist hurries along under a baking sun, the colourful, noisy, swarming crowds: children with their schoolmasters, acrobats, prominent men in sedan chairs or litters with their clients around them, soldiers, sailors, actors, passing travellers, slaves from distant provinces, well-dressed women on their way to the baths or a show, water-sellers, pedlars, porters, horsemen, all adding to the confusion – not to mention beggars and thieves. We should not forget the idlers gazing at the throng from the cool interiors of the barbers' shops and the customers seated at table in inn (*thermopolia*) and gaming-house. It is an accepted fact that in Mediterranean countries, the majority of business transactions take place in the

10   Paved street in Pompeii

street. What wealth was accumulated in this way! There was the whole range of activities from the luxury shops in the *strada dell'Abbondanza* to the humble stalls in the side-streets. The ruts left by waggons in the paving stones give some idea of how much traffic there was. However, some streets were reserved for pedestrians. Elsewhere, the watertanks, at cross-roads, and the street fountains must have been an obstacle to movement. We should also notice that, as in all Roman towns, under the paving there ran a carefully laid system of sewers.

If we now turn to Gaul, Augustodunum – present-day Autun – was built by Augustus between 15 and 10 BC at a junction of natural routes between the basins of the Loire, Seine and Rhône, in order to replace the former capital of the Aedui, Bibracte, in accordance with a consistently held policy. This was to move centres of population down on to lowland where they could be watched, while receiving at the same time all the benefits of Romanisation.

Autun was an important meeting-place of routes: roads led towards Decize, Orléans and Bourges; towards Avallon, Semur, Saulieu and Sens; towards Besançon, Chalon, Mâcon and Lyons. We should remember that the Autun mile-

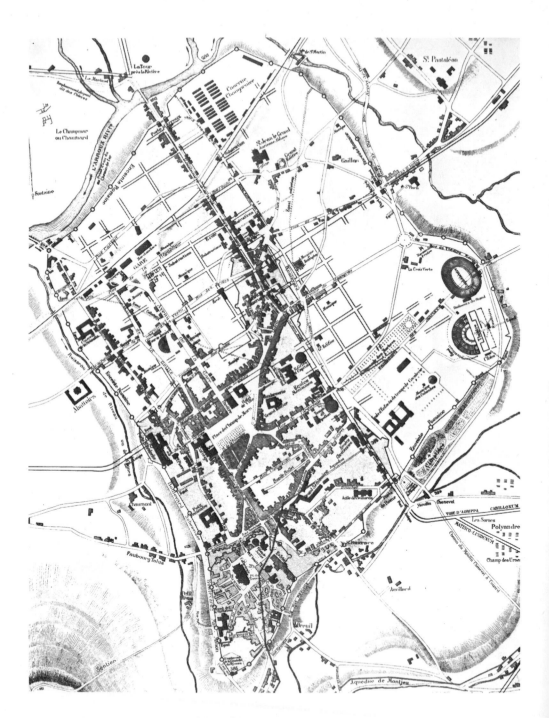

11   Map of Autun, ancient and modern

stone[31], a road sign dating from the beginning of the third century, opened up to travellers vistas of far horizons, with a road to Rome and a road to the Rhine. The *Antonine Itinerary* placed Autun on the road to the Ocean, leading through Auxerre, Sens, Lutetia, Beauvais and Amiens. Study of this road has shown how well its course was adapted to ground features. It was very carefully constructed; the agger was given flagstone kerbs, while sections have indicated that successive layers of metalling brought its height up to three feet[32].

Of the gates in the city walls, two have disappeared: that on the south (the Rome gate, with its foundations recognised in the sixteenth century and which was called in medieval times the gate 'of marbles', probably because of its wealth of ornamental stone) and the one on the west (the St-Andoche gate, excavated in 1850, so that part of its elevation is known). On the east side, the St-André gate is still visible, through which passed the road from the Loire to Besançon and Langres; it was defended by projecting towers. Finally, athwart the road from Sens to the north, can be seen the Arroux gate. Both surviving structures comprise double central carriageways with semi-circular arches supporting an upper storey and flanked by side-passages.

The surface of the Roman streets lies at a general depth of 1·6m. There is a filling of small pebbles in the gaps between the large flagstones. A section was recorded across the street to Rome when a cutting was dug for the railway in 1866–67. Apparently, after 270, the paving was removed from the *summum dorsum,* which was then rebanked with building debris and given fresh paving in the reign of Constantine.

The streets form a geometrical checker-board pattern such as we associate with the *colonia,* but somewhat adapted so that it is oriented to fit into the axes of the city's diamond shape (the main axis runs north–west by south–east). This may be recognised as the plan of a camp adjusted to ground conditions. It will be seen that the streets tie in with the towers in the city walls, whose circuit has been established. The *cardo maximus* comes from the direction of the Saône and goes as far as the Arroux gate. It is 1,250m long, but it continues for another 1,570m by a series of short straight sections that may indicate the edge of the *pomoerium.* The highway was 8m wide and had two pavements, each of 4m.

There were two *decumani* at right angles to the *cardo,* one reaching the west gate after a zig-zag (at the approach to the forum?), while the other, which was to become the road to Besançon, lay parallel, 300m away, aiming for the east gate.

The *insulae* were determined by the streets and their short sides ran parallel to the *cardo.* The areas of the *insulae* vary and this may be explained by the desire to have different sizes of land parcel or merely by a wish for variety, such as may be suggested by another important detail in the lay-out of the city: the visual effect of stepped building levels in the higher parts of the town.

Successive city plans (of which we have records since the sixteenth century) show that this geometric pattern, more or less abandoned in the Middle Ages, when there were two nuclei centred on the castle and the Marchaux, was unconsciously reused, although at a higher level, when new development took place in the town.

Similar regular street patterns survive in the majority of city centres in old French towns: Rouen, Orléans, Tours and Arles.

3 THE ROAD IN THE LANDSCAPE

Along the roads and outside the towns (beyond the *pomoerium*) lay cemeteries where monuments, in all their variety, put on display the success of the dead and their families and allowed the deceased, thought to be pursuing a more leisurely existence in the next world, a moment's awakening as the living went by. Among many inscriptions expressing this vague belief, at times bitterly and sceptically, we may quote: 'Do not overlook this epigram, O traveller, halt awhile to hear it and know it ere you depart ... All we ... dead are now nothing more than bones and dust. I have told you some home truths, be on your way, traveller, that I may not seem to you over-talkative for a dead man[33].' Propertius, on the other hand, waxes indignant against this social mixing: 'I am in no wise pleased to have my name on view in the middle of a road[34].'

Examples of these cemeteries must include, of course, the Alyscamps, along the road to Italy where it leaves Arles, one of the best-known sacred sites in the Roman West. In spite of damage in modern times and in spite of the artificial manner in which empty sarcophagi have been placed in line (the finest are in the museum), the site remains as thought-provoking as the *via Appia* in Rome. This Christian burial ground, with its series of 17 chapels and its thousands of graves, grew up around the tomb of St Geneseus. Such cemeteries of Gallo-Roman and Merovingian times were later to inspire many an epic legend, which saw the numerous tombs as evidence of mighty battles in the past.

Another example may be found outside Glanum, where the ancient Celtic road is lined by Gallo-Greek burials. Here the inscription on the *mausolée des Antiques* was turned to face travellers coming along the road from Spain and into the town through the municipal arch. Tombs may also be found in the open country, as in the case of the mausolea or tumuli (in Belgium), belonging to the great estate-owners, which made landmarks for travellers, even at night (there is an elegiac couplet, taken from Virgil, on a tomb south of Lambasa[35]). Relics of these holy places, whether they were cemeteries or centres of worship, have survived in unusual circumstances, often near cross-roads: thus, close to old roads in North Africa, still lie numerous tombs of 'holy-men' (marabouts). It is this sort of association that makes these isolated burial places so interesting archaeologically.

In addition to tombs, milestones and engineering works[36] formed part of the road landscape.

When agricultural land was developed, water-course and road sometimes came in for combined treatment. There is often an aqueduct beside a road, as for example from Novéant to Gorze where the underground section of the aqueduct (the

Sarrazin stream) and the old road lie parallel. Such is frequently the case in the Roman countryside. To quote Pliny the Elder: 'Agrippa brought the aqua Virgo a distance of two miles along the Praeneste road from the point where the side-road joins it at the eighth milestone[37].' To the south of Constantine, the aqueducts, with their characteristic courses, even seem to have been, in certain places, the main feature around which the entire human development of the landscape was set in motion. Usually aqueducts entered towns at the gateways. Short of an aqueduct, there were watertanks, troughs or wells for travellers to quench their thirst. As Pliny the Elder tells us once more[38]: 'Fertile land should be left as meadow and irrigated with rain-water from the public road.' Ancient tracks followed by livestock (transhumance roads) always have ponds strung out alongside them.

What about the vegetation cover around Roman roads? We know that woodland was avoided because of ambushes (cf. Book I of the *Gallic War* in which Caesar describes a long detour made in order to miss the forests and narrow glens of the Doubs valley). Roads often skirted woodland without going into it. But alongside many routes there must have been copses – where a halt could be made away from the sun[39] – and also sacred groves. Four relief sculptures at least from Gaul illustrate a horse-drawn vehicle passing a tree[40]. Does this merely symbolise the countryside or are we to visualise plantations beside the road? Pliny the Younger states that Romans were not unmoved by the magic of the landscape and his uncle sings the praises of the vines hanging from the young elms in northern Italy, one of the features of the Po countryside that were to be the delight of all foreign visitors. And it is well known that the Romans also liked to plant woodland walks on their country villas. While tree-planting in antiquity must remain a mystery to us[41], it plays an important part in the appearance of roads: Palladio considers that they should be lined by trees, while Sully and Gautier go on to recommend low, quick-set hedges, 'so that they would offer no advantage to brigands'; they would give 'the roadside beauty and firmness of line'.

Even away from the centres of population, there were sanctuaries along the roads, where people paid their respects to Hercules[42], Mercury, Mars, the Dioscuri[43], the *Lares Viales* (invoked by Plautus), and the divinities attributed to the meeting-point of two, three, or four roads (*Biviae, Triviae, Quadruviae*). These little places of worship were often sited at prominent features on the journey, such as cross-roads and fords, and might conceal earlier cults (in Gaul, for example, there are columns to the horseman-god close to fords, while Caesar in the *Gallic War* quotes the protection given to travellers by Mercury). A passage from Apuleius[44] tells us how varied these holy spots were: 'When pious travellers meet a sacred grove on their way or some holy place, they usually offer a prayer and an ex-voto, halting awhile . . .' Then a list follows: 'An altar garlanded with flowers, a grotto adorned with shady foliage, an oak tree bearing horns, a beech bedecked with skins, a holy mound enclosed by a wall, a tree trunk sculpted by an adze into a human shape, a patch of turf charged with the aroma from the burning of libations, a rock sweet-smelling from perfume.'

4 STREET PATTERNS AND COUNTRY ROADS.
CENTURIATION BOUNDARIES

The previous notes on city streets necessarily form part of our subject, since there is a close connection, at any rate in theory, and sometimes verified on colonial land, between the patterns of city streets and of those serving farmland. This is made clear by a text in Hyginus concerning Ammaedara (Haïdra, in Tunisia)[45].

At this point we should redefine centuriation, which as we know comprised a grid traced out on the ground. After he had marked on the two axes at right angles to each other, the *decumanus maximus* and the *cardo maximus,* the Roman surveyor (*agrimensor, gromaticus*) laid out in relation to these a series of parallels, which appear on the ground as lanes flanked by side-ditches or lines of stones cleared from the fields. The land divisions thus obtained were called *centuriae* (originally one *centuria* for 100 men) and were further subdivided in a geometric fashion by footpaths leading to the various lots, by drainage ditches or irrigation trenches and by lines of stones. The *centuriae* occurred in several dimensions, the commonest being composed of 20 *actus* each of 120ft, about 710m. The ideal arrangement according to the surveying manuals, was that the *pertica* or centuriated land as a whole should be divided into four equal areas starting from the very centre of the city; but this was theoretical only and scarcely applied except on the *colonia*. We know of one example at least: Ammaedara (Haïdra) in Tunisia. It is worth noting here that the orientation of

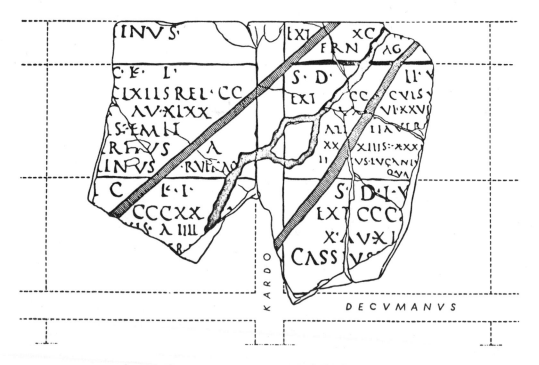

12   Part of the cadastral inscription from Orange (after A. Piganiol, 16th Supplement to *Gallia*, 1962, p. 109)

street grids, land-plots and main roads in relation to each other may date the successive stages by which colonisation took place. Thus, in northern Italy, centuriation which is tied in with the *via Aemilia* of 187 BC must be contemporary with it or later.

One of the most extraordinary inscriptions to have survived is the cadastral registry of Orange, which outlined on flagstones the boundaries of the *centuriae*; a few important landscape details; exact information about the siting of the lots in relation to the axes; the areas of tributary or colonial land; the land tax; and finally, the name of the official adjudicator. This material evidence, placed alongside the illustrations in the textbooks of the *gromatici*, proves that there must have been land registries in general use, involving some fairly exact map-making (and of the latter, the *Peutinger Table* gives only a sketchy idea).

Let us take as an example the centuria DDXVI-CKI from land registry B:

This fragment will fit exactly on to the modern map. The Roman engraver has marked the river Berre and the highway (the Agrippa road), which bridges it at the Logis de Berre. Then suddenly he has brought the road to a halt at the precise point where the edge of the plateau des Echirouzes rises from 73m to 124. The old road went up onto the high ground in the direction of Montélimar, for, 8km south of that town, the discovery of an inscribed milestone[46] informs us that Tiberius repaired that road in 31–32. So our engraver left off marking the course of the road where the straight stretch ended. At the Logis de Berre a milestone bears the name of Constantine . . . The Agrippa road is now the D-158 and at the Logis de Berre the modern road avoids going up on to the plateau des Echirouzes, but turns to the left towards Donzère, just where the ancient draughtsmen finished his line[47].

One of the most surprising things arising from the examination of maps and aerial photographs for traces of centuriation is the way in which *limites* have survived. One is struck by short sections of road, which do not fit in with the present-day network, and turn sharply or end suddenly for no clear reason. But these stretches of road, once projected, are found to be in alignment. They may be continued by a footpath, ditch or stream or by some local boundary, sometimes simply by the edge of cultivated land: these sudden changes show how far the old courses still persist. Such alterations in alignment to right or left, however slight, are evidence of the growth and development of farming but there is always a return to the original axes, striking proof how straight these were.

Place names like 'dismano' (from *decumano*), 'cardito' (from *cardo*) and 'limite' (from *limes*) – in Italy – provide extra evidence.

We must emphasise that these land registries covered large areas of the Roman world: almost the whole of Italy and Spain, North Africa (as far as agricultural land was concerned), Yugoslavia and the Danube valley, and Provence. There are traces in Greece, the Near East, Belgium, Germany and even in Britain.

There can be no doubt that on the ground the parcels were very clearly demarcated. The geometric checker-work pattern found in the provinces resulted from the lines set out when the land was developed, with the *centuriae* inscribed as it were on the surface; the *limites* are best revealed by the network of communications. One main road may serve as a *decumanus maximus* for one or several land surveys. Many other roads were built to fit in with those constructed for centuriation; as far as possible their courses were made to coincide with the *limites* of the centurial parcels. When it was impossible for the road to maintain a straight line because of unfavourable terrain, a detour was made to reach the next *limes* so as to avoid expropriating land or interrupting the system of *centuriae*. The roads were indeed the key to this economic set-up, with their posting inns and granaries.

It was not only on the main highways that road and countryside were in harmony with each other. The geometric lay-out of the secondary roads, which were also based on the cadastral survey, was the best method of ensuring that all land parcels had the same ease of access; exactly the same system was used when the American West was colonised. The road network was the means by which land was distributed and divided into lots and so formed the main feature whereby the estates were developed. Thanks to their stony metalling, often running alongside waterways, the old roads have survived, helped too by the fact that the tenancies of the properties through which they ran (the regulation *Iter populo debetur,* the subject of Saumagne's excellent study) did not allow trespass. It is for this reason alone that, accidentally, centuriation has persisted in the Vega de Carmona. It can be easily seen that tracking the details of the land registries which were probably in their day the best way of carrying out colonisation allows us to obtain a realistic estimate of the progress of both conquest and settlement, showing how thoroughly and permanently Romanisation took hold. The discovery of the land divisions will provide the only proper framework in which to plot random archaeological finds and, together with the distribution of the *villae* and *vici*, lay the basis of a statistical survey of both the demography and the economy, so enabling us to understand what Roman civilisation was at bottom: a framework for local initiative, which filled the gaps. The whole structure combining adherence to principle and flexibility in application gave stability to the land, which was the foundation of the economy of the ancient world. It is striking to observe how the guiding lines of the past, which were usually dictated by the very nature of things, still make their presence felt in the modern landscape. Modern developments take place at points geometrically determined by age-old coordinates. Roads and railways follow directions that avoid cutting across farmland, where the field boundaries still correspond to the ancient land divisions. Towns are still growing where the old axes crossed. Large farms lie close to Roman ruins, in the angles of *centuriae*. In this way, the land surveys, not very visibly, form the framework to living in many provinces. The unchanging landscape is one of the most certain facts in historical geography.

5 ROAD CONSTRUCTION[48]

It happens that one of the few ancient texts giving information on the different phases of construction of a Roman road is a poem by Statius in praise of the *via*

Domitiana, a short cut along the *Appia*[49]. Domitian had it built at great cost between Sinuessa and Pozzuoli, skirting the sandy, marshy coastline so as to avoid the roundabout route through Capua. The text reads:

> The first task here is to trace furrows, ripping up the maze of paths, and then excavate a deep trench in the ground. The second comprises refilling the trench with other material to make a foundation for the road build-up. The ground must not give way nor must bedrock or base be at all unreliable when the paving stones are trodden. Next the road metalling is held in place on both sides by kerbing and numerous wedges. How numerous the squads working together! Some are cutting down woodland and clearing the higher ground, others are using tools to smooth outcrops of rock and plane great beams. There are those binding stones and consolidating the material with burnt lime and volcanic tufa. Others again are working hard to dry up hollows that keep filling with water or are diverting the smaller streams.

These lines are very much to the point, in spite of the abrupt, rhetorical style affected by Statius, and Duval's useful commentary[50] is followed here. First it is clear that the strip of land involved in the road was marked out by furrows, so obliterating earlier tracks: there has been a view that the word *limites* could, technically speaking, apply to the byroads giving access to centuriation in Campagna. The road trench had to reach, if not bedrock, at any rate a sufficiently firm foundation, which was reinforced by ramming, piles or brushwood (*crates*). Sections were built at a time, as with modern motorway construction; this method of building may well explain the slight changes of alignment observable on the ground in the case of Roman roads. The trench was packed with materials brought from elsewhere, the bottom layers being made of stones, gravel and sand successively and the spine of the road cambered to aid drainage. The surface was given a covering of paving stones held in place by a kerb (*umbo*) formed of similar stones set on edge supported on the outer side by a stony revetment rather than a sidewalk. Other wedge-shaped stones (*gomphi*)[51] acted as clamps: they were jammed between the stones of the kerb as well as in the paving[52]. Many different trades were engaged in the work: woodcutters, quarrymen, carpenters, stonemasons and navvies. The surrounding hills provided flagstones, paving stones or rubble and in particular timber for reinforcing the foundations, for use in constructions of all kinds (new fords, bridges, suspended roadways) or again for heating lime kilns. Employing mortar (here made of lime[53] and pozzolana instead of sand) was unusual on roads, except on very difficult ground. The approaches to the road must have been kept well drained, but Statius does not mention side ditches. He next deals with the bridge thrown across the Volturno.

Two other technical sources must be noted dealing with road construction. The first was written by Julian and occurs in a letter to his friend and tutor Libanius just as the emperor was setting off on a campaign against the Persians[54]:

> In the territory of Chalcis, I came across a road running through the remains of

an Antiochan winter camp. This highway was, so to speak, half-marsh, half-mountain, and hard going withal. The marshy ground was crossed by a layer of stones, seemingly cast there by intent, but in an artless fashion, unlike other territories, where, in the case of roads, as for masonry, stones are rammed together into the built-up soil of a causeway, as if it were mortar in a wall.

Julian, keen strategist that he was, used to march at the head of his troops, keeping a watchful eye on the roads. A solidly built construction of stones set in soil as described here is not often found and was kept for difficult sections, swampy areas, deep glens and high ground exposed to snowfall; nevertheless it is a feature providing proof of a Roman origin. In modern times, the system of construction has depended on the use of graded stones, well packed and tamped.

The last quotation comes from the *Gothic War* by Procopius and describes the *Appia* between Rome and Capua, which was paved by Appius with stone from various sources: 'After much laborious smoothing, the slabs were cut into polygonal shapes and he then laid them together without using lime [some manuscripts say 'without metal'] or anything else. And they were fitted together with such care and the gaps so well filled that, to the onlooker, they appear to be the work not of man, but of nature[55].'

6 ROAD BUILDERS

We should remember at this point the text quoted earlier from Siculus Flaccus about the classification of roads, their construction and their upkeep.

In the case of the main roads, the importance of the army's role has already been emphasised, with its cadres of civil or military engineers, who were often veteran volunteers (*evocati*). These men did not rely on merely empirical methods, a fact amply demonstrated by the straightness of the boundaries of centuriation over dozens of miles, despite obstacles and interruptions imposed by relief.

It is not easy to visualise how the surveying was carried out, although manuals do contain ideas on triangulation. Sighting instruments had already been devised (*groma, dioptra*) which allowed signals to be picked up from one point to the next and overcame problems created by differences in level. This would be worth further investigation, starting with what is known from Greek science. It would be wise, too, to spot what has survived beyond the Middle Ages. Fustier's useful book[56], *La Route,* shows clearly the part played by surveying instruments in the development of road engineering[57]. Roman engineers certainly aimed at high points in the landscape, for from one viewpoint to the next it is possible to check the bearings of straight sections of road[58].

To carry out the work there must have been a work-force of some size, provided by the army and helped, of course, by conscripted civilians, as Cicero's *Pro Fonteio* tells us[59]: like Bugeaud's army in Algeria, the legion built the roads, established the land survey and registry, thus helping in the settlement of the natives and their

Romanisation. We have very few ideas about this large-scale work. Detachments were put at the disposal of the specialists responsible for undertaking the land survey and at the same time laying out roads: thus the milestones in southern Tunisia bear the name of the proconsul and the number of the legion that took part on the road survey: *Legio tertia Aug[usta] leimitavit, C. Vibio Marso proco[n]s[ule]*[60]. We also know of a land conveyance effected under Septimus Severus south of the Hodna Chott: the transaction, prepared by the freedman Epagathus (probably a Greek *mensor*) and the prefect's adjutant, Manilius Caecilianus, was negotiated by an *evocatus* in the Third Legion, M. Gennius Felix[61].

Another inscription worth quoting dates from AD 145 and was found on a rock-face in the gorges of Tighanimine (Aurès). It commemorates the work of a unit brought from Syria to face a native rebellion: 'Under the reign of the emperor Caesar T. Aelius Hadrianus Antoninus, Augustus, pious, father of his country, consul for the fourth time, and of Marcus Aurelius, Caesar, consul for the second time, by order of Prastina Messalinus, imperial legate and propraetor, the vexillatio of the VI Legion Ferrata built this road.'

It is noticeable that the majority of main roads were pioneered by military operations. For example, on its return from the first Samnite war (343–40), the Roman army did not come back along the *via Latina,* but followed the coast through the territory of the Aurunci, thus blazing the trail of the *Appia* on a line that had already been known to traders, at least since the hegemony of Etruria. In the early third cencentury, operations against the Umbrians of Mevania and Narnia and against the Senones took into account the route that became the *Flaminia.* Great strategic roads were built by the military in Gaul under Agrippa from BC 16–13 in Dalmatia and Pannonia under Tiberius from AD 6–9[62], in the Rhineland and the Danube valley under Claudius, and in Asia Minor under the Flavians.

These highways were policed from fortified posts, which soon developed into army colonies, both in Italy and in the provinces. Examples include the Roman colony of Terracina (329–26), guarding the most dangerous pass on the *Appia,* the Lautulae; the Latin colonies of Cales (337–34) and Fregellae (328–25) which protected the *via Latina* against the raids made by Samnites and other enemies from the south (Pyrrhus took this road as far as Anagni and perhaps Praeneste); the Latin colonies of Alba and Carsioli on the Apennine way; and the colonies of Dyrrachium, Pella and Philippi on the *via Egnatia.*

These posts had, when first set up, undeniable strategic importance, but soon became in addition centres of population and development. In the countryside between the large towns, there came into being a pattern of townships and markets based on economic factors, recalling once again Bugeaud's policies in Algeria – hence the existence of those *fora* created by roads, with names taken from the great colonisers: Forum Appi on the *Appia,* where Appius Claudius Caecus had been bold enough to erect a statue of himself wearing a royal crown[63].

In peacetime, the decision to open up a road lay with the censors[64], eventually with the praetors. Under the Empire the heads of state took a personal interest in the road system and commemorated new road construction by striking special

coin issues: thus we have the Augustan denarii of 16 BC variously displaying a milestone in celebration of repair work or two triumphal arches with equestrian statues
and trophies on a bridge or a double arch with *rostra* and a *quadriga* on a bridge, or
again a double arch or a fivefold one bearing a chariot drawn by elephants. This
shows the importance attached to roads by the government. As early as the eulogy
of Appius Claudius the building of the *Appia* was put on the same plane as military
victories or political deeds.

7 STRUCTURE AND FEATURES OF ROMAN ROADS

The possibility of digging test trenches may not often occur and results are not clear-
cut: it is seldom that datable material comes to light from the build-up of the road
or from the side-ditches. In any case, no construction can be regarded as typical. But
there are many ground exposures in quarries and public works which allow sections
of old roads to be studied, once they have been scraped clean, while it is simple and
cheap to carry out geophysical profiles of roads by electrical or magnetic methods,
such as at Izernore (p. 107).

In the early seventeenth century, in his *Histoire des grands chemins de l'Empire
romain,* written at the royal command[65], N. Bergier elaborated a theory that has been
popular for a long time, arising from the laying of floor surfaces and pavements
(*expolitiones*) and the building of tiled flat roofs. Bergier believed that he had been
able to establish that the following layers were laid in succession on beaten earth up
to a thickness of 1 or 1·5m.

> *statumen*, several rows of flat stones, bound with mortar or clay;
> *rudus* or *ruderatio,* a watertight foundation raft, made of a concrete containing
> small pebbles, broken stone and brick, well rammed down;
> *nucleus,* a finer concrete, with a lime and sand cement reinforced with broken
> tile, rolled out in layers;
> finally, *summum dorsum,* with a central camber, sometimes sloping straight down
> on each side, for drainage, made of gravel (as for *viae glarea stratae*) or paving stones
> (*viae silice stratae*).

Bergier's theory, which was to have wide acceptance by archaeologists, seems to
have originated as follows: whereas the word *pavimentum* had only one meaning for
Vitruvius and Pliny the Elder, namely the actual floor inside houses, Bergier connected the word with the French 'pavé', which signified the whole of a road, and so
followed a false argument. Since *pavimentum*='pavé', then all the information
given by Vitruvius in this respect must apply to Roman roads; the author's research
led him to believe he had identified the various layers making up the *pavimentum*.

There is a certain similarity between the build-up of roads and that of paved floors,
but a Roman road is not a 'buried wall'. Its structure is both more variable and more
complicated. As a general rule, what is seen is:

a foundation course (sometimes involving stakes), consisting of a rubble layer

with stones set on edge to aid drainage, always the concern of Roman engineers;
a build-up of resilient material[66] (sand);

a surfacing, not necessarily paved, especially in the earlier period (the first paving
appeared in 174 BC[67], but on the *Appia* not until the time of Hadrian) and in the
open country[68], usually along the easier stretches.

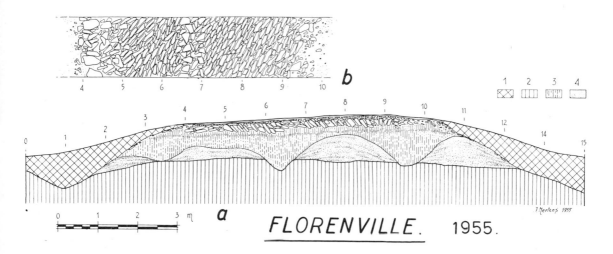

13 Roman road from Rheims to Trier: plan and section at Florenville. Details: (a) section: 1 recent
fill 2 undisturbed natural 3 clay 4 sand (b) plan showing surface metalling (after J. Mertens, 'Les
routes romaines de la Belgique', *Industrie*, no. 10, October 1955, p. 31)

Nevertheless the manner in which roads were built varied a great deal, even along
the same route, according to the firmness of the subsoil and the available materials.
The interpretation of most sections is complicated by the repairs and remetalling
that occurred on many occasions. Sometimes iron slag was used (cf. place names like
'vy Ferrat'). We should remember, too, Ulpian's distinction[69] between, on the one
hand, *viae terrenae,* mere surface roads, and, on the other hand, *glarea stratae* and
silice stratae, properly metalled roads.

Broise has recently published some detailed observations made in the Haute-
Savoie:

The road is made of successive layers of gravel, often reaching one metre in thickness, the result in many cases of a number of resurfacings. People have spoken
in the past of consolidated gravel and we have often noticed ourselves that the
gravel of roads in Boutae (Roman Annecy) had a binding of compacted clay of
thin mortar so as to make up what we would call today a rough concrete. Sur-
facings of large stones, whether or not roughly shaped, have also been noticed
over stone foundations; but the fact that there is no metalling today on the surface
does not mean that there was none originally, for paving, especially in the *vici,*
may have been torn up for later building-work.

This point will be noted later with reference to African roads.

When they passed through population centres, some roads included sidewalks (*margines, crepidines*) with a raised edge (*umbo*).

There are many raised causeways bordered by lines of shaped slabs set upright and possessing side-ditches.

Amongst the ditches, several types can be picked out with the aid of aerial photographs[70]:

quarry-ditches immediately alongside, which provided ballast and material for remetalling and drained the surface-water; the verges are then either side of the causeway or else 20m out, with a width of 1·1 to 1·7m, sometimes more. There are such ditches even within towns. They are not unique to Roman roads. We may observe that, thanks to the retention of ground moisture, even when these ditches are filled, they allow vanished roads to be seen from the air when the causeway has been destroyed (a practice which had official backing when major roadwork took place, as in the eighteenth century'. These ditches sometimes have legends attached to them, as at Cagny (Somme), where the bands of dew running along them are said to mark the way trodden by St Domitius and St Ulpha.

boundary-ditches lying 20m more or less on each side; their presence may explain the shape of elongated fields along the roads which correspond to strips of land that long remained uncultivated (they may well have a different colour). There may have been a ban on ploughing or on building (we know this from inscriptions on the edges of aqueducts)[71] or a verge may have left for road-users (a bridleway for horsemen, or a grassy belt for herds, as in Spain) or again the natives may have been forbidden to use a strip of land, at any rate in the early days and in woodland favourable to ambush. There is mention in Strabo of such measures of security along the Ligurian coast[72] and in more recent times we may note the practice of cutting down vegetation on either side of a road within musket-range[73];

finally, hollow-ways exist[74], lined by side-ditches lying a javelin's throw away which appear to be connected with former military camps and may have served to allow the safe movement of troops or the entry of water supplies, fodder and livestock. We have the example of the great depression linking the two Roman camps stationed in front of Gergovia. Raised banks, bundles of brushwood or palisades may have completed these bracchia-type ditches, which must thereby have acted as an obstacle to the movement of surface water.

Roads varied considerably in width.

Augustus had issued decrees (known through surveyors' writings) fixing the width of a *decumanus maximus* as 40ft (13m), that of a *cardo maximus* as 20 and of other *decumani* and *ordines* as 12. Byroads were allowed 8ft. If the widths that we see today corresponded to the original widths, then we might have a chronological guide. But the standards used varied with the importance of the road, and this changed with the times, as is shown by the differences in the width and thickness of the deposits visible in one and the same section.

In towns there is a connection with the openings through gateways (thus at Autun, 50ft, that is 8m, with two sidewalks of 4ft; an order of 1720 speaks of 60ft). Usually in the countryside roads are 15–20ft wide to allow vehicles to pass each other but we have to reckon with cases of narrowing where the terrain was difficult!

It is unwise, apart from the main strategic roads, to attempt any classification of the old highways.

Ruts, both in town (as at Pompeii) and in country, may have been the result of wear and tear, but where they are deep (6–30cm) and with sharp edges, clearly shaped by pick and hammer, they were obviously intentional. On awkward ground, close to a sheer drop, they served as rails, guiding the waggons, for these had front wheels higher than the actual frames, making independent steering impossible. Bends had to be negotiated therefore on a wide arc.

The use of these rails, sometimes in conjunction with transverse grooves to prevent horses from slipping[75], may have started earlier than the Romans. In some places, parking lanes are said to have been recognised, which raises the problem that this would involve one-way traffic[76]. Gauges have been claimed varying from 1·05 to 1·85m; the figures differ according to the way in which the measurements were made (from the centre line of each rut or between inside edges). Comparisons have been sought with the wheel-bases of ancient vehicles, prehistoric (waggon burials) or Roman, and with modern railway gauges. It is quite possible that careful study of the standards used could yield evidence about dating (1·3m in antiquity, 1·45m in the Middle Ages ?).

Alongside the paved way in use by heavy waggons, there often ran parallel tracks providing easier going for both walkers and riders, especially when faced with oncoming traffic. Palladio has pointed out these sand or gravel strips, which were separated from the higher traffic lane in the centre by lines of stones set on edge. We need only to travel in Spain, even today, to notice in the verges of many important roads the tracks followed by sheep in seasonal movements.

On each side of the *Appia,* close to Itri, Fustier has observed a line of prismatic boundary stones, like those edging the road. They are spaced out irregularly and mark out a beaten track $2\frac{1}{2}$ft wide for beasts of burden, so extending the band in public use to 32ft[77].

A strip of clay soil running alongside a paved road may also be evidence of an older road of mere beaten earth.

We should take special note of the profiles of Roman roads, both longitudinal and transverse. The builders avoided obvious problems and there was a preference for a course on dry level ground or along the so-called military crest, below the top of the slope, where one could see without being seen. Nevertheless difficult situations were tackled purposefully[78].

One such difficulty occurred on marshy ground, where the road was given a proper causeway, and not just an earthen ridge[79], upon dykes which later on in the Middle Ages may have been used to hold back ponds (as in the Sologne).

Professor Mertens has recovered some interesting information about the *via Mansuerisca* in the Hautes-Fagnes, Belgium: he found a wooden framework, probably in the native tradition[80], involving piles and culverts, overlain by a built-up causeway:

> Two rows of cross-beams were placed on the marshy soil for the whole length of the road. The distance between the beams was 2m. There was a gap between the internal ends of each pair of beams, while the external ends projected some 40cm beyond the basic timber seating. These outer ends were slotted to take vertical stakes so pinning the framework to the ground. On the cross-beams were fixed lengthwise with the road two lines of joists to carry the sides of the highway. The joists bore a transverse 'corduroy' of tree trunks and on this in turn there lay limestone flags cemented with clay, covered again by the road-metalling of gravel and pebbles. Tree trunks were discovered under other roads at river-crossings[81].

Other examples can be pointed out. In the marshlands of the Ems and the Hunse, wooden roads have been found with morticed timbers and at Kembs, near the old course of the Rhine, traces of duckboarded tracks. The 'Ferronne highway' in the valley of the Thérain, lying in the marshy country west of Clermont, had a foundation of stones laid chevronwise. Modderman has noticed a layer of timbers probably belonging to a road running along the bank of the Rhine[82].

Drouyn observed at a point at which a Roman road crossed swampy ground layers of tree trunks laid criss-cross fashion[83]. Caesar noted such construction close to Sens[84] and reference can also be made to the passage in Tacitus' *Annales*[85] describing the *Pontes Longi* at the mouths of the Rhine: 'Caecina received the order to cross at all

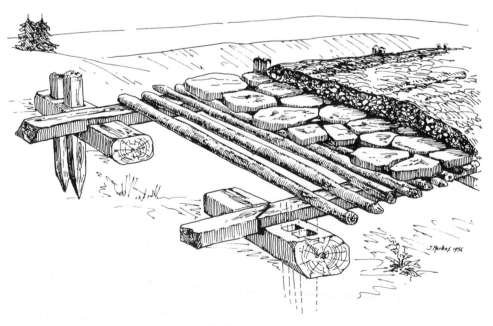

14   Section of a road built over on unstable ground: the *via Mansuerisca* in the Hautes-Fagnes
(after J. Mertens, op. cit., p. 39)

speed by way of the Long Bridges. This is a narrow highway in vast marshes, built in the past by L. Domitius; beyond it there is only slime and thick, tenacious mud, in which the waterways are difficult to make out; all around rise low wooded hills . . . Caecina was wondering how he could at one and the same time repair the time-worn bridges and drive away the enemy.' Place names like 'Pont-long' or 'Long-pont' may well take us back to similar structures. We should also note the timber roads (brushwood bridges) preserved in the peat of the La Brèche marshes west of Breuil-le-Sac (Oise)[86]; they were made of timber frames resting on a brushwood foundation held in place by stakes, fixture being made by wedges not mortices, the whole covered by a double floor of beams supporting wattlework and then by sand. Two stretches are known each of 600m, with a width of 3.9 to 18m and a thickness of 60cm. The course was forked, the eastern approach being paved. The supporting layer of brushwood was strengthened in some places by stout tree trunks and, close to the river, by quarry stones cemented with marl. The amount of material used per hectare has been estimated at 2,000 cubic metres of timber and 4,000 cubic metres of brushwood. Comparisons have also been suggested with a timber track in the peat bogs of Somerset (Meare Heath), dated to the local Late Bronze Age (750–500 BC) and with the 'road of life' in the Gironde marshes, but the age of the causeways at Breuil-le-Sec is much in dispute and the proffered dating ranges from a prehistoric origin to the Middle Ages. The interest of such structures is that they can be carbon-dated.

Engineering works proper will be discussed later.

It is useful at this point to compare descriptions of various roads, as they appear both on the surface and in section, from different provinces of the Empire.

The Syrian road from Apamea to Theleda provides one example[87]. It is 6m wide with a central spine and kerbs at the side or raised edges. In lower parts liable to flooding, it becomes a causeway, interrupted at intervals by a setting of large flat stones. The edges of the causeway slope gently down to the ground on either side. The stone setting, laid between the middle rib and the kerbs, forms a hard road surface of fitted paving. Crossing the marshland, the way is marked by a layer of flagstones, level with the surface of the water.

Another road worth describing is that from Bosra (Syria) through Damascus to Palmyra[88]. It is 5.5m wide and is composed of two strips, each sloping away from the centre to form a slight hog's back with a line of stones marking the middle rib. Two further such lines make up kerbs on each side. These three parallel features are constructed with roughly hewn slabs, rectangular rather than square in shape and set edge to edge. Between them there is a road surface of basalt slabs laid in an irregular pattern. The three lines of stones project about 15 or 20cm above this surface. When a wadi had to be crossed, an embankment was built to ease the gradient. The embanked sections are of the same width as the road and their sides are always sheer. They are constructed in dry-stone masonry. The external faces consist of roughly dressed blocks with side measurements between 30 and 50cm.

Caravan roads in the desert, beyond the *limes,* have left little ground evidence, for their courses were defined only when crossing stony country. In order to spare the feet of the animals in a camel train, small rocks and sharp fragments were pushed to each side to form parallel verges, which have survived as gently curving ridges[89]. But the style of building at the posting-stations; the method of establishing watch-towers which could exchange visible signals; the provision of water supplies (by well or tank); and finally the actual distances of the stages – all these factors show that the Romans were responsible.

On the whole, the roads follow the obvious course over the desert. When the going was not firm under foot, a higher route was sought, half-way up mountain spurs. Mostly, we simply find *viae terrenae,* humble beaten tracks with edges each side, and with eventual later improvements. Where floods were a threat. there occur at regular distances cross-ribs of flat stones laid athwart the normal longitudinal features, enclosing in effect a series of macadamised strips. The paving slabs used on the low ground are flat above, but on their lower sides bear a bevelled point.

There are, according to the author, two stone edges 12m apart which serve either to contain the surfacing material or simply to mark out the course of the road, at any rate in the interior of the province. Sometimes there are four lines of stones dividing the highway into three lanes, the middle one being 6·5m wide.

In general the impression is given of an organisation whose methods were firm, but not harsh, based on a sound knowledge of local geography (there were winter and summer roads) and carried out with flexibility. The map of Roman roads is the map of natural routes. They run straight with bends and detours when the ground requires. One is struck by the regularity of the stages and the wideness of the highway. There is no hesitation in tackling difficult terrain (swamps, lava-flows) at the cost of major works, but as soon as possible the road seeks out the easiest course, the most picturesque places and the watering-points.

It must be added, that as regards the materials used in the actual road construction, there is still a shortage of careful, on-the-spot observations backed by sample-taking for petrological analysis[90]. The study of sands by grading in particular should allow quarries to be identified, since special qualities of material may have to be obtained at some distance. In a few exceptional cases, details of interest have come to light, as, for example, the use of Euganean trachyte, which was transported by water to pave some roads in the lowland around Padua, in the same way that basalt from the Vivarais was employed in Gaul. It may well be that the systematic study of grades of material will enable some advances to be made in dating.

Model sections have been published by Mertens in Belgium[91] or in Italy (Alba, *via Valeria*) as well as by Fustier[92]. They bring out the variety of solutions adopted by Roman road-builders when having to adapt themselves to individual problems (in the Crau, a natural conglomerate was used, while elsewhere we find a mass of clay well rammed down, 'a technique as yet unrecorded for counteracting the absence of hard material by working up local substitutes'). In Alsace there is a road made of crushed Gallo-Roman titles.

Even in Italy, Fustier comes to the conclusion that there is no general theory. The course of a road is as much determined by geographical factors as are the materials to build it. There is also evidence for much reuse in the building and repair of roads[93].

The following is an excellent description of a section:

> The old road is built in a wide depression dug into the ground and filled with fine sand. The width of the roadway between the kerb-stones set on edge is 5·2m and the sandy sides of the depression each form *margines* (parallel tracks) of 1·5m, which may have served as bridle-paths. The foundation course is made of small slabs of local limestone, bedded on a scatter of other stones resting on the sand, so as to form a perfectly flat surface which shows no signs of wear and tear. The next layer, which rises to the level of the kerb-stones or just above, is slightly cambered and less even and has traces of remetalling. A rather loose paving lies at this level between the western *margo* and the edge of the side-ditch running parallel to it and some 1·5m away. An *as* of Constantine ii was found just above the second layer. At the higher levels, the side-path is no longer in service and the fifteenth-century highway takes on that cobbly appearance so often associated with farmyards. The later resurfacings have been dispersed by ploughing. The kerb-stones measure 28 by 12 by 4cm[94].

In conclusion, what must be emphasised is the great variety of approach to road construction in the past and the adaptability of road builders in planning a route and in using local methods, which is understandable, since it was the natives living alongside the roads who often built them and anyhow kept them under repair. We should remember, too, that on the ground the same road may pursue several courses in service at the same time or successively, as a result of changes in land use. Some branch roads lost importance, other roads were upgraded or downgraded for economic or political reasons and as a result or urban development.

8 ENGINEERING WORKS

BRIDGES

In the first place, we shall deal with the type of bridge that came to be built in many places, thanks to Roman skill in the construction of arches. *Opus caementicium* was used for the foundation and the framework of arches and piers, together with *opus quadratum* or *latericium* for the facing.

The method of building (similar to that for aqueducts), and the sites are known in a variety of ways: textual references, especially technical works like those by Vitruvius; commemorative coin issues; relief sculpture (notably Trajan's Column); mosaic floors (the Arles bridge); illustrations in old prints; archaeological finds (including the results of dredging, which may bring up oak piles, protected by shoes, flanged iron tips); and finally place names provided by maps and land surveys. Examination of a plan and analysis of the site on the ground may suggest the

15   A mosaic from Ostia: the Arles bridge

possibility of a bridge (for example, a vanished bridge over the Tiber along the line of a street in Rome and again the destroyed bridge over the Rhône at the point where the projection of the main axis of the Arles amphitheatre meets the river).

Building operations were carried out in two ways: in Mediterranean lands, the piers could be erected directly on the river bottom, when the bed was dry in summer. In North-West Europe, where there are no seasonal differences, piers were constructed with the aid of piles and timber scaffolding. In a chapter devoted to the problem of masonry construction in water[95], Vitruvius gives some details and we learn of the employment of artisan divers[96]. Roman engineers could not build flattened arches of great width, so, in order to avoid extra spans and piers, they raised the apex of the central arch well above flood level. This arrangement required steeply sloping approach ramps, which carried traffic across the river on a series of arches allowing free passage to boats and flood waters. The river banks sloped the opposite way to the ramps and the side arches were successively lower and narrower. The road over the bridge had therefore a pronounced humpback. Building details are of interest: pier-abutments serving as buttresses and cut-waters, very high vaulting (the rise corresponding to at least one-third of the opening), constructed from large blocks with offset joints or using parallel arch beams normally without ties, tympana linked by curved jointing, and, in the case of the small arches, tall slender voussoirs. Sometimes there can be seen holes for bronze clamps that have vanished, corbels that once supported timber centering and gaps for scaffolding. Attention may be given, too, to the sectional construction of the roadway, the type of parapet, and the decoration (cornices, lintel-courses, pilasters and capitals, inscriptions).

Such surviving evidence forms a useful comparison with classical texts dealing with bridge-building, in particular Caesar's famous description of the bridging of the Rhine [97]:

> He built a bridge in the following way: he coupled together pairs of timbers, one and a half feet thick, sharpened a little way up from the end and measured according to the depth of the river, so that they stood two feet apart. With the aid of rafts he lowered them onto the river bed and set them firm by ramming, not like ordinary piles in an upright position, but leaning over with the flow of the current. Opposite to these and forty feet downstream, he set two further timbers, coupled in the same way, leaning against the current. These two pairs of timbers had two-foot wide transoms set into them and across the gap; between them, one each side, braces were fixed to keep the couples apart. With the piles thus both splayed and clamped together in opposite ways, the whole construction had such strength, thanks to natural laws, that the greater was the thrust of the current, the more the structure held together. Upon the transoms were placed cross-pieces and upon these again battens and wattlework. Furthermore, downstream, sloping piles were fixed to reinforce the whole structure like a buttress and take the force of the river. Others were arranged a little way upstream from the bridge, so that if the barbarians sent down tree trunks or boats to destroy the construction, the shock would be lessened.

The bridges of Rome

We shall now sum up what is known about the bridges of Rome, following Le Gall's masterly treatise on the Tiber:

> The Sublicius Bridge (from *sublica,* pile or timber) was probably erected by the Etruscans, although it has been attributed to Ancus Martius[98]. It is famous for having been defended by Horatius Cocles against Porsenna[99]. Over it the Romans fled to Caere[100]. It was certainly an ancient structure, as evidenced by the superstition attached to it and the archaic style of building, which was respected to the point of tabu: no metal, beams with fixed ends (using wooden braces?), perhaps to allow easy dismantling. To Varro, of course, we owe the suggested etymology of *pontifex: pontufices . . . a ponte arbitror: nam ab his Sublicius est factus primum ut restitutus saepe*[101], and some have gone so far as to see this function as a survival from the lake-village culture, with the bridge having originated as a track borne on piles. But these explanations remain uncertain, despite medieval parallels (Order of the Pontiff Brothers, confirmed by Clement III in 1189, the Brotherhood of the Holy Ghost). The Sulpicius Bridge, often carried away by floods and restored, at any rate until the fourth century, is known through a coinage issue of Antoninus Pius (140–43), showing Horatius Cocles swimming in the Tiber, and through an issue of Marcus Aurelius (180). Its position, downstream from the Aemilius Bridge, has been established from an analysis of traffic conditions (city walls, ease of access).

The Milvius Bridge ('Ponte Molle') may date from the fourth century: after the capture of Veii, a way across was needed, in the first place made of wood. Then, having served the *via Veientana,* the bridge was used by the *Clodia* (late fourth century), the *Cassia* (second half of the third century) and the *Flaminia* (220). It is clear that local geography determined the exact site. There must have been an approach causeway over the swampy ground[102]. In 207 BC the people of Rome made their way along it to meet the messengers from the Metaurus. The bridge seems to have been rebuilt in stone by the censor for 109, M. Aemilius Scaurus, with each end of wood, thus being easier to destroy. In the *Res Gestae,* Augustus takes pride in having repaired all the bridges along the *Flaminia,* with the two exceptions of the *Milvius* and the *Minucius.* On that occasion, statues were erected to him upon triumphal arches at each end of the road, at Rimini and at the Milvius Bridge[103].

The bridge, after many repairs, still carries modern traffic.

The Aemilius bridge or *pons Lepidi,* of which one arch survives ('Ponte Rotto' was its name in 1598) downstream from the Isola Tiberina, was the first stone bridge in Rome. It owes its name to the censor for 179, M. Aemilius Lepidus, who built the Aemilia Basilica and who was responsible for the bridge-piers[104], carrying a wooden roadway, and destroyed by a storm. The arches were the work of P. Scipio Africanus and L. Mummius, censors in 142. We know of restoration at the time of Augustus (an entrance arch) and medieval repairs by the popes, who left a commemorative inscription. The remaining fragment is composed of travertine and peperino stone with vaulting of tufa from the Grotta Oscura. There are indications of corbels. A sombre note on Roman life: it was a popular spot from which to commit suicide[105], while Heliogabalus' corpse was thrown from this bridge into the Tiber[106].

The Fabricius bridge, built in 62 BC, links the left bank with the Isola Tiberina. An inscription informs us more than once: *L. Fabricius G. f. cur[ator] viar[um] faciundum coeravit,* and, on the central arch: *idemque probavit.* Another inscription: *M. Lollius M. f. Q(uintus) Lepidus M(anii) f. cos. ex. s(enatus) c(onsulto) probaverunt,* corresponds to a repair after floods in 21 BC. This was also a suicide spot[107]. The bridge, 5·8m wide, was decorated with herms. It is built of travertine in those parts exposed to view, but the rest of the vaulting is made of tufa; the facing of travertine and brick is of later date.

The Cestius Bridge must date from the end of the Republic (first century BC), since building initiated by emperors bears their name. A fourth century restoration turned it into the *pons Gratiani.*

The bridge of Agrippa or of Aurelius Antoninus (restored) corresponds to the present 'Ponte Sisto' (see below, *pons Valentiniani*).

Nero's bridge (its medieval name, the piles are known) led to the circus from the Vatican.

Hadrian's bridge (*Aelius*) is well preserved. It is dated to 133–34 by the inscription: *Imp. Caesar Divi Traiani Parthici filius, Divi Nervae nepos Traianus Hadrianus*

16   The Fabricius bridge in Rome

Augustus pontifex maximus tribunic(ia) pot(estate) XVIII, cos.III fecit. The structure comprises: three central flattened arches, two small ones on the right bank and three on the left serving to carry the approach roads; piers with triangular cut-waters; and in the bridge structure, iron ties covered with lead. The roadway, 4·75m wide, is paved with polygonal slabs of lava-stone and has two sidewalks

3·1m wide made of rectangular travertine slabs cramped together. Pilasters today carry Bernini's angels, but were preceded by columns bearing monumental statues: these turned the bridge into a ceremonial way leading to the mausoleum of Hadrian. There is a bronze medallion showing the bridge with three large central arches and two steep approach roads, each carried on two arches, balustrades made of stone slabs ending in little pilasters, and, on the right bank, a river wall and step. The access roads have been altered, as the town has changed. In medieval times the bridge was in heavy use, for it linked the city with the Vatican.

The *pons Valentiniani* underlies the 'Ponte Sisto', it was the ancient *pons Agrippae* (Agrippa built it and adorned it with statues), which was restored by Antoninus Pius, then by Valentinian and Valens. A whole arch has been found lying in the river and fragments are known of the architectural and epigraphic detail, coming from a triumphal arch erected by Antoninus at the entrance to the bridge. The inscription announces:

> To the emperor Caesar, our lord Flavius Valens, very great, pious, fortunate, victorious and triumphant, always Augustus, the Senate and the Roman people, for the foresight which has always been common to him and his illustrious brother. The honour of dedicating Valentinian's bridge, set up according to the needs of the Eternal City, after its completion has been handed over by decision of the very great princes to L. Aurelius Avianus Symmachus, a most worthy man, former prefect of the town.

The latter must have directed the work during his prefecture, which was completed on 10 March 365[108]. Pieces of gilt-bronze statues have been found (first to third century).

The *pons Gratiani*, dating from 370, was demolished only in 1885–89. The orator Symmachus spoke about it in his eulogy of Gratian[109] and, addressing the Rhine, he declared: 'Well, O horn-bearer[110], take care not to think thyself the equal of Tiberinus, since you both sustain monuments of Princes; he has been crowned and thou art under the yoke.' This bridge, made of reused materials, involved one of the largest known arches (length 48m, opening 23·65m), with a system of iron cramps set in grooves and sealed with lead, earning it the name of 'ponte Ferrato'. Concerning the *pons Theodosi*, known through medieval sources and near the Aventine Hill, according to the order followed by the list in which it is mentioned, we simply know that artisan divers[111] were employed and the construction had given rise to jobbery.

As for the *pons Probi*, there was a restoration of Nero's bridge.

There must have existed bridges of which we have no knowledge (in particular, wooden bridges over the Tiber). Nero had thought of the scheme which involved a bridge between Palatium and the Capitol[112].

Roman bridges in Italy

Among the most unusual were:

Augustus' bridge at Rimini (AD 14–21) which carried the Flaminia on five low arches and five high ones (the central span measuring 32m) and was embellished with triumphal arches;

the Savignano bridge over the Rubicon, which survived until the recent war;

the Narni bridge over the Nera (AD 10);

the Ascoli Piceno bridge[113] over the *via Salaria*;

Domitian's bridge, close to the mouth of the Volturno, described by Statius;

the ponte Leproso, at Benevento, on the *Appia*;

the Fossombrone bridge (third century AD);

the very fine bridges in northern Italy (Ivrée, Pré-St-Martin, Val de Cogne, Aosta, St-Vincent, Châtillon);

the bridge of Porto Torres in Sardinia, a humpback structure with seven arches.

Roman bridges in Gaul

There is no complete inventory for Gaul[114], although the evidence exists for native Gallic bridges – through place names[115] and through Caesar's text – at Lutetia[116], at Melun, on the Aisne, at Genabum[117], at Geneva, on the Allier[118], and at Ponts-de-Cé[119]. We may note by way of example, the following bridges: at Ascain over the Nivelle (Pyrénées-Atlantiques); Flavian, close to St-Chamas; Julian, near Apt; at Vaison over the Ouvèze; at Viviers over the Escoutay; at Champagne (Charente-Maritime); at Saintes (decorated with the Germanicus arch, now removed), destroyed under Louis Philippe; the bridge of boats at Arles with arches and milestones, known through a mosaic in the Place des Corporations d'Ostie; at Narbonne, used as a foundation for houses; and, of course, the bridge–aqueduct at Gard.

Other remains are found at Ambroix on the Vidourle, at Domqueur, Ganagobie, Lavoute, Mane, Mondouilloux, Outremecourt, Pont-Serme, Rolampont, St-Thibéry on the Hérault, Ste-Colombe, Sommières, Tarascon, Vendelais, and Le Vignau. According to Blanc, there appear to be the ruins of 15 bridges in the ravines of the Ardèche.

The Roman bridge at Geneva, which replaced its Gallic predecessor (cut by Caesar in 58 BC)[120] a little upstream on the axis of the decumanus, has been described by Blondel. There is knowledge of a masonry pier and the piles of another pier in the layer of clay, serving as a foundation for a timber framework which must have supported the masonry (square oak posts and wrought-iron shoes with square nails). The structure, which dates from the end of the second century and was twice restored in antiquity, rested on both banks, formerly set back, and on the island in the Rhône. The wooden roadway, 5·5–6m wide, was carried between the piers on such stout trestles that they lasted until the sixteenth century. The 19 spans of 12·8m gave a length of 220m, with a bend in the course at the island. The crossing was guarded by a fortlet on the left bank and a tower on the island.

Other bridges in the Roman world

In Belgium, there are possible examples at Arlon and Montignies-St-Christophe.

In Germany, the army established a number of bridges for military operations, in Caesar's train[121]. The crossing at Pfalzem-Stadtbredimus, in use since prehistoric times, has yielded the piles of a pre-Roman bridge, dated by dendrochronology to 168–149 BC. This small bridge was followed by a Roman one in 30 AD similar to that at Coblenz. A lead medallion illustrates the Rhine bridge at Mainz-Kastel.

But the bridges that have been most carefully studied are those at Trier (by Cüppers, 1969). Their siting has been explained with reference to local geology and surface drainage, the road network and the development of Roman technique, not to mention other crossings over the Rhine and Moselle and their tributaries and bridges in the Danubian lands, Switzerland, France and Britain.

At the point at which the valley is widest and both banks are favourable to human settlement, a massive bridge was built about 44 AD, with ashlar piers resting on a system of piles. As the river level is changeable, construction had to be on a large scale where there was a junction of vital roads. This first bridge was mentioned by Tacitus in his account of the Batavian war[122] (70 AD: the Moselle bridge linking the colony with the other bank).

Remains of the bridge were found during work on the bed of the Moselle and they conformed with what we know of the roads and constructional details. The piles were made of oak trunks 50cm in diameter, their tips protected by iron shoes. Seven piers were found resting on these piles, set in rows to form a pentagonal base measuring overall 10·2m by 19·5m. Flat planking had been laid over a clay floor well rammed down with broken stones into the gaps between the piles. The whole foundation supported the ashlar blocks which stood to a height of 8m and bore a wooden superstructure.

53942

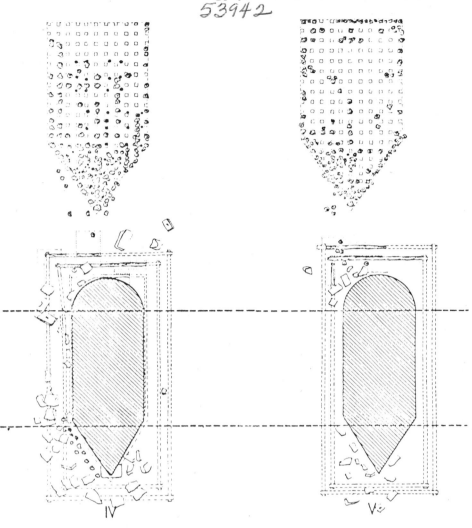

17   The Trier bridge: piers in plan and elevation (after H. Cüppers, *Die Trierer Römerbrücken,*
1969, p. 152)

This early bridge served as a construction platform for the new one, whose foundation course was composed of squared stone placed directly on the river bed. Caissons had been used for the seven piers and the western bridgehead (there was evidence of repairs). The space between the double walls of the caissons was filled with well-packed clay. The piers stood 12m high and were made of blue limestone from the Moselle, Eifel basalt and Trier sandstone. As the building technique is reminiscent of the *Porta Nigra,* a dating bracket has been suggested between the first and the fifth centuries. In fact, the date is around 140 AD, judging from pottery found in the caissons. The wooden bridge was set on longitudinal timbers supported by corbels on the piers.

Among the small finds from close by were iron tools used in shaping wood and stone. The bridge was included in the city fortifications and furnished with gates and defensive towers. In the second century AD, when the wall circuit was shortened, a new bridgehead was built, using lead-sealed cramps. Other repairs in the Roman period were revealed by different sizes of stone. In the fourteenth century, the wooden roadway was replaced by stone arches. Further repair was carried out in the eighteenth century, but the piers of the famous Römerbrücke are certainly Roman. Cüppers emphasises not only the close links that the bridge has had with the development of the town (which grew up close to both the navigable waterway with its river port and the road crossing) but also its intrinsic aesthetic appeal.

We shall limit ourselves to mentioning a few other famous bridges of the Roman world. In Spain, the Roman bridge at Salamanca; the bridge-aqueduct of Lladenet near Barcelona; the bridge of Martorell; the Alcantara bridge over the Tagus, built by Apollodorus of Damascus under Trajan (220m long, 18 arches, destroyed by the Moors in the eighth century) and in whose construction the cities of Lusitania took part; the bridges of Andujar, of the Rio Chaves and of Toledo. Others exist at Alconetar, Bande, Besalu, Caceres, Cange de Onis, Cordoba, Dancella, El Garro, Lavera (two), Lerida[123], Lugo, Medellin, Merida, Monistrol, Puebla de Trives, Santiago, Siviglia, Tres Puentes, Vadillo, Ventas de Capara, Villa del Rio and Villodas Alava.

Another bridge attributed to Apollodorus, over the Danube (20 piers bearing superstructures in wood and brick), is known through Trajan's Column. A letter from Pliny the Younger, admitting that Caninius was right in wanting to write a poem on the Dacian War: 'Thou wilt celebrate fresh bridges thrown across rivers'[124], shows the impression that that undertaking made on the public.

This was the same search for prestige as in the case of Caesar overcoming the Rhine, Caligula claiming a triumphal march across the waves thanks to a wooden bridge thrown over the bay of Baiae[125], or Nero building bridges over the Euphrates[126].

Bridges were therefore vital points in the road network. Milestones (Arles) were often set up on them and they were embellished with triumphal arches and honorific inscriptions.

By way of example, we may quote the inscription from a bridge along a road in Lycaonia, trodden by St Paul:

The emperor Titus Caesar, son of the divine Vespasian, Augustus, high pontiff, in his tenth term as tribune, fifteen times hailed emperor, father of his country, consul for the eighth time, nominated for the ninth, censor, and Domitian Caesar, son of the divine Vespasian, consul for the seventh time, nominated for the eighth, priest of all the colleges, prince of youth, have built this road through the agency of Aulus Caesennius Gallus, consul, member of the commission of fifteen responsible for sacrifices, propraetorian legate of Augustus[127].

The titles used date the text to the end of 80. The princes had had a track converted into a paved road through the intermediary of the governor of Galacia–Cappadocia–Lycaonia.

It would be worth while completing and elaborating the inventory of Roman bridges that Gazzola outlined in 1963 by studying the place names to which they gave rise (El Kantara in Algeria, the river Alcantara in Spain). Light can be thrown by small bridges with their own names and we should refer back to what has been said about the value of place names. It must be borne in mind that bridges were usually named after their builder or restorer (under the Empire, the emperor) and this may have resulted in successive changes (cf. p. 95 in the case of Rome). An inventory should also be made of literary references[128] and of monuments depicting bridges, such as Trajan's Column.

As they were generally built with great care, and maintained and fortified because they allowed the exaction of tolls at compulsory river crossings, Roman bridges survived a long time, at least until the Middle Ages. Evidence for them can be found in the documents of those days: thus in England, Bede wrote of the ancient remains of bridges still visible in the eighth century, of which some were in use even in the twelfth. Many old bridges were replaced only in the eighteenth century, when there were changes in the water flow following river control.

Naturally, even along old roads, many so-called 'Roman' bridges are medieval. The latter can be recognised by the manner of building; they are erected on semi-circular arches or triangular arches, the roadway is narrow, the thoroughfare is guarded by towers and occasions the payment of a toll. A decision can often be made by establishing the unit used (length of foot). The bridges of the Renaissance have flattened, segmental arches, for their foundations were constructed within coffer-dams made of pile planks firmly secured by ramming; in the eighteenth century, such was still the case and the spans were now equal, while parapets were added.

It must not be forgotten that in addition to bridges there were ferries. Some are mentioned in literature, as , for example, the ferry at Cavaillon[129], with *pontones* or *rates* moved by *ratiarii* using oars or a tow-rope. Where rivers have to be crossed, we often find travellers in recent times writing of ferries that have been functioning since antiquity. Such ferries are still numerous in Spain.

APPENDIX

Roman bridges in the provinces[129a]

We complete here the information given above by classifying in alphabetic order of countries and places a number of the 293 bridges listed by P. Gazzola:

Algeria: Constantine (on the Rhumel), Duperré, El Kantara, Hippone, Tébessa.
Austria: Graz, S. Dionysen.
Iraq: Kakho.
Iran: bridge-dyke of Shushtar.

Lebanon: Beirut, Tyre.
Libya: Wadi Zuara.
Luxemburg: Echternach, Wasserbillig.
Palestine: Jisr el Majani-Samaria (on the Jordan), Lydda-Samaria.
Portugal: Alter do Châo, Chaves, Segura.
Rhodes.
Rumania: Turnu Severin.
Syria: Aleppo (3), Bosra (2), Er Rukkad, Kiahta.
Tunisia: Ad Pertusa, Aïn Hedja, Aïn Mounès, Bulla Regia, Djedeida, El Knatir, Grichel Oued, Kairouan, Kasserine, Maktar, Medjez el Bab, Oudna, Siliana (valley of the), Souk el Arba, Souk el Khemis, Sousse, Teboursouk.
Turkey: Aizani, Kutahya, Laodicea, Mersin, Pergamum, Sakarya.

Other engineering works

Besides bridges, we must not overlook fords[130] and dykes. One of the best examples is provided by the stone causeway of *Pons Zita* (Tunisia) running for 6km between the island of Djerba and the mainland, with a town at each end: Zita and Méninx on the isle of Lotus-eaters. Alexander the Great had already provided prototypes[131].

Important engineering developments included:

retaining walls, for example along the Roman road from Carthage to Thevesta close to Aïn Younès, perforated to allow water drainage;
raised banking, sometimes forming a herring-bone pattern, is a certain sign of Roman construction;
worked rock-faces on which tool marks can be made out (cf. place names like Rochetaillée, au Lautaret, Pierre Pertuis, Incisa in Italy), with refuges for pedestrians, niches for the statues of gods, slots to take the supports for a wooden roadway with an overhang, at Pisco Montano near to Terracina for a height of 36m, and at the Iron Gate on the Danube (likewise of Trajanic date);
and even tunnels: Porte Taillée at Besançon, the Roman gate of Bons, the Terracina arch, Mont-Grillo (Domitian), the tunnel at the *Campi Phlegraei,* the Furlo pass on the *Flaminia.*

The last of these made an impression on Montaigne who spoke of it in his *Journal de voyage*:

It is a way cut through a rock; and because Augustus was the first to undertake this mighty work, there was an inscription in his name, which time has effaced, and another can be seen at the far end, in honour of Vespasian. Around can be seen much building arising from the depth of the water, below the road, rocks cut and smoothed of great thickness, and all along the road, which is the *via Flaminia,* leading to Rome, there are traces of their heavy paving, buried for the most part, and their road which was forty feet wide is now no more than four[132].

This paragraph is interesting for its exact details. Roman engineering on a grand scale had here a profound effect on Montaigne: the spot was called by the Ancients

18   A road cut through rock: the 'route des Gaules' in the Aosta valley

petra pertusa (or *intercisa,* cf. the French Pierre Pertuis) or *forulus,* whence the present name ('galleria del Furlo'). Vespasian had this tunnel dug in 76–77 AD at the narrowest point in the Candigliano gorge, through a hard stratum in the Lower Lias. The chisel marks are clear.

Movement along the *via Flaminia* was made much easier (there are remains of several bridges in the area). Above the north-east entrance to the tunnel may be read the inscription: Imperator Caesar Augustus [Montaigne confused this imperial title with the name of the Emperor Augustus [Vespasianus Pontifex Maximus, tribunicia potestate VII, imperator XVI, pater patriae, consul VII (I), censor faciundum curavit[133]. The ancient section of the tunnel is 38·3m long, 5·47m wide and 5·95m high. It must be pointed out that another shorter tunnel had been dug earlier by the

Umbrians. Part of the roadway preceding the Furlo tunnel may still be discerned, as Montaigne must have seen it, reinforced by an old retaining wall. The French writer certainly saw how the road level was raised and its width made narrower.

Another example may be quoted from the Val-de-Fier (Haute Savoie, following the surveys made by Broise and Dufournet): along this 4km-long gorge, the road can still be seen in four stretches totalling 300m. The course has been cut into the rock, there are stout retaining walls, the road surface is rutted and at bends refuges have been created. Such engineering feats are frequently mentioned on inscriptions[134]. They made a deep impression on contemporaries, as is shown by the following words of Pliny the Elder, expressing disapproval in this case of Claudius' public works: 'I pass over in silence the harbour at Ostia, the roads constructed through the mountains, the mole separating Lake Lucrinus from the Tyrrhenian Sea and so many bridges built at such great expense[135].'

It is essential to locate the sites of engineering work in order to re-establish the course of an old road: the destruction of a bridge may have brought about considerable changes in its line[135a].

9 GROUND EVIDENCE AND METHODS OF LOOKING FOR OLD ROADS

METHODS: SOME EXAMPLES FROM THE FIELD

An example of ground reconnaissance: the Roman road of Agrippa to the north of Langres

We shall consider here a section of the great military road running from Montigny Wood to Meuvy. It is clearly marked on the IGN map and the writer has himself traced the various forms that it takes on the ground. At the spot known as La Croisée, west of Montigny Wood, the Roman road is today a well-rutted farm track; farther on, 500m west of La Villeneuve, it turns into a mere path between two thick rows of shrubs, which tend to obstruct it and, beyond, it becomes a broad dense growth of trees and bushes looking impenetrable from the outside. But if one plucks up courage to go into this wilderness, within can be seen a rather higher and more compact bank lying virtually exposed between two walls of vegetation. A fresh transformation occurs northwards: along the road alignment, there is simply a watercourse, lined by trees and forming a field boundary, then a slight ridge with trees on it that from a distance casts a shadow on the sunlit meadows. This ridge becomes more pronounced over a stretch of waterlogged ground; in some places it has been cut to allow streams to flow or represents an enclosure boundary. Finally, in sight of the church tower at Meuvy, we come across a narrow lane, left high above the neighbouring fields because it has been spared from ploughing. Elsewhere again, all that has survived is a fence line between estates or even the boundary, unmarked on the ground, separating two communes or two parishes.

Since then, the writer has had the opportunity of filming this section from a helicopter. The result well illustrates how valuable air photography can be in linking sections of an ancient road that have survived in a variety of ways (8mm film of the IPN).

Examples of geophysical traverses

The writer gives examples of those that he has personally carried out and checked by cutting a section, at several points along the Roman road linking the district of Valromey (Ain) and Besançon, close to the cross-roads with the route running from Lyons through Nantua to Geneva. South of the *vicus* of Izernore, the course of the road is still marked on the flat ground by a farm track called 'battle-lane', then, on the outskirts of the township, by a line of property boundaries, which the farmers call a 'ridge', as they have noticed that there was a strip of drier soil causing differences in crop growth.

Three resistivity traverses were made in July 1965 by the Schlumberger four-probe method (using a constant distance of 10m between the current input electrodes and 1m between the voltage electrodes, the horizontal interval being 1m). The resultant resistivities display lowest readings over ditches, subsequently checked by excavation.

Three magnetic traverses were carried out in August 1965 and July 1966 with a proton magnetometer of the Elsec type made by Littlemore (readings to a depth of 1m, horizontal interval 1m). The results, which present steadier variations than with the resistivity survey, are more useful, although displacement has arisen in the readings owing to the orientation of the road to magnetic north and the differences between the two ditches.

In July 1966, a mechanical digger opened up a control trench across the road and revealed, immediately below the plough soil, two very broad ditches (the west ditch being possibly double), filled with brown soil which stood out clearly against the light subsoil. Between the ditches, the foundation of the road is represented by an even layer of light-coloured gravel without large stones, the top of which has a steady camber. The material for the build-up is derived from the immediate subsoil. The main dimensions of the road profile are: width of causeway, 4–5m; width between ditch bottoms, 7m; average width of the ditches, 3m; depth of top of causeway below modern surface, 0·35m; depth of ditch bottoms below modern surface, 0·85m.

This part of the road was laid on a subsoil composed of free-running but resistant material, lying undisturbed on flat, well-drained ground. It seems therefore that two ditches were enough to ensure the run-off from a slight causeway, built up from local gravel and perhaps covered by surface metalling that has now vanished.

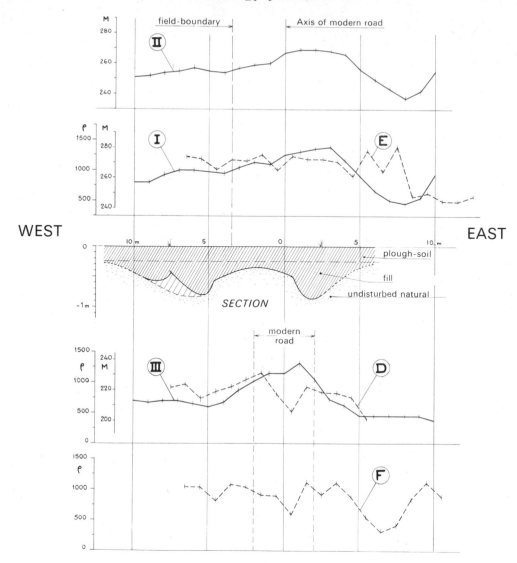

19   Geophysical traverses across a Roman road at Izernore in the Ain department. Details: *D, E, F*: traverses resulting from a resistivity survey; I, II, III: traverses made with a proton magnetometer. Key to scales: apparent electrical resistivity: in   m; magnetic field: *M* = (reading on magnetometer) 52,000 in   (Source: G.A.A.–T.C.F.)

Identification of road stations

An important methodological problem is to establish the sites of road stations. A number of clues must be brought to bear:

> calculation of distances, if possible with reference to milestones or road itineraries, but taking into account the nature of the ground (shorter stages in hilly areas, necessary river crossings, favourable sites like hill slopes, springs, cross-roads); place names;

survival of settlement (but watch out for cases of changes of site);
sites of Merovingian mints (along important roads), chapels, medieval cemeteries and fairgrounds[136];
archaeological evidence (building remains, burials, inscriptions).

Matherat[137] has proposed a geometrical method of locating road stations and it has been found of use by Boyer and Février[138]. Given two known road stations, A and B, we require to locate a third unknown station, X. AX and BX are distances known from itineraries and their sum, for argument's sake, exceeds the actual distance AB on the ground. The method is briefly:

(a) An ellipse is drawn having as focal points A and B with a major axis in length $AX+BX$. Then X cannot lie outside the ellipse.

(b) Two arcs are then drawn, centred on A and B and with radii equal to AX and BX respectively. If, in this extreme case, the missing stretches of road (AX and BX) are both straight, then the intersection of ellipse and arcs provides two solutions for the siting of X.

(c) Two further arcs are drawn on either side of the major axis to join A and B, each measuring in length $AX+BX$. These arcs represent the other extreme case where the missing Roman road is a curve or a series of short straight stretches approaching a curve. Then X will lie within the quadrilateral formed by the four intersecting arcs. The remainder of the procedure comprises fieldwork to establish the exact site.

The absence of a station from an itinerary does not signify its disappearance. Care is needed. Each itinerary does not mention all the stations.

Useful information about the courses of the old roads and particularly about the stations along them may be forthcoming from medieval establishments: abbeys, priories, leper houses may have followed the ancient staging-points, sited on land in public domain[139], as a kind of survival of the *cursus publicus*. Houses belonging to military orders, such as the Hospitallers of St John of Jerusalem, were almost always located close to the busiest highways, next to bridges and passes, which wayfarers were obliged to cross. A category which may be most enlightening in this quest is that of the *xenodochia* or basilica-hostels which formed a transition between Late Antiquity and the Early Middle Ages. An example is the one at Montferrand (Aude)[140], which, taking the place of an older *mansio*, used to welcome travellers crossing the Naurouze pass (Carcassonne Gate) on the *via Aquitanica*. It probably stood on the site of the *vicus* of Eluso. Its buildings (dormitories, refectory, baths) and cemetery (fifth to sixth century) have been excavated. *Xenodochia* are also to be found at intervals along the Roman roads in northern Italy (along the *Emilia*, but not the northern part of the *Postumia*, which shows that it was out of use).

RESEARCH TOOLS

Publications

If we can re-establish the road network of a region, which formed the basis of

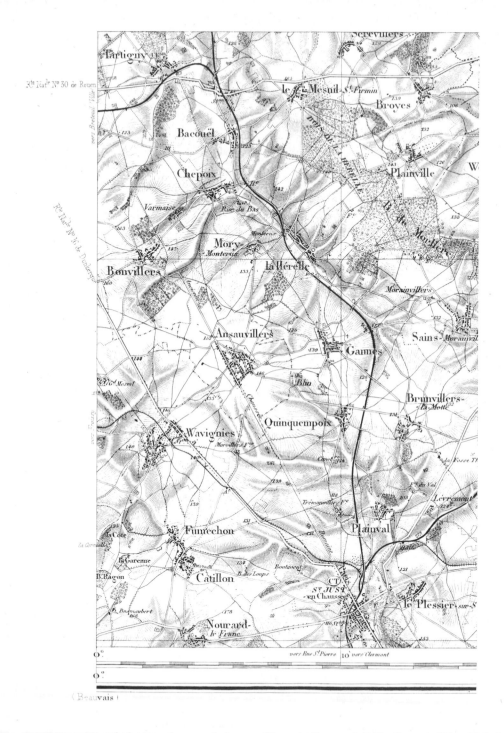

20   Use of a large-scale map: St-Just-en-Chaussée (Source: I.G.N., Carte de l'Etat-Major)

land development and human settlement, then we can begin to group scattered finds and to direct our research which otherwise would be lost in detail. Thus in practice we are recreating the structure of a whole area.

What tools do we have at our disposal for this purpose? Grenier has written a manual devoted to roads[141] and there are a number of papers, hundreds of them since that time, in a host of local periodicals that are not easy to obtain. These articles are accompanied by plans that are difficult to use by anyone who would like to have a personal view of the problem on the spot. The scale of these sketch maps (1/500,000 or 1/1,000,000) does not allow one to say that a road goes through points *A* and *B* and so they can be linked by a line to give a course that is true on the ground. Furthermore when giving map references, places named on land surveys that cannot be located on a small-scale map, must be avoided; modern grid references must be the norm.

As things are, existing material showing the topography – namely maps and air photographs – can in many cases prepare the way for and curtail the length of fieldwork.

We shall show the results of research using maps and photographs, before tackling the problem of dating; people are in the habit indeed of talking of Roman roads, when they should really be talking of old roads.

Topographical maps

It is perhaps surprising that topographical maps should already virtually display as they are the system of old roads. If we compare a number of maps that have been drawn up at intervals down through the years, we notice that the courses of some roads have changed but little until the major developments of the seventeenth and eighteenth centuries. Cassini's map allows doubtful cases to be eliminated: it clearly reveals straight walks and carriage drives built in the eighteenth century, avenues leading to châteaux or through parks and hunting paths and sometimes shows in addition roads that have been improved or not yet built. It ought to be possible to use older maps when they exist, especially when they yield information on parish boundaries.

A map has another advantage in that it offers an overall view of a wide area, in particular the map on the 1/200,000 scale – a useful factor when we are dealing with the changing pattern of the old roads. It is easy on a map to seek out gaps in a road alignment, for example along the edges of land holdings, and to make a preliminary assessment of circumstances that may be favourable (natural geographical routes, like ridges on marshy ground)[142] or unfavourable (natural obstacles).

Maps also give us information about place names[143]. Such evidence can come from estate plans or land surveys, allowing us to give close attention to unusual features in the holdings or the local boundaries, which may have archaeological bearing in the close study of place names, but do force us to work parish by parish.

The advantage of old maps (earlier than road developments in the eighteenth century and above all earlier than the arrival of railways) is that they rid the research

21 Vertical air photograph of a Roman road (Source: I.G.N.)

22 Oblique air photograph of a Roman road (Source: J. Mertens, Actes du colloque international d'archéologie aérienne, 1954)

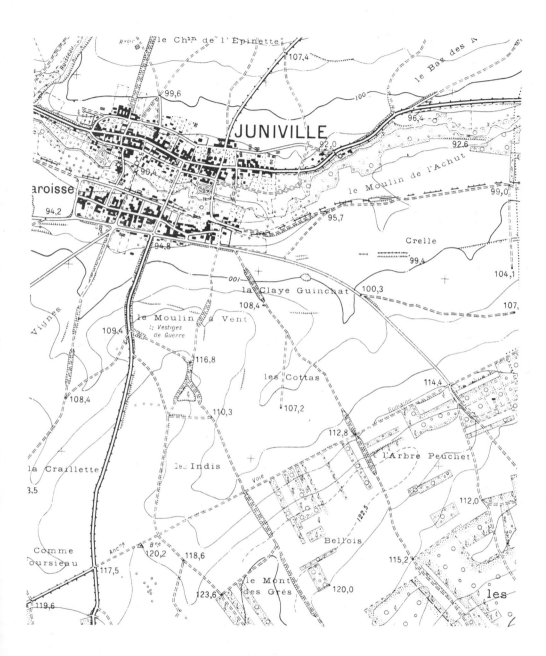

23   Use of the 1/20,000 large-scale map: abandonment of a Roman road in the neighbourhood of a settlement. The road is in use as far as spot height 177·5 and then joins another road which takes traffic towards the village of Juniville to link with a through route running along the north bank of the river. The Roman road survives here as a field boundary between woodland and arable, particularly along the 'military crest' (Source: I.G.N.)

worker of his subjective view of the modern network; they may show the way in which roads were classified (though a watch must be kept for roads only at the planning stage). Some are very valuable, such as the Sardinian land survey (Savoy), which reveals the division into holdings, with the farm and parish boundaries. The best method is to compare maps of different periods which have been photographically reduced to a common scale, thus avoiding arithmetical errors caused by converting old units of measurement into metric equivalents. By comparing dated maps, we may be able to eliminate various details in turn and so begin to set up a chronological framework. It is noteworthy that at the present time secondary roads used for bypass purposes often take us back onto old roads[144].

As a result of mapwork and the search for place names, we shall find ourselves with sections of old road that are apparently discontinuous; these stretches with their sudden gaps are highly important.

Air photographs

Air photography[145] now plays its part in checking and aligning these stretches of road which have survived in such a variety of ways that their interconnection cannot always be recognised either on the ground or even on the map. From above we may see groups of trees or clusters of bushes fitting into a common line, whereas to the ground observer they seem to be growing anywhere without rime or reason.

The air cover shows us a river flood plain where a road may have disappeared under recent alluvium and at a glance reveals wetter areas (darker), avoided by the old road.

Examining the photographs without any set objective in mind may yield results that are independent of the map, but the latter should be studied first if time is not to be wasted.

STUDYING OLD ROADS

What general conclusions can we reach about the appearance, course and importance of old roads – Roman and otherwise?

The road in its geographical setting

The best-known characteristic of Roman roads is their straightness. They are straight when natural obstacles allow them to be. The Imperial road tried to maintain a direct course, while at the same time respecting the lie of the ground, so that it more resembles a bent line. As for secondary roads, they often follow the gently curving tracks of Gallic or pre-Celtic times.

It has also been asserted that the Roman road was a ridge-way, because visibility was better, there was less danger and the going was firmer. It is more likely to be a road along the military crest, just below the actual ridge, whence it is possible to see the surrounding countryside without being seen, keeping as far as possible to the

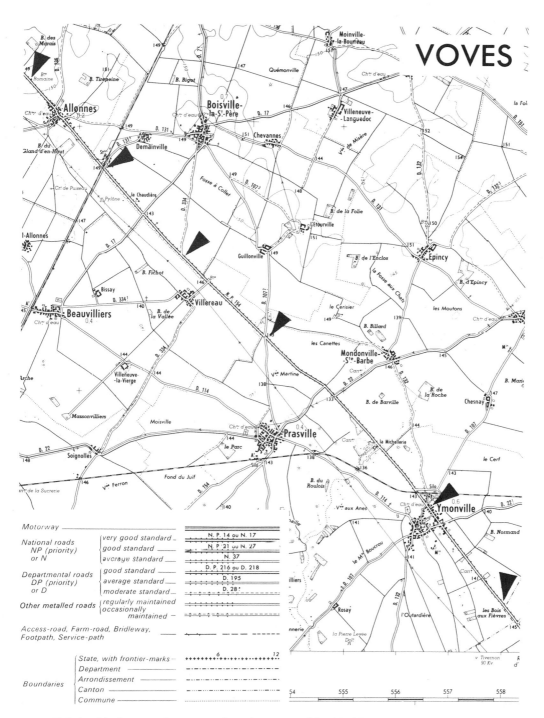

24 Relationship between Roman road, settlements and land-holdings at Voves (department of Eure-et-Loir) (Source: I.G.N.)

same height[146] and out of the wind. But one frequently finds the course of a large river closely followed by an ancient road.

It is vital to give attention to the connections between roads and water drainage. The majority of large valleys have a main road on each side (cf. below p. 197). But whereas the modern highway passes over the alluvial soil on the valley floor, the ancient road tried to keep away from ground subject to flooding and maintained a course outside the less stable alluvial deposits where construction and upkeep would both have been more difficult. Roman roads avoided in the same way land that was damp[147] or marshy in order to obviate costly embankments. However, if the road was important enough, there was no hesitation in building causeways (Sologne, Vendée), which have sometimes been used to dam artificial lakes in recent times.

The course of the road had similarly to take into account the need for water supplies, of great importance when there were pack trains on the move; this may explain the behaviour of some roads in Beauce, which 'rebound' when they reach the top of the valley, for the construction of engineering works would thereby have been avoided. Let us remember, too, the position frequently found where a road ran tangentially to meanders, either still existent or abandoned.

To cross water, a secondary road often used a ford. Photographs show the track coming to a stop, then continuing on the other bank, on a slightly staggered course. On the way down to the ford and out of it (where there may be more stones, but there is the possibility that the river bed has shifted), a splaying of tracks like a bird's foot probably means that conditions were difficult underfoot. When a deep valley has to be crossed, the Roman road bends sharply to take the slope at an angle, then once at the top, it resumes a straighter course.

River crossings attract certain types of settlement, for example posts for *utricularii* and their rafts, as well as watermills in recent times.

The Roman road and settlements[148]

As a rule, earlier sites are avoided by Roman roads, especially the great Imperial highways, which were unconcerned with local interests and small settlements. However, along these roads, posting-stations and markets were set up, which, as time went by, developed into townships. Some remained one-street villages, others grew in size. The road often attracted the village, but when the ancient road itineraries name a *civitas*, it does not mean that the route went through the town itself: occasionally it simply skirts its territory. The *statio* or *mansio* stood at a junction where a *diverticulum* led off to the town placed on a defensive site some distance away. We may understand what happened in the past in old countries like France[149] from the recent experience of newly developed lands: a road attracts people for a variety of reasons – sight-seeing, excitement, news and novelty, useful ideas and information, fashions and slogans, the variety of goods on offer. The fact that people could satisfy each other's needs and move easily around was the key to the many-sided development of town life. The initial grouping of population centred on the road was followed by a second phase in which there grew up a system of scattered settlements linked by short antennae to the main road.

The course of a Roman road is often directly connected with the foundation of *fora,* each with the name of its builder, both in Italy (Forum Appi, Aureli, Clodi, Corneli, Livi . . .) and in the provinces (Aquae Sextiae defending the strategic road from Italy to Spain, Lyons and Augst defending the Rhine road, Nyon controlling the road over the Grand-St-Bernard).

Amongst the population centres directly created by Roman roads and their junctions there appear a certain number of holy places[150] which included 'theatres', particularly in Gaul.

What about population distribution in the countryside? Whereas in recent times we find old farms freely stationed along ancient highways, the great farming establishments of antiquity (*villae*), which may have given rise to villages, used to avoid main roads. These *villae* often lay several hundred yards away, even though some possibly provided an inn or were themselves attracted by the presence of the road (*villa* of the Quinctilii on the *Appia*). But on the whole Roman roads served as axes along which population was distributed, then grouped and stabilised, to such a degree that a road network has often been re-established from a map showing settlements, especially mints or other centres of specialised products and markets.

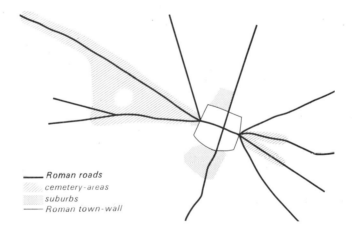

25 Plan of the road system at Bologna, Italy: the 'bird's foot' phenomenon

—— Roman roads
/// cemetery-areas
▒ suburbs
—— Roman town-wall

The connection between road and settlement may suggest some relative dating: a village built on a Roman road is a street village. If the road is earlier than the village, then the latter was built on it and it should go through the village without the slightest deviation. In addition, in the case of large towns, road forks of the 'bird's-foot' type at the gates (or at the bridges)[151] often allow successive phases of town expansion to be made out. A bird's foot implies the existence of a barrier either earlier in date or contemporary and so post-dates the city walls. It is also possible to follow how the courses of the roads changed as the city walls developed[152].

Roman roads and land holdings

Air photography makes its greatest contribution in helping to decipher the relation-ship between roads and land holdings. The right approach to this research is to tackle it under the regional heading of the *civitates*. We are dealing here with the basic features of the agricultural scene. Indeed, even if two or three lanes in turn take parallel bites out of the neighbouring fields, or if, as is often the case, gradual encroach-ments lead to the disappearance of a farm road, what has survived is, on the whole, remarkable, for such roads, in themselves subject to right of way, 'were the vital features in the operation of the land survey . . . the unchanging framework on which our countryside was built' (Roupnel). So it is understandable that even a road which has vanished can survive as the end boundary of two series of holdings lying parallel or perpendicular to it. What has been said earlier about centuriation[153] applies to all types of land holdings more or less geometric in shape and tying in with roads.

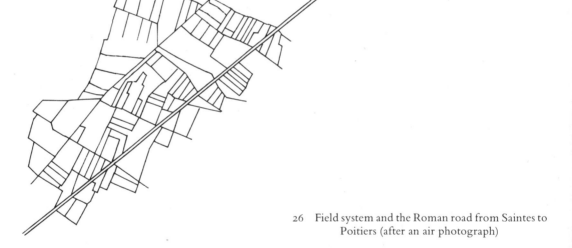

26   Field system and the Roman road from Saintes to Poitiers (after an air photograph)

The course of the latter always gives some indication as to how the land was occu-pied. As early as 220 BC in Italy, the construction of the *via Flaminia* fitted in with the law promulgated by Flaminius concerning the sharing of Picenian and Gallic territory among private colonists (232). The widespread use of milestones along roads dates from the time of the tribune C. Sempronius Gracchus, who promoted agrarian reforms and the *lex Sempronia viaria*. The moulding of the farming landscape began with the roads, as the module that they created was transposed as it were into the surrounding countryside. Today we are discovering that surveyed land holdings existed alongside many important road routes. Such as the case with Agrippa's road from Lyons to the Rhine[154], where milestones not only marked a point on the route, but also served as boundary indications for farming estates. The same development has been noted in eastern France (work by Dupuich), in the Loire valley (Liger and Clos Arceduc), near Rheims (Legros), Amiens[155] and Chartres.

A recent theory has been built up on these links between roads and land holdings[156]: every mile byroads, *diverticula*, joined the highway at an angle of 60°, with others joining at right angles every half mile, so that taken together equilateral triangles were formed having sides one mile long. What makes this 'triangulation' even stranger is the fact that it is not mentioned in surveyors' texts.

If we wish to analyse the system of holdings we must in fact go beyond a search for a geometrical pattern in farming. The periodical *Photo-interprétation*[157] has given many case examples of land holdings, taken from air photographs and offering possibilities of relative dating. A thesis being prepared under my guidance (Liger) will go much further by showing how the space–time analysis of the relationship between superimposed grids[158] or of the manner in which they should be fitted together must be considered in a four-dimensional context capable of being computer-programmed[159].

Let us limit ourselves here to the statement that on a cadastral map, a road or track separating two land parcels is usually ancient and that, despite its double role as a link between settlements and as a bound in land tenure, an old road can have a divisive effect: Mademoiselle Soyer has noticed[160] that when circular enclosures of farmland have been intersected by a Roman road, each part went on to develop independently. This explains how the road may have a stimulating influence or, on the other hand, may depopulate an area that is already under-developed and underpeopled: the appearance of a landscape really depends on the traffic of buying and selling, which controls human settlements and the pattern of daily contact.

Roman roads and boundaries

Some *civitas* boundaries[161] may come to light as a result of studying a road grid: distance-units marked by stones may vary, while twists and bends can be revealing. It is a well known fact that many recent boundaries (enclosures, cadastral divisions, parishes, communes and cantons) follow old routes which started as the boundaries of great estates. The *limes* is one particular example.

SPECIAL FEATURES OF AIR PHOTOGRAPHS

The characteristics so far discussed have common qualities pictorially in photographs, on maps and in written description. What then, to complement these, are the purely photographic characteristics? What does a Roman road look like in black and white on a photograph? Often an air view will give results that were quite unsuspected on the map.

In some cases, it may be useful to have at hand oblique shots which bring out alignments and perspective. In general, the factors that explain why air photography reveals so much about the system of Roman roads are the same as in the case of other archaeological features. Slight changes in ground relief may give shadows appearing as differences of intensity in the photographic reproduction; when it is crossing a freshly ploughed field without crops, which looks grey on a photograph, the road shows as a white line. On land covered by crops and appearing dark, the feature is seen as a pale line, provided it is free of vegetation or even if it is buried in a field under crops.

If the road has a vegetation cover, it then appears as a dark line amid light fields. In North Africa, where roads are bare, they show up as a white streak when crossing regions that are mountainous or very dry, but they can look black in marshy or damp areas.

The nature of the ground itself is of course a vital element in preserving this evidence: damp or friable soils, clays and sands, which were not a ready source of road metalling, are less helpful than, for example, a limestone bedrock.

Vegetation covering old roads is different from that in the country around: they tend to support a vigorous growth of conifers, gorse, broom and spiny bushes. When there has been paving or metalling, the ground is unfavourable to crops and becomes overgrown: we find silica-loving plants adapted to drought and stony conditions or, in limestone districts, blackthorn bushes and rank, tough grass. Often a road appears as a stretch of fallow, an abandoned area, given over to its own particular flora, showing distinctly as a dark line on photographs, contrasting with the rest of the landscape, which is light-grey or dark-grey.

While they are a striking anomaly against an even-hued background, Roman roads are less visible in broken country, such as woodland.

In forests, there are noteworthy cases when the tree cover looks thicker or different[162], along a road lined by conifers. Elsewhere one could have a white line, with the result that a Roman road may be discovered easily in woodland, especially since, with the decline in use, its appearance has changed less. Of course, in examples like this, winter views show more details more clearly. Unless forced to do so, the Romans avoided going through wooded country: the road would skirt the forest rather than enter it; on the other hand, tracks of Celtic times and earlier often vanish into a forest to end up at a clearing where worked stone is visible[163].

As they often lay in close association with roads, then any building remains or human settlement, villages, camps, holy places, theatres, known or not, are valuable evidence in supporting a hypothesis. These sites show up well on photographs as a faint, but clear tracery. They have more or less distinct outlines and are of a different shade, usually being lighter than the surrounding fields. Having been picked out on air photographs, such sites can be identified only by examination on the ground.

Very often, a Roman road acts as a field boundary, in which case the enclosures are aligned with it and are grouped methodically on either side, whereas a modern road cuts straight through at random. That is one criterion for judging the age of a track: when it crosses an area that has never been out of cultivation, the enclosures lie at right-angles. The case is otherwise where the land development is of recent date (plantations, former marshlands, moors). It may even happen that the old road and the narrow strip separating it from a new highway survive together as a long narrow band.

Tracing a Roman road on a number of photographs may reveal all the characteristics we have mentioned, either in combination or in different places. It is unusual for an old road not to possess nearly all of them.

Pitfalls

But examining air photographs can present snags. First there is land regrouping, which destroys country lanes, so that they easily look like lost Roman roads, though only for short sections. This movement towards larger fields may leave behind buried traces of old roads and boundaries that have vanished on the surface but remain in the ground, a fact likely to cause confusion. An effort should be made to compare the modern air view with earlier documentary evidence. France possesses several series of air photographs published at roughly eight-year intervals by the *Institut géographique national* (IGN).

Furthermore, road alterations bring about new land boundaries whose regularity could be deceptive. What should be borne in mind in awkward cases is that much can be solved by common sense and a close look at the problem in its setting.

Warfare has complicated matters, especially in eastern France, by creating fresh ruins and fresh ground features, such as new roads out of the blue, unconnected with human settlement, and craters left by bombs and shells. Building remains cannot be dated simply from air photographs.

An abandoned aqueduct may well show up as a white streak, in the same way as a Roman road. But careful reasoning will distinguish the two. Water supply flows down on a steady gradient and heads towards a tank or a bath house and in many cases the aqueduct begins at a stream. A Roman road, on the other hand, takes little notice of changes of height and links up settlement sites, recognised stretches of road or present-day farm tracks which seem to peter out in the fields.

A watch should be kept for buried cables and pipelines, which run very straight with sharp bends. They may have branches leading to reservoirs and in the future will present pitfalls to investigators. Watch out, too, for the disused narrow-gauge railway which fulfils the same requirements as a Roman road and shares some of its characteristics: the track, which avoids small villages or runs alongside a main road, makes use of embankments and seeks a straight course. But if the railway is betrayed on slopes (which it has to take on a wide curve), there is nothing more like a Roman road in lay-out, colour, width and general appearance[164].

Use of measurements

There are many cases where examining the course of a road on air photographs is not enough to give a conclusion. This most frequently arises when a modern road has been exactly superimposed on the old road, so masking it completely. In addition, we may hesitate over the attribution of an ancient road: was it Roman or pre-

Celtic? In very hilly areas the Roman was sometimes glad to take advantage of a pre-Celtic track, even if it was not straight.

This should make us look for a new criterion. The techniques described until this point have all been qualitative by nature and nowhere make use of measurements. There is only one metric test that can be applied to roads: the spacing of the distance stones. The one possibility of relocating where they stood lies in the fact that, for centuries, they were the main feature in the road system, acting both as a landmark and as a boundary stone. They consequently influenced the lay-out of the grid of local roads that were built later than the Roman road and were subsidiary to it. So, along a genuine Roman road, it should be possible to pinpoint a number of places, such as turnings onto minor roads, local administrative boundaries and sometimes tree clumps or old crosses, between which distances measured along the road are an exact number of units (leagues or miles, Roman or Gallic)[165]. In fact, during an age when the density of population in the countryside was not high, the distance stone was an outstanding feature in an otherwise characterless landscape. It was often hidden in bushes or a copse that avoided clearance. As time went by, with a cross occasionally replacing the stone on the same site or even being erected on the stone itself, the spot retained its prominence. Thus we can draw up a list of features, such as spinneys and crosses, which may commemorate vanished distance stones.

Let us imagine, on a given road, a Roman boundary stone, left, or assumed to be left, in situ; in place of a stone, we can imagine some landmark or another (a cross-roads with a cross or an old chapel). Then if, by using this stone as a zero point and measuring out along the road distances equal to units of one Roman mile or one Roman or Gallic league, we come upon other landmarks (always allowing for an error of up to 100m), then we may conclude that the road in question was measured out in miles or leagues and that this system was a basis for a road lay-out, either local or private; that the distance stone is still in situ or that the zero point represents the site of a former stone.

When metric coincidences occur in rapid succession, then, by probability theory, the degree of certainty is high enough practically to exclude error.

We may imagine the case of a road along which there are 25 cross-roads in a distance of eight Roman leagues, that is three for each league of 2,222m. This frequency places three cross-roads on the average within range of each presumed league stone. With the league corresponding roughly to 22 hectometres, each of these cross-roads has one chance in 22 of lying in an any given 100m band. So, all in all, in the example chosen there are three possibilities in 22 (or 1 in 7) of finding a crossroads within 100m of a marker stone. If we discover five coincidences at the same time, that signifies one occurrence in $7 \times 7 \times 7 \times 7 \times 7 = 16,807$ that chance could have brought about such a situation.

For convenience in investigation, a scale should be prepared graduated in Roman leagues and eased along a straight stretch of road of sufficient length in the search for points of coincidence[166].

If there are two sets of coincidences in interval-distances, intermediate stones may be suspected. However it would be unwise to look too systematically for a series of landmarks separated by a particular fraction of a league or a mile. Unless a side road left the main highway opposite a distance stone, it would not be expected to lie exactly on a level with it. The junction occurred, therefore, just before or just after it, the distance being small, but variable, and greater at an oblique turning. This distance doubles the possible inaccuracy between two successive side-roads, hence the figure of 50m, increased for the sake of argument to a margin of 100m, and used in the previous example. If the absolute error is 50m, the relative error in one league will be only 1 in 44, but it is higher when dealing with fractions of a league. It is advantageous, therefore, to seek out coincidences only on a 'wavelength' of one league, when we are trying to determine if the modern highway is following a Roman road.

In order to make an investigation like this possible, it is vital, of course, that the Roman road in question should have had an important role in the settlement and development of the area. The side roads branch off from the sites of former stones only if, at some time in history, they were deliberately made to do so. This assumes that ground relief is not the major determining factor (along a steep-sided valley, branch roads can lead off only at side valleys).

Ideally, the area on which one is seeking these metrical coincidences should be flat, provided its agricultural development took place when the distance stones were still in position. The local road grid then lies at right angles to the Roman road and place names ending in 'ville' are numerous. Where there was a choice of several roads from which a system of roads and land division might emanate, then for obvious convenience in farming, the one following a valley was selected.

Often two sets of distance markings will be found deriving from two periods of use and sometimes from two different zero points.

The method described allows demarcation to be checked with the aid of a scale which may be nothing more than a strip of tracing paper graduated in the chosen series of units. Essentially it is a matter of looking for intervals of approximately the same length. It is effective when the coincidences along a line are spaced regularly. If the course of the road is not straight or if there are no distance stones in position, it may be impossible to carry out the search by this method.

Whatever is said, the method does not allow us to take into account relative error at each subdivision of the road. Such error may have many causes: a mistake by the original surveyor, wrongly sited distance stones, slight but inevitable alterations in the location of these as time went by, not to mention any error made in map compilation and in the results obtained therefrom.

These considerations have been taken into account by Dubesset, Guy and Liger, who have put forward a general approach to the numerical analysis of road systems (particularly useful in the case of land divisions). It can be simply stated: if there is a system of distance marking corresponding to a metrical scale (U); if the maximum error agreed for an interval is equal to E; if O is a distance mark or a boundary mark: then the distance between this point taken arbitrarily as zero and any other such division mark is equal to a multiple of U plus or minus E.

Furthermore, if, taking O as zero, we find two distances measured from O that satisfy the first condition, then the difference between these two distances must also satisfy it and this, through the combination of errors, is far from always being the case.

Any series of data in the same plane and along a given line which satisfies the stated conditon may represent surviving elements in a system of land measurement.

The calculations involved in following through these two principles are intricate and time-consuming. Thirty distance intervals mean more than a thousand arithmetical sums and an equal number of checks. Programmed and put through a computer all this work takes only about a second and the cost is minimal. By this means a real drive could be started to verify the courses of Roman road itineraries, under acceptable economic terms.

The computer makes it possible to go beyond this first stage and to tackle distance measurement more broadly and accurately: after a more advanced programme, we can learn the unit or units that have served as the basis for land division. The computer provides both the value of the unit and the list of distance marks. We might hope in this way to learn the different values given to a unit such as the Roman league, in keeping with the site itself, its date, or the surveying methods that were used.

There are further ways in which our general approach could be applied. It might locate the junction of a road and a land division or the most likely course of a stretch of road that has now disappeared.

The software for the solution of these problems is now available.

THE PROBLEM OF DATING

Dating is a difficult matter and air photography, we are often told, does not establish it. In fact, relative dates can perfectly well be obtained by a little logical reasoning when we examine the relationships between two or more features in the landscape. Byroads that form an integral part of land divisions and serve only a local estate or area were probably included in the original lay-out. But roads cutting across a field system are not earlier, which proves that there was no general scheme such as we find with the regular grid resulting from Roman land surveys. The checkerboard effect, however, is often succeeded by a star pattern radiating from a village that grew up on a road and required links with neighbouring settlements. An additional dating possibility arises from comparing a countryside checker-board with an urban layout. When the section of a main road going through a settlement is not aligned with the sections on either side of the town, or if, in other words, it bends just as it is going to become the *decumanus maximus* of the town, it is obvious that the settlement had already been built with a street plan on a different alignment and this had to be taken into account.

It appears that the majority of the routes in Gaul had already been established by the time of Caesar. Certainly an early date must be accorded to old roads running along each bank of a river. Waterways were the first means of entry into a forested region. Pre-Celtic trackways are lined by tumuli, dolmens, and menhirs (which were for long held in respect). The road of Gallic times had settlements all along it, whereas Roman roads avoided them. Roads that can be traced back at least to medieval days, such as pre-Roman tracks, are usually secondary routes, linking small villages and taking a more arduous course with many more sharp bends. It has been asserted, too, that medieval roads were probably not lined by ditches. The presence of chapels, hospitals and places named after saints provided surer clues[167].

To conclude, all these methods should be used *pari passu* to reach the common objective.[168] Tracking Roman roads in the way shown will yield clues, working hypotheses and even probabilities, but every time the last word must lie with inspection of the ground and, if possible, excavation, which may expose in the road build-up or, in association with it (in ditches or close by), datable finds (pottery, coins, burials, horseshoes, wood, reused material or structures that have been sectioned, like rubbish-pits, even buildings), all of which will have to be included in the general story.

PRACTICAL ADVICE

Initial steps

If the methods so far described are to lead to results, they must be followed consistently. It is advisable to use map sheets on a scale of 1/50,000 (20km × 27·5km). For an overall view of the topographical setting, the 1/200,000 map should be used and, for those areas for which it has been issued, the 1/100,000 map (representing four sheets on the 1/50,000 scale), giving the best compromise between area, amount of information and legibility.

The procedure to take is as follows:

1   Initial study of the topographical setting on the 1/100,000 or 1/200,000 scale: possible major lines of communication, river-crossings or passes, geographical obstacles. Note should be made of any series of roads, lanes and local boundaries in alignment: these will be the first linear features to study.
2   Second stage: examination of the 1/50,000 map cover, with special attention to the details of the course taken by any possible road: continuity of the line, street villages, relationships with relief and relevant data concerning alignment.
3   Finally, inspection of the air photographs. At this point, this should concentrate on gaps or doubtful cases. It will reveal straightaway the relationship between the presumed Roman road and field divisions, thereby enabling certain dating possibilities to be eliminated. Once examination of the air cover has ruled out these hypotheses and at the same time, as often happens, brought new discoveries, another look can be taken at the 1/50,000 map.
4   Assembling on a smaller scale (1/100,000 or 1/200,000) results that were first recorded at 1/50,000 gives once more an overall picture.

Cross-checking must constantly take place between photograph and map.

Field-work

1   Investigation will begin with the present condition of the road: stretches now

included in a first-class road, local road, farm track or footpath, vanished sections identifiable from lines of bushes (enclosing a bare strip', isolated trees, field boundaries, earth banks. Estimate the length of these stretches. Is the original road material visible (causeways or cuttings helping with difficulties of gradient, fords, flagstones, gravel, signs of constructional work)? What factors explain its disappearance (nature of soil, relief, ploughing)? Observations will be made under a variety of conditions (different viewpoint and time of year, watch for erosion after heavy rain). At river-crossings, special attention will be given to dragging and seasons of low water.

2   Investigation will then extend to the vicinity of the road: duplication of a section of road where the ground was difficult, possible forks and branches, evidence in the fields (fallow strips, ridges, lines of stone known as 'murgers' often scattered or disturbed up by the plough, anomalies in the soil or in the flora), sherds of pottery, coins, worked stone exposed by chance disturbance (road-widening, pipe-laying, burrows, marshy ground, watching for material exposed in spoil-heaps). Is the layout of the farmland based on the road? Are there close by any wells or springs that have been diverted? Keypoints will need close observation (intersection of modern and Roman roads – the latter elsewhere buried in vegetation may become visible – edges of woods, wherever anomalies occur, as when a stretch of road zig-zags and so on). Are there no old crosses or recumbent boundary stones?

3   In the course of time, information can be obtained from local people and local land-registries in order to list special place names not appearing on maps, legends, traditions about the use of an old road or about past discoveries (coins, burials in side ditches) and any other useful facts (difficulties with ploughing or growing crops, ridges and mounds, stony patches).

4   According to circumstance, the list can be extended to include the whole of the surrounding area: interesting historical monuments (earlier than the seventeenth century). Note the position in relation to the road network of castles, churches and chapels (which was their patron saint ?), any of which may stand on the site of a Roman road station[169], tumuli, mottes, isolated burial grounds. Keep an eye open at farms (flagged roads may have been taken over as threshing-floors or field boundaries, worked stone reused in various ways, stone coffins serving as pig troughs[170], and flagstones that possibly originated from a road or a building becoming walls for fields or gardens). Quarries (whether abandoned or still worked, quarry ditches close to the Roman road).

All observations must be noted on the spot, map in hand. They are improved by being illustrated with photographs or sketch maps.

Entries can be made using abbreviations provided they are clear. There must be a firm distinction between positive evidence (course certain) and hypotheses (course probable).

These distinctions must emerge on the final overall map. There need be no hesitation about showing a road with several variants, if these have been noticed: an old road is not usually single, but is formed from a bundle of tracks (this is the reason why the Ho Chi Minh trail proved so adaptable and useful). Side by side there can often be seen a Roman road going straight through, then a local road for the people of the district, or a ridge road, never waterlogged, and a valley road, liable to flooding. The Roman stations lay where these variants meet.

Finally, one needs paper and instruments for drawing and simple survey in order to record cross-sections and profiles, tapes 2m and 10m long, plus a compass to take the bearings of discoveries and a camera.

10 ROMAN ROADS AND PLACE NAMES

The quest for road names is exciting but fraught with dangers. Through its misuse by scholars with insufficient philological knowledge[171], place-name research is today somewhat discredited.

Place names must be traced as they developed through time, particularly in the case of localised place names, if we are to interpret them correctly. We must also know of the dialects or patois of the region under study.

Maps alone do not supply enough place-name material: only three or four names per sq km on the 1/20,000 scale, less than one on the 1/50,000. It is vital that an analysis of maps should be completed by the examination of estate plans and land surveys, for local place names are extremely revealing, and also vital that a thorough search should be made of old maps and documents. Often the etymology of a place name can be recognised only in its earliest forms. A systematic perusal of dated documents could provide a stratified series of place names: thus a name like 'chaussée Brunehaut' (Brunhilda causeway) without a preposition is earlier than another 'chemin de César' (Caesar's way) although both may refer to remains of the same date[172].

Here it is possible to give only a few examples of road names, at the same time emphasising that they merely furnish clues in advance of inspection of the ground.

Roads: history and legend

Names given in troubled times, when the metalled roads left by the Romans were exercising such an effect on people's minds that they connected them with the most important or most popular figures in history or legend: Devil's Way, Caesar's Way, Brunhilda Road, the Jacques Coeur Road . . .

Roads and gods

Celtic divinities: Grannus→Grand.
Roman divinities: *fanum Martis*→Famars.
Holy places: *lucus*→Luc.
Christianity: *ecclesia*→(E)glisolles, *monasterium*
→Moûtiers, *oratorium*→Ozoir, Louzouer; saints' names: Père,

Pierre (Peter) *ad vicum*→St-Péravy, chemin roumiou=(pilgrims') road to Rome.

Roads: justice and death

feudal justice beside busy roads: le Gibet (gibbet), le Pendu
(the hanged criminal).
Roman or medieval cemeteries beside roads: la Tombe (tomb);
common nouns indicating burials: *atrium*→(Vieil)-Atre; *martyretum*→Martroy; Cinq-Mars-la-Pile.

Words signifying various aspects of roads

in Celtic: camminos→chemin=way (variously described as:
chaussée=trodden, pavé=paved, perré, ferré=stony, blanc=
white,vieux=old,deCésar=Caesar's,desRomaines=Romans').
in Vulgar Latin: *ruga*→rue, *via*→vie (which may be;
vieille=old, grande=big, main).
in Germanic: Strasse, Weg.

Road structure

Calciata via (*calx*, lime)→chaussée, Cauchy;
ferré (meaning uncertain) P(i)erré, Perreux . . . pavé.
strata (*lapide*)→Etrée, Estrée . . .
la Cavée (sunken road), le Turail (embanked road), haut (high),
haussé (raised), levée (dike), a sloping road: la Montée.
adjectives: *alba via*→Aubevoie, rouge (several possible meanings), vert (green), Longroi, ancien, vieux, grand.

Bends and forks

curva via→Courbevoie
cross-roads: Croix (cross), Fourche (fork), Etoile (star).
tres vias→Tresvées
meeting of four roads: *quadrivium*→Carroi, Carrouge.

Clues from place names may arise from the Roman road, in its immediate area.

Milestones and road distances

Columna→Colonne, Colombe (St-Péravy-la-Colombe)
millière (cf. milliaire)→la croix de Mille Heures, pierre (several
meanings), Pierrefitte (*ficta*), Pierrefritte, Hitte (in the southwest).

Numbering of mile- and league-stones

ad tertium lapidem→Thiers.
tertia leuga→Tiercelieux
> Quart, Quint, Sixte, Septème, Oytier, Peyrat-la-Nonière, Dième . . .

leuga→Leu, Lègue.

Roadways and waterways

Presence of watering-points:
> Fontaine; *puteoli*→Puiseau(x) *rivus*→Rieu/Riou tributaries: *condate*→Condé

Importance of fords (in Celtic: *ritos*), Chambord=ford on a bend, vadum→Wé, Gua.

River-crossings: ferries
> *trajectus*→Maastricht, Utrecht.

Bridges: (in Celtic: *briva*→Brive, Salbris (bridge over the Sauldre); in Latin: *pons*→Pontivy (*pons vetus*), Pontoise.

Tautology in two languages: pont de Bricques (Germanic: Brücke)

Road-users and their destinations: grand chemin (highway) from
> X to Y, ancien chemin (old road) from X to Y, chemin des Bourguignons (Burgundians'), des Lorrains (Lorrainers'), des Rouliers (Waggoners'), des chasse-marées (of the fish-carts), du vin (of wine), saunier (salt-maker), des boeufs (of the oxen), des moines (monks'), des Gens d'Armes (of the men-at-arms) . . .

Road stations

Maison Rouge *balnea*→Bagneux *capanna*→Chavanne *casa*→Chèze *cella*→Celle *civitas*→Cieutat, Ciotat *fabrica*→Faverge *figulina*→Féline *forum*→Fréjus (*Forum Julii*), Feurs, Fourvières (*Forum vetus*) *hospitale*→Hôpiteau *maceriae*→Mazères, Mezières *magus* (Celtic)=market: *Noviomagus*→Nogent, Noyon maladrerie (leper house) *mansio*→maison *mansionile*→Mesnil moulin (mill) *mutatio*→Muizon, Mudaison poste (post) relais (relay) remise (mews) *stabulum*→Étalle, Étoles *tabernae*→Tavernes Saverne *vicus*→Vic, Vix, Neuvy *villa*→ville (common in compounds)

Other estate names were formed with the suffix (in French) 'court' and with the owner's name completed by the suffix 'acum'.

Military settlements

colonia→Cologne
Alains→Allaines, Alamans→Allemagne, Francs→Villefrancoeur (villa Francorum),

Germains→Germagne, Goths→Gourville, Marcomans→Marmagne, Sarmates→ Sermaise, Vandales→Villevendreux (*villa Vandalorum*)

Roads and fortifications

in Celtic: *briga* (fortress), camp, *castra*→La Châtre
castellum→château, castellare→Châtelard
in Celtic: *dunos*→Dun, *firmitas*→Ferté
la Garde, la Motte, *podium*→Puy, rocca→Roche, turris→Tours.

Roads and land boundaries

basilica (market, sanctuary)→Bazoche, Bazeille   *confinium*→Confin   *fines*→Fins.
in Germanic: *marca*→la Marche (cf. Celtic *morga*)
mediolanum= the clearing in the middle, Milan, Meillant, Miolans, Montmélian
in Celtic: randa (cf. German: Rand). Equoranda (water-frontier)→Aigue-
rande, Ingrande, Ingrannes, Yvrande   *terminus*→Terme
planted trees: épine (thorn), houx (holly), orme (elm).

Customs posts

camera (toll-post)→C(h)ambre
fiscus→Fesches
quadragesima→Carême

Caesarodunum 1970 contains a summary of *The Roman roads of the civitas of the Aedui* (E. Thévenot), Brussels, 1969, with a series of place names related to the roads of Burgundy, classified as above.

3

Roads in the
Roman Empire

The limited scope of this book prevents equal treatment from being given to all the provinces and it is not possible, for example to describe here the 372 roads (85,000km) recorded under Diocletian. In addition, our knowledge varies from region to region. We shall confine ourselves to a rapid survey of the chief routes, suggesting a chronology for their development and emphasising those road networks that seem most significant and have received most study.

Starting, logically enough, with Italy, we shall pass to Greece and thence, in a clockwise direction, move round the Mediterranean via Asia Minor, Egypt, North Africa and Spain, then on to Britain, before dealing with Gaul at some length and ending with Germany, the Alps and the Danube valley.

1 ITALY

EARLY ITALY

There were roads in Italy before Rome, the work in particular of the Etruscans and the Greeks.

Seasonal rhythms, dictated by transhumance[1], between the coastal plain and the mountains, were a feature of life throughout the peninsula. The *via Salaria,* used back in protohistoric times, is an example of one of these 'tratturi' which air photography has shown to be numerous around centres of population in Apulia.

The roads of Etruria itself have been studied on air photographs and on the ground by the British School in Rome, under the guidance of Professor Ward-Perkins. They already involved engineering work. 'Colonial' Etruria also had its own communications: small finds occur spaced along a master line aimed at the Alpine passes and skirting the Apennine Hills, from the point at which the Reno road emerges, controlled by Marzabotto, then to Casalecchio and Felsina (Bologna) as far as Mantua and beyond, while Bologna was certainly linked to the busy commercial centre at Spina, at the mouth of the Po. Travel across the damp Paduan plain was at times by river and lagoon or else made use of the raised banks or coastal dunelands.

Southwards, the Etruscans reached Campania via the natural route from Veii to Fidenae on the Tiber, then on to Praeneste (whose importance in the seventh century BC is brought out by graves richly furnished under Eastern influence), then along the course first of the Trerus (Sacco), then of the Liris (Garigliano), in competition with the coast road. The inland route, later the *Latina,* must still have been used by the Etruscans, even after Rome gained her freedom, in order to reach their colonies in Campania. From there, they had contacts with the Greek colonies in southern Italy along packhorse trails, which, keeping to the wide valleys with their seasonal water-courses, formed a link between both seas.

A recent congress on Greater Greece (Tarento, 1962) gave consideration to the roads of southern Italy. It was emphasised how much the landscape has changed in historic times, in particular the river systems; rivers with estuaries that were navigable and had a steady régime today have deltas and a régime subject to drought and storm. River-mouths have moved through the effect of subsidence ('bradisismo'). Offshore traffic or even direct sailing lines may obviously have competed with the land route (the 'Heraclean' coast road), allowing for the fact that roads taking the valleys across the isthmus provided short cuts which conveniently avoided the dangers not only of the strong currents in the straits of Messina (Charybdis and Scylla) but also of certain city states holding political and commercial sway. In general, there seem to have been two great traffic axes alternately to the fore. From the seventh century, with the expansion of Tarento, the east–west road was dominant, following the route taken by the people of Oenotria in their heyday. The north–south route was the one along which the Sabine people thrust when they separated from the Samnites, following tracks taken by Greek colonists into the heart of Lucania. Later this was the principal line of movement of the Roman army, for whom the Sulmo–Luceria–Venusia axis formed a vital strategic link. The *via Appia* gave fresh stimulus to the east–west passage until the time of the Lombards.

These roads witnessed the arrival of subtle influences in Italy: Devoto has shown that Greek words reached Rome by sea (Cumae) or by land (Tarentum) according to their Ionian or Doric source.

But enough has been said about developments before the Roman conquest.

The main Roman roads in Italy

We have dealt earlier with the site of Rome and the road grid radiating from the city.

Road-building came in the wake of the conquest and the subsequent political unification and economic development of the peninsula (colonial settlements, land survey and centuriation). The road-builders were often consuls or provincial governors, who gave their names to the highways and the new towns along them (M. Aemilius Lepidus and the *via Aemilia*).

Rome first turned her attention to Campania. The *via Appia,* first major link with the south, was planned by the censor Appius Claudius Caecus in 312 BC, originally as far as Capua. It was then extended (via Trajana) via Beneventum, Aeclanum, and

Venusia, Horace's homeland, Tarentum, to Brundisium (264), the embarkation port for Greece (in Epirus, the route was continued by the *via Egnatia,* see below). Horace' lines illustrating his journey to Brundisium along the *Appia* have already been quoted. Trajan built an alternative route from Beneventum, where a triumphal arch marked the beginning of the new *Appia-Traiana,* to Canosa and Egnatia (112–17). From the *Appia* there had already branched off at Sinuessa the *via Domitiana* (AD 95) which led across the marshy ground of the Volturnus and Liternum to Cumae, Puteoli and Naples. A poem by Statius commemorating the building of this shortcut, with interesting technical details, has already been mentioned.

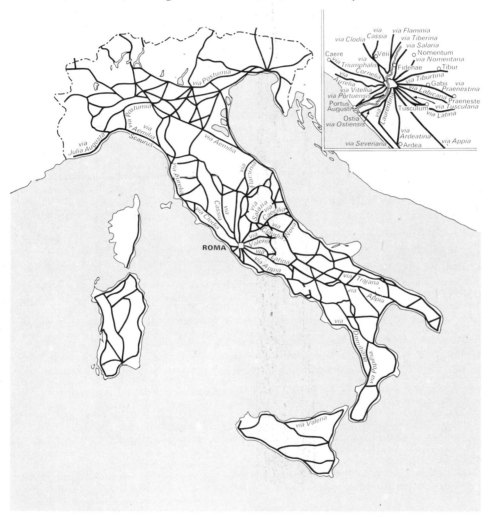

27   The main Roman roads in Italy (after *Atlas of the Classical World,* Amsterdam–Brussels, Elsevier, 1959, p. 128)

If the *via Appia* followed the coast, the *via Latina,* for its part, went along the interior through the land of the Hernici (Anagnia, Ferentinum, Fregellae, Cales).

From Capua the *via Popilia* branched off towards Lucania and Bruttium (Eboli, Sala Consilina, Rhegium). A well-known inscription at Polla shows that the builder (the consul Popilius?) was responsible for building bridges, milestones and posting-stations over the whole stretch of 320 miles, at the same time causing the shepherds to make way for ploughmen[2].

With the conquest of northern Italy, the *via Flaminia* (220 BC) passing along the valley of the Tiber, through the land of the Falisci and Umbria, on to the Adriatic coast (Pisaurum), reached Ariminum[3] whence the *via Aemilia* led to Placentia (187 BC). In the same year, a road was constructed linking Arretium to Bononia. In 132, one could journey north from Ariminum to Adria along the *Popilia*, and this was followed by the *Annia* as far as Aquileia (131). The *via Postumia* (148–47 BC) ran from Cremona to Verona, and from Padua to Aquileia. The *Valeria*, planned as early as 307 by the censor M. Valerius Maximus, went obliquely across the territories of the Aequi, the Peligni and the Marrucini as far as Teate, Ortona and the sea. The *Salaria* passed through the land of the Sabines and Picenum (Reate, Asculum) likewise reaching the Adriatic, the coastline of which could be followed by a link road.

On the Tyrrhenian shore, the *Aurelia*, and inland, going through Volsinii, Clusium, Arretium and Florence, the *Cassia* (completed between 154 and 125 from Arretium to Florence and Pisa) both linked up at Pisa, from which town the *Aemilia Scauri* (109, from Pisa to Genoa and Tortona) and the *via Julia Augusta* aimed for the Maritime Alps, Gaul and Spain.

The islands seem to have been neglected: one road only in Corsica, on the east coast. There was a road going round Sicily, known as the *Valeria* (210) on the north coast and as *Pompeia* on the north-east where it passed through Messina. Secondary roads linked Agrigentum to Panorma, Catana to Thermae Himerae, Gela to Syracuse.

Knowledge can be advanced in this sphere only by detailed studies giving a synthesis of information on the history of the landscape. Piganiol has offered this advice in his *History of Rome*: 'Each Roman road must be examined carefully, so that we can rediscover the native way that it replaced or bypassed.' For the main high-ways the *Real Encyclopädie* provides the list of improvements (*via Cassia* paved in 171) and repairs (in the case of the *Flaminia*, Agrippa had 15 bridges rebuilt, one being over the Nar).

We shall now look in detail at the roads of northern Italy which played such a vital part in the Romanisation of Central and Western Europe, before tackling the ever-present problem of crossing the Alps.

Let us not forget that links with Spain first of all took place by sea, then via the Alpine passes before following the coastal route.

Roman roads in northern Italy

For the pre-Roman period there is evidence for one road only from literary sources: Pseudo-Scylax mentions the Etruscan road from Spina to Pisa (3 days).

Before Romanisation, the road system apparently remained in a fragmentary state. The Romans were no doubt responsible for straightening roads and linking them with each other in addition to carrying out more permanent engineering work.

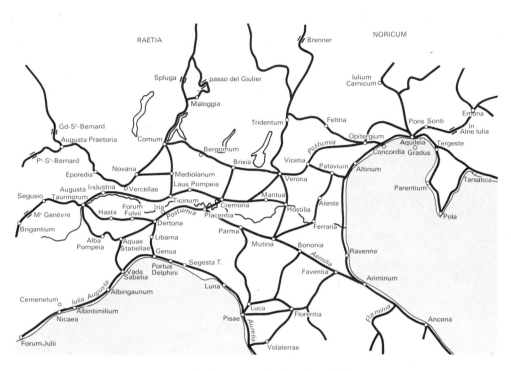

28   The Roman roads of northern Italy

The ground search is helped by place-name study. We come across again in Italy the names found in France: Strada, Stra (and compounds), Agna (from *Annia*), Loreggia (from *Aurelia*), Postioma, Postaime, Costuma (from *Postumia*), Strada Regina, Strada Antica (Collantiga), Pagana, Paganorum, del Diavolo, Via Ungaresca/Ungarorum, Romea, Romera, Francigena, di Orlando, via Pelosa, Selvatica, Erbosa, Persa, Stradazza, Maltravers, Arzere (from *agger*), Campagna, Levada, via Petrata, Silicata, Calcata; place names derived from distance stones: Ottavello, Tavello, Tavo, Tho; Trebbio (from *trivium*), Codroipo (from *quadruvium*); Taverna.

Roads were built, just as colonies were set up, for strategic reasons.

In 282 BC the consul L. Aemilius Papus attacked the Boii who had come from Gaul. Ariminum (Rimini) was colonised in 268 and 222. Clastidium in 222, when Cremona and Placentia were founded.

The *via Flaminia* reached Ariminum in 220.

The *via Aurelia* reached Vada Volaterrana (Torre di Vada) from Rome in 241.

197: Placentia and Cremona were colonised afresh.

189: A colony is set up at Bologna.

187: the consul M. Aemilius Lepidus laid out the *via Aemilia* from Ariminum to Placentia, the military value of which was emphasised by Livy[4]: it went through the territory of the Boii and took the savage Ligures in the rear. It was also an important trade artery, following the course of a route for Etruscan traffic that skirted the valleys after emerging from the Apennines. The *via Aemilia* was to give its name to the Eighth Augustan legion, the *Aemilia*[5].

All the road construction of the second century BC occurred about this axial line. Of the same date- the *via Flaminia minor*: Bologna–Arretium.

175: *via Aemilia* 'altinate': Bologna–Altinum (Quarto)–Aquileia.

148: first stage of the Postumia from the Tyrrhenian Sea to the Adriatic via Placentia.

132–31: *via Popillia–Annia*: Ariminum to Aquileia (see below).

This triangle of roads reflects both the geographical conditions and the progress of the military conquest.

The *Flaminia minor*, planned by C. Flaminius Nepos, consul in 187[6], followed an ancient Etruscan track along the valley of the Reno towards Pistoriae (Pistoia), Florentia (Florence), Arretium (Arezzo) where it joined the *via Cassia* (towards Rome).

One road went from Arretium to Ariminum (where the town *insulae* are aligned with it) along the valley of the Marecchia and through the Viamaggio pass.

Another left Sassina, homeland of Plautus, to go down towards Caesena, along the Savio valley.

The *via Faventina* (or *Ravignana*, its name in medieval days) joined the valleys of the Arno and the Lamone.

These three roads, with those linking Luca and Parma, Luna and Placentia, were, in part at any rate, earlier than Rome and were used at the time of the conquest. This seems to be confirmed by the fact that they do not bear their builder's name.

In 175 M. Aemilius Lepidus must have constructed the *via Aemilia Altinate* from Bologna to Hostilia on the Po, Ateste (Este), Mons Silicis (Monselice), Patavium (Padua), Altinum, Concordia and Aquileia. The first stretch is in any case uncertain. One theory takes it through the site of Ferrara. This was a road with a strategic rôle: it linked Rome with her allies in Venetia and with her distant colony of Aquileia (181 BC).

The western region, Liguria, resisted for longer. The colonies of Luca and Luna date from 177.

In 148, the consul Spurius Postumius Albinus conceived the scheme for a great rock-cut road from Genua (Genoa) to Libarna (Serravalle), Dertona (Tortona), Stradella, Placentia, Cremona, Verona, Vicetia (Vicence), Tarvisium (Treviso), Opitergium (Oderzo), Quadruvium (Codroipo), Aquileia.

Finally, the *via Popillia–Annia* carries the name of both its builders, the consul for 132 BC, P. Popillius Laenas, and the praetor T. Annius Rufus, (131). Less interest was then being displayed in strategic advantages than in the agrarian policy of redistribution of the land. The *Popillia*, from Ariminum onward, was following a coastal duneland. It may have been double-tracked north of Adria (cf. on the shore of the

Venice lagoon the medieval place name 'Pupilia' with traces of agger and the 'Agna' place names close to Padua, explicable perhaps to the name having extended along a *deverticulum*).

M. Fulvius Flaccus, consul in 125 BC, the first to cross the Alps with an army, was responsible for the line of the *via Fulvia* from Dertona to Forum Fulvii (Villa del Foro), Hasta (Asti) and, later, Turin.

In 109, the *via Aurelia* was extended along the coast by the censor M. Aemilius Scaurus from Vada Volaterrana to Pisae, Luna, Genua, Vada Sabatia (Vado), Aquae Statiellae (Acqui), Dertona (the *via Aemilia Scauri*).

We must date from the end of the Republic the road sections joining Ticinum (Pavia) and Mediolanum (Milan) to the Alpine Lakes, likewise the Piedmont road between Verona, Brixia (Brescia), Bergomum (Bergame), Leucerae (Lecco), Forum Licinii, and Comum (Como), birthplace of the Elder Pliny and his nephew.

A local *Aurelia* (initiated by the consul in 75, C. Aurelius Cotta) linked Patavium and Acelum (Asolo).

After the disorder caused by the civil wars, Augustus gave great attention to the restoration of the road network. In 27 BC he was *curator viarum* for the *Aemilia*.

Consequently the triumphal arch at Ariminum commemorated road repairs, at the junction of *Flaminia* and *Aemilia*. The year 25 saw the start of the wars against the people of the Alps, in 12 a treaty was concluded with Cottius, in 16 Augustus gave funds to the public treasury (*aerarium*) for the purpose of restoring roads (erection of several bridges and milestones) and constructing new ones through the Alps. Once again new colonies were being set up at the same time.

In 13–12 the *via Julia Augusta* was marked out along its western stretch, starting from Trebbia (Piacenza) and coinciding with the *Postumia* as far as Dertona, then with the *via Aemilia Scauri* as far as Vada Sabatia. Passing through Albingaunum (Albenga), Albintimilium (Vintimille), in Alpe Summa (La Turbie, on the frontier between Italy and Gaul, where the trophy commemorates the pacification of the Alps), and Arles, the *via Domitia* was reached (796 miles from Rome to Gaul along the coast) on the way to Spain.

From Augusta Taurinorum (Turin), Placentia was the destination along the *via Fulvia*, while by following the left bank of the Po, through Ticinum (Pavia), Duriae (Dorno), Laumellum (Lomello), Cutiae (Cozzo), Carbantia (Balzola ?) and Rigomagus one arrived at Segusio (Suse), Matrona Mons (Mont-Genèvre) and Brigantio (Briançon).

From Cutiae, passing through Vercellae (Verceil), Eporedia (Ivrée), Vitricium (Verrès), Augusta Praetoria (Aosta), it was possible to reach the Little St Bernard (Alpis Graia) or the Great St Bernard (Summus Poeninus).

One road ran from Milan to Como, passing by the lake at Clavenna (Chiavenna), through the Spluga pass (Cuneus Aureus), then on to Curia (Chur) to reach Rhaetia and the upper Rhine.

After the campaigns of Drusus, a main road followed the Adige and went through Tridentum (Trent), Pons Drusi (Bolzano), and the Resia pass. It is named after Claudius: *via Claudia Augusta* (AD 46–47). From Hostilia, one reached Verona and

Tridentum. Augustus built the section Mutina (Modena)–Colicaria–Hostilia, called the *via Claudia Augusta* in the Po valley.

Altinum gives its name to the *Claudia Augusta* of Altinum (cf. the causeway termed the Lagozzo or Agozzo of *Augustus*) in the Piava valley: the San Boldo pass, Feltria, the Valsugana and Tridentum (course uncertain). There was a road from Feltria to Bellunum, going over the pass of Monte Croce di Comelico down into the valley of the Drava.

In 2 BC Augustus was again at work constructing the eastern *via Julia,* from Aquileia or Concordia to Ad Tricesimum (Tricesimo), Julium Carnicum (Zuglio) and the Carnic Alps. From Aquileia, an important meeting-place of roads, one went to Julia Emona, Lubiana, by the inland route (valley of the Frigido) or, along the coast, to Fons Timavi (San Giovanni), Tergeste (Trieste) from which place another road, also Augustan, reached Tarsatica (Tersatto). In 78, Vespasian completed the coastal section as far as Pola (*via Flavia*).

At the time of Augustus, therefore, there came into being the major road-links across the Alps. At a later date, we should notice activity under Trajan and Hadrian, restoration at the time of Valerian, the tetrarchs and Constantine. With the Later Empire Milan assumed greater importance as a centre of communications, a role then assumed by Ravenna until the end of the Western Empire.

We must complete this study of the road network in northern Italy by looking at communications by sea and river, while remembering how the landscape has changed since Roman times, especially at the mouths of the Po[7].

There the lagoons were linked up by cutting through the lines of dunes lying along the coast and the river banks in order to make canals (*fossa Augusta* from Ravenna to the mouth of the Primaro and to Spina, *fossa Flavia* from Spina to Adria, *fossa Clodia* close to Chioggia).

There were river ports at Bologna, Piacenza, Verona, Brescia, and Milan, which sometimes continued in existence until modern times.

The *Antonine Itinerary* (126, 6) mentions a mixed route on the *cursus publicus*: a highway partly by road, partly by lagoon, from Ravenna to Altinum, as well as across Lake Como (279, 1), while in the *Peutinger Table* we find such a route from Ravenna to Hostilia.

The use of these waterways continued, in particular with the decay in the road network. This is shown by the widespread trade, for which archaeology has provided the evidence, in stone from Istria, marble from Verona and Euganean trachyte (*colli Berici*) and by literary references: Strabo[8] (two days and two nights from Piacenza to Ravenna), Vitruvius[9], Sidonius Apollinarius in 467[10] (a journey from Pavia to Ravenna on board a boat belonging to the *cursus publicus,* with a relief crew at Brescello, fifth century) and Cassiodorus[11].

The Po, passing through a landscape that retained more forest cover than today, flowed with a more regular régime. According to Polybius[12], it was possible to sail upstream for 2,000 stadia (355km), as far as the Tanaro, and according to Pliny the Elder[13], as far as Turin. The situation must have been improved by Roman water engineering, carried out in connection with land division (centuriation). The tributaries of the Po and the major lakes also came into use: Catullus went along in his *Phaselus* following the course of the Mincio from the Adriatic to his villa at Sirmione on Lake Garda[14].

From inscriptions we know of a *corpus naviculariorum maris Hadriatici,* a *collegium nautarum* at Adria and Ravenna, and boatmen's guilds on Lakes Garda, Como and Mantua.

Recent studies, making use of medieval sources, have shown the importance of the salt trade from the saline marshes inland, Comacchio having inherited an advantageous position that made it in effect the pre-Roman Ravenna.

Finally, local shipping was active along the coasts.

An example of a great Italian road: the *Aurelia*

A study of the *Aurelia,* running from Rome to *Forum Aureli,* has been carried out under Professor Castagnoli by a team from the Institute of Ancient Topography in the University of Rome, resuming the tradition of Plinio Fraccaro. The authors have used every kind of evidence at their disposal: literary texts, iconographic records, ancient surveys, maps old and new, air photographs and their interpretation of the material. Fieldwork concentrated on:

surviving features of the road (pavements alongside, remetalling and paving as seen in sections, bridges, branches going to Etruscan cities inland and to coastal colonies, milestones and inscriptions);

all the ancient structures lying in proximity to the road: building remains, especially those of a number of large villas, the area once covered by a *pagus,* wells and tanks, drainage *cunicoli,* aqueducts, tombs, altars, towers, architectural fragments and other finds (sculptures, mosaics, furnishings, millstones, pottery picked up on the surrounding farmland).

As in the case of Gaul, one is struck by the way in which the old itineraries have changed and by the accelerated speed of their destruction, factors raising the problem how the landscape is to be conserved. Those responsible for town planning in Rome are trying to keep a green belt for the Eternal City, the framework of which will be formed by the circuit of Aurelian's wall and the first stretches of the ancient highways. Concern over these matters is regularly expressed in the excellent periodical *Capitolium* published by the city authorities in Rome.

It would be a worthwhile task to rewrite Italian history simply from the point of view of the roads. We shall limit ourselves to quoting a few examples involving the generation from the Social War to Caesar:

Corfinium was chosen as the chief centre for the revolt because it occupied a key position on the *via Valeria* between Rome and the Adriatic;
in the summer of 82 Carbo confronted Metellus on the *via Aemilia*;
in 69–68, skirmishes took place with pirates on the *Appia*;
in January 62, Q. Metellus Celer moved along the *Aemilia* to bar the way to Catalina;

in 61, Pompey returned in triumph along the *Appia*, with his following swollen in numbers at every halt;

on 19 April 59, on the same road, Cicero met Curio, Caesar's 'agent provocateur', at the *Tres Tabernae*;

on 1 January 52, again on the *Appia*, close to Bovillae, Milo, on his way to Lanuvium with a band of gladiators, clashed with Clodius (had he not already had a scuffle with Hypsaeus the year before on the Sacred Way itself?);

we could re-establish in the same way the main roads used by Caesar when he conquered Italy, taking possession of key points like Arretium on the Cassia.

2 GREECE

The relief of the country with its many subdivisions, indented coastline and islands encouraged movement by sea. The main Roman road, the first built outside Italy, was the *via Egnatia* (148 BC), which went from Apollonia to Thessalonica, following an ancient highway whose western part was used by the army from 199, and then was extended as far as the river Hebrus. Cicero on his way to exile, Pompey, Antony and Octavius all took this road.

From Corinth, famous for its *diolkos*, where the isthmus could be crossed, it was possible to go on to Epidaurus and Troezen, Cleonae and Argos, Sicyon and Phlius. There was a road along the coast towards Megara, Athens and Boetia. Another led from Argos to Mantinea and Sparta. From Mantinea one reached Messenia, Olympia and Elis. Corinth was linked with Patras, Dyne and Elis by way of Pellene and Aegae.

There were also roads between the following towns: Apollonia–Thessalonica; Apollonia–Nicopolis–Thebes–Athens–Corinth; Athens–Thebes–Larissa–Thessalonica and thence towards Moesia. Along the Thracian coast one aimed for Philippi, Perinthus and Byzantium.

The journeys made by Pausanias suggest that there were many other secondary roads, marked by piles of stones left by each traveller in turn.

It is well known that Greece and particularly Athens enjoyed a high reputation amongst the Romans[15]. The cultural trip to Greece, with the object of visiting one of the Schools or a philosopher on an island or on the peninsula, forms an interesting theme, which Marrou has developed in his *History of Education in Antiquity*[16].

3 ASIA MINOR AND SYRIA

The peninsula had known great empires before Rome, splendid empires that had developed their own communications[17] trodden by many a merchant before the legions.

The mountains in the north and south established the lines of the natural routes.

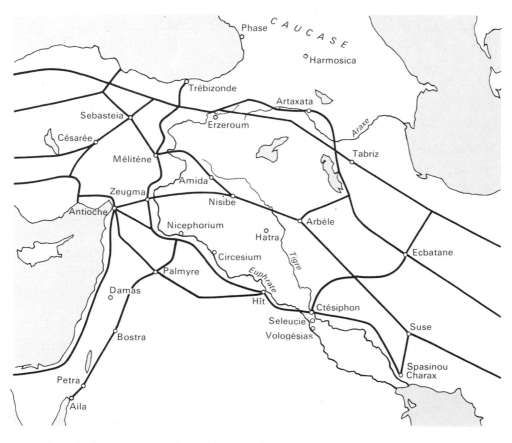

29 The main Roman roads in the Middle East (after A. Poidebard and R. Mouterde, *Le 'Limes' de Chalcis,* Paris, 1945, Fig. 1)

The Romans, concerned with putting down piracy, first of all repaired the old royal way from Ephesus to Laodicea and Apamea via Tralles. Pompey founded stations in the valleys of the Lycos and Halys, while Augustus installed colonies and garrisons in Isauria and Lydia to watch over the southern road. There were military roads linking these places and running to the sea: Iconium to Lystra and Laranda, Side and Apamea to Selge and Cremna. Vespasian laid a road between Satala and Melitene. The Romans held the crossings of the Euphrates at Zeugma, Samosate and Melitene.

From Ephesus, a road ran to Tralles and then, following the Meander valley to Laodicea and Apamea, Antioch of Pisidia, Philomelium and Iconium: thence to Laranda and to the gates of Cilicia, Tarsus, Antioch of Syria or to Zeugma. From Sardes, one went up the Hermos valley towards Philadelphia, Synnada, Pessinonte, Ancyra, Tavium, Megalopolis, then Melitene or, northwards, Satala and Nicopolis.

From Nicomedia a southern branch went through Juliopolis to Ancyra, a northern branch to Amasia through Claudiopolis and Cratia, then on to Comana, Satala and Nicopolis.

There were cross-country roads: Sinope–Tarsus through Amasia and Tavium or Comana and Megalopolis and links between Ephesus, Sardes, Smyrna, Thyatira, Pergamum and between the colonies in Pisidia.

In Syria the road system was based on that of the Seleucids and thereby dated back to the Persian empire.

From Egypt, Gaza could be reached and from there Petra to the east, or the coastal ports: Caesarea, Tyre, Berytus, Seleucia and, from Trajan onwards, the Bosphorus, or Jerusalem, Emesa, and Antioch or Damascus. From Leukè Comè on the Red Sea, it was possible to go to Petra, then to Gaza and the Mediterranean or, through Philadelphia and Canatha, to Damascus. From there, a caravan trail led to Palmyra and the Euphrates, another to Epiphania, the Orontes and Antioch. By way of Chalcis and Berea one reached Zeugma on the Euphrates or Cilicia. Antioch was a very important road junction, on the route to Cilicia and Byzantium, Palmyra, the Euphrates and Babylon, Samosate and Zeugma. Other roads linked Antioch and Selucia, Apamea and Laodicea, Emesa and Aradus, Damascus and Sidon, Jerusalem and Caesarea. The importance of Antioch must be emphasised, as the centre of the strategic frontier system between Rome and the Parthians, which was to remain until the Arab conquest the hub of communications between Asia and the Mediterranean. The roads from Antioch linked it with all the major crossing-points on the *limes* of the Euphrates and the *limes* of the Palmyran area and their courses were extended eastwards in the direction of Ctesiphon and Lower Mesopotamia along the Tigris and the Euphrates. As for Chalcis, it lay at the keypoint of the eastern *limes* and of the forward defences of Antioch and was at the focus of two great strategic routes running along the axis of the Euphrates and that of the Orontes: it therefore commanded all the advance roads towards the two *limes* of the Euphrates and Palmyrenia and all the enemy invasion roads from the direction of Mesopotamia.

Activity in road construction under Trajan must be noted, connected with the war plans against the Parthians (the *via Trajana* built by the Legio IX Hispana under its legate Cladius Severus, from Emesa to Philadelphia and Gerasa, Bostra, Damascus and Palmyra). The *strata Diocleitana* linked Sura, Resafe, Palmyra and Bostra. The conquest of Arabia was aimed at safeguarding the land route between Palestine and Egypt and the Arabian trade.

Roman roads, as well as the whole system in the Syrian desert, have been the object of original research by the pioneer in air photography, Father Poidebard. After becoming acquainted with the Near East during the 1914–18 war, he received the mission from the Geographical Society of looking for waterholes and lost irrigation works in High Syria. Immediately, this army-reserve officer, as an air observer, realised the contribution that the aeroplane could make to archaeological knowledge, fought for the new method, and won the interest of the Institute of France, which appointed him to search for 'the trail of Rome in the Syrian desert'. This was the title of a book published in 1934, completed by *The 'limes' of Chalcis* (1945) and by numerous papers. The first series of discoveries, from 1925 to 1932, traced the *limes* of Imperial times from Bostra to Palmyra and to the Tigris, while a second campaign (1934–42) established how the rear defences were organised between the Euphrates and the Orontes. In 550 hours of flying, over an area measuring 1,000 by 300km, Father Poidebard found hundreds of kilometres of road and some 400 structures either of military origin or connected with water supply. With the help of the French army and air force in the Middle East, he checked his findings on the ground, questioning leaders of caravans and tribal chiefs on 'the man-made tracks connecting historic sites in the region'. A long time was spent in perfecting the method used: it involved following up evidence from original sources, then actual observation, photography and ground survey. Aircraft in those days could fly very low so that a milestone might be recognised in situ, could land anywhere or rise to 2,500m to obtain a panoramic view. Father Poidebard took advantage of shadow effects created by low relief, against the light, and also the differential growth of vegetation: after the autumn rains, the desert is greener at first along the depressions of ancient roads and filled ditches, whilst remaining lighter over structural remains. The same results are produced when the spring sun begins to scorch vegetation: 'Scarcely visible at ground level, the old road system stands out clearly when one gets up to 1,500m . . . At Ledja, air photographs taken from 2,000m give an overall view and solve problems by revealing the Roman road running across the lava fields.'

Amongst the important information recovered was first and foremost the plan of the old roads. From 1925 onwards, by observing from the air successions of tells that fitted in with the positions of ancient towns and with river-crossings, Father Poidebard managed to put back on the map thirteen itineraries and three cross-roads. Causeways today robbed of their paving show up clearly, even where every trace of surface metalling has disappeared, thanks to the shadows thrown by built-up ridges, the kerbs of basalt blocks and the lines of flints removed from tracks to protect the feet of camels of burden. These edging lines are only a few centimetres high, but, although covered over by windborne sand, they become visible in an oblique light. After rain, depressions brought about by the movement of caravans in the past remain damp and show up from above as even bands of greenery.

Father Poidebard carried out every type of check needed in looking for old roads: the great age of the natural routes between lowland and high plateau, pinpointed by worked flints; the importance of water supply from wells or tanks; concern, too, with handy grazing for transport animals; the vital role of a system of visible signals, so that traffic was always moving within sight of watch-towers; the different routes taken in winter and summer; the disappearance of paving, only where the road crossed marshy ground; the sites of vanished bridges shown up on either side of a river by sloping earthworks of regular shape and similar height. With a stopwatch, Father Poidebard was able to demonstrate how the tells were evenly spaced out, often forming bridgeheads at river-crossings and he thus identified major stages of about 50km, usually subdivided to give three stations, facts which allowed him to make this comment on the *Peutinger Table*: 'I now have in my view the whole network of ancient roads, with the tells lying along them at intervals, once the centres of farming communities, fortified settlements and military defence posts.'

When he extended his investigations Father Poidebard was to turn naturally enough from the roads to the *limes*. This word first meant a track, then a fortified

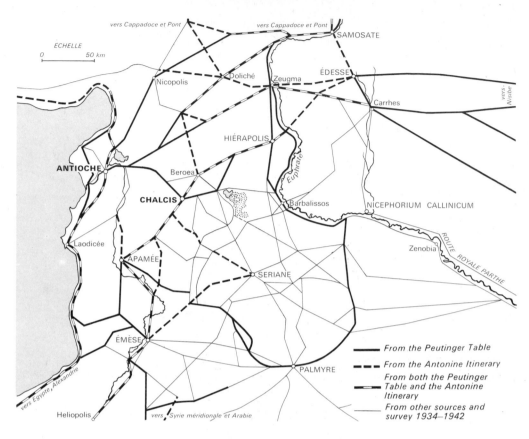

30   The Roman road system in the area of northern Syria (after A. Poidebard and R. Mouterde, op. cit., map 1)

military road, before being understood as an Imperial frontier, a frontier, however, in the sense of a broad zone, organised under a plan that was carried out with patience and flexibility and based on a deep understanding of the geographical and political factors. In Syria the Euphrates and the Tigris formed permanent invasion routes; Roman forts had merely to be built where Assyrian and Hittite strongholds had stood. The *limes* linked the keypoints of Bostra, Damascus, Palmyra, Circesium, Thannouris, Singara and Amida and with the support of high ground and stretches of river-line the frontier system cut diagonally across the desert between the 100 and 250mm isohyets. This historical fact arose from a major geographical principle, for the map showing the arrangement of the Roman *limes* can be closely integrated with the rainfall map, which is very apparent to airmen at the change of seasons in spring and autumn: the hill-ridges which have been mentioned attract cloud and mist, forcing a climb in altitude.

Furthermore, the tribes used to move in summer towards the mountains, outside and around the region of the desert, and the *limes,* cutting transversely across the belt of transhumance and the caravan trails leading towards Arabia and the Persian Gulf, kept watch on the passes through the highlands and on the fords over the water-courses. Thus it enabled effective control to be exercised over the nomads and the caravan routes along which there travelled spices, aromatics, ivory, ebony, sandal-wood, pearls and precious stones from Arabian, Parthian, Sassanid or Persian markets on their way to the Mediterranean ports of Syria: in this respect the commercial rôle of the *limes* was no less important than its military one.

The boundaries of the *limes* were defined by Diocletian, who increased the number of *castella* in order to ward off the swift raids of Sassanid and Saracen horsemen and settled locally recruited troops on land concessions. Thus the *limes* remained until Byzantine times and the Arab conquest.

From 1925 to 1932 the map of the *limes* was drawn up in this way, showing its full extent between Bostra and the Tigris, over a length of 750km and a depth of 100 to 200km, re-establishing the Roman military and economic system. The main road, along which lay at intervals the control centres of the army of occupation, made its way through well-defined passes. Every 10 or 20 miles there were police posts, connected by a system of visual signals. Every 30 miles larger *castella* represented staging-points for camel caravans following the age-old desert trails. The main highway was doubled on each side by parallel strategic roads. Finally forward routes into the desert kept watch on water sources and areas where nomads used to gather, the whole system being knit by further roads running transversely.

Father Poidebard observed many details that throw light on tactics and strategy: branch roads, for example, going deep into the territory of allied or subject tribes; the outermost line of the *limes* acting as a barrier for customs checks; sites that might have been a starting point or a defence position on river bends at bridgeheads sited in Persian territory; possible weaknesses in defence or lines of invasion; a defence system in depth, involving fortified agricultural settlements on river banks behind the line of *castella,* amidst a steppe in which could be seen the man-made ridges and vales left by irrigation canals, later destroyed by Arab and Mongol invasions; the tactical segmentation of high ground in hostile territory; the surveillance of grazing land and sources of water.

4 EGYPT

Communication by water was important in the delta, thanks to the system of canals, of which the main one linked the eastern arm of the Nile, by way of the Bitter Lakes, with Arsinoé, a harbour on the Red Sea, whilst a branch led to the Pelusiac mouth. Trajan cut a new canal as far as Clysmon from Memphis. Various canals led from the Nile to large towns.

There were roads across the mountains giving access from the Great Valley to reach the Red Sea at Berenice or Myos Hormos, distant 11 or 7 days from Coptos, or at Leukos Limen. This highway was divided into stages with watertanks, overnight halts and police posts, the course being marked out by reeds stuck in the ground[18], a useful procedure in case of sandstorms[19]. A track ran across Sinai. From the left bank of the Nile, caravan trails, this time marked by cairns of stones, went out to the oases (temple of Ammon, Thebes). We should not forget the great coast road towards Cyrenaica and Africa (3,500km from Alexandria to Tangier), another from Antinoé to Myos Hormos, which was the work of Hadrian. There were also private roads serving quarries for granite and porphyry.

From both texts and representations we know that the camel was used in Egypt and then later in North Africa.

Alexandria held a vital position as a trading port, between the Mediterranean and the Red Sea, thus gaining access to the Indian Ocean. We should remember that the monsoon was discovered by western merchants during the time of Augustus. Pliny the Elder relates the story of a freedman of Annius Plocamus, who was working for his master, a tax farmer in the region of the Red Sea; one day, in the course of tax collection as far south as Aden, he was surprised by the monsoon and swept away to Ceylon[20].

Pliny's words may be quoted concerning the route to India[21], a journey by both land and sea, clearly comparable with the *Periplus* of the Arabian Sea (*Mare Erythraeum*):

> Two miles separate Alexandria from the town of Juliopolis. From there, sailing up the Nile, one reaches Coptos, 309 miles away, with the help of the etesian winds, in 12 days. From Coptos, camels are used and the stages allow for fresh water supplies. Thence, in 12 days one reaches Berenice, where there is a port on the Red Sea. Sailing starts in early summer . . . The return journey begins in December . . . which permits the round-trip to take place in the same year.

Even more than other countries of the East, Egypt always exercised a great effect on Roman imagination. Its politics and religion were always full of interest, as well as its scenery and geographical curiosities such as the mystery of the Nile floods and the source of that river, the canals, the fauna and flora, and even the oases. Archaeology created admirers: Alexander's tomb, the Pharos, the Pyramids, the temple of Ammon, hieroglyphs: all these were mentioned in Lucan's *Pharsala*, while from Pliny the Elder, we learn how visitors to Thebes marvelled at its size, orderliness and sheer age[22]. Exiles took up their abode in those parts as well as invalids seeking health (Seneca, Zosimus, the freedman of Pliny the Younger).

An example of this Grand Tour is the journey taken by Germanicus[23]: 'He went to Egypt to find out about its monuments. Being the provincial governor was only an excuse . . . He embarked at Canope to go up the Nile . . . From there, he reached the neighbouring river-mouth which was dedicated to Hercules . . . Then Caesar visited the vast ruins of ancient Thebes. Enormous buildings still stand bearing in Egyptian characters the full story of its past glories . . . But Germanicus did not feel it was enough to gaze at these wonders; yet others drew his attention, above all the stone statue of Memnon . . . the mountain-like pyramids . . . then the lakes dug in the soil to receive the bountiful waters of the Nile; finally the river gorges and the mighty depths which no human gaze has plumbed. From there, he went on to Elephantina and Syene, formerly outposts of the Empire, which now extends as far as the Red Sea'.

The inscriptions left on the Colossus of Memnon by the tourists of antiquity make it plain how inquisitive they all were, like Servius Sulpicius, who was in command of the *ala* of the Vocontii. Then again, there are examples along the road running up the narrow Nile valley to Coptos, at the ten posting-stations built under Augustus. Each has its towers, barracks, store buildings, tanks or wells and is sited at a keypoint, where the valley widens or natural routes merge; each, too, has its graffiti left by travellers, passing traders or soldiers and displaying a medley of languages, writing, beliefs and cultures, that bring alive for us these out-of-the-way trails in the desert sands.

5 NORTH AFRICA

Observations of the same kind as those made by Father Poidebard in Syria have been published in *Fossatum Africae* by Colonel Baradez[24] on the subject of the military roads of southern Algeria. There, by the use of constructional skills, roads were built to take the shortest course as far as possible, but there was no hesitation about deviating from the straight line whenever tactical considerations made it advisable: water supply, relief, poor visibility and insecurity, risks of ambush or of being cut off, unstable ground, gullies. Furthermore, the main roads were doubled by emergency tracks that allowed an alternative route to be taken when a stretch of the former was temporarily out of use.

The investigation of the *fossatum* was based on air photography and fieldwork and began with examination of the tactical siting of all the forts that have been discovered in southern Algeria. Each one could be justified – defence of water supply, protection of a cross-roads or a bend: many of the fortlets were sited in natural gaps which they aimed at controlling or overlooking, the entrances or exits to narrow valleys; they were often on low-lying ground, but were paired with observation points on high ground, so placed as to complete a system of visual intercommunication. Each pass had its tower keeping guard to the front and to the rear. Each road was lined on both sides by watch-towers, which were placed all the closer when the road ran in a depression or where local visibility was limited. The chief forts were consciously placed where there was a change of slope ensuring easier sighting.

All these installations were part of a scheme (grander than either the Great Wall of China or the Maginot Line) staggered for a depth of 60–80km and extending for a distance of several hundred kilometres between Morocco and Tripolitania. Along this frontier zone can be picked out a belt of territory in which it was possible to engage the enemy in a war of movement and another belt which had to be defended at all costs, as it lay on the edge of the farming areas with their stable population. This second belt was protected by a continuous fortification, a wall or ditch of adaptable form, which even in adjoining sections, made use in turn of a variety of constructional methods, according to the nature of the ground that was being crossed and the materials that lay within reach. Some irregularities in course can be explained by the need to defend some settlement or other. Occasionally wadis or salt lakes were incorporated in the barrier. But the wall-ditch always made tactical use of the ground surface, clinging to the relief, keeping to the near side of a slope, out of enemy gaze, and flanked by towers for defence or to maintain a watch (as many as eight to the kilometre), which were built where there were changes of terrain or slope.

It is impossible to find fault with the course taken by the *fossatum* or with the siting of the towers: no single point was out of view. Some towers were located a little way forward or rearwards so as to enjoy better visibility where there was danger. Others, if we are to judge by the view from them, were clearly intended to transmit signals. In some places, the *limes* was protected against attacks from the rear; the gaps in it, to allow the movement of caravans or of herds, are narrow and controlled by a military installation. And it was probably to prevent some seasonal transhumance or to keep an eye on a troubled sector that the *fossatum* was built around particular highland areas.

Forward of the *fossatum*, there was a safety zone 60km deep, within which enemy parties could be hunted down by mobile units, while forces of any strength were split up by the systems of defence works provided by the forts in staggered formation, so that their attacks were checked and nullified. The first of these fortifications formed a discontinuous line of static surveillance and housed mobile units who provided the active surveillance that safeguarded the whole system. At the same time, a complete network of communications (main roads from the rear, link roads, parallel strategic roads) made it possible to reinforce very rapidly any points that were threatened or, if things came to the worst, to fill breaches created by the enemy in the defence lines. Advanced posts kept a watch on water sources which would have offered a hostile force the last vital supplies before tackling the Roman positions. The fortlets in the outermost defence line were constructed on points projecting into friendly or even enemy territory like antennae with which Rome sensed and tested the Barbarians, regulating their movements and displaying the power of her presence.

Thus by looking at strategical problems from the enemy point of view, Colonel Baradez was successful in establishing the various sectors of the *limes* and their boundaries, as well as resolving what had been their general intention, the final defence line to hold at all costs, the line of surveillance and the part played by the mobile units, the main through and secondary roads, the strategic roads, the transverse roads, the keypoints and the strongholds in the rear able to direct reinforcements in whichever direction was necessary.

This strategical study of invasion threats and defence measures has shown that Rome faced up to problems in space and time by finding solutions one after another or at the same time: first, deployment in the defence zone of a number of well-entrenched garrisons; second, extensive patrolling by mobile units with the support of a system of water supply, camps and forts; third, a defence set-up that was staggered in depth.

The very choice of such a system may enable conclusions to be made about the psychology of the military: those who felt the need to be cocooned in a host of little towers and to get reassurance from the close presence of their neighbours were second-rate soldiers and not professionals. A military scheme based on mobile units and on an offensive outlook is suggestive of material and moral strength. On the other hand, a policy of timidity, springing from a completely defensive view-point, showed that the fibre of a people was aging. As a consequence, when passively organised behind defence works, the army could only deteriorate physically.

To give an exact date to these developments, a close look was required at the various circumstances that may have led at any particular time to the original concept of the *fossatum*, why it was needed and how it was carried out. It was, to be sure, because of the unchanging rules of strategy, that, when Marshal Rommel decided to protect the most vulnerable stretch of the Tunis–Gabès–Tripoli road against raids coming across the Saharan wastes, he cordoned off the Tebaga corridor with a long anti-tank ditch, so restoring the Roman *limes*.

But what Colonel Baradez has revealed above all is that the way the army was organised in the areas bordering the Sahara was closely related to their administration and their economic and political life. One simple fact: it is highly significant that the defence line of the *limes* cuts diagonally across the transhumance belt. By intercepting and keeping a watch on various trails, this frontier allowed effective surveillance and control to be exercised over the nomads' movements and so it maintained considerable political pressure on them.

As the final barrier in a frontier zone based on defence lines organised in depth, the *fossatum,* together with its parallel strategic road, was the boundary between, on the one hand, a more-or-less barren zone valuable only tactically to defence units relying on their mobility and elasticity and, on the other hand, the inhabited zone that had to be protected without thought of retreat. In this way Colonel Baradez discovered on the edges of the Sahara one million hectares of land capable of cultivation, forming terraces or irrigable strips, together with many unknown towns and villages which had originated in camps – in other words a complete military system. He demonstrated the extensive schemes for storing and supplying water constructed in Roman times all along the foot of the hills (djebels), following the north–south alignment of the salt lakes (schotts). Economic reasons sometimes carried the day when the *limes* was set up: an obstacle supplied by nature was given up in favour of man-made fortifications in order to include in the protected-area oases and population groupings that Rome wished to defend.

Very similar conclusions emerge from a study of other sectors of this fortified frontier of the Roman Empire that we call the *limes* and we shall meet it again in England (Hadrian's Wall), Germany and the Danubian lands, just as we have met it in the Near East and North Africa.

But now we must take a wider look at the whole of the road network in the latter area.

Salama[25] has given attention to the phases of its development and these are well known, thanks to some 2,000 milestones.

One of the first tasks of the Romans was no doubt to construct a road along the coast linking the Punic colonies: Carthage–Utica–Hippo Diarrhytus (Bizerta).

Have not the Carthaginians been credited with the invention of metalled roads[26]?

Under the Republic there was also a way up the Bagrada valley, from Carthage to Sicca Veneria (Le Kef) and Theveste (Tebessa), while another road led across Cape Bon from Carthage to Neapolis (Nabeul).

The Augustan colony at Simitthu (Chemtou) must have been connected to Carthage. It was also possible to go from Carthage to Hippo Regius (Bône, today Annaba). As the allowances to colonists increased, so must the number of roads.

The year AD 14 saw the beginning of the first strategic road leading from the HQ of the legion stationed at Ammaedara (Haïdra), where the Third Legion Augusta had perhaps been established after a war against the Gaetuli, ending in AD 6. This road led to Tacape (Gabès) and 300km of its course were completed by the pro-consul for Africa, Asprenas.

The first major contributors to the African road system were Vespasian, who also set about restoring affairs in the province, and his two sons. In AD 75, the army HQ is moved to Theveste, from where a road ran to Hippo Regius. The road from Carthage to Hippo Regius was repaired by Vespasian.

One road was pushed out on the north side of the Aurasius highland (Aquae Caesaris, Vazaivi, Aquae Flavianae, Lambafundi, Lambasa, Lamasba (Mérouana) and Zaraï, in the direction of Auzia).

Trajan, no doubt advised by Frontinus, conceived the idea of organising the *limes*, thus completing what the Flavians had planned. Problems of organising and defending the frontier then took first place.

After Timgad was founded (AD 100), a new military way was laid out on the southern flank of the Nemencha and Aurasius Ranges. The fort of Ad Majores was set up. A strategic road was started towards Thabudeos. There were links between Lambasa and Tacape, through Theveste, Thelepte (Médinet-Kédima) and Capsa (Gafsa) and, farther southwards, through Thabudeos, Ad Majores and Tusuros.

In 122, a through road was operating to Mauretania. In 128 the great camp at Lambasa was established. From Sitifis (Sétif), it was possible to go to Saldae (Bougie, today Bejaia) and Igilgilis (Djidlelli). Simitthu sent its marble in the direction of Thabraca (Tabarka). Hadrian connected Cirta (Constantine) with Rusicada (Philippeville, today Skikda), Sitifis with Djemila, surfaced the road from Carthage to Theveste and gave his assistance to many towns, following a policy of settling the nomads and trying to set up small-holdings and a free peasantry.

Antoninus Pius opened up the pass through the Aurasius and a road reached Medjedel in 149.

Under Commodus a start was made to the *limes* in Tripolitania. Numidia received a new frontier. Castellum Dimmidi was established. The word *praetentura* was then given to a covering strategic road in Mauretania, an integral part of the *limes*.

There was much road-building under Septimius Severus and Caracalla. But already, by 238, Castellum Dimmidi was given up, and we must not be deceived by the many milestones erected in the third century. From 285 to 302, there took place in the provinces a process of subdivision, with a shortening of frontiers and with internal lines of communication being put on a military footing.

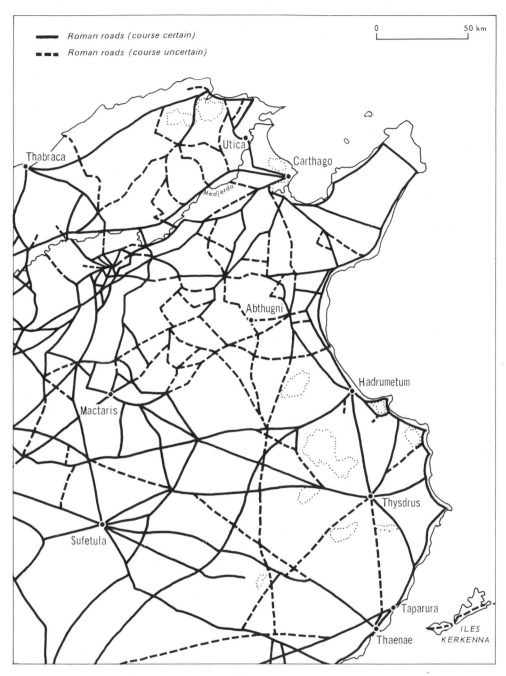

Roman roads (course certain)
Roman roads (course uncertain)

0   50 km

31   Roman roads in the province of Africa (after P. Salama, carte du Service cartographique, Algiers, 1949)

Salama has emphasised that the network of communication was important in the first place to the government and the army, then later to traders: the roads were well suited to the geographical conditions, not only as regards terrain and climate, but also because there were no inland waterways. The road moved forward with the army. It was a military road as long as conditions were insecure. Roads gave mutual cover and the same journey could be made by several alternative routes. Highways were built in conformity with official policy, in particular the emperor's own wishes. After safety, which was above all the main objective, government interests were considered: the great highway from Carthage to Lambasa linked the residence of the proconsul for Africa with the HQ of the governor of Numidia, who was both the civil commander and garrison commander at Lambasa until the end of the third century. Likewise a major government road ran east–west, through the new chief towns of Cirta and Sitifis, to join Carthage with Caesarea, the seat of the governor of Mauretania.

But the development of the road system went hand in glove with the growth of towns, especially since it aided the transport of building materials. There were many roads in the highly Romanised areas where towns had the space to multiply thanks to natural factors and strategic or economic considerations.

From the economic point of view, we should notice how vital were the north–south axial routes, linking mountains, lowlands and coast. These roads were primarily needed to cope with the *annona*. They were mainly planned to export corn, oil (with chains of *horrea*), wood and marble, wild beasts intended for the amphitheatre – trafficking which is illustrated on the mosaics of the Square of the Corporations at Ostia. Some roads even became specialised. Transport movements also occurred, of course, for the purpose of internal trade.

The tariff list from Zaraï (Zraia), on the Ngaous–Sitifis road, the main trunk road from the Gulf of Syrtis Minor to the Mauretanian frontier, via Gafsa or the Southern Djerid, then the Biskra Gap, corresponded to a traffic flow along an extensive route, already very ancient by that date, AD 202. It mentions commodities that were in transit: sponges, *garum*, woollen cloth, dates, slaves, resin and pitch, livestock and leather, wine, dried figs, but it is not known if the text is complete.

As a whole, the road network in North Africa had the following structure:

a great coast road from Cyrenaica to Tingitana (used by Apuleius[27]), going round the shoreline of the Gulf of Syrtis Major, then Oea, Sabrata, Tacape, Syllecte, Hadrumetum and Carthage;
a longitudinal road, running east–west through the chief towns and involving the choice of two alternatives: either Carthage–Cirta, Sitifis, Auzia, Caesarea or, farther south, Hadrumetum, Theveste, Lambasa, Sitifis or Auzia;
in Mauretania Caesariensis, the road from the Chélif towards Volubilis;
Morocco (Tingitana), apart from a main road from Tingis to Sala by way of Ad Mercuri, with a branch to Volubilis, chiefly relied on transport by sea and looked towards Spain;
important cross-country roads had the ports as their destination, the total length of all the roads being some 15,000km (20,000 according to Picard).

To all this should be added the army communications in the *limes*, in Mauretania, Numidia and Tripolitania, together with advanced posts along the caravan trails leading in the direction of Black Africa – the oasis of Cydamus (Ghadamès) was, for example, linked to two ports on the Libyan coast. With reference to these trails we may quote from Pliny the Elder[28], who, in company with others, shows how the wars of conquest were the motive force behind geographical discovery: 'Until the present, there has been no proper road to the territory of the Garamantes, which is strange considering that, if one knows the whereabouts, it is possible to discover without much digging wells that the rogues of that tribe have covered over with sand. During the last war that the Romans waged against the people of Oea, in the reign of the Emperor Vespasian, a new route was found, shorter by four days; this way is called "Beyond the top of the crag".' These caravan routes have long existed. The rock-paintings and rock-carvings in the Tassili n'Ajjer and in the Hoggar lie alongside very ancient tracks leading from Tripolitania to the Hoggar. We should look at recent finds in the Saharan strongholds of Bu Njem, Gheria-el-Garbia and Ghadamès, which controlled the main trails giving access from the coast to the Fezzan, the territory of the Garamantes, where Roman influence and trade have clearly left their mark. Rebuffat[29] has been able to trace the old routes by having faith in the fact that caravan itineraries have not changed with the years. In the now dried-up valleys of wadis, he has found prehistoric evidence overlain by strata containing Roman pottery and quernstones. The Roman fortress at Bu Njem (dated by an inscription of 202 and occupied until the fifth century) forms a rectangle with rounded corners measuring 138 by 93m and having four gateways, a praetorium, a hall with the sacellum, and bath-buildings. A township with an area of 15 hectares and a wall 1km in length, lies buried in the sands, surrounding the military site on three sides. The discoverer considered that 'the aim had certainly been to protect the flourishing civilisation of the regions closer to the sea against the dangers in the desert. At the same time life and travel in the wilderness was to be brought under control as far as tracks and wells allowed.' And the writer went on to emphasise 'the dynamic spirit and readiness to adapt that carried Rome along the roads into the very heart of the country and brought a mutual exchange of benefits: Rome contributed to the country she discovered and that country in turn contributed to an imported civilisation which provided the means of self-expression.'

In general, the road system in Africa developed chronologically as follows: the network, which was still fragmentary and piecemeal under Tiberius (to whose reign can be dated the oldest bridge in Roman North Africa, on the Wadi Beja, south of Vaga) was extended by the Flavians and assumed under the Antonines more or less its final structure. Completed by Septimius Severus and Caracalla, it was still being maintained in the third century, but was gradually abandoned in the fourth. All the same, Roman roads in Africa, in spite of the Vandal occupation, served in the sixth century as a framework for the organisation of the Byzantine armed forces, which made an effort to reintroduce the *annona* for the benefit of Constantinople. The roads, too, were to help the Arab invaders.

A comparison may be made with the French system of roads, in which Gafsa, Constantine and Sétif remained important cross-roads.

Schmitt's careful studies of Ptolemy's maps have shown that it is possible to identify the majority of the Roman stations, if we take into account the geographer's individual point of view which may vary according to whether the itinerary being used as a source was by land or by sea and also if we use Arab geographers and chroniclers. The roads often followed the courses of protohistoric tracks, lined, in Morocco especially, by megalithic monuments, and the Arabs were guided along them, in turn erecting at the roadside the tombs of holy men and sages called marabouts, whose local name may recall the name of a vanished town.

As regards the features and build of the Roman roads of North Africa, Salama has noticed, in addition to their normal straightness and their preference for a course on high ground (the military crest), that they are very varied and adaptable, even to the point of idiosyncrasy. They do not present a constant width: 4 to 5m for carriage roads, 2·5 to 3m for secondary roads. Usually, the metalling is composed of small rubble. Sometimes, it was laid on ground that was naturally flat, with the course of the road arranged ad hoc and provided with culverts to carry the water of the wadis underneath. Even the great highway from Carthage to Theveste, paved by Hadrian, was never more than 67cm in thickness, yet this was a causewayed road. Sections show that it was built up of four thin layers: on top of the foundation of large fragments of stone had been run a bed of mortar, part of which had flowed down between bits of the foundation material. Above there was a deposit of pebbles and on these had been set, not flagstones, but very irregular stones that were not even cobbles. There was a central camber. A road section from north of the Aurasius yielded the following details: width 6m, with stratification from base to top; a bed of sand, 0·1m; a bed of mortared flagstones, 0·2m; concrete of crushed stone, 0·15m; concrete made from gravel, 0·15m; a surface of coarse mortar with kerbstones along the edges, making a total of 0·8m. These *gomphi* occur frequently, every 3 to 6m where the road is embanked. When there are storms they can be seen sticking out of the sand or the snow. Amongst the engineering works in North Africa, we may mention roads that have been carved out of solid rock; like the road through the Aurasius and quarry roads. To the south of Tebessa, in the Wadi Refana gorge, the road has been cut through the rock for more than 2km, with deep ruts, and it bears the local name of 'Triq el Karetta', or waggon-way. There are also cols where a cutting has been made for the road, causeways across marshes, substantial retaining-walls, drainage schemes and numerous bridges and dykes, such as that at Djerba or the great viaduct linking the two Kerkenna islands[30]. Associated structures may include wells and watertanks, watch-towers and forts.

A few points are worth adding about the relationship between roads and centuriation, the details of which are in the *Atlas* published by the writer and A. Caillemer. In the northern part of the province of Africa especially, roads must have been built to fit in with the land divisions: their straight stretches often coincide with the boundaries of centuries. It would have been impossible, for a long distance and on any kind of ground, to mark out parallel stretches of road lying at multiples of 710m from each other unless a rectilinear pattern of holdings had already been in existence. If the roads are aligned along the boundaries of centuries, it is not merely because a straight line is the shortest path from one point to another. When the ground prevented a road from maintaining a straight course, the builders diverted it to reach the next *limes*. It is clear then that the road line was set out with the obvious intention of avoiding land expropriation or rather, in the first place, of avoiding splitting up the centurial grid. Even when there are several roads, as in the country around Sousse, their courses, first forking off as diagonals in the rectangular land divisions soon fall into alignment with the system of boundaries. The road leaving Thysdrus, close to the amphitheatre and aiming for Sullectum follows for 605km the *decumanus* which goes through Mahdia and marks the north-west boundary of the centurial block at Chebba. However, if, in the north of the country, roads observed the pattern of land division, the opposite was the case in the central and eastern areas, where it was the orientation of the earlier roads, themselves taking the major natural routes, that determined the alignment of the land divisions. As one went southwards, the main concern became organising water supply for the land. The growing disarray of the cadastral checker-board on the edge of the semi-desert and desert is due to the changing geographical conditions. The breakdown in the land system ties in with the general policy of settling nomads, which was first thought up in the early days of the Empire and was to show its effects particularly in the third century.

Milestones provide a striking example of the increasing importance of regionalism, for we can certainly attribute centralisation to the early Empire. The road from Carthage to Theveste remained the great Imperial road, with only one system of numbering the milestones; on other roads, however, the milestones, which under Augustus and even under Hadrian had been marked counting from one direction were being reckoned during the times of Caracalla and Maximinian from each end. Thus the distance tally between the winter camp and Tacape starts at the latter town and does not seem to have gone past Gafsa. Theveste and Thelepte were each considered to be the finishing points for their sections of road; it was a similar case with Ammaedara and Cillium. Likewise, along the Gafsa–Turris Tamalleni road, after the pass at Djebel-el-Asker, it was the second of these towns that built the road and numbered the stones, which explains why there are 1,740m instead of 1,480 between stones numbered 26 and 27 from Capsa, the 27th being also the 34th from Telmine. It is noteworthy, too, that there is a special mile measuring 1,625m on the Haïdra–Gabès highway.

From these observations it can be seen that milestones throw light on changes of policy. The case of Tripolitania, studied by Goodchild, strengthens the point: out of the 41 milestones known there in 1948, only one is as early as Tiberius. The others, sometimes in groups, date from Caracalla or are later, the year 216 having been the start of a system of marking that lasted until 276 and was a reflection of military activity in connection with setting up the local *limes*. Roads outside the towns were nothing more than tracks.

6 SPAIN

The basic natural routes run along the east coast, a region of importance to Greek and Punic settlements, and up the valleys of the major rivers: Ebro, Sucro, Tagus,

Durius, Anas and Baetis. Road construction began with the conquest and there are milestones dating from the end of the Republic.

It is to Republican times that we can date the coast road (120 BC), from the Pyrenees to Carthago Nova (Cartagena), through Saguntum (Sagunto), and then on to the river Baetis (Guadalquivir) and the road from Barcino (Barcelona) to Ilerda (Lerida) and Osca (Huesca, mines). The road in the south must have reached the Baetis: the bridge at Corduba (Cordoba) is earlier than Augustus.

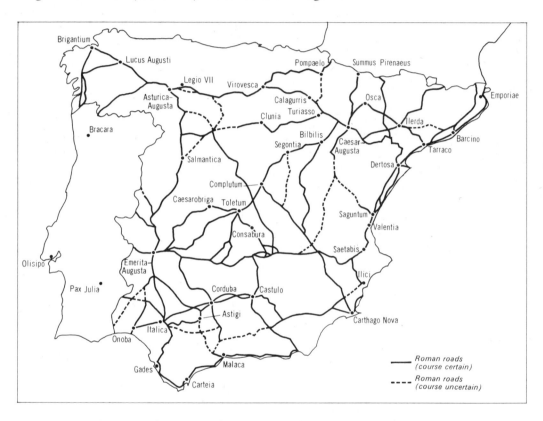

32   Roman roads in Spain (after *Atlas nacional de España,* Instituto Geographico)

The latter, in his anxiety to pacify the province, initiated an active policy of road construction that encircled the country and sent spurs inland from ports to mines. He repaired the road from Tarraco (Tarragona) to Carthago Nova through Valentia and also the one along the Baetis (Corduba–Hispalis–Gades). Dion[31] has shown how extra evidence from the milestones along the *via maxima,* later the *via Augusta* (covering 1,500km from Le Perthus to Cadiz) has thrown light on the *Res Gestae* of Augustus (XXVIII–XXXIII) by indicating the distances AD OCEANUM[32]. The *Res Gestae,* indeed, were recording the ultimate destination of that enterprising ambition that drove Mediterranean societies, throughout antiquity, towards the Atlantic seaboard, along routes chequered by the legendary wanderings of Heracles. Cadiz was the final destination of the ancient Heraclean way, then of the great land road linking Rome to southern Spain by northern Italy and the pass of Mont-Genèvre.

The many settlements created by Augustus, distinguished by the title *Augusta,* all had their outlet onto the east coast.

Milestones make it clear that there were also other roads set up by Augustus: from Bracara (Braga) to Asturica (Astorga) through Lucus Augusti (Lugo); from Caesaraugusta (Saragossa) to Juliobriga (Regnosa), from Emerita (Merida) to Hispalis (Seville), from Carthago Nova to Castulo (Cazorla), from Ilerda to Caesaraugusta–Turiasso–Clunia (Peñalva del Castro)–Ocelodurum (Zamora)–Asturica–Bracara–Caesaraugusta (two possible routes), Emerita–Salmantica (Salamanca, bridge over the Tagus), Corduba–Castulo–the Montes Mariani (Sierra Morena)–the territory of the Oretani, and the repair of the *via Augusta* from Ossigi (Maquiz) to Hispalis.

Claudius repaired the road from Carthago Nova to the Pyrenees, did work close to Castulo and between Emerita and Salmantica, and Asturica and Bracara.

Nero reconstructed the road to the West through Clunia, repaired the *via Augusta* and the highway from Emerita to Salamantica.

Vespasian did likewise for the Bracara–Asturica road, reconstructed the *via Augusta* in Baetica, laid out a cross-country route from Emerita to Caesaraugusta passing through Augustobriga (Talavera la Vieja), Toletum (Toledo), Complutum (near Alcala de Henares), and Segontia (Siguenza) – a road repaired by Trajan – as well as from Salmantica to Emerita. He also built roads in Lusitania and in the region of Castulo.

Here is a summary of the Spanish road network[33]:

from Gaul to Tarraco through Emporiae and Barcino (*via Domitia*);
from Bordeaux to Pompaelo (Pamplona) and Virovesca, where a road joined from Tarraco to Asturica, coming along the Ebro valley and through Juliobriga;
from Asturica to Brigantium (Corunna) by way of Lucus Augusti;
from Asturica and Bracara to Olisipo with a branch to Pax Julia (Beja);
from Emerita to Hispalis;
the *via Augusta* along the Baetis to Laminium (Fuenllana) and Tarraco; the coastal road: from Carteia (El Rocadillo)–Malaca (Malaga)–Carthago Nova–Saetabis (Jativa)–Valentia–Saguntum–Dertosa (Tortosa)–Tarraco;
the cross-country road from Caesaraugusta to Emerita via Bilbilis, Complutum, Toletum and Emerita.

Three regions in Spain were of particular interest to the emperors: the rich valley of the Tagus, the north-west and the mines of Baetica and the Montes Mariani.

We have referred earlier to the discovery of the Astorga tablets and the use of a local unit for the mile, two important details concerning Spanish roads.

A personal look at centuriation in the Guadalquivir valley and the Vega de Carmona (July 1970) has convinced the writer that in those areas river navigation was of importance. It is known that sea-going vessels could come up as far as Hispalis. Maps and air photographs in combination show that many ancient roads have vanished, together with transhumance tracks and tell-tale place names, comprising series like those in other parts of the Roman world (Camino Viejo de los Toros, Aldo Camino, la Estrella, las Horcas, Cruz, Casarrubia, Desman, and names of estates or derivatives of numbers representing road distances and cadastral measurements).

Centuriation has survived in many places despite the Arab conquest and the reconquest and this is probably due to land-abandonment which allowed ancient boundaries between holdings to survive and also because the services required of tenants were from the very first bound up with the public road system. There are regions where one has the feeling that the landscape has not changed for 2,000 years (olive trees composed of three or four trunks growing on immense stocks, possibly going back to antiquity). But when land has been redivided and developed these old survivals have been obliterated.

Reference has already been made for Spain to the significance of the pilgrimage routes and the Vicarello goblets (pp. 47, 55–6). Another point worth watching is the traffic with Mauretania across the Straits of Gibraltar.

7 BRITAIN

In spite of Caesar's landings, Romanisation was a late development and Rome had to give up the idea of occupying the northern regions, beyond the Antonine Wall and Hadrian's Wall.

The road system has been closely studied on the ground and there are some revealing place names: Watling Street, Stone Street, Pedlar's Way, Stane Street, Stanegate, Ermine Street, Port Way, Ackling Dyke, Fosse Way, The Street, Dere Street. London, both a sea and river port, early became an important trading centre, with roads first to Camulodunum (Colchester), then to Kent and the Channel ports and to Lincoln and Chester.

There was a road along the north coast of Wales, another towards Carlisle and the north and a third to the north-east through Leicester and Lincoln.

A road led to the south-west from London to Dorchester and Exeter by way of Calleva (Silchester) (whence it was possible to reach Winchester, Gloucester, Bath, Caerwent and South Wales) and Old Sarum. Another went to St Albans, Wroxeter and Chester, then to North Wales and Caernarvon, Lancaster, Carlisle and the Lakes. The east was served by a road through Caistor, Lincoln, York and Newcastle in the direction of Hadrian's Wall.

Secondary roads linked London to the Channel ports and Colchester or brought supplies to the main centres of population.

We should notice the role played by the roads leading from mining districts and by strategic routes (the main north–south road and the strategic roads behind the Walls) with perpendicular spurs notably from Hadrian's Wall (Solway–Tyne)[34], along which the stations can be given names, thanks to the Amiens patera. The man responsible for the line of the Wall was A. Platorius Nepos, who had been *curator* of four Italian roads: the *Cassia*, the *Claudia*, the *Cimina* and the *Nova Trajana*.

In his *Agricola*, Tacitus made two revealing remarks amongst others about

Britain, emphasising that the Roman world was first opened up by traders and then by the army: XXI: *tertius expeditionum annus novas gentis aperuit* ('the third year of campaigning revealed new tribes.) and XXIV, 3: *melius aditus portusque per commercia et negotiatores cogniti* ('the approaches and ports are already known, thanks to trading contacts and business men').

These words, which hold true for Gaul (there are many hints of this nature in Caesar), are also valid for other provinces: in Greece, for example, traders were used to serve as army guides[35] and, Perseus, in his flight from Samothrace, tried to use the services of a Cretan who knew the Thracian coast, having traded there[36].

33   Roman roads in southern Britain (based on the Ordnance Survey)

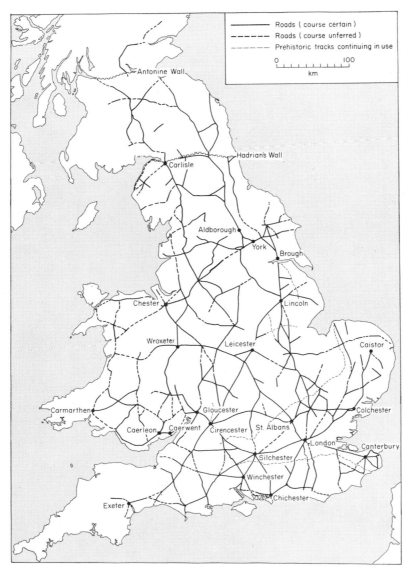

8 ROMAN ROADS IN GAUL

It has been seen earlier (p. 15) that Caesar's conquest of Gaul was aided by the prior existence of established roads and ports. In no other way can we explain the speed of some of his movements.

As for transport by water, evidence comes from the building or requisitioning of boats.

These pre-Roman roads used major geographical routes, following the valleys of the great rivers, which were separated by easy passes. There is the well-known page from Strabo[37] who, in the footsteps of Posidonios and taking up ideas inspired by traders, emphasises the number of rivers in Celtic Gaul and the convenient directions in which they flowed, speaking highly of 'the harmony between land, rivers and sea: the territories through which they run are for the most part flat or else hilly regions cut through by navigable waterways. Furthermore, the rivers are so happily disposed in relation to each other that they ensure in both directions transport from one sea to the next, with the goods scarcely having to be carted by land at all, and then only over flat ground easily crossed. Most often they are transported by water, some rivers being chosen to go downstream, others to go upstream.'

River traffic was to remain a vital factor in France until the nineteenth century. We shall return to it.

The oldest road built by Rome is the *Domitia* (running from the Rhône to the Pyrenees, that is from Tarascon to Le Perthus through Nîmes, Béziers and Elne), the work of the proconsul Domitius Ahenobarbus, who has left us the oldest milestone in Gaul, marking the distance of 20 miles to Narbonne. The consul, who had remained in Provence as governor after the foundation of Narbonne in 118, then established the land link between Italy and the province of Spain, the administration of which dated from 197 BC, 80 years before Gallia Narbonensis. He also founded a settlement, *Forum Domitii* (Montbazin).

Road developments as important as these meant sizable public schemes and heavy expenditure and government representatives had opportunities for malpractice. This was the case of the proconsul Fonteius, defended by Cicero (*Pro Fonteio*, 69 BC), who had made provincials pay for the construction and upkeep of roads by increasing tolls, especially on wine, of which the Gauls were particularly fond. For information about this wine trade and about the road to the Gironde with its occasional scatter of amphora sherds, the reader should consult Etienne's important work[38].

After the journey made by Augustus in 27 and the decision to make a land registry – we should emphasise once more the connection between roads and centuriations – Agrippa was given the responsibility of carrying this out, necessarily incorporating existing stretches of road, developing the highway itself and introducing new engineering schemes. The new road network formed by the four great military ways took full advantage of the geographical opportunities in the isthmus of Gaul. With its centre at Lyons, it was based on the axial line following the rivers Rhône (with roads on both banks), Saône, Moselle[39] and Rhine, whilst one could go from Lyons into Aquitania and towards the Gironde. A direct road led to Saintes,

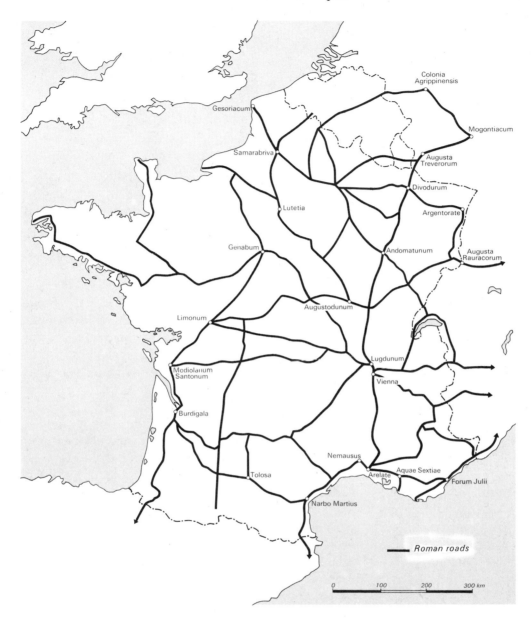

34   The main Roman roads in Gaul (after F. Benoit, *Art et dieux de la Gaule*, Paris, Arthaud, 1969)

provincial capital of Aquitania, by way of Roanne, Vichy, Clermont, the Sioule valley, Limoges (with an alternative from Lodève to Rodez), Cahors and Périgueux. Dion has demonstrated the political reasons (the collaboration of the Santones with the Romans against the Veneti)[40] explaining why the region around the mouth of the Charente was Romanised so early. The inscription from the amphitheatre at Lyons mentioning Caius Julius Caii Filius Rufus, priest of Rome and Augustus, and the dedication by the same person of the arch of Germanicus at Saintes can be understood, at such a distance apart, only by assuming that the great road already quoted was in existence.

Strabo's famous words on the matter must be given in full:

> Since Lugdunum occupies the centre of Celtica[41], and is to a large extent its capital, lying as it does at the confluence of rivers and within access of the different parts of the country, Agrippa made it the starting point for the main roads: one going over the Cévennes Mountains to end in Aquitania and the territory of the Santones; the one to the Rhine and the one to the Ocean, which is the third and leads to the lands of the Bellovaci and Ambiani and finally the fourth, the one leading into Narbonensis and as far as the Marseilles coast. But one can also, by passing on the left Lugdunum and the territories upstream from that town, fork off into the Poeninus itself, crossing the Rhône or Lake Leman to reach the plain of the Helvetii and, from there, through a pass in the Jura mountains, arrive at the territory of the Sequani and Lingones, where the road divides into two branches, one going to the Rhine, the other to the Ocean[42].

This text brings out the connections between Agrippa's strategic road system and the waterways, on which traffic was in the hands of corporations of *nautae, ratiarii* and *utricularii*, who propelled rafts made buoyant with inflated bladders. Sea traffic, be it noted, went upriver to Arles, a town with a double port[43].

In northern Gaul, Langres, Rheims, Trèves and Bavai[44] had cross-roads of even greater importance than Paris, owing to the manner in which the army organised the *limes* along the Rhine and the travel links with Britain.

The West remained apart, which explains why Romanisation took longer there.

On the whole, then, the system of roads, serving an even distribution of towns, was less centralised than the modern one, and had several nodal points, such as Lyons and Bavai, a concentration of roads along the frontiers and a variety of routes from one major settlement to another.

Claudius, himself a native of Lyons, completed the establishment of the road system, as many milestones bear out[45]. The Emperor was interested in the roads to the Rhine, but did not neglect the West and planned a road from Chartres to the Cotentin peninsula, opposite the Isle of Wight. It was from Gesoriacum (Boulogne) that he embarked for Britain in 43 AD. The excellent provincial administration set up by Tiberius and Claudius could not fail to come into conflict with the governing class, but it was road development that hastened the process of Romanisation. The roads along the Rhine came into being with the building of the Flavian *limes*. After the *Agri Decumates* had been annexed, a road was taken straight up the Neckar valley. Trajan completed the strategic roads (Mainz–Baden–Offenburg, Mainz–Cologne–Vetera, and the one to Nijmegen).

Rome took great interest in the mouths of the Rhine, particularly the navigation canals. The subject has been reconsidered by Dion in his study of Roman commercial undertakings in north Gaul[46]. They made use of navigation along the Rhine[47] and coastal shipping in the shelter of the Flanders banks. Transport of troops by water made it possible to carry out combined operations aiming at pincer movements along the coast, then on the one hand up the Ems and the Weser and on the other up the Lippe. Such manoeuvres, aimed at the heart of Germany, were set in motion by Drusus, Germanicus and Corbulo. The last-named, who conquered the Frisians, made it possible once more to sail on Lake Flevo and the river arms connecting with the Rhine and the sea. Drusus had dug a canal[48] to provide a shipping link between the main course of the Rhine and Lake Flevo. There appears to have been[49] a sunken weir (*moles*) at the beginning of the Vaal, intended to divert towards the right – into the Rhine properly speaking – a greater proportion of the flow, held between dykes (*aggeres*) in the direction of the present Ijssel. The weir was destroyed by Civilis[50].

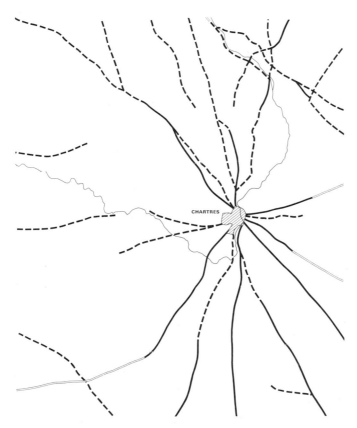

35 Early road system around Chartres (information from I.G.N., Service de documentation technique)

Antoninus saw to the repair of roads in Gaul (Arles–Vienne, Trèves–Cologne, Avenches–Lausanne) and added secondary roads. Other roads were restored, according to milestones, in the time of Septimius Severus.

There are many stones in Belgium, Switzerland and the Rhine valley dating from Caracalla, but distances were henceforth measured in leagues of 2,222m. The road itineraries were being compiled, we may recall, from this time onward.

Whilst the Gallic emperors did not neglect roads, the latter must have acted as invasion lanes, for many hoards have been found along them. We can understand the campaigns of the Emperor Julian, if we relate them to the road system.

There are many place names of value at this stage, commemorating, for example, the settlement of barbarian troops to guard roads or colonies of soldier-farmers generally known as *laeti* along the main invasion paths[51].

Finally, the progress of Christianity took place, of course, following these same itineraries, with their folk memories today of St Martin and other devout people.

Examples from different regions

The civitas *of the Aedui*

The Roman roads of the Aedui have had the advantage of being excellently summarised by Thévenot, working in a region well known to him. He has shown how, in the eighteenth century, research made headway when land was inspected in advance of road improvements, surveys were undertaken for the Cassini maps and there was a general upsurge of interest in Greek and Roman antiquities. In the nineteenth century, we owe more progress to better cartography, the active enthusiasm of Napoleon III and the work of the Commission for mapping Gaul, and finally the foundation of many local societies. Thévenot has used every source of information, such as we have earlier explained, and in the process has sifted out a great quantity of miscellaneous but useful material.

It was with the trade in flint that the territory of the Aedui was to act as a threshold for the first time between the valleys of the Loire and the Saône. This function was continued by the amber trade. With the coming of metals, the transport of goods over long distances demanded routes with greater security, whether for the trade in salt or tin, which must have taken a variety of routes in space and time.

When independence ended there arose political factors such as alliances and tolls, while vehicles and waterways came into general use. Connecting roads must have existed between the five native population centres of the Aedui (Bibracte, Chalon, Mâcon, Decize and Noviodunum), as well as between Bibracte and the neighbouring *civitas* capitals, a fact made clear by Caesar's movements and those of his enemies. To a large degree road courses did not change and the Romans maintained them with slight straightening when they answered a real need. We may consider as pre-Roman a road with settlements along it as revealed by place names or lined up with other stretches known to be pre-Roman or perhaps associated with sacred sites of native origin.

Thévenot has studied the roads from Lyons to Boulogne through Chalon-sur-Saône and Autun, from Autun to Besançon, Langres, Troyes, Orléans, Clermont, Bourges and Feurs, the road running beside the Loire, the roads from Autun to Mâcon, Belleville, Beaune, Dijon and Auxerre, those radiating from Chalon and and Bibracte, as well as a series of 23 secondary roads. The method adopted for each study is the same: general remarks and bibliography, an examination of the course of the road, its organisation (build, width, milestones, posting-stations and relays), and its history (origin, construction, use and survival).

It seems likely, according to Thévenot, that Agrippa's road was closely based on the Gallic road to the Channel, passing through the lands of the Aeduan allies before the conquest and linking the native capitals, by way of Chalon, Autun, Sens, Beauvais and Amiens. The name 'British way' may commemorate its early destination. On the other hand, the road from Langres to Rheims would appear to be a later alternative. The route that is suggested is important in its own right and has the stamp of officialdom; it is the only road in Gaul, of those that are described in the *Antonine Itinerary*, measured in both miles and leagues. It must have been constructed between 20 and 10 BC to serve the Aeduan community, in keeping with the new settlement at Autun.

The road junction at Lutetia

The area lying between the Seine, Meuse and Escaut was the base for making contact with the Rhineland and Britain and in every age has attracted traffic.

Duval has described[52] the Roman roads radiating from Lutetia, itself already an important junction of routes. There were two roads upstream along the Seine valley towards Melun, and one downstream towards Rouen, with branches going to Senlis, Dreux, Chartres and Meaux. The road to Orléans is typical. Traces of it have been found in the rue St Jacques. It was nine metres wide in the Late Empire and often repaired. Where it left the town (rue Pierre Nicole), there lay alongside it a cemetery of the first to third centuries, which gave rise in the Middle Ages to the legend of the Issoire Tomb. The pilgrimage to Compostella made the 'rue St-Jacques' (St James's Street) famous and farther on at Linas some of the old road-surfacing survives. There was a bridge (*Urbiensis* – a reference in 583) over the Orge, while Châtres, near Arpajon, derives its name from a *castrum* and Saclas (the *Salioclita* of the *Antonine Itinerary*) has a few remains.

Roman roads in the Alps

Roads known to us through the texts date from the schemes of Augustan times. These great strategic roads with their distant connections were in use, to some extent at least, during the proto- and even the prehistoric period, simply because geography made only one route possible (as with passes and cross valleys). Artemidoros and Posidonius, two of Strabo's sources, may have known of such tracks (along the valleys of the Durance, Drôme and Isère), which would have been followed by immigrant tribes (the Celts from the sixth to the fourth centuries, like Bellovesus[53]), by armies (Hannibal in 218 BC[54]) and by traders.

As early as the second half of the third century BC, Pseudo-Aristotle[55] tells us that movement along one Alpine way was ensured by paying tolls to Celto-Ligurian peoples who lived beside it. Dion[56] has demonstrated that this must have been the Mont-Genèvre road, with which are associated some typically Celtic names: Caturiges (Chorges), Eburodunum (Embrun), Brigantio (Briançon) and Segusio (Suse). The Celts kept control of this great through route and it must have been they who were responsible for the system of protection mentioned by Pseudo-Aristotle.

The texts make it clear how the Romans increased their geographical knowledge of the Alps: we know of the advantage that Hannibal obtained through using a northern pass until then unknown to the Romans.

Polybius (about 150 BC) knew of only three ways through the mountains[57]: those lying in the territory of the Ligures, close to the sea, the Taurini (Mont-Cenis) and the Salassi (St Bernard).

Varro quotes five, two of which seem to be identical[58], so giving us Strabo's four[59]: the *Alpes Maritimae*, the *Alpes Cottiae*, and the two St Bernard passes.

The coast road

Polybius was the first to mention the Ligurian trail through the *Alpis Maritima*[60]. It was difficult because of the relief[61] and the local brigands[62]. Rome needed 80 years of guerrilla warfare to open up this route to her armies (Sextius Calvinus, founder of Aix). But the submission of the Ligures was achieved by Augustus only in 14 BC. Fortunately coastal shipping allowed movement from Genoa to Marseilles and the Rhône[63].

The road, once constructed, was named in 13 BC the *Julia Augusta*. It went from Piacenza to the Var, then along the valleys of the Argens and the Arc (*per Alpes Maritimas – Alpis summa* or *maritima*)[64].

The frontier between Italy and Gaul lay at La Turbie, where the Augustus trophy (*Tropaeum Augusti*) commemorated the victory over the Alpine peoples. The inscription has been accurately restored by comparing fragments that have been discovered with the version recorded by Pliny the Elder[65]:

> To the emperor Caesar Augustus, son of the divine Caesar, high pontiff, imperator for the fourteenth time, invested with his seventeenth tribunician power, the Senate and the Roman people have raised this monument, because, under his leadership and his auspices, all the tribes from the Higher Sea (Adriatic) to the Lower Sea (Tyrrhenian) have been subjected to the authority of the Roman people.

There follows a list of 21 tribes. The list of coastal towns is provided by the sea section of the *Antonine Itinerary*.

Other secondary routes were, of course, used:

> the valleys of the Var and Paillon through the Braus, Brouis, Tende and Fenêtres; the Madeleine pass (or the Larche or Argentière passes), the two latter being controlled by the customs post (*Quadragesima Galliarum*) of Pedo (Borgo S. Damaso); the St Autaret and St Véran passes, Agnel (recognised *stationes*); the Mont-Genèvre pass (*Alpis Cottia, Mons Matrona*; the station refuge was called *Druantium* or *Summae Alpes*). It was the shortest way between the valleys of the lower Rhône and the Po along their tributaries, the Durance (which was navigable)[66] and the Doire Ripaire, usable in winter (cf. the crossing made by Vitellius). It was said to have been opened up by Heracles, whose name seems to have be-

come associated with all the passes of the Western Alps, showing the extent of Greek penetration in the West[67]. 'Passing from Celtica into Italy [the Hero] went across the Alpine mountains', wrote Diodoros of Sicily (IV, 19, 3–4, inspired perhaps by Posidonius), 'and eased the harshness of the track and its obstacles, so that it became possible to cross the pass with an army and its baggage. The barbarians dwelling in those mountains were accustomed to harass and pillage armies crossing over; he subjected them all and having killed the brigand-chiefs ensured the safety of those travelling that way.'

This road to Spain was established about 120 BC by Domitius Ahenobarbus and was named after him: *via Domitia*. Pompey, who claimed to have opened it 77, must have carried out some improvements[68]. Cicero saw it as only a track (*semita*). It was used by Caesar on so many occasions that probably for that reason the Mont-Genèvre route was known as *saltus Alpis Juliae*[69], his *proximum iter in ulteriorem Galliam per Alpes*[70] between Genèvre and Gap. Augustus organised this route with the collaboration of King Cottius, who saw to its upkeep and security. Their contemporary Strabo[71] considered that it was the shortest and busiest way from Italy to Gaul. This was a situation that was to endure. The main posting-stations after Turin were Avigliana (Ad Fines, a station collecting the Gallic 'fortieth') Susa (Segusio), Exilles (Scingomagus), Oulx (Ad Martis fanum), Cesana (Gaesao/Tyrium), Genèvre, Briançon (Brigantio), whence one could reach Vienne by way of Grenoble (Cularo), Embrun (Ebrurodunum), Chorges (Caturigomagus), Gap (Vapincum); then from there towards Valence through Luc (Lucus), Die (Dea Voncontiorum), Auoste or else towards Beaucaire and Tarascon through Sisteron (Segustero), Apt (Apta Julia), Cavaillon (Cabellio), St-Rémy (Glanum) and St-Gabriel (Ernaginum).

Farther north, the passes of La Roue, Fréjus, the Little Montcenis, Le Clapier and L'Autaret were in use from the eve of the conquest (Hannibal used the Mont-Cenis or Le Clapier[72]), then in the early Middle Ages.

The ancient name of the Little St Bernard (*in Alpe Graia*), because of its similarity to *Graecus,* has given rise to some fanciful etymology: Heracles has been said to have passed that way. C. Gracchus is supposed to have built a road there in 122. The Salassi of the river Dora Baltea looked after the road, but levied a heavy toll[73]. They were subjected by Augustus in 25 BC. In the view of the Augustan geographer, this was the only road between Aosta and Lyons worthy of vehicular traffic[74]. At the top of the pass, a local deity, Graius, was venerated, together with Hercules and Jupiter.

The road stations from Vienne to Aosta (Augusta Praetoria) were: Bergusium (Bourgoin), Augustum (Aoste, Isère), Labisco (Les Echelles), Lemincum (Le Lémenc, at Chambéry), Mantala (near to St-Jean-de-la-Porte), Ad Publicanos (close to Albertville-Conflans), Obilonna (Arbine, by La Bâthie), Darantasia (Moûtiers), Axima (Aime), Bergintrum (Bourg-St-Maurice), Alpis Graia, Ariolicum (La Thuile), Arebrigium (Pré-St-Didier).

From Aosta, it was also possible to reach the Great St Bernard pass (*Summus*

Poeninus) but heavy carts could not get as far. The god Poenius was the object of worship in the pass, then was replaced by Jupiter (hence the medieval name of 'Mont-Joux' from *Mons Jovis*) and finally, with Christianity, a hostel was set up in the eleventh century. From there, the road went down towards the upper Rhône.

The main towns were linked to one another by secondary routes known through literary sources, epigraphy, place names, archaeological remains actual or suspected, religious sites and medieval survivals. There were such roads from Vienne to Geneva, Aosta to Geneva, Arles to Aix by way of Marseilles, Aix to Riez (Reii Apollinares), Sisteron to Fréjus. There was in particular a north–south road in the Pre-Alps.

The Alpine passes. Some historical notes[75]

The value of the passes to transport and so to the nations concerned depended on two factors. Firstly, their height determined both the period of use when they were not closed by snow (we know little about the climate of antiquity) and the ease or difficulty with which the climb could be made. The second factor was the general location of the passes in relation to the Alps and the surrounding countries. Present-day roads, however, are deceptive and throughout history there have been a number of secondary routes across the Alps in use at various times. Account should also be taken of communication within the mountain massif. Although the Alps have seen human occupation since the earliest times, not a great deal is known about the lives of the inhabitants. The increased number of occasional finds dating from the Bronze and Iron Ages allow us to establish the routes used to cross the highest mountains. The access roads leading to these show up clearly on the distribution maps for certain characteristic objects (Early Bronze Age flat axes, Italic brooches of the Late Bronze Age and the beginning of the Early Iron Age, wine flagons with clover-leaf spouts and bracelets with oblique incised decoration).

The Celtic element underlying the history of the passes is important. In a book entitled *Les Peuples préromains du Sud-Est de la Gaule*[76], Barruol has shown how Celtic settlement took place in Ligurian territory along the routes through the Alps (the evidence coming from names of tribes, family names and place names, for example, Caturigomagus – Chorges, Scingomagus – Exilles, Eburodunum – Embrun).

All the arrangements made by Rome took into account the main traffic routes that needed maintenance and control; changes in administration correspond closely to changes in roads. The kingdom of Cottius was unique in exercising power on both sides of the Alps, for it held the only passes that could be used in winter. There was a Jupiter cult in the high passes of the western Alps and some fusion of worship around native Celtic deities, in particular a sky-god, sometimes associated with companion deities (the *Matronas* of Mont-Genèvre, *Mons Matrona*). The Joux column on the Little St Bernard may be compared with that of Cussy-la-Colonne (a snake-footed horseman), since the cult seemed to be connected with thunderbolts and thunder-storms.

Literary sources and inscriptions indicate that while Augustus introduced many schemes, those of Claudian times were more vital.

The passes played an important role in the movement of armies and goods (the latter either in transit or locally produced, like ores), and had a role too in the spread of ideas and changes in taste and fashion. If we compare the difficulties of the various ways over the Alps, we shall understand in some degree why there are differences in the Romanisation of the Alpine and Transalpine provinces.

The Romans took special care with their defence belt along the right bank of the Rhône between the Alps and the Jura, for it was significant to the Rhône valley and, since the opening of the two St Bernard passes, to northern Italy, too.

Over the years there was clear evidence that Roman strategy aimed at maintaining in this sector covering forces of sufficient strength. Thus Caesar sent the Helvetii back into their deserted villages, then, later, colonies were set up at Augst, Nyon and Avenches (under Vespasian). Diocletian granted a constitution to the province of Sequania, which became *Maxima Sequanorum*, lying at the junction of *Rhaetia* and *Germania Superior*. Later still, in 443, the Burgundians were conceded by Aetius the territory of *Sapaudia* (the word from which we get Savoy).

It is important to notice how far waterways and land routes were in competition with each other or complementary. Before Rome came along, it was the river system that took the traffic, hence the significance of tolls. For a system of land routes to operate, some political unity is required. Thanks to their engineering skill and their policy of unification, the Romans were able step by step to build a road network over great distances. The medieval state of affairs was quite different from that of Roman times. Waterways gradually came back into favour and this encouraged a return to the early itineraries. In the Late Empire, Roman administration was based on rivers: the flotillas that we note at important points were simply merchant craft taken over by the army.

Political power was broken up piecemeal, creating of necessity a multiplicity of feudal services. The Middle Ages saw a return to the pre-Roman situation.

With the interconnection of land and water routes again of first importance, a vital role was played by the road and river junction at Seyssel. This was a site where transshipment had to occur. It had close links with Geneva, towards which two main lines of communication converged: one, coming from the north, from Germany, reached the Rhône through Helvetic territory, while the other came down from the Great St Bernard and passed along the left bank of the Rhône and the lake. Seyssel (Condate) may be considered to have been the outer harbour of Geneva on the open Rhône flowing down to the sea. It was down this river that the stone went used in building Lyons and there came up river, in another age, amphorae from Italy and Iberia. Trade was shared out among the *ratiarii* of the upper Rhône and the *nautae* of the lower Rhône, in association with those of the Saône.

Particular points to notice are:

firstly, the major geographical influences (the rôle of transhumance, seasonal movements);
secondly, the part played by historic individuals (Napoleon, in Caesar's footsteps, reopened the route along the left bank of Lake Geneva);

thirdly, the involvement of local people: even in antiquity, if there was the possibility of exercising permanent control, one trail was chosen rather than another that might be more favourable for transport: those living alongside vied for the right to act as guides over the various stretches of road. Since the earliest times, portage was offered before tolls were demanded and the great standby for the inhabitants near the Alpine routes has always been to exploit the traffic: so it was that the *Arimani*, Lombard warriors, were given the responsibility of looking after roads and bridges in exchange for land concessions. They used to raise horses at Milan for the revenue authorities. Travellers' tales from the four-teenth to nineteenth centuries indicate that the *marrones* of Novalaise and Étroubles, who enjoyed franchises and were the distant ancestors of modern guides, found it quite possible to get soldiers across the mountains in the heart of winter.

The various periods of history throw light on each other. We need to be acquainted with the Middle Ages, if we are to understand Roman and pre-Roman traffic movements; medieval man did not usually travel along Roman roads. For roads responded, as they always have done, to individual needs. Their courses became modified as their rôle changed and resources varied. In medieval times there was little traffic and it was unreliable. The Great and Little St Bernard passes, with only local traffic, gave way to the Mont-Cenis, itself in decline in the fourteenth century, then an increasing part was played by the Simplon and the St Gothard, which was opened about 1237. The fall of the Roman Empire and the advent of the Barbarians had considerable influence on movements across the Alps. During the Early Middle Ages, traffic depended in the first place on each new political set-up, with its frontier barring the entrance to the valley leading up to the pass, a vital strongpoint where travellers had to negotiate. In addition to military expeditions (Carolingians against Lombards), there were religious exchanges (pilgrimages, import of relics) and trading movements, of which little is known. The Middle Ages did see a certain number of exports (cloth, salt meat and salted fish) and there was an international trade in spices and silks. During the twelfth and thirteenth centuries, these exchanges were at their peak in respect of the western passes, with goods making their way to and from the fairs in Champagne. These trading relations increased at the end of the thirteenth century, but other routes intervened: competition now came from sea shipping and the passes in the Central Alps.

We should note finally what kind of political groupings were created around the passes and the roads, and, in particular, the successful experiment of the kingdom of Savoy between the eleventh and fifteenth centuries.

Gallia Belgica

The Belgian network is structured around the major axis from Bavai to Cologne. It radiates from several important road junctions and has been the subject of close study by Mertens:

Bavai (Bagacum) is a nodal point with seven branches going towards Tongres and Maastricht, Arlon and Trèves (Trier), the north and Flanders by way of Blicquy or Gand (Ghent);

Tongres (Atuatuca Tungrorum) with roads to Maastricht (Trajectus), Liège, Bastogne, Taviers, Tirlemont and the North;

Arlon (Orolaunum vicus) on the highway from Rheims to Trèves, with a branch towards Metz;

Tournai (Turnacum) in the direction of Arras (Nemetacum), Cassel (Castellum, two roads) and Bavai.

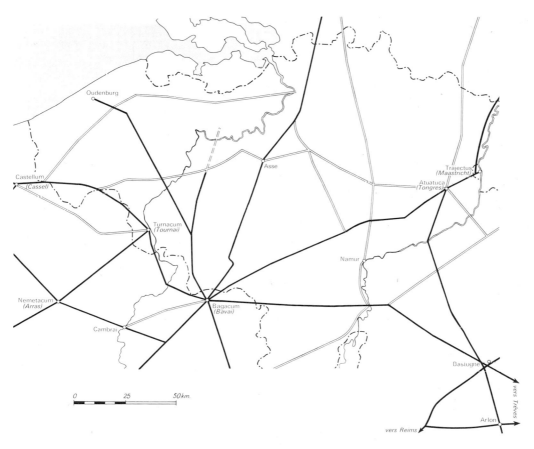

36   Roman roads in Belgium (after J. Mertens, 'Les routes romaines de la Belgique', *Industrie*, IX, 1955, no. 10)

Several roads went through the Ardennes. Trèves, be it remembered, was part of the province of Belgica and reference should be made to what has been said about bridges over the Moselle[77]. This is not the place to examine the secondary roads and we shall notice simply a few distinctive details about Belgium:

the existence of a number of *vici* and *castella*, some of which have been researched (Morlanwelz, Liberchies);

the positioning of *tumuli* along the roads, the tombs of wealthy Gallo-Roman landlords;
evidence of Roman centuriation in Limburg;
many road-sections, of special interest where roads were built on wooden piles and cross-pieces (*via Mansuerisca* in the Hautes Fagnes, cf. pp. 89–90);
a number of interesting survivals due to local legend (place names in particular: chemin de Brunehaut, Chaussée-Notre-Dame, chaussée du Diable, Strée, Straimont, Taviers, la Pirée, Katzy, Oude Baan, Waalse Baan, Tourinnes-la-Chaussée, Cherau de Charlemagne).

Ternes has made a close study of the Belgian system of roads in its eastern part (corresponding to modern Luxemburg), especially around Dalheim. This writer, who has also tackled the problem of pre-Roman highways, emphasises that there were a number of roads with alternatives available and that the fords over the Moselle had a vital rôle.

9 THE GERMANIES

There was a major road along the left bank of the Rhine. Starting in Cisalpine Gaul, it went through Rhaetia by way of Curia (Chur) and Brigantium (Bregenz), then along the south bank of the lake and on to Turicum (Zurich), Vindonissa (Windisch) and Augusta Rauricorum (Augst), where it was joined by a road from the Alpes Poeninae, Lousonna (Lausanne) and Aventicum (Avenches). Shortly after, it came to the fork with the road from Cabillonum (Chalon) and Vesontio (Besançon) and continued towards Argentorate (Strasburg), Tabernae (Rheinabern), Noviomagus, (Neuss), Borbetomagus (Worms), Mogontiacum (Mainz), Confluentes (Coblenz), Rigomagus (Remagen) finally to enter Germania Inferior: Bonna (Bonn), Colonia Agrippina (Cologne), Novaesium (Neuss), Vetera (Xanten), Ulpia Traiana, Trajectum (Utrecht), Lugundunum Batavorum (Leiden?).
    There were also cross-country roads: in Germania Superior, Lousonna–Vesontio–Andematunnum (Langres) and then towards Belgica; Chalon–Langres, then Noviomagus, Solimariaca (Soulosse), Belgica (Trèves–Trier) and thence to Mainz or Cologne; Argentorate–Tres Tabernae (Saverne)–Divodurum (Metz) and Belgica; the strategic road Gesoriacum (Boulogne)–Geminiacum (Gembloux?)–Perviciacum–Aduatuca (Tongres)–Cologne or Xanten.
    In the angle between the Rhine and the Danube (*Agri Decumates*), a road ran along the right bank of the former river from Augusta Rauricorum to Aquae (Baden), Logodunum and Mainz, with a parallel road to the east of the Black Forest through Vindonissa, Arae Flaviae (Rottweil), Sumelocenna (Rottenburg) and Grinario. When the *Agri Decumates* had been organised, the old road from Augst to Windisch was joined by two new ones: to Mainz along the Neckar and to Strasburg along the Kinzig.
    A number of spur roads branched off from the Rhine towards the *limes* and the

Danube – they cannot be detailed here – and towards Germania Magna, as is shown by the expeditions of Germanicus and Corbulo. Chiefly they went up the valleys of the right bank of the Rhine (Lippe), along which they can be traced by scattered finds of potsherds.[78]

After the year 90, the Danube river-line played a more significant rôle: in future, troops were to be constantly on the move along that strategic route in response to army demands.

In the case of the Germanies, the Rhine bridges were, of course, vital: Caesar's bridge, built in ten days in 55 BC between Andernach and Coblenz[79], Constantine's bridge (about 310 AD), about 420m long, linking Cologne to the bridgehead of Divitia (Deutz). Regarding the lower Rhine, reference has already been made to the engineering schemes initiated by Drusus (p. 163). These did not bring the Frisians out of their isolation and that tribe, living as it did away from the main continental routes, kept for long its style and way of life and played no part in political developments.

The plans for a canal from the Saône to the Moselle shows how far-sighted were the views of the Roman authorities. It is worth quoting these words from Tacitus: 'Vetus, the army commander in Germania Inferior, was planning a canal between the Moselle and the Saône, linking these rivers, so that goods brought up by the Rhône and the Saône from the Mediterranean could then pass along the Moselle to reach the Rhine and so go down to the Ocean: this would have avoided the difficulties of land transport and there would have been a direct waterway between the northern seaboard and the Western Mediterranean. But this great project was foiled by the jealousy of the governor of Belgica . . .[80]' Yet Roman know-how was probably quite in a position to tackle the problem, judging by other schemes either planned[81] or actually carried out (a canal of 23 miles in length dug between the Meuse and the Rhine by Corbulo[82], the dyke and canals constructed by Drusus at the mouth of the Rhine[83]).

10 THE CENTRAL AND EASTERN ALPS (RHAETIA AND NORICA)[84] AND THE DANUBIAN LANDS

The roads leading from Northern Italy to the Rhine and the Danube were essentially intended to allow the swift deployment of troops. From Milan, after going past Lake Como, the Rhaetian Alps were crossed in the direction of the Rhine valley to reach Lake Brigantia (Bregenz) and Augusta Vindelicorum (Augsburg).

From Verona a road went along the Athesis (Adige) to reach Tridentum (Trente) and Endidae (Egna). This line of communication formed the Brenner route to the territory of the Vindelici and was planned by Drusus and completed by Claudius. Farther west there were ways over the *Cuneus Aureus*: the Splüger pass and the Maloja-Julier pass.

From the sizable port of Aquileia, at the head of the Adriatic Sea, it was possible to travel to Virunum (Maria Saal) and Noreia (Neumarkt) over the Carnic Alps

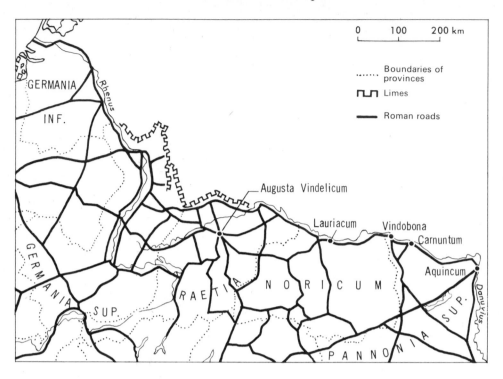

37 Roman roads between the Rhine and Danube (after H. Bengtson and V. Milojcic, *Grosser Historicher Weltatlas,* Munich, 1958, p. 35)

(Predil pass) and the Noric Alps, and to Lauriacum (Lorch) on the Danube.

The road over the Julian Alps (Alpes Juliae–Birnbaumerwald) was easier: the Ocra pass (Nanos), Nauportus (Ober-Laibach), Emona (Laibach), the Sava valley as far as Siscia (Siszek) and Sirmium (Mitrovitza) or else the Drava valley as far as Celeia (Cilli), then Poetovio (Pettau) and Carnuntum (Petronell) or Vindobona (Vienna) on the Danube, close to the customs station of Brigetio (W. Szoeny).

The Danube carried heavy traffic, which was doubled almost from its source by a road running down the right bank to serve the forts along the *limes* and in particular passing through Castra Regina (Regensburg), Castra Batava (Passau) on the frontier between Rhaetia and Norica, then Vindobona, Carnuntum, Arrabona (Raab), Brigetio in Upper Pannonia and Aquincum (Buda, Lower Pannonia). The road to Pannonia was constructed immediately after the reign of Augustus[85].

The lower Danube, with the *limes* parallel to it and spur roads running up the Marisus and Alutus valleys, was followed by a road from Sirmium to Singidunum (Belgrade), Viminacium (Kostolac), Naissus (Nish) – with a branch to Ratiaria (Artchar) – Serdica (Sofia) and Thrace, where ancient Histria was worried by the *portorium ripae Thraciae.*

The famous site at the Iron Gates of Orsova, with its wealth of prehistoric, Roman and medieval remains, has been submerged in the waters held back by the giant dam at Djerdap. The Roman road was carved out of the rock and widened by cantilevered planking. The *tabula Traiana,* inscribed on a rock-face, carried the regulations for shipping on the Danube and established for the canal of Sip, now modernised, its rôle in the transport system. To keep this exceptional inscription out of the water, it has been cut from its position and raised 20m.

Downstream from the present dam, on the frontier of Yugoslavia and Rumania, there could still be seen about 1850, when the river was low, 16 stone and brick piers belonging to the famous bridge by means of which Trajan united Moesia and Dacia.

11 BEYOND THE IMPERIAL FRONTIERS

There were trading routes even beyond the frontiers of the Empire. Some at least had been properly planned and given facilities, others simply followed natural lines of communication, in particular major river valleys, their precise courses varying with time. Mediterranean merchants[86] probably did not go beyond the free trading-posts available, while middlemen must often have been unaware of the beginning and end of the chain. Some tribal chiefs, like Maroboduus, king of the Marcomanni, were in favour of these exchanges of goods.

The origin of many of these trails is lost in the mists of time, like the routes taken by Baltic amber[87], or by gold and African ivory. The ways traders carried out their dealings on these routes left some strange survivals, as for example the 'dumb-show bartering' known to Herodotus in respect of African Cernè (isle of Mogador ?). Carcopino relates that, according to sixteenth-century Arab chroniclers, such customs have persisted until recent times in what was Roman Morocco.

In his fascinating book *Rome beyond the Imperial Frontiers,* Sir Mortimer Wheeler has shown how these routes carried Roman products far and wide (coins, gold and silver vessels, bronze objects – *paterae, situlae,* wine-flagons, bowls – glassware and *terra sigillata*), although it is sometimes difficult to distinguish in Europe between imports, diplomatic gifts, spoils of war and strays.

We are taken into Germany, Denmark, Scandinavia, Eastern Europe, Africa (cf. p. 147 sq) and Asia, over the legendary routes of the trade in spices, precious gems and silk, for which Isidorus of Charax lists the relays between Zeugma and Bactriana. Then there is the extraordinary mention in the *Annals of the Hans* of the arrival in the Chinese court of an ambassador from An-Toun (Marcus Aurelius).

It is well to reflect on the immense scope of the geographical exploration that took place under the Empire: 'From the woods of Hertfordshire to the palmgroves of the Coromandel, these red-glazed cups and dishes symbolise the routine adventures of tradesmen whose story may be set only a little below that of King Alexander himself.' Pliny the Elder also was an admirer of those men 'who venture unarmed, boldly yet peaceably, in search of fortune'[88], even to farthest Ethiopia[89]. He tells us the story of a Roman knight who was sent to seek amber by the promoter of Nero's gladiatorial displays and who scoured the Baltic seaboard and the markets of that region[90] or again the exploration made by a military tribune accompanied

by praetorian guards who were sent by Nero himself, bent on an Ethiopian expedition, in order to reconnoitre the coast as far as Meroe[91]. From these far-off travels,
people brought back plans drawn on the spot, as in the case of the Caspian Gates[92].

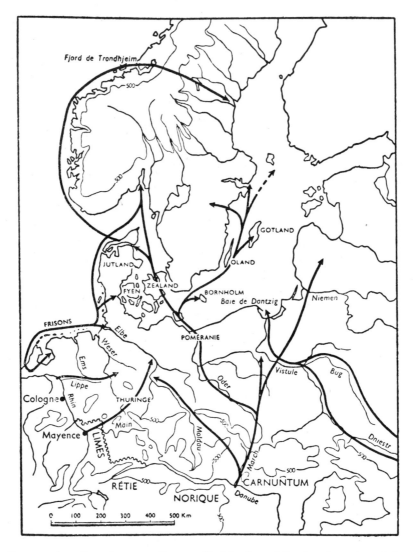

38   Trade routes into Free Germany (Source: Sir Mortimer Wheeler, *Rome beyond the Imperial
Frontier*, London, 1954)

If we compare this reference to maps of a key strait with what has already been
said about the careful lay-out of *colonia* there seems to be confirmation for the remarks of Vegetius about military maps[93]: 'A general must have perfect descriptions
of routes in all the regions where he makes war, so as to know not merely distances
measured in paces, but also the standard of the tracks, the shortest ways and the
most devious ones, the mountains and rivers . . . Some have gone so far in seeking

this information as to possess for the provinces where they will be campaigning road itineraries that are not merely described but also illustrated, so that they can conjure up and see before their eyes the road they must follow.'

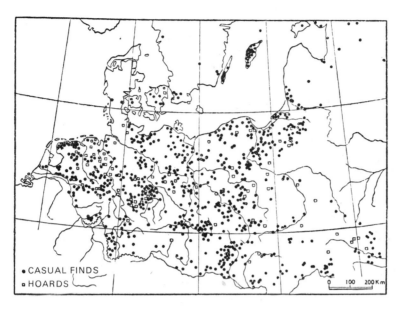

39 Finds of Roman coinage in Free Germany (Source: Sir Mortimer Wheeler, ibid.)

Commercial dealings inevitably brought with them religious and artistic influences that gave rise to some astonishing hybrids, like the art of North-West India and Afghanistan, where Greece had led the way for Rome.

We should not be deceived furthermore about the feelings that lay behind geographical discovery in those days: Romans did not have any understanding of objective exploration for learning's sake. 'Geography does not take into account what lies beyond the inhabited world', wrote Strabo[94].

4

Life on the road

1 VEHICLES

In Roman times people travelled a great deal, walking and riding on horseback or in a vehicle. Very long journeys were made on foot[1].

The horse, mule and donkey[2] were used as steeds or as pack animals[3]. They wore light shoes, hipposandals (iron *soleae*), rather than ordinary horse-shoes[4] and in preference to the hard metalled road, kept to the sandy tracks alongside.

We have already noticed the high degree of skill attained by Celtic coach-builders, just as in the case of other nomadic tribes. It is not surprising that Gaul should have provided Rome with many vehicles to copy, together with their names, such as the following:

benna (cf. French 'banne' or 'benne' = coal cart), from which was derived 'bagnole' (truck, car), by analogy with 'carriole', (light cart) a vehicle for several passengers (*combennones*)

carpentum, a two-wheeled covered gig, used by women (like the *pilentum*, which had four wheels); the root of the French 'charpente' and perhaps of Carpentras (Vaucluse)

carrus (which replaced the Latin *currus*), chariot for warfare or racing, the source of many derivatives: 'char', 'charron' (cartwright), 'charrue' (plough), 'charger' (load), 'carrosse' (coach), 'carriole'; to be compared with *carrago*, a waggon-laager and *carruca*, luxury chariot and *carracutum*, high waggon

rheda (*raeda*), four-wheeled waggon for the Imperial Post (same root as *Redones*[5], the tribe of the modern Rennes)

petorritum (same root as *quattuor*), also four-wheeled

plaustrum, country-waggon with solid, creaking wheels, mentioned by Virgil[6].

We also find:

angaria, four-wheeled, for postal purposes (a Persian word that passed into Greek)

arcera, an open cart
birota, two-wheeled (French 'brouette' = wheelbarrow)
capsum, open
cisium, two-wheeled chaise or gig
clabula (rium), heavy ox-cart, military transport waggon
colisatum, Celtic ?
covinnus
essedum, two-wheeled
ploxenum, used in Cisalpine Gaul
sarracum, with low, solid wheels, for moving timber[7]
tensa, show chariot.

Dion[8] has suggested how to understand the uses to which various conveyances were put: one should notice the suitability of the vehicle to the highway in question[9], the dimensions of the road and its state of upkeep and, in general, the policies underlying the development of the farmland and its division into parcels. A worthwhile point of interest is that there may be local survivals: the immense farm carts of Emilia-Romagna, late nineteenth century in date and conserved at the Ethnographic Museum in Rome (EUR), are very reminiscent of the vehicles from the French waggon-graves (northern Italy was, of course, another Celtic region) and the author has seen waggons with solid wheels in the Sardinian countryside.

40 A horse-drawn vehicle (Relief of Maria Saal, Landesmuseum, Klagenfurt)

Some vehicle bodies were light and flexible (relief sculptures suggest the use of wickerwork[10]) and there existed a number of technical devices (brakes ? hood), but suspension must have left much to be desired: one hardly can have gone out for pleasure rides on bumpy roads in vehicles lacking springs. That would explain the private *ambulationes,* shady, gravelled avenues for riding, such as we learn about from the descriptions of villas in Pliny the Younger. A traveller who was not in a hurry and was anxious for his own comfort made use of a litter borne by men or mules.

There has been much criticism levelled against the method of harnessing. Des Noettes thought he had proved that the Roman harness, which involved a supple non-rigid collar bearing on the neck and not on the shoulders, risked choking the animal and so limited the tractive effort to under 500kg. He made the bold suggestion that this irrational device had helped to maintain the system of slavery. It took until 1957 to demonstrate[11] that he was in fact basing his argument on incomplete evidence and that his theory had been accepted simply because historians and archaeologists were ignorant of mechanical science . . . Indeed, the Romans had not omitted experimenting in the matter: Columella[12] advises that animals should never be yoked by their horns, Vitruvius[13] considers the problem where two animals in a team are of different sizes and yokes were available, in addition to horse-collars. Furthermore, did not Ausonius mention waggons drawn by 30 horses (for the movement of quarry stone ?)? On the whole, teams seem to have been harnessed abreast rather than in file.

The fact remains that the *Theodosian Code*[14] limited loads to between 200 and 600lb in the case of light carts and to between 1,000 and 1,500lb (429kg) in the case of heavy carts used by the post[15]. Even if this were only a chance reading, not found in the *Justinian Code,* the restrictions can be explained in various ways: unsuitable teams, vehicle bodies of insufficient strength, slowness of land transport, poor road-surfacing. What is certain is that the development of the shoulder-collar in the twelfth century, by allowing heavier loads, caused the remains of Roman roads to deteriorate more swiftly. One thought that emerges is that there is a relationship (emphasised by Fustier and valid for every age) between the type of vehicle and the construction of the road, particularly its surfacing and profile. It has been possible to make use of bends with a shorter radius and so to climb slopes more gently, because vehicles have been so much improved. The progress of this technical revolution is full of interest: the appearance of the pivoted front undercarriage in the sixteenth century, then the suspension of the body and so on. There is another detail that will cause a smile: Roman roads, we have noticed, had strategic importance in the first place, especially for the movement of lines of heavy waggons ('artillery', supplies). Every general staff is worried by the problem: will the roads be adequate? Today, for example, we need think only of heavy tanks. In this respect, on the maps compiled by engineers-cum-geographers like the Naudins, it will be seen that the roads considered capable of taking army convoys and guns are Roman roads. This reveals how useful old military maps can be for our purpose.

There are many illustrations from the past showing the variety of vehicles that used to be in service. Thus we find, in the case of Gaul and Germany, the following relief sculptures reproduced in Espérandieu-Lantier's standard work:

at Avignon (musée Calvet) and found at Vaison: a ceremonial waggon decorated with heads (a vehicle belonging to the town or a funeral-hearse ?);
at Dijon (archaeological museum), men leading horses;
at Klagenfurt (Maria Saal), a travelling-carriage;
at Langres (musée St-Didier), a four-wheeled cart bearing a large barrel, drawn

by two heaving mules, led by a driver holding their reins and equipped with a whip:

at Saintes (archaeological museum), a horseman, formerly part of a tomb whose stones have been reused in the wall around a late third-century fort;

at Strasburg (archaeological museum), a late first-century stela, showing a soldier in the transport corps, carrying whip and sword and leading a cart drawn by two mules;

at Trèves (Trier) (Landesmuseum), the Neumagen ostlers;

on the Igel tomb, scenes depicting the transport by land and water of bales of cloth.

To the above may be added a bronze votive offering from Alésia (in the Museum of National Antiquities), dedicated by Satigenus, son of Solemnis, to the goddess Epona, protectress of horses (one, at least of her attributes). It represents a fast two-wheeled vehicle drawn by a mare. The list lengthens every year[16].

There is similar evidence from North Africa:

a stela (Boglio) from the late third century showing three waggons bringing in the harvest;

a mosaic (St-Marie-du Zit, late fourth century) portrays a small cart drawn by two horses and carrying a workman and the shaft of a small column.

2 THE CURSUS PUBLICUS AND NEWS COMMUNICATION

Thanks to human ingenuity, there were many ways of transmitting messages: shouting (in use amongst the Gauls[17]), tom-toms, visual signals, which were at an early date passing communications between *oppida* in the same defensive line. Every empire in the past was forced for political and administrative reasons to set up a system of messengers. The Persians made them part of the army and the idea, according to Herodotus and Xenophon, was credited to Cyrus the Elder, who used to send horsemen (*angaroi*) hastening night and day along the royal roads. In the Egypt of the Ptolemies, however, messengers were regarded as civil servants. Rome was much inspired by the way that matters worked in that country (calendar, financial set-up, land survey), especially after Caesar's visit. In his day there was no official system: the dictator hired vehicles for long journeys[18], probably from establishments which had understandings from town to town. Before Pharsala, he must have taken care himself to have relays of horsemen ready to carry the news of his victory to all parts[19].

This was the setting in which Augustus created the *cursus publicus*[20]. Suetonius made note of the original arrangements:

So that there might be swifter news of what was going on in each province, he organised relays of runners, then of chaises, at intervals along the military roads. The second proved a more satisfactory idea, since when the letter arrived at its destination, the bearer could be cross-examined on the situation if need be. The first seal used by Augustus for diplomas, dispatches and letters was a sphinx, then the head of Alexander the Great and finally his own head, cut by Dioscorides. This has been in service with all his successors. Augustus added to all his letters the exact time of the day or night when he wrote them[21].

From this detailed information it appears that the Roman Imperial Post served as a government information service in which safety counted more than speed. The runners mentioned by Suetonius were young townsfolk – at any rate the sons of notable families – organised in *sodalitates juvenum,* which were known from inscriptions to be pre-military groupings, the Latin equivalent to the Greek gymnasium. They apparently ran the stretch between two relay stations and we should notice a Chinese reference of the fifth century to a relay system in the West about 400 years earlier involving changes every 'ten li' (miles) with a staging-house every 30.

The term *viae militares* (military roads) is explained by Cicero's allusions to the *via Egnatia*[22], with camps strung out along it, and by an inscription[23] which tells of a road built in the reign of Hadrian from Berenice to Antinoupolis and served at intervals by watering-points, post stations and forts. Yet another, of Nero's time[24], mentions that in Thrace, the governor, on the emperor's orders, constructed *tabernae* and *praetoria* along the military roads. The first of these words signifies private inns, leased to *caupones,* the second staging-points maintained by *civitates.* Those with land adjacent to the main highways were indeed obliged to furnish supplies to VIPs, a heavy burden imposed by the state.

Gradually, after Augustan times, messengers were in action up and down the roads and their career was officially recognised.   . .

The way in which the Imperial seal evolved was characteristic and reflected the development of the powers of Augustus. Alexander's example enjoyed widespread respect.

The seal was needed to authenticate diplomatic passports issued by the Imperial chancellery and giving their bearers the right to travel by the imperial post. These 'diplomas' comprised certificates inscribed on bronze (in the shape of folded tablets) or written on papyrus or parchment, and intended to avoid forgery. However fraud was undoubtedly commonplace, if we judge by epigraphic evidence: for example, there has been found in Arcadia[25] an edict of Claudius (earlier than 49–50) in which the emperor is stated to be expressing the wish of relieving from the burden of providing relay horses not only the colonies and towns of Italy, but also the provinces and all their cities. Similar abuses have been noted from Egypt.

Book x of Pliny the Younger's letters, those exchanged with Trajan when he was governor of Pontus-Bithynia (111–12) allow us to reconstruct how the passport system worked. Each governor's office received a batch of warrants a year in advance (Pflaum, whose argument we are following here, estimates that in Pliny's case it was about 50) and the person responsible was quite free to use these to transmit important information (one subject per letter!). The emperor could delegate his seal to the praetorian prefect.

In the first century, there was not as yet any regular corps of messengers. No doubt the job was done by slaves from the Imperial household or soldiers. A coin of Nerva shows two mules standing unharnessed behind a cart and bears the legend: *vehiculatione Italiae remissa*. This was progress and later, under Trajan, the post became a civil-service matter[26], for in his reign, there appeared the first government officials in charge of the organisation, namely freedmen responsible for vehicles (*a vehiculis*[27]): Hadrian chose a knight as departmental head[28] and separated the prefecture of posts from that of the *praetorium*. In fact, the burden still lay heavily on provincials, who paid the *mancipes,* henceforth responsible, instead of the municipal magistrate, for supervising messengers. Each municipal 'post office' was put up for auction, in the way that the Romans farmed out matters like tax collection. The successful bidder (*manceps*), having been accepted by the prefect responsible for vehicles, had the choice of acting on his own behalf or being the figurehead of a company. He had supreme control over the slave muleteers (*junctores jumentarii*).

From the reign of Septimius Severus onward, vehicle prefects, originally 'centenarians' (they had emoluments of 100,000 sesterces) took over transport as well. Inscriptions reveal their growing importance: careerwise they advanced all the more rapidly since they often obtained in addition the procuratorship *ad silices,* then the control of army supplies[29] – *cura copiarum exercitus* – which was definitely combined with the prefecture of the post under Commodus. The latter position came to the fore in the time of Marcus Aurelius: it became 'bicentenarian' (salary of 200,000 sesterces) under Septimius Severus.

There were far-reaching changes in the latter period: 'He caused the responsibility for vehicles to pass from the individual to the imperial treasury' (report the *Scriptores Historiae Augustae*[30]). Because of the devaluation of the coinage and the consequent loss in purchasing power, the troops demanded to be paid in kind. This is why the military *annona* came into being, a harsh tax on land, theoretically reserved for wartime, then soon made a permanency. It will be discussed below. As the transportation of these supplies created serious problems – towns exhausted by civil war could not have done anything – the Emperor had to take the post over on his own account. In practice, the increased cost of the *cursus* was raised from the annona itself. As the services expanded, so their administration was decentralised and the cursus became independent financially. It was only in part of the Empire that the State took over the expenses. As an institution the *cursus* went on, but private citizens paid, as the *Theodosian Code* makes clear.

The chief of the central office in Rome and the vehicle prefects in the districts of Italy received their running costs from the Treasury in order to pay the *mancipes* and maintain the road stations. Steeds were provided by the Imperial stud. Besides the muleteers (*muliones jumentarii*), each station had a staff of scribes (*actarii, numerarii*) and a company of troops who were 'stationed' there (*stationarii*), on special duty for the postal service and the maintenance of army supplies and acting as dispatch-bearers and road police.

At the start a civil organisation, the *cursus* thus became more and more militarised, with the road stations serving the post and the police no longer differentiated, first in Italy, then after the mid-second century, in the rest of the Empire.

The prefect of vehicles, who might have been a lawyer or an army officer, was an important man at court and could even end up as Emperor like Macrinus. He had to follow up the engagement of the *mancipes,* when they were paid for by the towns, choose them himself for the next five years, look after the road stations and keep check on waggoners and drivers.

The issue (*evectio*) of diplomatic passports was made by the Emperor, the praetorian prefects and, within limits, governors of provinces. They were drawn up by the secretariat *a memoria.* We must imagine bronze tablets bearing the words *tabellarius diplomarius* attached to horses' necks or fixed to vehicles. The *evectio,* a kind of letter of credit, stated what the bearer could requisition. There were forgeries and there were heavy penalties, too.

The messengers were organised in a semi-military fashion, officered by *decuriones.* There is evidence for *equites* (mounted couriers, used in the district of Rome), *Numidae* and *commentarienses.* But each administrative grouping had its own liaison-team: *tabellarii*: slaves or freedmen, *geruli*: city ushers, and in Rome, *cursores,* the place of each of these in the hierarchy being uncertain.

The Emperor could also employ soldiers from his guard (praetorian *speculatores*), a genuine private police force, akin to the *beneficiarii,* non-commissioned officers, with the duty of watching junctions on strategic roads. There were also *frumentarii* and, in Diocletian's reign, *agentes in rebus.*

Diesner has recently shown[31] that until the coming of the Vandals Roman roads were kept up and the post survived. Some light is thrown on the way the *cursus* worked by the travels of bishops on their way to *concilia.*

3 THE MILITARY ANNONA

In his study of the military *annona* in the Roman Empire during the third century[32], Van Berchem has demonstrated that there was a clear relationship between the amount of food doled out to the army (corresponding to a change in the form of pay, owing to inflation) and the use made of taxes in kind.

During the first and second centuries, the Treasury disposed of revenue from the Imperial provinces, in which the legions were garrisoned. In provinces, where normal taxation was levied partly in kind, the army authorities obtained food supplies for the troops directly from public granaries, while the *civitates,* with the aid of wealthy private citizens, had the duty of giving billets to soldiers en route for active stations. In each province, the commissariat depended on the governor and the procurator and their staff; in wartime, an officer was posted to see to supply movements. Septimius Severus took special interest in roads and stationed military units (*beneficiarii*) at important junctions to ensure the safety of traffic and in his reign a *procurator annonae* first appears. As early as the end of the second century, Egypt saw the introduction of a tax for the *annona.* This form of revenue is known through the receipts which were handed to taxpayers by the collectors (*ostraka* and *papyri*) and was an exceptional levy in origin, intended to supplement public funds when there was a war. However, as hostilities continued it became a permanent feature and merged with other taxes. The *mansiones* (there was one for each *civitas*) were road stations organised for the Imperial post and equipped with storerooms for supplies requisitioned from the provincials. In this light, we may recall that the *Antonine Itinerary* would appear to comprise a list of *mansiones* connected with the levying of the *annona* and serving as cantonments for soldiery on the move (a common occurrence in the third century). As against the *mutationes*, the *mansiones* (some were walled *villae*), lay at varying distances from each other, for their siting was determined by the presence of local taxpayers. These granaries were intended to supply the military, whether the supplies for the *annona* were handed out on the march or sent to the standing garrisons. It was on this reserve that both the army and the public services depended, for government officials in the fourth century were equally interested. The employment of *beneficiarii* to defend the road stations also had the effect of showing the mailed fist to local people obliged to pay their contribution to the public granary.

An inscription[33] survives giving an edict of a governor of Thrace, who founded the *emporium* at Pizos in 202, the year when it was visited by Septimius Severus. The station was under the control of local dignitaries and the *curiales* in office and the town magistrates were responsible. A military unit was on duty. The inscription shows that as a class decurions put up with the burden of the *annona*. There is no doubt that handing over supplies and managing granaries was a crushing state imposition. In times of war, management was passed to the army.

The *annona* was thus another service to be added to the Imperial post, putting increased powers in the hands of the praetorian prefect during the third century: each commanding officer, within his own sphere, controlled both troops and vital supplies and tended to become independent of central authority. The change in the way soldiers were paid occurred at the same time as strategy was transformed in conformity with the development of the *limes*: units were more and more static, living off the local territory. The arrangement was extended by Diocletian to all the provinces. Even Italy had to be assessed, an essential procedure if taxation had to be recovered in kind. But the annona was to be demilitarised by Constantine, without losing its impression of being an emergency wartime measure.

4 ROAD STATIONS OF THE CURSUS

The *Theodosian Code* makes no distinction between the words *mansiones, mutationes* and *stationes,* which originally had special meanings:

mansio meant a stopping-point, for an overnight stay, in particular, a halting-place for the Emperor or an important relay, later the distance covered in a day, and a group of lesser dwellings, neither *civitas, oppidum* nor *vicus*;
mutatio was a relay (fourth century);

statio, first a sentry, then a sentry-post or a squad, this being the term given by Tiberius to units raised for anti-brigand patrols, road police, finally a relay.

It would be useful at this point to study the corresponding Greek terms. The names of the relays were taken from:

distance marks: at the fourth milestone – *ad*[*talem*] *lapidem* (*miliarum* understood)[34];
a prominent landmark: *ad fines, ad fluvium, ad pontem*, summo (Poenino) = at the top of the pass;
a town name, although the relay was often some way off (in the same manner, we find railway stations at the foot of hills or spurs on which lie the towns they serve at La Roche-Migenne, Les Aubrais, St-Pierre-des-Corps)[35];
we shall note examples of inns possibly giving their names to road stations.

What was the distance between these? Vital as the answer would be for the purpose of siting, there is no accepted figure.

According to the *Itinerary from Bordeaux to Jerusalem*, in which stages are carefully indicated, the average distance between *mutationes* and/or relay changes was apparently 8,333 paces. If we judge by the cases where names of *mutationes* are based on the distance to the next town (*Ad X . . .*), the commonest interval was somewhere between 7,000 and 12,000 paces.

A text of Procopius informs us that 'in a single day's travelling a good messenger might cover eight stages, sometimes less, but usually never less than five[36].' Everything depended, naturally, on the density both of the traffic and the population[37] and on the nature of the road: often relays are found at fords or at the bottom of steep hills where horse teams had to be doubled. The intervals were shorter in mountainous country than on flat ground.

The average distance between *mansiones* or overnight halts seems therefore to have been from 30 to 36km corresponding, says Vegetius[38], to the normal stage of a legionary.

There has often been confusion between average speeds and records, a point dealt with below.

The burden of constructing and looking after the public buildings of the Imperial post fell to the towns[39]. Until Severan times, the relay service was managed by *mancipes*. Management was put up for auction by the towns, but *mancipes* too could conclude a contract with the treasury.

To ease matters for some provinces, Septimius Severus handed over the service to troops (*stationarii*), by making the post the responsibility of police squads raised to fight brigands. The *Theodosian Code* shows that this change-over was completed, with the main road stations having been the first no doubt to be controlled by the military[40].

It is worth recalling the inscription from Pizos mentioned above, reproducing an edict issued by the legate *pro praetore* of the Thracian province with a view to setting up markets. The new *emporia* were to have their garrisons, whose commanders would be on an equal footing with the new quasi-magistrates in having responsibility for public buildings (*praetoria, balnea,* a reminder of the little illustrations on the *Peutinger Table*). Regulations were laid down for the settlement of new citizens with their privileges (freedom from supplying horses and services to the *cursus*) and for the control and upkeep of the public buildings.

Septimus Severus enlarged the road stations by adding *horrea* for the storage of corn and of army supplies. An edict[41] issued by Severus Alexander two months before he left on campaign reproduces marching orders, laying down stages to be covered and the store bases. The services provided by the road patrols and the post were thus complemented by those involved in the collection of the *annona*. As mentioned earlier, the *Antonine Itinerary* comprised a series of routes arranged in the first place for Caracalla in the early third century and the stations listed therein represented the overnight halts of the Imperial party as prepared in advance by local inhabitants. In the *Itinerary,* too, *saltus* or great imperial estates named after former owners were used as road stations. Once in being, 20,000 to 24,000 paces apart, these halts were changed into permanent relays, then fortified by *castella.*

Archaeology is unfortunately not very informative about arrangements at relays, for the basic problem in excavation has been to identify the purpose of each building exposed and its date (*praetorium* or travellers' hostel, baths – water supply was a vital factor – stables, sheds, barns for fodder, grooms' quarters, forges).

At Thézée (Loir-et-Cher), the 'Tasciaca' of the *Peutinger Table,* substantial remains of brick walls and herring-bone masonry have suggested the existence of a *villa.* But the site was probably that of a road station, the first in the *civitas* of the Turones, on the Roman road from Bourges to Tours, along the right bank of the Cher. The structures included a great courtyard 80 by 60m, surrounded by a wall, with, on the east side, evidence of living-quarters (stables ? stores ?) and, at the far end, a large hall, 38 by 13·5m, with two other buildings and a rear room with an entrance. The hall, of basilican type, (cf. place names like 'Bazoches' and 'Basouges', derived from the Latin *basilica* and often found on the boundaries of *civitates*) had some interesting openings with semi-circular arches and square windows, these with flattened arches. The chronology is uncertain. The site could be a *praetorium,* an undefended station, also used as a market or bonded warehouse, a law court for the governor or a tax-collection centre for treasury officials (*basilica*).

Maybe the building called 'the palace of Pépin le Bref' at Vouvray (Vernon) was really a similar establishment.

A fortified station, on the other hand, has been found at Jublains (Mayenne), dating from the third century. It consisted of a *castellum* situated at a cross-roads, with a double defence circuit, a *vallum* and a wall with towers. It received its second line of fortification after being ruined in 256, but was finally destroyed in 275.

Test excavation has taken place at the station and township of Elesiodunum, lying in the Carcassonne (or Naurouze) gap between Toulouse and Narbonne. It was mentioned in Cicero's *Pro Fonteio.*

A station has been dug on the Little St Bernard (*in Alpe Graia*): a large building was used as an inn, with an enclosed courtyard and rooms giving on to it, a porched entrance, first-floor wooden *cubicula,* stable, forge and vehicle-shed.

From the Great St Bernard there is a dedication of 222 AD addressed to the *Genius Stationis* by M. Sulpicius Marcellus of Cologne, who belonged to the military police. The *mansio Martis* on Mont-Genèvre was built in Caligula's reign.

At Einöd (Carinthia), a station is known, equipped with a kitchen, heated rooms, and rooms with wooden partitions.

The Logis-de-Berre has revealed a walled *statio* athwart the road[42].

Identification as *mansio* or *mutatio* in uncertain, especially since one category could slip into the other. Conclusions can be drawn from the amount of traffic concerned, distances travelled and the geographical location[43]. Relays placed at road junctions and serving several routes were clearly more important.

Several texts give information about stables: Procopius[44] speaks of 40 horses. The *Theodosian Code*[45] shows that a *vicarius* could not mobilise more than 10 horses and 30 mules and gives some details about what went on at a station: the staff included a farrier (until recently a key figure in our countryside), cartwrights (*carpentarii*) able to repair vehicles damaged by jolting, a veterinary surgeon (*mulomedicus*), a groom (*mulio*) for each group of three animals. The *manceps* or *stationarius* checked the messenger's passport (*diploma*) and kept the books.

The groom took the whole team on to the next relay and came back with the vehicle: it was forbidden to pass a relay without stopping.

The *manceps* leased the stations for five years in the Early Empire and the *muliones* were their slaves until the Late Empire when they became *servi publici*. The law protected them from harassment, but they could not take tips.

Relays that were situated at water-crossings where there was no bridge must have had a post providing a service of *utricularii*.

Earlier we have seen that Father Poidebard's investigations into the Syrian *limes* took account not only of roads, but also of the structures alongside. In the *Limes de Chalcis,* he goes on with a collaborator to describe many types of defence-work, so building up a series that starts with a humble guard post, watching water-points (*turris, burgus*), then passes on to strongholds in the semi-desert (*praesidia, castra, castella, centenaria*) and ends with defended towns or towns with a regular garrison.

The military posts, sited on hilltops, have sides measuring about 20m in length and walls 1m thick, doubly faced in coursed ashlar and unmortared, together with guard towers. Adjoining one gate is an enclosure for a caravan park.

A more important[46] defended site is the fort at Amsareddi, dating from the late second or early third century. It is square with sides of 87m, an external ditch, walls 1m thick, square angle-towers with 5m sides (of which 4m project externally) and gates with flanking towers. Within, buildings lie spaced out on either side of the two streets crossing one another at right-angles. There are also two chapels, a guard-room and three enclosed annexes, without counting remains of other structures and evidence of a water conduit close by.

The fortified *horreum* at Et-Touba[47] served an estate that was in existence between 326 and 353. It has three ground-floor rooms with vaulted ceilings. The building itself has three floors and comprises a rectangle of 27 by 8·5m constructed of basalt blocks to give walls 0·9m thick. There is a surrounding wall 10m away with towers looking out on the desert and, within the enclosure, a watertank. The central room measures 5·3 by 4·5m and gives access to the stores. A staircase once led up to the second floor and to the steward's apartment, which had a gallery, like those seen on third and fourth century African mosaics.

In general, the stages occur at regular intervals along strategic roads, that is every 20,000 paces (30km), the stations being linked by a system of visible signals; in the case of caravan trails, the distance is 30,000 paces (45km), with relays every 10,000 paces.

In all the selected examples, Father Poidebard observed evidence of earlier human occupation (protohistoric tells) or later (Byzantine reoccupation, judging by inscriptions, fortified monasteries, finally Ommiyah dwellings).

The defended sites lying along the Roman roads emphasise thereby the vital strategic importance[48] of roads which started as the means whereby a country was pacified and penetrated after its conquest and ended up by being the last refuge and defence line of the Roman troops. Romanisation, which had spread by relying on the road network, was now in retreat and defending itself in the *castella* along the very same roads.

The *burgarii*, quartered in the *burgi*[49], were militarised units, a road militia responsible for maintaining and policing highways, particularly the great military roads close to frontiers. This knowledge allowed von Domaszewski[50] to establish the road system along the Rhine–Danube frontier from inscriptions left by army detachments posted at cross-roads. Fustier claims to have discovered such a police post at Lay (Loire), a kind of guard-room measuring 12 by 6m at the northern side of an old road[51], in a wooded mountainous district.

5 PRIVATE ESTABLISHMENTS

In addition to the relays belonging to the *cursus,* there existed a whole series of privately run establishments, which it is not easy to arrange into a significant order of importance.

The hostelries offering board and lodging were known by the terms *deversorium* (sometimes a private abode built by wealthy Romans on the way to their estates), *hospitium* (a word revived in various senses during the Middle Ages) and *caupona* (used pejoratively). *Stabulum* meant an inn with a stable.

Inns and ordinary places for eating and drinking were called by the name *taberna* (with the added epithet: *deversoria, vinaria*), which gave many derivatives, and *popina,* an Osco-Umbrian borrowing. But one also finds: *cenatio* (the normal meaning is 'dining-room'); *ganeum* and *gargustium,* mere hovels, together with loans from Greek, like *thermopolium* for the sale of hot drinks and *xenodochium.*

The intended purposes of premises like these emerge from the manner in which they are laid out and equipped, as revealed by excavation. Thus from the discoveries at Herculaneum and Pompeii it has been possible to draw up a traveller's guide, as it were, to the inns and eating-houses: there are details like a kitchen with an oven, a *triclinium,* single rooms, stalls with tether-rings for animals, counters with casks or amphorae inset into them. The same typology can be applied to the bars as to the shops: the majority were probably let by landlords, who also could instal bars on their land alongside main roads, following Varro's advice: 'If there should happen to be on a property close to a high road a site convenient for welcoming travellers, it would be a good thing to build a tavern there[52].'

These inns were attracted by the official *mutationes* and *stationes* of the *cursus,* a fact which explains the names of some of the stages of the itineraries: *Tabernis, Tres Tabernae* (from which are derived Saverne and Rheinzabern). The relays whose original purpose was to provide government messengers with steeds came to hire them to ordinary travellers. The guilds of *cisiarii* (*cisium*-drivers) and *jumentarii* (pack-horse drivers) must have had a stranglehold on business at the gates of towns (there are today similar transport concerns at the exits from Rome). Besides the inns, there were shops, a bath establishment, a chapel (for example, the road station Ad Aesim in the Apennines had a temple to Jupiter Apenninus[53]), forming the kernel of future population centres. Modern Spain has comparable developments taking place along its expanding road network.

The names of Roman inns are known from road itineraries and inscriptions and are of various types:

> *Ad Stabulum, Taberna,* expressed or understood (hence Etaules), with an adjective: *Taberna frigida, Ad Novas, Ad Medias, Ad Veteris, Ad Pictas, Ad Rubras* (one thinks of the 'Red Houses' associated with Roman roads); *Ad Decem Pagos,* the meeting-place of ten provinces (the 'Continental Hotel' of its day);
>
> a person's name in the genitive or the name of a class of people: *Ad Fratres, Ad Centuriones;*
>
> names of tools presumably used as inn signs: *Ad Rotam* (sign, like the modern 'Les Routiers' or a waterwheel ?), *Ad Ensem;*
>
> names of animals: *Ad Aquilam, Ad Gallum Gallinaceum, Ad Draconem, Nigropullo;* and of trees: *Arbore felice.*

Inscriptions have preserved for us examples of the wording of inn signs: *Mercurius hic lucrum promittit, Apollo salutem*[54].

Both literary texts and inscriptions tell us of the fittings and furnishings, as for example the advertisement from Pompeii: 'Accommodation to let, room with three beds and all conveniences' (*hospitium hic locatur triclinium cum tribus lectis et comm*[*odis omnibus* ?])[55].

Tenants included many freedmen, of Greek and Eastern origin. Some may have been acting as managers of their residence and there is a possibility they were organised into guilds. Legal references suggest that there was a class of people, both despised and mistrusted, who were commonly thought to be rogues and misers[56]. The innkeeper is a traditionally comic character with a long literary history, known to foreign visitors in Italy from the sixteenth to the nineteenth centuries. Stories of crime frequently had their setting in taverns and innkeeper's wives were reputed to be witches[57].

Customers did not rate very much higher: commercial travellers, muleteers, sailors, hetaerae, suspicious individuals. A Roman of quality stayed with friends when journeying. On occasion he might even take with him tents, crockery and food[58].

All this explains the cautions and adverse remarks made by Christian writers, especially directed against inns being set up next to religious houses.

The inn trade, in general, was regulated by imperial ordinance, which imposed restrictions on opening hours, with local inspection first by the aediles, then by the town prefect.

It would be outside the subject of this book to talk of food, drink, internal decoration (excavations have revealed many frescoes), furniture and pottery, entertainment offered (music, dancing – cf. Copa) – and prices. Colourful details can be found in the works of Horace and Martial and some vivid description in the *Satiricon* or the *Metamorphoses*. It is enough at this point to notice the unusual inscription from Aesernia, reproducing a conversation between a departing traveller and the inn-keeper: *Copo, computemus. Habes vini sextarium unum, pane[m], assem unum, pulmentar[ium], asses duos. Convenit. Puell[am], asses octo. Et hoc convenit. Faenum mulo, asses duos. Iste mulus me ad factum dabit*[59] ('Innkeeper, let's settle our account. One measure of wine and bread, one ass; some stew, two asses. Agreed. The girl, eight asses. That, too, is agreed. Fodder for the mule, two asses. That animal can take me to my destination.')

There is a graffito from Pompeii to the effect that: *Vibius restitutus hic solus dormivit et Urbanam suam desiderabat*[60] ('. . . slept alone here, very much missing his Urbana'). A mosaic found at Ostia invited the guest to drink his fill: *hospes, inquit Fortunatus, [vinum et cr]atera quod sitis bibe*[61].

6 THE TRANSMISSION OF NEWS

In antiquity, the speed with which people travelled[62] and the speed with which news was transmitted were one and the same problem. It was an important aspect, difficult for us to understand in the era of telecommunication.

The matter can be basically illustrated by examples taken from Livy, Books XXVII to XLV, and emphasised by quotations from other sources.

The ancients themselves were aware that there were contradictions in their sources owing to problems in transmitting information and the distances involved and we should realise that a general on campaign and a governor of a far-off province had to be almost independent, at any rate under the Republic.

XLIII, 4, 6: So little was known in those days about what was happening at the gates of Rome that at that time the praetor was in his country house at Antium, enjoying his ill-gotten gains . . .

XLIV, 32: The Illyrian war, the end of which was learnt in Rome before people were even aware that it had begun.

XLI, 1: [After the victory over Perseus] the messengers sent to announce the victory in Rome did so with all possible speed, but the good news outstripped them.

XLV, 18 (decision about affairs in Macedonia): Only the main guidelines could be fixed by the Senate: 'The rest was left to the good sense of the army commanders and the commission members whose presence on the spot put them in a better position to decide with more certainty what measures were necessary[63].'

The day's march remained the traditional unit for estimating distances:

XXXVIII, 59: That whole region, in length 30 days' march and in breadth 10 . . . was taken away from Antiochus.

Who carried the news before the *cursus* was set up?

everywhere, traders. Caesar remarked: 'Townsfolk surround merchants and force them to say where they have come from and what they know[64]';
private individuals with distant friends;
XXXIV, 17 (concerning the decree of the Senate on the Bacchanalia): 'Fear swept through Italy in every direction, when letters were received from people in the city telling their friends in country towns about the senatorial decree';
in the case of important news, official representatives:
XLII, 4: N. Fabius Buteo (a praetor going to his province) died in Marseilles when on his way to Hither Spain. The news was brought by delegates from Marseilles.

The following give some idea of travelling speeds, but the distances covered are not always indicated:

IX, 9: From the territory of the Samnites (Caudium) to Rome, three days' swift march;
X, 39: Between Aquilonia and Cominium, the messenger took the daytime to reach his destination and came back at night;
XXXVIII, 13: Three days' march by the army from Gordiutichos to Tabes;
XXXIX, 21: The Senate sent off a messenger with orders to reach the praetor C. Calpurnius at the harbour of Luna . . . He arrived on the fourth day.
XLIII, XXII, 24: Perseus took two days going to Stratus from the frontier of Aetolia;
XLIV, 1: Troops leaving Italy put into port at Corcyra the following day and on the third day reached Actium, the port for Acarnania;
leaving his ships in the Gulf of Corinth, the praetor went overland across Boeotia. After one day's rapid march, he joined the fleet at Chalcis.
XLIV, 30: A praetor went from Apollonia to the camp on the river Genusus in three days;
XLIV, 45: From Amphipolis, Galepsus was reached the same day and Samothrace the following day.
XLV, 1: After the victory over Perseus, a messenger arrived on the 13th day

following the battle (the 10th of the Calends of October); the consul's couriers, whom the messenger had preceded, arrived on the 6th of the same Calends (however it has been seen above that the news was officially broken in four days). XLV, 33: Aemilius Paulus, who had been camping a mile from Amphipolis, reached Pella in five days, two days later was at Spelea and in 15 at Passaron (Epirus);

XLV, 41: (speech by Aemilius Paulus): 'When I left Italy, I embarked at Brindisi at dawn; about the ninth hour I was off Corcyra with my whole fleet. Five days later, I was in Delphi . . . From Delphi, I took five days to reach the camp.'

The following are quoted for comparison:

Appian, *Civil War*, II, 5, 32: Caesar sent a letter to the Senate and it was borne with such speed by Curio that in three days he covered 1,300 stadia. *Civil War*, II, 14, 98: After Thapsus, events were announced in Utica in under three days.

Cicero's letters show that, in the case of the battles of Forum Gallorum and Modena, the news took eight days arriving in Narbonensis from Modena, whereas 14 to 15 days were needed to go from Rome to the same province.

One letter from Rome was 50 days in reaching Cicero at Cybista (Cappadocia). When he wrote to his son studying in Athens, some letters required three months.

The news of Gaius Caesar's death in Limyra (Lycia) was known at Pisa after 36 days (four days from Rome to Pisa).

Pflaum has noted the following statistics:

Cato the Elder travelled from Brindisi to Rome in five days (Plutarch, 35) or from Otranto to the capital in the same time (Livy, XXXVI, 21); Cato the Younger was 30 days crossing the Cyrenaican desert; the news of Nero's death[65] passed from Rome to Spain in six days (a land journey of 332 Roman miles in less than 36 hours); the disaster at Aquileia was known in Rome after four days, that is 130 to 140 Roman miles per day[66]; in the Late Empire, it required five days and a half to cover the 1,247 Roman miles between Antioch and Constantinople[67], 54 days between Rome and Alexandria and seven between Rome and Brindisi.

A good example of the transmission of news by means of the *cursus* was provided by the accession of Pertinax (1 January 193), which was made public by the prefect in Egypt at Alexandria on 6 March, an interval of time that must have represented, at the worst season of the year, overland communication.

Charlesworth has also assembled some examples, these being for Asia Minor[68]:

one day from Ephesus to Tralles[69]; two more days to Laodicea; four or five further to Philomelium; three more to Iconium;

eighteen at least as far as the Euphrates (that is, 30 days on horseback or more than 35 on foot, but it was possible to use the *cursus* non-stop in 21 days);
one day's travelling from Sagalassos to Apamea[70];
six from Mazaca to the gates of Cilicia[71];
three from Sinope to Phasis[72].

The government service seems, as usual, to have taken much longer: in the Late Empire, 66 days from Milan to Rome, more than five months from Milan to Carthage.

Special tables would be needed to cope with sailing times, since the speed going by ship could reach a hundred miles a day. As an example, Livy mentions: from Dyrrhachium to Corcyra, three days, and from Neapolis to Cephallenia, five days[73]. A crossing from Ostia to Tarragona in four and a half days was a record.

What makes the matter more difficult is that some writers in modern times have tended to mix up average speeds with cases that were exceptionally fast, the latter having been more worthy of note by the ancients:

Tib. Sempronius Gracchus (Livy, XXXVII, 7), using previously prepared relays, arrived at Pella three days after leaving Amphissa, showing incredible speed, according to the historian;
Caesar, sleeping in a waggon or a litter and with his secretaries in attendance, managed to cover 150km per day in a *cisium*[74];
Tiberius went 200 miles in 24 hours from Pavia into Germany[75];
but he was beaten by a standard-bearer who did the journey from Mainz to Cologne, 108 miles in 12 hours[76].

Average speeds were clearly much lower, especially when numbers of people were travelling together.

The *iustum iter* of the Roman army was 10,000 paces, that is 15km, with the *magnum iter* 30km[77], one day in four being rested (*iter intermittere*). Of course, by lightening the load of four legions (*expeditae*), Caesar managed to get them to cover a return journey of 75km in less than 30 hours[78]. He took 27 days to go from Rome to Iberia 'having travelled a very long way with a large army'[79]. But on heavy ground or with baggage, everything altered:

XXXVIII, 15: The army, laden with booty, could scarcely make five miles in the course of a day.
XLIV, 3: In an area of broken terrain, the vanguard of the legions, although lightly armed, could cover only with difficulty 15 miles in two days[80].

The *cursus* speed was something like 75km per day, an average equivalent to that of the Emperor Silvanus taking 28 days, in the fourth century, to move from Milan to Cologne by way of Geneva (about 2,000km), but the ordinary traveller could hardly have exceeded 45km, if we are to go by the very exact figures for Gaul given in the *Itinerary from Bordeaux to Jerusalem*.

Not enough attention, it seems, has been paid to the fact that diplomats were offered average time in which to act[81], although time to make ready must also be allowed for:

> XXXVII, 7: Advice to the Aetolians to ask for a six months' truce in order to dispatch an embassy to Rome.
> XLII, 48: Perseus' ambassadors were informed that they had to leave the city limits of Rome immediately and Italy within 30 days.
> XXXVII, 1 and 49: A decree from the Senate instructed the Aetolian ambassadors to leave Rome that very day and Italy within fifteen days.
> XLII, 36: Ambassadors who had been dismissed had 11 days in which to leave Italy. A magistrate kept an eye on them until they embarked . . .

These figures may be compared with averages and records of modern times: in the sixteenth century a mounted messenger could cover 37 to 47km, while Napoleon went 200km daily for 13 days to travel from the Berezina to Paris.

7 CUSTOMS SERVICES

De Laet[82] has made a close study of the *portorium*. The word, meaning both a right of way (*portus*) and a transport duty on the movement of goods, covers not only the idea of customs (a tax paid at the frontier), but also town dues (paid at city gates[83]) and tolls (for roads and bridges) and is more concerned with money-raising than with the protection of home trade and the taxation of luxuries. Rome did not see the system as a method of regulating the exchange of goods, but rather as a source of public revenue. Once the customs organisation was in being, the *portorium* was levied: at the State frontiers, on the boundaries of customs areas, at the gates of some large towns, at important road junctions, on passes and bridges and at fords. It was closely connected with the network of communications.

From the very beginnings of Roman trade, *ad valorem* taxes were exacted on Greek lines, but our evidence comes mostly from the Early Empire. We know that, in the first century BC, throughout Italy Rome was leasing customs offices (*stationes*) in the main ports or trading centres inland. The collection of the *portoria* by the publicans gave rise to abuses, such as Cicero reveals in the cases of Sicily (*Verrines*), Narbonensis (*Pro Fonteio,* concerning a duty on the movement of wine) and Syria. Some towns in favour were able to enjoy the fruits of their customs, which were leased out locally, under Roman inspection. The customs system spread steadily with the conquest. At the beginning of the Empire there were large tariff areas that took in several provinces, but no customs barriers with limits coinciding with provincial boundaries. It is impossible here to go into the details of the administration. Sufficient to say that in the Early Empire there was a tendency towards land unification and state control, in which government services were centralised and both regulations and tariffs were combined. The end of the first century AD saw tax-gathering companies replaced by farmers-general, then by Imperial civil servants, with a system of direct taxation in which the revenue passed to the Treasury (a development starting in the reign of Hadrian). Let us take as an example the *Quadragesima Galliarum,* which involved Narbonensis, Aquitania, Belgica, Lugdunensis, the two Germanies, the Alpes Maritimae, Cottiae and Graiae, part of Rhaetia, the Atlantic and Channel coasts and the bank of the Rhine. In the first place there were four clearly marked-out regions, with the Pyrenees forming a tariff barrier, in addition to some inland customs points (Lyons, Langres, Saône). The rate was 1/40 or 2·5 per cent (it was different elsewhere). Coins of Galba with the legend *quadragesima remissa* show that this tax had been suspended – albeit temporarily – between Gaul, Italy and Spain. The siting of the customs points, which has sometimes given rise to place names (*Ad Portum, Ad Publicanos*), was almost exclusively determined by geographical factors: natural barriers like mountain ranges and rivers, and places like bridges and major road junctions. The *stationes* were accompanied by military posts, but it was the civil authority that was responsible for levying the *portorium.*

In Africa, arrangements were different: the *IV Publica Africae* with customs points at Carthage, Rusicada, Chullu, Caesarea, Zaraï and Lambasa, took in the *portorium,* the *vicesima libertatis* (5 per cent on the emancipation of slaves), the *quinta et vicesima venalium mancipiorum* (4 per cent on sales at auction) and the *vicesima hereditatium* (5 per cent on inheritances).

In addition to the ports, there were inland customs points. The tariffs at Zaraï[84] and Lambasa[85] were town dues. In the outlying districts, some town dues had continued from the past where there was a long tradition of city life, as an Imperial favour, granted according to time and circumstance.

A few more details: we learn from Quintilian[86] that the *instrumenta itineris* (animals and vehicles) did not pay taxes, nor did personal property, goods belonging to the Treasury and the Emperor, supplies and equipment being sent to the army by the State, certain commodities depending on local arrangements and festivities.

There was a prohibition on the movement of corn, salt, iron and whetstones, which were not allowed to pass into hostile hands. All those who dwelt in the Empire were in effect liable to the *portorium,* but the Emperor could grant immunity (to governors and to soldiers and veterans). Regulations existed to protect merchants and travellers and punish fraud. There was special jurisdiction in the case of disputes. In the fourth century, customs zones gave way and the distinction between customs points operating on the Imperial frontiers and those inland disappeared. Some towns continued to collect dues. Little is known about the effect of *portoria* on internal and external trade. Some industries had probably moved to avoid paying taxes levied between provinces.

There are a number of texts and inscriptions on the subject of customs. A list of tolls was engraved on a stela by order of Mettius Rufus, Egyptian prefect[87]. The following constituted the demands for payment by the publicans of the detachment working from Coptos; these collectors were responsible under the Arabarches for indirect taxes and controlled the military road from Coptos, on the river Nile, to the Red Sea: for a Red Sea ship's captain; 8 drachmas ... for a sailor, 5 drachmas ... for women plying the trade of courtesan, 108 drachmas ... for soldiers' wives, 20 drachmas ... for a donkey, 2 obols ... for a small cart with a hood, 4 drachmas.

The following tariff of town dues (*portus*) regarding goods passing the gate of Zaraï (Numidia) is dated to the third consulate of L. Septimius Severus (202): Regulations for taxes per capita: for each slave, one denarius and a half; for a horse, mare, jack-ass, mule, donkey, ox, half a denarius; for a pig, one sesterce; for a piglet, two asses; for a sheep or goat, one sesterce; for a kid or lamb; two sesterces. There were rates for foreign clothing, leather (of different qualities), glue, sponges, amphorae of wine or *garum,* dates, figs, nuts, resin, pitch and alum[88].

Philostrates in his *Life of Apollonios*[89] describes an amusing scene at a customs point: the Magus, on his way to India, goes through the frontier post at Zeugma on the Euphrates where people had to pay one quarter of the value of their goods according to a list (*pinakion*) displayed outside the customs office:

> The publican in charge of the post took him in front of the tariff list and asked him what he had to declare. Apollonios told him: 'I have with me Temperance, Justice, Virtue, Continence, Worth and Patience! . . .' So the publican said: 'Write me down a list of these slaves.' Whereupon the other replied: 'That's impossible; they are not slaves I have with me, but mistresses.'

Finally a quotation from Pliny about incense, camel-borne from Arabia, on which taxes were claimed by priests, kings and their scribes, police, soldiers, bearers and servants in general. 'Wherever you go, you have to pay, here for water, there for fodder, for halting overnight, for tolls of all kinds . . . Along our sea coast, you still have to pay the farmers in this Empire of ours[90].'

This distinction between commodities is confirmed by the tariff at Palmyra[91], which includes slaves, animals (horses, sheep, camels), foodstuffs (corn, wine, salt, vegetables, oil, fats, salt fish), some raw materials (wool, myrrh, skins, bronze) some trades (butchers, cobblers, clothiers, whores), but excludes silk, gems, ivory, ebony, spices, which by passing through Palmyra created its wealth and were certainly subject anyway to Imperial taxes.

8 INTERDEPENDENCE OF LAND AND WATER COMMUNICATIONS

Only a few pages can be given to this theme.

Water, both a source of life and a means of defence, has eased communications and located settlements, with rivers large and small playing a major rôle. Roads have been attracted across waterways at points favoured by geography:

> the head of a river, close to its source, before the valley deepens, so making a cross route more difficult. Likewise, a road will take a course round the head of a bay, while the head of an estuary is always an important situation[92];
> the place where a river emerges onto low ground from its mountain tract, always a strategic site exercising control over movement and exchange between regions with different and complementary soils and production;

the head of navigation (which may have changed since early times)[93] and so the transshipment point. Roanne, for example, is the former head of river traffic on the Loire, whence it was possible to reach Lyons by easy porterage. It is vital to look for river ports, where the mode of transport had to change, places engaged in ship construction and raising pack animals, lying at the junction of roads serving the hinterland.

Once we know of an important site along a water-course, it is possible to re-establish the chain of stages every 30 or 40km. There will be many places as at Tours, at the junction of Loire and Cher, where tributaries create a convergence of routes. On the Seine, the Parisii had a powerful advantage in controlling two tributaries, the Marne and the Oise, both important trading highways.

Those places which still felt the influence of tides or up to which sea shipping could reach were likewise key points in human settlement. At the limits of sea and river shipping there often lay a bridge, in the first place a bridge of boats as at Arles[94]. These first bridging points (London, Rome, Seville, Bordeaux, Nantes, Rouen) kept their significance until the nineteenth century, when the requirements of ocean vessels favoured the establishment of ports on estuaries.

Wherever it was possible to effect an easy river-crossing was obviously a key position: originally these were fords, as place names may remind us (derivatives of *ritos* and *vadum*), or islands (Rome, Paris, Sens, Melun, Metz, Amiens). At Paris, a flood-free terrace, on the right bank, made it easy to cross the alluvial plain. At Koenigshoffen and Schiltigheim, the loess terrace overlooks the island that was the cradle of Strasburg; the Roman road took advantage of these open, level rises, which were above the marshes, in no danger from floods and crossed only by occasional streams.

When building his first roads, man was attracted to these old river terraces, out of reach of floods, and he also had an eye for a spot where the valley narrowed and there was a high crag on which to site a stronghold and set the abutments of a bridge. Alsace, where there runs close beside the Rhine a highway used since the Bronze Age times and in fresh service for the Roman road from Basle to Strasburg, and the plain of the Saône, which was followed by Agrippa's road, provide two examples of river terraces, where towns and villages lie along ancient routes, at the junction of different soils offering complementary products. Lines of *oppida* show the historic rôle of some through routes, like the Ornain valley (the Champagne Gate), the valleys of the Avre, lower Seine and Somme, and the Chagny Gap.

Settlement patterns can often be understood if we look on water-courses as lines of communication, especially where they meet land routes, clearly advantageous for trading purposes. Very careful study of a limited area certainly leads to the conclusion that each of these has been an asset to the other since the very earliest times. Strabo noted that, as the Rhône was a difficult river if one wanted to go upstream, an alternative porterage road was available[95]; the Garonne was a similar case and, according to Dion[96], Diodoros of Sicily was referring to this river when he spoke of caravans of pack horses bringing British tin[97]. Ausonius described the rivers of

Gaul as being duplicated by tracks[98]. As far as topography has allowed, great rivers have always been followed on both banks by roads[99], which in particular made use of natural levées (alluvial ridges turned into towpaths), edges of alluvial terraces and the healthy terrain half-way up hill slopes, a favourite site, too, for villages. This explains the long country roads lined by settlements that lie along the crest of the little hills in the Val de Loire. The old road tries to remain at a constant height above flood level, so it avoids low, marshy ground and cuts across the necks of meanders[100]. As for the road along the river bank itself, this must in recent times have been turned into a dyke in order to ensure all-the-year traffic. Dion has studied this transformation and shown how the modern road along the levée, set on dykes, took the place of the metalled road on the low terrace or the old upper road on the slope. With the arrival of railways, the close connection between routes by land and water has been severed.

On the whole what Vidal de la Blache said is correct: 'The courses of Roman roads mainly follow the chief river valleys. We can see translated into reality the governing idea that the ancients formed of our country as a natural link between Italy and the Ocean[101].'

No less important as factors in the establishment of settlements able to encourage and control human movement are the overland routes. Circumstances have determined that certain of these are assured of a place in history: these are the major geographical gaps in France, the Carcassonne Gate and the Burgundy Gate.

If we want to understand properly why some river crossings are important, we should trace back the land routes converging on them, particularly those helping to create political ties over long distances. We shall thus appreciate, for example, the great value of the river markets, Gien and Orléans, lying at each end of the Val de Loire, within easy reach of the Seine: similarly, Sancerre, Rheims, controlling a number of valleys, Tours, a nodal point for both roads and rivers, Metz, Limoges, and, above all, Paris, focus of several waterways and close to lowlands and open plateaux across which roads could easily forge ahead towards far destinations: Paris lies where the Seine meets a natural track ('route des seuils' – the road through the gaps) that runs over the western plains of France from the lands by the North Sea to those facing the Atlantic (Dion). Only the site of Lyons stands comparison.

Once the broad principles that govern the general setting have been recognised, a closer look can be taken at the actual location of a town. Alongside the main valley there may be dry side valleys or gentle spurs giving easy access to higher ground and aiding movement by road. Did the town develop along the river – this was the case of Paris, although the old Celtic bridge has suggested how the *cardo* was aligned – or did it turn away from the river, as at Rome? We must look, too, to see which came first – town or port – and we must study the dating of the bridges (the oldest being where the river crossed ancient highways) and their order of importance, according to whether they served local needs or long-distance communication. Dion has shown how, in the Val de Loire, bridges or ferries used by overland routes gave rise to settlements at those points where they reached the alluvial ground towards the flood plain. Artificial mounds were raised to take the bridge abutments. There were streets, even districts laid out in line with bridges that have sometimes vanished, in Rome and in Arles (where the amphitheatre was aligned on the bridge of boats). Bridgeheads have played an important part in city development. On many great rivers, such as the Rhône and the Rhine, both banks were significant. Lyons was a long time passing to the other bank of the Rhône, but gradually the bridgehead on the left bank acted as a magnet for the roads coming over the mountains.

Looking for surviving evidence of a man-made crossing must centre on the possibility of sunken causeways or bridges, traces of which may be found by dredging or exposure at low water. The remains of old bridges should not be always sought in present-day river beds, which may have shifted. They may be revealed by the embanked access roads, which may be visible running over marshy or soft ground. The possible remains that survive include: iron-shod oak stakes for supporting piers; wooden shuttering to take concrete foundations; spurs or reinforcements for piers; worked masonry; keystones; ribs; and fragments of decoration.

Old ports should be surveyed in a similar way to establish in their vicinity the relationships that existed between sea traffic (either direct or using lighterage) and land routes. This would involve tracing the roads that converged on ports of call or followed the coastal dunes and bringing out links between these ports and inland towns. There may have existed several landing places for the same port, either at different periods or simultaneously, where, for example, either side of a headland could be used according to wind direction.

It was quicker to move by sea over long distances (nine days from Rome to Alexandria, going via Utica or Messina to use the etesian winds)[102] and was convenient for heavy goods. But it was dangerous (many references to disasters at sea are confirmed by underwater archaeology) and services were suspended in winter[103], season of the *mare clausum*. People then had to go a long way round: so it was that Mucianus, in order to avoid a sea crossing in winter, made Vespasian's troops go through Cappadocia and Phrygia instead of embarking them from Greece. On his way to Rome, St Paul was forced for the same reason to winter at Melita. In any case, many journeys took in more than one form of transport, especially for those passing through Greece[104] or those who came from the East and landed at Brindisi or even Pozzuoli. There is a notable example in Tacitus[105]: Piso landed at Ancona, then passed through Picenum to reach the *via Flaminia*. From Narnia, he went down the Nar, then the Tiber.

The various forms of communication were complementary to each other rather than competitive[106] and sometimes specialised in different traffic. However, towards the end of the Roman period, movement was tending to be by water, not by road. This brought about the decline of towns that were route centres, but not situated on rivers, with a consequent shift in urban life.

However, it was possible to complete by water those land journeys that did not involve speed or heavy goods and so, for the Roman period at least, there is no need to join the pessimists who claim that the stagnation of local trade meant shortages and slump with greatly fluctuating prices and uncertain returns on farming[107]. All that can be concluded is that, as methods of transport became more limited, so production became less centralised. But the trend towards self-sufficiency was apparent only in the Late Empire. A host of factors will need to be examined, such as the problem of deciding whether there were outlying areas that could have acted as markets.

The function of Roman roads

This is the point at which to sum up the various types of traveller who used the main highways: military leaders and their forces, emperors with their train, high dignitaries accompanied by their staff, envoys from afar or the provinces[1], messengers employed by the *cursus,* sailors from the fleet, whom Suetonius[2] shows us had to take their turn marching from Ostia to Pozzuoli to Rome in order to hoist the *velum* at the amphitheatre, and, of course, private citizens. These included people travelling on business (merchants in search of supplies or fairs[3], itinerant craftsmen such as masons, sculptors and mosaicists, gangs of seasonal farm-workers, in the style of the famous 'Mactar harvester'[4], theatrical performers, teachers or lecturers such as Apuleius) litigants or those sentenced to exile and poets, similar to Martial, looking for a patron. There were the sick on their way to drink healing waters or to breathe healthier air, pilgrims seeking a holy place and Very Important Persons off to consult an oracle, just as Tiberius visited that of Geryon, near Padua[5], meeting on the road groups of strolling priests and a host of quacks. Some travelled to satisfy their scientific curiosity (Polybius, Pliny the Elder, Plutarch – all intellectuals who went to study in Greece) or merely for their pleasure (Pliny the Younger, tourists in Egypt . . . people who were going to see a play or the games at the amphi-theatre forming a party from one district, courtesans[6], sometimes the funeral procession of a great man who had died far away[7]).

On the road all these folk would meet commercial traffic: foodstuffs moving towards the towns from the countryside, wares from local workshops, raw or finished materials on their way to far destinations along roads which traders were always first to tread before soldiers and settlers and, finally, in conquered territory, convoys of waggons bearing the military *annona* to the public granaries. Famine could be staved off in fact only by the movement of corn.

We should note in passing that carrying supplies for the *annona* to army quarters must have been a local burden at the suit of the *curiales,* in addition to managing the granaries, at any rate in peacetime. This was a duty little appreciated by provincials and appeared amongst British complaints, if we are to believe Tacitus, usually well-informed: 'In order to put the British in their place, they forced them to wait at closed granaries . . . they had to take their corn to warehouses that were distant and hard to reach[8].'

In the same way, a major tax burden arose when army units moved around living off the country. Traditionally, the Emperor and his suite were given hospitality by the people of the district that he was visiting[9].

There is no better illustration of this intense activity than the few lines from Tacitus: 'After crossing the Dalmatian Sea Piso left his ships at Ancona, then reached the *via Flaminia* through Picenum, where he caught up with a legion that was being transferred from Pannonia to Rome before moving to quarters in Africa[10].'

The traffic provided a living for a crowd of humble folk whom it attracted along the wayside and who were responsible for 'services': renters of horses and vehicles, innkeepers, landlords of hostelries, blacksmiths and even peasants and shepherds selling produce beside the road[11], such as can still be seen in Italy or Spain.

Roads, which were originally built by, and for, the army to aid speedy movement and heavy transport ('artillery' and supplies) and then were developed by successive governments for sending dispatches and general administrative purposes, also gave assistance to trade.

In this respect, 'the history of roads is making least headway, when it could be of greatest value, throwing light on their use and evolution and on the density of their traffic[12].'

Of course, this is a subject for which the evidence is imprecise. What facts have we at our disposal?

It is true that there is information from the road material itself: thus resurfacing means that there was a policy of maintenance; deep ruts suggest traffic intensity and the width and straightness of the roadway are evocative of an important destination, far off. It is true, again, that milestones and dedications commemorative of engineering feats are signs of Imperial interest. But none of this is enough. Nor can we really count of finds made in the build-up of the road and in the side-ditches. As for buildings and other remains found on either side, the distribution of which is often our main clue to the line of an old road, how far away do they have to be for us to conclude that they are connected with the highway? Early texts giving details about the use of roads are few and far between. Inscriptions are sometimes more helpful; the Zaraï tariff, for example, allows us to draw up a balance sheet of trade in the province: it lists, we should recall, amongst the articles currently on sale, slaves (from the desert), livestock, clothing, leather, furs, wine, condiments and fruit, in exchange for which the town imported salt, iron, copper and flax.

The most useful information may come from the structural remains of houses alongside the road, provided the evidence is stratified and properly recorded. If finds such as coins, glassware and pottery from a variety of sources are to have real significance, the details must be subjected to statistical procedure. A comparison of percentages can then give us some idea of the relative importance of the different elements of trade. Thus, at Izernore (Ain), amphora sherds of Iberian origin are evidence that oil was imported from Spain up the Rhône valley, which has similar finds all the way along it (cf. excavations at St-Romain-en-Gal), like its extension, the Saône valley. Etienne has likewise published details of the route taken by wine amphorae through the Carcassonne Gate, a trade earlier than the first vineyards at Bordeaux.

The Rome–Ostia complex, though exceptional, has left some impressive evidence at Monte Testaccio of mixed trade carried on by land and particularly by sea and river. By analysing texts, inscriptions and amphora stamps, Le Gall[13] has been able to draw up an impressive list of imports, including: corn from North Africa, Egypt, Narbonensis, Spain, Sardinia, Sicily and Crete, vegetables, meat, condiments (pepper re-exported from Egypt, *garum* from Spain), cheese, fruit, fish; and in addition to these foodstuffs, manufactures and raw materials such as: pottery, clothing and textiles, papyrus, metals, marbles and decorative stone, wood, wax, pitch, incense, ivory, red lead – and slaves. Only by referring to such lists, like the one that Broise has compiled for the *vicus* of Boutae (Annecy), could one really come to appreciate the part played by lines of communication. Even then it would not be easy to decide the relative importance of land transport and water transport and to give a list of goods a quantitative interpretation. Overall, there is no doubt about the connection between the state of the roads and the level of economic activity. This aspect will not be pursued further, for it would mean re-assessing the whole of Roman economic history in relation to Roman roads. This is not possible in a book devoted to roads mainly as structural features.

It must be accepted then that the extent of Romanisation was closely connected, both as cause and effect, with the system of roads. Roads, indeed, formed the essential framework for human settlement and land-division and, by easing the transport of commodities, led to the accumulation of wealth. But, at the same time, as men and goods moved from place to place, there came in their train influence of a subtler nature[14], in the realm of art and religion, which tended to unify the whole Empire. Roads brought innovation but they also conserved and unified.

Pliny the Elder was clearly aware of the moral effects of roads, when he gave vent to his feelings, old Roman that he was: 'Which way was vice introduced if it was not by the public road? Which other way indeed could ivory, gold and precious stones have passed into private use?[15].'

A few themes worthy of further attention include:

(a) In literature, the spread of the conquerors' language, with its ways of thought and popular myths, particularly as a result of public displays.

(b) In the artistic field, the movement of craftsmen with their design books and working methods, and of works of art with the fashions they created.

We may take as an example the conclusions reached by Hatt in *La Tombe gallo-romaine*[16]: in the course of the first century, the prototypes and techniques of sepulchral sculptures slowly moved through Gaul, following the main roads, especially that leading to Germany. In the second century, economic decline in the south caused labour to transfer towards the south-west, centre and north-east, and mausolea came to be built at busy cross-roads to Germany. These tombs spread along the highways taking the trade in cloth and wine, from Bordeaux to Trier and from the Saône to the Rhine. Regional funerary sculpture made its way from Narbonensis, along the roads of Aquitania, the various artistic features being blended thanks to the contacts of internal trade. In a similar manner, note may be made of the spread of the *ascia* and religious names. Evidence can come to light at certain important road centres or termini. Account must be taken of a multitude of influences and especially of markets and customers' tastes; so it was that centres of pottery-manufacture in Gaul settled down nearer to consumer markets along the *limes*. We should consider how long these movements took, involving time-lags that might stretch to a generation between Rome and the farthest provinces, depending on the art and craft in question. Rome was not the source of all inspiration, for the city, be it noted, also received from the provinces. Exchanges could return by roundabout routes following the strategic frontier lines, notably the Danube valley along which the *limes* of the Rhine received Syrian glass and Danubian cults. Seaways, too, brought many influences and changes of taste.

Similar phenomena in medieval times have been the focus of interest. Theories have been put forward with a variety of emphasis to account for the character and growth of epic legends (cf. the title of 'Le Charroi de Nîmes') along pilgrimage routes (Bédier, Paris). Some would have it, for example, that the St James roads ('les chemins de St-Jacques') inspired a series of churches with recognisable, if stereotyped, plans, which were built on an impressive scale for large congregations and presented unusual elevations with a wealth of sculpture to arouse religious fervour. Other medieval influences included wandering pedlars and epidemics.

(c) In religion there are often close connections with literature and art. We can note here the spread of new religions, pagan at first, and particularly the cults of eastern origin, coming up the Rhône or Danube valleys or *via Aquileia* and the Alpine passes. Then, later, the advent of Christianity, first observable in the towns, was in close association with Roman roads[17]. Everywhere along the roads in Gaul there are traces of men like St Martin, a mass of places named after saints and, at intervals, early deaneries. It was along these roads that bishops made their way to a council and along them that the Church built its own establishments for receiving guests, so as to avoid the worldliness of taverns and to cope with increasing numbers. In no time chapels sprang up at roadsides, replacing pagan shrines, or were erected over the graves or relics of saints. There were so many of these chapels in the fifth century that an African council had to ban them. The very same routes were to come back into use for the great pilgrimages to St James of Compostella, Rome or Jerusalem.

When all is said and done, the main unifying factor was the political one, summed up in the famous dictum: 'All roads lead to Rome[18].'

The 53,638 or so miles of main roads (Diocletian listed 372 of them), forming as they did the line of advance for army and commerce, the binding force between races and cultural influences, and the essential basis for the settlement and development of land and its colonisation and survey, served to unify the Roman world and so, at long remove, to create modern Europe. This thought aroused enthusiasm in Pliny the Elder: 'Roman power has given the world unity. All must recognise the services that she has made to men, by improving their contacts and making it easier for them to enjoy in common the benefits of peace[19].' And again:

> Is there anything more wonderful than to witness this never-ending exchange between different parts of the world [in this case, the trade in plants with healing properties]? We owe it all to the noble immensity of the Roman peace, that peace that enables the most distant shores and nations to know not only men but also frowning mountains high in the clouds, together with their crops and plants. May it last for ever, this gift from the gods, who seem to have presented the Romans to the world like a second source of light[20].

Several generations later, at a time of crisis, the Gaulish poet Rutilius Namatianus (*De Reditu suo*) echoes this feeling 'Hear me, O magnificent queen of the world subject to thy laws, O Rome, who hast taken a place beside the gods in heaven. Thou has welded the most diverse nations into one country. Thou hast offered conquered peoples a share in thy civilisation and made one city of what was the universe[21].'

This is a work on Roman roads only. However, the study of a road system cannot be conveniently dealt with in chronological divisions. For any given period, only relative judgments can be offered on its functions and often it is a delicate task sorting the tangled skein of tracks.

One of the main contributions of Fustier's work already quoted is to have provided comparative tables showing features of the road network at different times (general direction, lie of the land, appearance of the road on the ground, place names, alignment and engineering work, plans with profiles and cross sections, details of construction with measurements and road-distances). All these criteria must, of course, converge. One point worth remarking is that more study might profitably be made of the unit of distance, as suggested earlier, the only criterion scientifically placing a limit on possibilities.

A FINAL LOOK AT THE ROADS

It is always instructive in any given region to see how the Roman roads fared, whether they survived or fell into disrepair: after the Late Empire the situation did in fact vary from one province to another. The Gaulish *Panégyriques*[22] indicate that the military roads were out of use, but they were still to guide the great invasions[23]. In many places they were taken over or destroyed, in others they were maintained, as in the case of the *Flaminia* by the kings of the Goths[24]. Survival was sometimes a conscious act. Here, for example, is what Leo the African observed about Rusicada: 'Sucaicada is a very ancient town, built by the Romans . . . Between this harbour and Costantina (Constantine) there is road paved with black stones, such as one can sometimes see in Italy, where they are called Roman roads. This is a great argument in favour of Sucaicada having been built by the Romans.' Sometimes it is local knowledge of the road that falls into disrepair. This has already been noticed in respect of place names. A better understanding of affairs in Roman times might come from a process of carefully working back from the present in order to analyse the position for later periods when abundant source material exists. From the khân of the Middle East, the posadas of Spain and the fondaci of Sicily, we could trace back to the original road stations.

Medieval documents, in particular land charters and grants to abbeys, show that the Roman ways were still sufficiently in use to demarcate areas of jurisdiction, manors and tithe boundaries, and to apportion land for parishes and communes. The rôle of certain brotherhoods ('Frères Pontifes') hospices, fairs[25], and forced labour, with the sharing of responsibility between central government and regional and roadside authorities, suggests similarities with Antiquity.

This is not the place to enter into controversy regarding the reuse or disappearance of Roman roads in the Middle Ages. Each branch of knowledge tends to look at matters from its own point of view and to be unaware of what has gone before. Some eminent medievalists have pronounced against the 'myth that Roman roads continued in use': Imberdis considers that medieval roads did not coincide with Roman roads, for the latter were difficult to modify and so not easily kept in repair[26]. Bautier[27] thinks that, exceptional cases apart, people moved around in the Middle Ages on roads which were planned and constructed at that time. Against these views, one could set many examples of the continued use of Roman roads: Fossier has pointed some out in Picardy in the thirteenth century[28]. In the Landes, Roman roads serving pilgrimages were maintained until the fourteenth century. Bloch has written with feeling[29]:

> How many castles used to stand alongside roads built by the Romans! For these roads saw the passage of merchants, who were, at different periods or even at the same time, protected, exploited, and robbed by the lords of the castles. Along the Roman roads travelled the medieval pilgrims on their way to the great shrines of Christendom; along them travelled the minstrels, weaving into their verse chronicles legends picked up at churches as they went on their way or tales that the ruins of the monuments of old had inspired in people's imagination. It might have been a Roman tomb, lying, like the more famous tombs of the Alyscamps or the *via Appia*, beside a road, close to the gates of a town, perhaps the 'tombe Isore', which used to be pointed out as one left Paris, on the way to Orléans, and which a medieval epic saw as the grave of that king of Conimbra killed by Guillaume d'Orange. Not that it did not sometimes happen in the Middle Ages for merchants and pilgrims to turn aside from the roads that Rome had built them.

And the author also quoted the example of merchants travelling between Paris and Orléans, who apparently made a diversion to avoid a feudal stronghold.

It would clearly have been absurd for anyone to attempt to replan the roads from scratch, especially when administration had become decentralised and economic conditions were uncertain. Even in the eighteenth century voices were raised against giving up a Roman road for a new line. A memorandum from Berry preserved in the Bibliothèque Nationale notes: 'I cannot observe without emotion an old road being given up still threequarters gravelled or paved, on which stand villages and inns, in order to build a new one a little way off, cutting straight through woods and destroying farmland', words whose sentiments are repeated by Barailon (1806): 'The military way from Bruère to Bourges is perfectly preserved for two-thirds of its length; it puts the new road to shame in that it is dry and passable at all times, whereas the new one, in winter, is nothing but an unpleasant, muddy track from end to end[30].'

Generally speaking, as regards the medieval period, regional studies tend to show that topography came into its own again and there was a return to a pre-Roman state of affairs with a flexible system of communications running between all the minor settlements, often passing along valleys and making do with improvised construction.

A little closer to modern times, we should notice that Louis XI set up posthouses, a distant imitation of the *cursus,* while in 1571 there was progress in the operation of the mail with a trial service between Paris and Orléans. Only in the mid–seventeenth century did people consider regular passenger transport across France at relatively fixed times. The regulations governing the royal mail throw light on how the *cursus publicus* worked.

Of particular interest are the rediscoveries made by the architects and engineers of the Renaissance: Palladio, struck by the aesthetic quality of the remains of Roman roads, was inspired by them to provide villas with access roads[31]. Looking into the military value of roads, he rediscovered a Roman principle: 'Roads can be made safe by taking them along high ground.'

In the same way, one can follow the progress of the building code (regulations in the eighteenth century advocated straight lines and established widths) and of techniques. Macadam (1756–1836) went back to Roman ideas: the need to drain the subsoil, and the importance of grading materials which had then to be packed in layers, a procedure apparently forgotten in the Middle Ages. More recently still, with moving vehicles driven by wheels in contact with the road surface, a return has been made to the Roman practice of constructing embanked highways.

Other points of interest include the development of terms associated with the road system, accounts and statistics and travellers' descriptions (cf. Montaigne's diary, examined earlier). Fustier quotes as an example Misson's observations showing how stretches of Roman roads in Italy were almost impassable, compared with the road he was using, built by the Renaissance popes.

Economic and social aspects need to be considered. Thus, in the eighteenth century, as they passed through an important geographical gap, convoys of waggons from Condrieu on the Rhône to Roanne on the Loire were reviving a portage section of the early tin routes[32]. There is also the case of the peasants from La Semine (Haute-Savoie), who were ruined by the construction of the new road to Geneva and the road labour associated with it, an event that must often have taken place in antiquity.

This overall look at matters shows that the Roman road, in its very shifts of course, through times of prosperity or decay, has had a life of its own and its history is a reflection of history in general, with ups and sometimes downs. In Roman times and in the Middle Ages alike, the road system was restored when the central power was strong. With Paris as its centre, Colbert revived the centralised network of roads that Agrippa set up centred on Lyons. The pattern is dense along the frontiers and in major industrial and commercial areas and frequently the railways have re-discovered age-old routes, such as the Rome–Apulia line, which follows the course of the *via Appia*.

One last hope: destruction of old roads is going on apace, with major schemes involving new alignments[33] (for example, the Roman road from Cambrai to Amiens, cut through by the motorway to the north close to Bapaume[34]). Some countries have adopted conservation measures (Switzerland has an archaeologist working on motorway developments). Could not both France and Italy protect some stretches of their ancient roads by turning them into long-distance footpaths or bridlepaths? We have suggested to the Touring Club de France that some of these routes should be waymarked as an experiment.

References

Introduction

1 *Annuaire du Collège de France,* 1960, pp. 376 sq.

2 *Gallic War, IV,* 33.

3 12, 35–7.

4 Paris, Fayard, 1962, p. 113. Comparisons are essential with other burials, cf. R. JOFFROY, 'La tombe à char de Pernant (Aisne)', *Gallia,* 1963, no. 1, p. 1.

5 Cf. G. CHAPOTAT, 'Le char processionnel de la Côte-Saint-André (Isère)', *Gallia,* 1962, no. 1, pp. 33–78.

6 Cf. R. DION, *Annuaire du Collège de France,* 1960, p. 363; 1962, pp. 383–403.

7 Cf. R. SENAC, *Bulletin de l'Association Guillaume Budé (B.A.G.B.),* 4th ser. Dec.1965; cross-checks possible with the early sources of the *Periplus* of Avienus.

8 'Le Danube d'Hérodote', *R.Ph.,* 1968, pp. 7–41. Cf. *Annuaire,* op. cit., p. 1967, p. 461.

9 The importance of these fairs cannot be over-emphasised, their dates following on from one country to the next, with the development of trading exchanges, right until the present day.

10 Cf. R. DION, *Annuaire,* op. cit., 1959, p. 485.

11 Cf. Ch. PICARD, 'Les voies terrestres du commerce hallstattien', *Latomus,* 19, 1960, pp. 409–28.

12 Cf. G. BARRUOL, *Les Peuples préromains du Sud-Est da la Gaule,* Paris, 1969.

13 Cf. the tolls exacted by the Salassi in the Aosta valley. Tacitus pointed out the habit of providing 'escorts' amongst some German tribes (*Germania,* XXI).

14 Cf. D. VAN BERCHEM, 'Du portage au péage, le rôle des cols transalpins dans l'histoire du Valais celtique', *Mus. Helv.,* vol. XIII, 4, 1956, pp. 199–208.

15 *Annuaire,* op. cit., 1968, pp. 503–18.

16 *Germania,* III, 5.

17 *Art et dieux de la Gaule,* Paris, Arthaud, 1969. The author suggests that statues of the Entremont type (third–second century BC) represent the last stage of a statuary extending along the coast on either side of the Rhône, following the land axis of the Heraclean Way, the main link between Italy and Spain.

18 Cf. G. DE.BEER, *Alps and Elephants. Hannibal's March,* London, 1955 and 1967; R. DION, 'La voie héracléenne et l'itineraire transalpin d'Hannibal', *Hommages A. Grenier,* Brussels, I, 1962, pp. 537–43.

19 *Gallic War,* VII, ii, 16.

20 P. LEBEL, 'Gués et voies protohistoriques', *R.A.E.* IV, 1953, p. 353, thinks it is possible to trace back to the Bronze Age. Cf. the distribution map in *Gallia-Préhistoire,* III, 1960 (61), p. 120, by P. Fustier (Origin and movement of bronze in pre-Roman Gaul) who has demonstrated series of finds linking centres in Brittany and the Gironde region, along the Garonne, Loire, Seine and Saône valleys, to casting workshops of which the most important lay beside Lake Bourget. We get some idea of comings and goings in proto-historic times from the tinkers frequently seen before the war in the French countryside and the wandering braziers and iron merchants of the Ancien Régime (the 'Bocains' of Villedieu-les-Poêles). In the same field, much information can be obtained from general surveys of ancient mine-workings, often still in medieval use. Even before the metal roads, there was long-distance traffic, suggested by distribution maps of typical finished work, cf. J.-P. MILLOTTE, *Précis de Protohistoire européenne,* Paris, A. Colin, 1970, pp. 198 sq. The author thinks that the amber road, between the Baltic and the Mycenian world, but with branches to southern Britain and the Rhine and Rhône valleys, dates back to

1500 BC. A thorny problem in protohistory is the connection between routes and megaliths, for example in Brittany. Here it can only be mentioned, cf. R. OLIVIER, *Norois,* Jan.–Mar. 1968, pp. 57-77.

21 Roads leading to the *oppida* are obviously protohistoric.

Chapter 1 Evidence from literature and inscriptions

1 'Les noms latins du chemin et de la rue', *R.E.L.,* 1950, pp. 104-34.

2 Used by AMMIANUS MARCELLINUS, XVIII, 6, 10; RUTILIUS NAMATIANUS, 39; *Theodosian Code,* XV, 3-4.

3 A close examination of Polybius or Tacitus would bring the same conclusions.

4 Some interesting details can be found in this historian, cf. Julian's journey, XVI, ii, 3-8.

5 A quotation from the same *Life* of Tiberius (XXXI) – below – says much about the place that luxury spending occupied in Roman thinking.

6 *Civil War,* I, 3-23.

7 Cf. VIRGIL, *Georgics,* I, 276-86: the ninth day, of ill portent for brigands, was favourable to travellers; PLINY THE ELDER, *Historia Naturalis* XXVIII, 21: Caesar used to utter a magic spell that he thought would preserve him against danger, every time he rode in a vehicle.

8 Cf. descriptions of Italian roads given by travellers in the sixteenth to eighteenth centuries; cf. MONTAIGNE, quoted below, DE BROSSES and others.

9 For these unpleasant features of travelling by road, cf. another text from APULEIUS, *Florida:* 'Let us imagine travellers in a hurry to reach their destination, who have preferred to go on horseback rather than sit in a carriage. It allows them to avoid all sorts of things: the handicap of luggage, ponderous vehicles with slow wheels, jolting over ruts, not to mention piles of stones, projecting tree roots, streams on low ground and steep hills. They have rid themselves of these causes of delay by taking a stout mettlesome horse...' Concerning dust on roads, cf. CICERO, *Ad Atticum,* V, 14, 1: *pulverulenta via;* PLINY THE ELDER, *Historia Naturalis,* XV, 81: dust along busy roads; STATIUS, *Silves,* II, 2, 32 sq. That was why travellers found baths essential. Those who have walked in columns along country roads are well aware of this.

10 For the length of journeys and discomfort of overnight accommodation, cf. SYMMACHUS, XX (XV).

11 An interesting topographical note: villas were seldom very close to the roadside, but rather at a distance of a few hundred metres. This was what agronomists advised. Cf. for example COLUMELLA, *De Re Rustica,* I, 5: 'The neighbourhood of a main road is not a very suitable place to site a farm, as much because of the damage passers-by may do to crops, as because of the frequent calls that may cause inconvenience.'

12 This subject is constantly recurring in Latin literature, cf. PLAUTUS, passim; PROPERTIUS, *Elegies,* III, 16, 1: 'Shall I go off into complete darkness and risk some night-attack?' A commentary on inscriptions can be found in A. MOCSY, 'Latrones Dardaniae', *Acta Antiqua Ac. Sc. Hung.,* XVI, 1968, pp. 351-4: epitaphs mentioning *interfecti a latronibus.* Example of a *praefectus* or *praepositus adversus ladrones, Année épigraphique,* 1968, p. 109.

13 Paris, *S.E.V.P.E.N.,* 1966.

14 No less colourful details of a similar type can be found in journeys described in APULEIUS, *Florida* and PETRONIUS, *Satiricon.*

15 Travellers in modern times have often reflected on this passage. Cf. J. LALANDE, *Voyage d'un Français en Italie fait dans les années 1765 et 1766,* Paris, 1769, VI, p. 398: 'Reading classical authors gives us an interest in the places where these people have lived and is one of the things that most increases our curiosity and pleasure when visiting Italy. Like everyone, I have read Horace' fifth satire, in which he describes his journey from Rome to Brindisi, but I was never able to be very enthusiastic about the travel details. It was when going from Rome to Naples that I had pleasure in rereading Horace's journey.'

16 A town close to Lake Nemi, 16 miles from Rome, that is about 23·7km, the Roman mile being about 1,480m.

17 A metrist of this name is quoted by MARIUS VICTORINUS, (*Gr. lat.,* V, p. 91, 6 Keil). It is not known if he should be identified with Horace's person and also with the author of a poem on the *Marvels of Italy* (Ἰταλικὰ θαύματα), from which STOBAEUS (*Anthologium,* 100, 6) quotes a few lines about a sulphurous spring discovered on Cicero's villa shortly after he died, at Pozzuoli.

18 Town founded by Appius Claudius Caecus, 27 miles from Aricia (39·9km), the starting place for a canal across the Pontine Marshes, ending 16 miles farther on at the Temple of Feronia, close to Terracina.

19 This road ran from Rome to Brindisi. Between Forum Appi and Terracina, it was often eroded or even cut through by torrents coming down from the Apennines, and people preferred to go by water.

20 Note the elevated style of this sentence (OVID,

Metamorphoses, XI, 309: *Nox coelum sparserat astris*); it forms a deliberate contrast with the everyday language of the next few lines: a common device in heroic-comic style.

[21] I do not think we need to look on *nauta* and *viator* as collective nouns, since Horace goes on to say that the boatman (and then one only is meant) unhitches the mule and goes off to sleep. But is *viator* taken in its ordinary meaning and does it signify a pedestrian walking beside the boatman responsible for leading the mule? Or, by giving the word the sense of *vector,* could we apply it to one of the passengers? I incline to the latter view.

[22] The details given about the croaking frogs, thin thrushes and cool evenings and nights point to springtime, when the fourth hour fell between 9 and 10 am.

[23] The canal ended 3 miles from Terracina (4·4km), close to a spring dedicated to an old Italian goddess, protectress of freed slaves and having affinities with Juno.

[24] Volscan name of Terracina.

[25] L. Cocceius Nerva, jurist and deputy consul in 39 BC and probably brother of M. Cocceius Nerva, the emperor's great-grandfather. With Maecenas, he had already negotiated the treaty of Brindisi between Octavius and Antony (40 BC).

[26] C. Fonteius Capito, deputy consul in 33 BC, Antony's legate in Asia. The perfection alluded to by Horace must refer, I think, to the impeccable correctness of his bearing and manners. The perfection is signified by a recognised metaphor, used by sculptors who ran a finger-nail over the marble to make sure that all roughness had been removed.

[27] 13 miles (19·2km) from Terracina.

[28] Formiae, 13 miles from Fundi. The Mamurrae were natives of that town; one of them, a friend of Caesar, is well known through the gory epigrams of CATULLUS: (29; 41; 43; 57; 94; 105; 114 and 115).

[29] Concerning L. Licinius Varro Murena, see *Odes,* II, 10. He was not present, but opened his house to the travellers.

[30] 17 miles (26·6km) from Formiae. After Virgil's death, Plotius Tucca was, in company with Varius, to edit the *Aeneid.*

[31] From Formiae to the Campanian bridge, on the border of Latium and Campania, the distance was 27 miles (39·9km); from the bridge to Capua, 17 miles (25·1km) and from Capua to Caudium, 21 miles (31·1km).

[32] In his *Journey in Sicily* (*Iter Siciliense,* Satire III, v. 117 sq. Marx), Lucilius described two gladiators who insulted each other before fighting.

In the present case, everything is reduced to a battle of words, a favourite sport in Campania, the region where the *Atellana* or *ludus oscus* had originated. The nickname given to Messius means 'cockerel' according to the Glossaries (Κίκιρρος ἀλεκτρυών, says HESYCHIUS II, 481, 2647 Schmidt); Messius played the well-known part of a man disguised as a cockerel in his local comic plays (cf. DIETERICH, *Pulcinella,* Leipzig, 1897, p. 94).

[33] Sarmentus had been the slave of M. Favonius, who was put to death during the proscriptions (scholium to JUVENAL, 5, 3). With the rest of his master's property, he passed into Maecenas' hands, by whom he was freed. But Favonius' widow was still alive.

[34] The reference is not to a rhinoceros, but to a unicorn, described by PLINY (*Historia Naturalis,* XVII, 76) as having a horse's body, a stag's head, an elephant's feet, and, in the middle of the forehead, a black horn two cubits high: clearly a fabulous animal.

[35] Apparently the Campanians frequently bore on their forehead large warts or wens which left scars when removed.

[36] We do not really know what Messius means, if Sarmentus had really been included in Maecenas' share of Favonius property.

[37] Or else: 'In a word, we were a merry company over that meal.' The emphasis in this line repeats the emphasis at the opening.

[38] From Caudium to Beneventum, the distance was 11 miles (16·3km).

[39] Presumably including both him and his house.

[40] Travellers left the *via Appia* at Beneventum, for it went on to Brindisi by way of Venusia and Tarento, whereas they continued towards Barium and the Adriatic coast across the Apulian mountains.

[41] A local wind characteristic of Apulia, as the Iapyx was of Calabria: cf. SENECA, *Naturales Quaestiones.* It is called today the Altino.

[42] 25 miles (37·03km) from Beneventum.

[43] Another rendering would be: 'amid the smoke of a weeping wood'.

[44] The distance quoted (35·5km) suggests the place was *Asculum Apulum,* today Ascoli.

[45] On the water shortage in Apulia, cf. *Odes,* III, 30, 11 and *Epodes,* 3, 16.

[46] On the Aufidus, 35 miles (51·81km) from Asculum.

[47] Or perhaps, 'stony', because of grit in the flour from poor-quality millstones.

[48] According to legend, Diomedes, having been driven from Argos after his return from Troy, reached Aetolia, then Apulia, where he was welcomed by King Daunus and founded several towns.

[49] The distance from Canusium to Rubi (Ruvo) was 23 miles, as much again from Rubi to Barium (Bari), and 37 (54·8km) from Bari to Egnatia (Torre d'Agnazzo).

[50] As there was water at Egnatia, the meaning must be that the inhabitants were *lymphatici,* that is to say the nymphs had disturbed their minds.

[51] Meaning any Jew.

[52] A serious imitation or a parody of LUCRETIUS (v, 82 and VI, 56)?

[53] Egnatia was 31 miles from Brindisi.

[54] This band of territory can be compared to modern 'air corridors'.

[55] The place names and administrative divisions are those of the Early Empire: *Genabum* and not *Aurelianum,* which gave Orléans, (likewise *Avaricum* for Bourges), but the stages are already calculated in leagues and no longer in miles. Besides, the map shows the loss of the Rhine right bank, which took place later than 256, and has the late names, *Francia* and *Alamannia*; these appear to be later part corrections, proven by the survival of names that disappeared at that time; finally a precise reference to the three capitals of Rome, Antioch and Constantinople takes us to 337–38. Christian glosses reveal other modifications. The *Table* carries a number of descriptive legends, for example: *Susa, fines exercitus Syriaci et commercium Barbarorum.*

[56] There were certainly earlier maps which could have served as models (Eratosthenes). For the successive copies and variants, cf. J. R. WARTENA, *In leiding op een Uitgave der Tabula Peutingeriana,* Amsterdam, 1927 (according to allusions to historical events and comparisons with other pictorial evidence). In that author's view, some maps were distorted because additional names and roads of late date had to be included.

[57] An idea to which R. DION has constantly returned in his lectures at the Collège de France, cf. *Annuaire* from 1959 to 1968. As a result, no exact topographical meaning need be given to the location and bearing of the various entries.

[58] Since stages between *mansiones* or *mutationes,* but not between *civitas*-capitals, were usually homogeneous on the same itinerary, it is right, when one distance is out of place in a series, to alter a letter so as to obtain a figure of the same order of magnitude.

[59] In his *Fossatum Africae,* Paris–Algiers, 1949, and in an article: 'Réseau routier de commandement, d'administration et d'exploitation de la zone arrière du *limes* de Numidie', *Limes-studien,* Vorträge des 3. Intern. Limes-Kongr., Bâle, 1959, pp. 19–33.

[60] Contrariwise, the *Table* can mix up various courses of a single road: the routes may have varied according to season, return journeys, direction of the sun and so on.

[61] *Berytus,* 1949, p. 91.

[62] It is usually thought that each bend represents one: when the name of the station, through lack of space, had to be placed higher than the bend to which it corresponded, the scribe then marked the distance.

[63] Like stage-coach itineraries marking Fossard, but not Montereau. When a road guide shows a place on two itineraries, there is a fork. The termini at the end of itineraries are chosen precisely because of their value as cross-roads.

[64] There is another point of view expressed by R. ETIENNE, *Bordeaux antique,* Bordeaux, 1962, p. 61: the *Table* is said to show long-distance trading routes using valleys separated by narrow gaps crossed by portage. It would have incorporated earlier special road lists, giving merchants information on the trading roads leading from transit ports into the interior of the country.

[65] A. and M. LEVI, *Itineraria picta. Contributo allo studio della Tubula Peutingeriana,* Rome, L'Erma di Bretschneider, 1967.

[66] The size depends on the available space. A close look at recent maps shows that 'cartographic artists' like filling empty spaces.

[67] The *Itinerarium provinciarum* was completed by an *Itinerarium maritimum* of later date, giving distances in stadia from European ports of the Western Mediterranean to North Africa. A sea route is marked from Rome to Arles.

[68] The omission of an important site might mean that it was destroyed at the time of the first invasions.

[69] Regarding the identification of stations, it will be noted that the *Itinerary* often gives an example of a road going through a dwelling site: *in medio Salerno,* but confusion between *mansiones* and *mutationes* is frequent.

[70] 'L'annone militaire dans l'Empire romain au III siècle', *Mém. S.N.A.F.,* 1936, pp. 117–201.

[71] Which would explain why some distances in Gaul are reckoned in miles, others in leagues.

[72] In the view of E. KIRSTEN, *Erdkunde,* 13, 1959, p. 414, an isolated extract like this that did not involve public itineraries could be simply explained as the plan for a journey.

[73] *Inscr. de Bordeaux,* II, pp. 203 sq.

[74] In 679–82, Arnulf, bishop of Gaul, made a pilgrimage to the Holy Land and the East, of which he has left an account, dedicated to the king of Northumbria. From the thirteenth century onward, we have records of a pilgrims' itinerary from London to Jerusalem . . .

[75] U. SCHILLINGEN-HAEFELE (*Bonner Jahr-*

bücher CLXIII, 1963, pp. 238–51) believes that the source was on the other hand an itinerary that did not show the courses of roads, which would explain the confusion between stations on neighbouring routes.

76 We should realise the importance of breaks in the itineraries caused by waterways, which had to be crossed more often by ferry or a ford than over a bridge. This was a very significant factor for travellers until recent days.

77 There must clearly be no confusion with the geographical or sea mile, one-sixtieth part of a degree of a global great circle (1·852m), or with the English mile (1,609m). In the texts, *lapis* may signify mile.

78 The Greek foot varied from 0·27 to 0·35m and the length of the stadium from 162 to 210m, being 185·5m in Magna Graecia.

79 Cf. ESPERANDIEU, 4035, 5268, p. 451, 7725.

80 Like the finely expressed thought of SIDONIUS, *Carmina*, 24 (farewell to his book): *vetustis columnis nomen Caesareum viret*: (the old road along which) Caesar's name grows green on ancient columns – a reference to an old military road with milestones along it bearing the emperor's name.

81 Cf. ISIDORUS of Seville, *Metrol. Script.*, II, 137, 15: *stadialis ager habet passus CXXV, id est pedes DCXXV, cuius mensura octies computata miliarium facit qui constat V milibus pedum.*

82 Cf. PLUTARCH, *C. Gracchus*, VII, 2.

83 The total increases each year. Cf. for example for 1968 *Année épigraphique*, pp. 13, 146, 309, 313, 396, 496. For Gaul, cf. indexes of *Gallia*.

84 Distance stones can also occur in other places and at other periods, cf. STRABO, XV, 1, 50 (708) (after Megasthenes): in the kingdom of the Indies, columns are erected every ten stadia to indicate forks and distances.

85 Or hammered. Examples of reused milestones ('palimpsests') *C.I.L.*, VIII, 10023 = D 151 (Tiberius); VIII, 22567 (Septimius Severus–Caracalla); VIII, 10021, 10047 = D 488 (Maximus). There are also cases of additional lettering, when roads were repaired.

86 As a rule, the town or settlement boundary, cf. M. BESNIER, 'Le point de départ des grandes routes de la Gaule romaine à Lyon', *B.A.C.T.H.*, XLI, 1923, pp. 75–96. In the third century, place names could be in various cases: nominative, accusative, locative, ablative.

87 An Egyptian example: *Année épigraphique*, 1925, p. 95.

88 Examples of equivalents between leagues and miles on milestones: *C.I.L.*, XIII, 9065–7; a milestone with distance in leagues at Soulosse-St-Elophe, *Année épigraphique*, 1968, p. 313.

89 One of the oldest mentions of this unit seems to have been made by Posidonius: Luern of the Averni tribe was having enclosures constructed for festivities, measuring 12 stadia along each side (*FHG*, III, p. 261).

90 Cf. AMMIANUS MARCELLINUS (XV, ii, 17): 'At that point (where the Saône joins the Rhône) lies the frontier of the Gauls and from there roads are measured no longer in miles, but in leagues', which echoes MELA, II, 78, describing the confluence of the two rivers as the beginning of Gaul (cf. STRABO, IV, 6; II, 208) because thereafter the roads are reckoned in leagues, and also the *Peutinger Table* which mentions close to Lugdunum: *usque hic leugas.*

91 AMMIANUS MARCELLINUS (XVI, 12) gives the equation: *quarta leuga signabatur et decima, id est unum et viginti millia passuum*, that is, 14 Gallic leagues for 21 miles.

92 *C.I.L.*, I², 638 = X, 6950.

93 *Année épigraphique*, 1968, p. 607.

94 As in the case of the *via Domitia* restored in 3 BC: 11 milestones of Augustus, plus 15 of Tiberius, 20 of Claudius and about a dozen of Antoninus.

95 Cf. H. ROLLAND, 'Un nouveau milliaire de l'Itinéraire de Peutinger', *C.R.A.I.* Jan.–Mar. 1962, pp. 676–80.

96 We have found survivals of this kind in Italy in the case of stones acting as limits of centuriation and often replaced by wayside oratories. Old maps, which show crosses, may help to relocate milestones.

97 *B.C.T.H.*, 1943–45, p. 567.

98 Could careful excavation possibly locate the foundation deposits, the buried charcoal, mentioned by the surveyors?

99 The most recent study, whose results we have used, has come from J. HEURGON, 'La date des gobelets de Vicarello', *R.E.A.*, 54, 1952, p. 39 (quoting previous research); cf. R. THOUVENOT, *Essai sur la province romaine de Bétique*, Paris, 1940, p. 479 and L. MAS GOMES, 'Los vasos Apolinares', *Museo de la Ciudad de Sabadell*, III, 1947, 5.

100 *Annuaire*, 1965, pp. 475 sq. Cf. supra.

101 Cf. the milestone standing in front of the mosque at Cordoba; cf. *C.I.L.* II, 4701, 4703, 4712, 4715, 4716.

102 There is a possible allusion to the Columns of Hercules.

103 We may compare present-day arguments on the course of a motorway.

104 This phenomenon is well known in Gaul, whereby there was a general disappearance in the early Empire of the names of the native peoples, which reappear later: Caesarodunum–Turones–Tours.

105 The longer distances on the fourth goblet seem

to have been the result of copying errors (Susa is also left out) rather than to a detour. The first three goblets have errors in figures, wrongly transcribed lines, omissions and alterations in place names.

106 Following J. HEURGON, in *C.R.A.I.,* 1949, pp. 125–8, *Gallia,* 1969, p. 103 and *Monuments Piot,* 46, 1952, pp. 94–115.

107 Cf. J. D. COWEN, I. A. RICHMOND, in *Archaeologia Aeliana.* Soc. of Antiq. of Newcastle-upon-Tyne, 4th se., XII, 1935, p. 310 (*C.I.L.,* VII, 1291; J. M. C. TOYNBEE, *Art in Roman Britain,* London, 1962, p. 174). The object appears to date from the middle of the second century AD.

108 Thought has also been given to the possibility of offerings made by pilgrims at a road station close to a cult site.

109 *C.I.L.,* XIII, 3497.

110 Cf. M. BESNIER, in *Bull. hispanique,* 1924, pp. 4–26 = *Année épigraphique,* 1921, pp. 6–9.

111 *C.I.L.,* XIII, 9158. Cf. A. LANCIER, 'La pierre milliaire de Tongres', *Bull. Com. Hist. Nord,* XXII, 1900, pp. 135–50; H. BAILLIEN, 'Dokumenten over de Romeinse mijlpaal te Tongeren', *Limburg,* XXXVIII, 1959, pp. 1–10.

112 *C.I.L.,* XIII, 2681c. Three fragments are known. In this respect, we may recall the map of the Roman world painted under a portico at the Maenian schools in the Autun university (EUMENIUS, *Pro restaurandis scholis,* 20).

113 J. VANNERUS, 'L'indicateur routier de Macquenoise', *Bull. Ac. roy. Belgique,* Cl. Lettres, XXXVI, 1951, pp. 468–98 (regarded as recent, after an ancient original); P. LEBEL, *R.A.E.,* III, 1952, pp. 43–51: J. HEGLY, in *Bull. Soc. arch. champenoise,* 1959, pp. 1–8.

114 In the view of A. DEMAN, 'Die Strassenkarte von Momignies', *Altertum,* XI, 1965, pp. 115–24 (résumé *R.B.Ph.,* XLI, 1963, p. 1326) it is a copy, dating perhaps from the early seventeenth century, of an original of the second half of the second century AD. See also M. REUTHER, 'Die Tontafelkarte von Momignies im Lichte der historischen Kartographie', *Altertum,* XIII, 1967, pp. 50–65.

115 G. PONTIROLI, 'Rinvenimenti archeol. fatti in Cremona', *Boll. Stor. Cremonese,* XIX, 1954 (55), p. 169.

116 *C.I.L.,* XII, 5732.

117 According to H. J. HEURGON, 'La fixation des noms de lieux en latin d'après les itinéraires routiers', *R.Ph.,* XXVI, 1952, pp. 169–78. Cf. C. PALLU DE LESSERT, 'La syntaxe des routiers romains et les déformations des noms de lieu dans l'Afrique romaine', *M.S.N.A.F.,* 1905, pp. 115–38.

118 It is known that inscriptions were cut with greater or lesser care according to their official status.

119 Cf. J. HUBERT, *Les Routes de France,* Paris, 1959. Medieval studies may produce information, as for example J. RICHARD, 'Passages de Saône aux XIIe et XIIIe siècles', *Annales de Bourgogne,* 1950, p. 245 (reuse of a Gallic road adopted by the Romans). We should note that the existence of a Merovingian mint at a particular point may fit in with a surviving ancient road.

120 It should be possible to establish relative dating in the hagiography of each region.

121 Cf. P. GRAS, 'Un itinéraire bourguignon au Ve siècle', *Annales de Bourgogne,* 1964, p. 185. Another example: we learn from the *Life* of St Quentin that his body was thrown into the Somme after his martyrdom (fourth century): *iuxta fluvium . . . ubi transit agger publicus qui venit de Ambianensium civitate.*

122 Cf. E. RENARDET, *Légendes, contes et traditions du pays lingon,* Paris, 1970, p. 102 sq.

123 Cf. J. LE GOFF, *La Civilisation de l'Occident médiéval,* Paris, Arthaud, 2nd ed. 1967, pp. 172 sq.

124 This aspect has been taken up again by R. Louis, who has shown (cf. *De l'histoire à la légende: Girart, comte de Vienne dans les chansons de geste,* Auxerre, 1947) that epic legends were centred on ancient cemeteries, especially those alongside Roman roads, like the Alyscamps at Arles. It is known that in Paris the legend of the 'Tombe-Issoire' (and the street named after it) perpetuates the memory of a Gallo-Roman burial ground lying beside the main road to Orléans. For the east of France, there are allusions to roads in the geste of Garin le Lorrain.

125 And also in the case of the Cistercians, Templars and Knights of Malta. Temples, commanderies, hospitals ('Maison-Dieu'), leper houses, and the like frequently are found along Roman roads in the same way as place names drawn from the healer-saints (St Ladre = Lazare, St Roch, St Sébastien, Ste Madeleine, Ste Marthe).

126 Cf. R. OURSEL, *Les Pélerins du Moyen Age,* Paris, Fayard, 1963.

127 Y. BOTTINEAU, *Les Chemins de Saint-Jacques,* Paris, Arthaud, 1964; cf. also P. FUSTIER, op. cit., pp. 152, 154: the local branch roads bringing the pilgrims together were secondary Roman roads that had often followed pre-Roman routes.

128 Cf. supra, the Heracles legend in the case of protohistory.

129 Cf. J. BEDIER, 'Les chansons de geste et les routes d'Italie', *Romania,* XXXVI, 1907, pp. 161, 337; 1908, p. 47, which inspired the present text.

130 Play of words on local place names or the result of drawing conclusions from ruins: thus, Charlemagne was supposed to have built a stone gate-

way, perhaps a remnant of the Roman town of Fidentia, at the church of Donino, on the *via Aemilia*. Donino was one of the patrons of the 'roumieux'.

131 Cf. the *Voyages de Villamont,* Lyons, 1606 (with a guide to the roads to Hierusalem, Rome, Naples, Loreto and Egypt) etc.

132 A doubly erroneous historical reference: the title *Itinerarium Antonini Augusti* dates from Caracalla (212–17) and the *Geography* is by Claudius Ptolemy (cf. supra), who had no connection with the Ptolemaic dynasty. But Estienne's intention is the same as that of the early itineraries, offering one route amongst several. In the sixteenth century as in antiquity, cartography came after these road lists.

133 The stages were 6 to 7 × 2 leagues per day (double for riders).

134 Cf. Sir GEORGE FORDHAM, *Les Routes de France. Etude bibliographique sur les cartes routières et les guides routiers, 1552–1850,* Paris, 1929 (cf. *Bull. section de Géographie,* 1919, pp. 213–55).

135 Written in 1580, but discovered only in 1770. The pagination used here is that of the edition by Ch. Dédéyan, Paris, Les Belles Lettres, 1946.

136 Cf. in the case of the Alps, what Strabo wrote of the Salassi: 'Their brigandry caused great harm to travellers going over their territory to cross the mountains. So, when Decimus Brutus fled from Modena, they made him pay one drachma per head for himself and his men.'

137 Cf. R. AGACHE, 'Archéologie aérienne de la Somme', *Bulletin no. 6 de la Soc. de Préhist. du Nord,* Amiens, 1964.

138 Cf. PSEUDO-ARISTOTLE, *De mirabilibus auscultis,* 85, quoted supra.

139 IV, 6, 6.

140 IV, 6, 11.

141 Concerning the difficulty of the passage across the Apennines, cf. TITUS-LIVY, XXI, 58 '(at the first signs of spring), while Hannibal was crossing the Apennines, such a violent storm arose that it exceeded almost all the horrors of the Alps (rain, wind, hail, snow) . . . Many men, many horses and seven of the elephants that had survived the battle of the Trebia died there.' TACITUS, *Histories,* III, 59: 'A severe winter gave the army a harsh test on crossing the Apennines and these troops . . . although their columns were not disrupted, had much trouble in overcoming the snows.'

142 126, 5–6 Ravenna. *Inde navigatur Septem Maria Altinum usque* (lagoon navigation). There were also ships on the rivers and canals (many literary references: CATULLUS, 4; STRABO, V, 1, 11, 217c; PLINY THE ELDER, *Historia Naturalis,* III, 16, 118; SIDONIUS APOLLINARIUS,

Letters, I, 5; CASSIODORUS, IV, 45, and epigraphs (colleges of *nautae*).

143 For haulage along the Tiber in Roman times, cf. J. LE GALL, *Le Tibre, fleuve de Rome dans l'Antiquité,* Paris, P.U.F., 1953, pp. 257 sq. and index.

144 Similar observation by DE BROSSES, VII, 1, 82: 'We cross the Po on a ferry which somewhat resembles a bridge of moving boats.'

145 Cf. place names: Le Péage (toll), (La) Chambre/Chéméré/Chemery (from *camera,* customs posts), and likewise, those signifying: – guard posts: La Garde, La Bastide, La Tour, La Maison des Gendarmes; – type and destination of traffic and nationality of traders: chemin Brabant, des Allemands, des Lorrains, des Français, tracks (carreyres and drailles) used for transhumance, salt routes (chemins saulniers).

146 For example a charter of 1274 transferring fiefs at St-Riquier: 'From the lazar-house at Wirench as far as the Authie, passing along the Brunehaut causeway'. A charter of 1205 issued by the lord of Douriez mentions land lying *iuxta calceiam Brunehaut.* The commune charter of Rue in 1210 establishes the limits of the town-outskirts *ad calceiam.* The official examinations fixing communal boundaries (about 1815–30) were in the same tradition. Commune records reveal many disputes about paths.

147 Under Louis XVIII, the minister of the interior had requested 'the precise documentation in all departments of monuments and antiquities in them'.

148 Cf. the communications made by Father F. de DAINVILLE to the Colloque international sur les cols des Alpes (Bourg, 1969; Orléans, 1971), and to the Colloque international sur la cartographie (Paris, 1970); Tours, 1972). The most useful documents from our point of view include the road plans of France (*Atlas de Trudaine*), drawn from 1745 to 1780, together with remarks made on the back.

Chapter 2 The Archaeology of Roman roads

1 *De Condicionibus agrorum,* ed. Lachmann, p. 146, 1; ed. Thulin, p. 111, 1.

2 For example, roads built in Gaul by Agrippa (16–13 BC), in Dalmatia-Pannonia by Tiberius (6–9 AD), in the Rhine and Danube basins by Claudius and in Asia Minor by the Flavians.

3 *Historia Naturalis,* XVIII, 111.

4 Quoted by the *Digest,* VIII, 3, 1.

5 This width was needed because four-wheeled waggons had no pivoting fore-carriage. Cf. ibid., 8: the *viae* allowed two vehicles to pass abreast. To this width were added strips along both sides, belonging to the public domain and edged by small boundary stones, for pedestrians and pack

animals. The *actus* was 4ft wide, the *iter* two and the *semita* one.

[6] Quoted by Hyginus, *Constituo Limitum,* ed. Lachmann, p. 194, 9; ed. Thulin, p. 157, 9.

[7] *De Limitibus,* ed. Lachmann, p. 111, 9; ed. Thulin, p. 71, 3.

[8] *Historia Naturalis,* XVII, 169.

[9] Paris, P.U.F., 1953.

[10] Cf. PLINY THE ELDER, *Historia Naturalis,* XXXI, 89: salt was highly esteemed as the name *via Salaria* shows, so called, because the Sabines had a treaty right to bring their salt along it.

[11] *M.E.F.R.,* 25, 1905, pp. 203–328.

[12] But the gates in city walls were not in every case necessarily the departure point for roads.

[13] Cf. PROPERTIUS, *Elegies,* IV, 7, 81–6: Cynthia is to be buried close to the road and its sounds: 'May my epitaph be short and may it be readable by the horseman galloping out of town!' Cf. PLINY THE ELDER: the tomb of Thessalus on the Appia (*Historia Naturalis,* XXIX, 9), the funeral pyre of a tame bird two miles from Rome along the Appia (X, 122); PLINY THE YOUNGER, *Letters,* VII, 29: funerary monument to Pallas on the *via Tiburtina.*

[14] *Satires,* III, v. 235.

[15] *Epigrams,* XII, 57.

[16] Pliny the Elder (*Historia Naturalis,* XIX, 23) observed that the dictator Caesar had the *via Sacra* draped in linen-cloth from his house as far as the slope up to the Capitol – a procedure which must have made it look like an Eastern bazaar.

[17] PLINY THE ELDER, *Historia Naturalis,* III, 66.

[18] XV, 43.

[19] In *M.E.F.R.,* 1965, pp. 349 sq.

[20] One of the advantages of Greek cities was tree-planting. In the fourth century, Carthage still retained this aspect: the *Anonymi Orbis Descriptio* shows the city taking pride in its orderly streets and squares, with trees planted along its straight perimeter roads.

[21] *C.I.L.,* CXVI, 1598.

[22] *C.I.L.,* XIV, 2922.

[23] *C.I.L.,* I, 206 (before 43 BC). More attention should be paid to perimeter-roads around towns.

[24] *Historia Augusta:* Hadrian (XXI) and Marcus Aurelius (XXIII) forbade vehicles and riders from entering towns.

[25] For the Early Empire, cf. *C.I.L.,* VIII, 7046 at Cirta: in the second century the town had to have statues removed that were impeding traffic. *Digest,* XLIII, 10, 2: Papinian (praetorium prefect of Septimius Severus) had to forbid the digging of holes in city streets; ibid., XLIII, 10, 4: 'The aediles will take care that nobody puts anything in front of shops, so that a vehicle can always pass, exceptions being made for fullers who are drying their cloth and wrights called outside by their trade.'

[26] *Theodosian Code,* XV, 1, 39.

[27] *Justinian Code,* VIII, 2, 20.

[28] II, 35 (96).

[29] VARRO, *De Lingua latina,* V, 143.

[30] *Ad Aen.* I, 422.

[31] *C.I.L.,* XIII, 2681c.

[32] Cf. *B.A.C.,* 1922, 5.

[33] *I.L.S.,* 8156.

[34] *Elegies,* III, 16, 25; cf. IV, 7, 4.

[35] *B.A.C.,* 1942, 95.

[36] Cf. pp.   and   .

[37] *Historia Naturalis,* XXXI, 42.

[38] Ibid., XVIII, 258.

[39] Cf. SUETONIUS, *Augustus,* XCIV, 11, the wood at the fourth stone along the via Campana.

[40] ESPERANDIEU, 4043, 5138, 5268, p. 449, 5299.

[41] We saw in note 20 that avenues in some Hellenistic cities were lined by trees.

[42] Cf. *Année épigraphique,* 1968, p. 451.

[43] Cf. the Domazan altar on which a Dioscouros appears as an ostler. After a long journey people did not fail to make an offering *Fortunae Bonae Reduci,* cf. *Année épigraphique,* 1968, p. 233, or to the *Deus Rediculus.* Note, too, the formula of good luck on inscriptions: *pro itu et reditu* with two pairs of footprints facing opposite directions.

[44] *Florida,* I (exordium of a speech by Apuleius in a town where he is passing through).

[45] Ed. Lachmann, p. 180: *Decumanus maximus et cardo maximus a civitate oriuntur et per quattuor portas in morem castrorum ut viae amplissimae limitibus diriguntur.*

[46] *C.I.L.,* XII, 5554.

[47] Cf. A. PIGANIOL, *Les Documents cadastraux de la colonie romaine d'Orange,* Paris, Editions du C.N.R.S., 1962, p. 236.

[48] The technical term is: *munire viam.*

[49] *Silves,* IV, 3, v. 40–55.

[50] In *B.S.A.F.,* 1959, pp. 176–86.

[51] The word has provided the French 'gond' (hinge). These projecting stones were used to reinforce the road edges, perhaps to help riders in mounting and to guide travellers in snow or sandstorms and can be spotted mainly in North Africa and sometimes Gaul (P. LEBEL, in *R.A.E.,* 1951, p. 192: *gomphi* were still to be seen in the eighteenth century near Langres, along Agrippa's road; also between Mâcon and Autun several have come to light).

[52] Elsewhere similar boundary stones, alternately flat and semi-circular, have been noticed, placed edge to edge. Close to Itri, the paving on the Appia (P. FUSTIER, in *R.E.A.,* 1960, p. 95) is lined by two rows of prismatic limestone blocks, measuring 1ft each way and spaced irregularly.

53 Check can be made by reaction to an acid.
54 This passage can be paralleled by the words *lapidibus perpetuis*, used in the *lex Julia municipalis* of 49 to describe road-surfacing. Some information can be gleaned elsewhere, cf. VITRUVIUS, x, 2: use of stone-rollers to smooth out paths around *palaestrae*.
55 XIV, 6–11.
56 Paris, Picard, 1968.
57 And, of course, the importance of training a technical staff: engineers and foremen.
58 F. ULRIX (in *Latomus*, 1963, p. 157) believes he has discovered how the course of a Roman road was set out. From high points, stakes were aligned every Roman mile, sometimes there being a discrepancy through difficulty in sighting or error by the surveyors, so giving a slight zig-zag, with the bends often one mile apart. This seems reasonable, but the rest of his argument is hypothetical. By a system of triangulation, it is claimed that branch roads (*deverticula*) forked off at 60°, with others midway along at right angles to the main road, the whole forming equilateral triangles with sides of one mile in length. On the undoubted relationship between roads and land-holdings, cf. infra.
59 VIII, 17: 'All were obliged to share in the work . . . Nobody was exempt.' This text shows that, in the phase of colonial exploitation following the conquest, there were administrative abuses (to the cost of construction and upkeep were added soldiers' billeting and various customs duties and tolls) and business abuses as well. According to records from early excavations, labourers were organised in chain-gangs. From legal sources in the Late Empire, we learn that provincials were always held responsible for repairs to roads, bridges, relay posts and road stations serving the imperial post. Senators and veterans were exempt. With the authority of the emperor, taxes could be paid in kind.
60 *C.I.L.*, VIII, 22786, a, f, k.
61 Cf. L. LESCHI, in *B.C.T.H.*, 1943–45, p. 325.
62 Cf. TACITUS, *Annals*, I, 20: maniples sent to Nauport for work on roads, bridges and so on.
63 SUETONIUS, *Tiberius*, 2, 5.
64 CICERO, *De Legibus*, III, 3, 7.
65 Following information in VITRUVIUS, *Architectura*, VII, 1; and PLINY THE ELDER, *Historia Naturalis*, XXXVI, 25, 184–87.
66 This was an important concept. In Syria, for example, where the local black basalt was found to be too hard, the roads were given a more elastic build-up.
67 Cf. LIVY, XLI, 27, 5.
68 An example is provided by PLINY THE YOUNGER, (*Letters*, II, 17): to go to his villa near Laurentum, he took 'a lane that was in part gravelled and was something of a hindrance to vehicles'.
69 *Digest*, XLIII, 11, 1, 2; LIV, 41, 27.
70 Cf. R. AGACHE, 'Presence de fossés parallèles à certaines voies romaines . . .', *Bull. de la Soc. des Antiquaires de Picardie*, 3rd number, 1968, pp. 258–64. The triangular shape of the *pala* (spade) may enable Roman ditches to be identified by their profile. The function of the ditches was sometimes assisted by banks that prevented surface drainage from flowing onto the road. In some cases, the road structure involved ditches along the axial line itself, cf. *R.E.A.*, 1956, p. 290: the highway from Rheims to Trier: (Fig 13): the stony metalling rests on three ditches, smaller than the side ditches and filled with clay, sand and gravel. This substantial build-up was intended to prevent the road surface from giving way at critical points (the centre and the edges). The longitudinal furrows and the rough foundation-layer kept the overlying road material in place.
71 These services established by law were long respected (cf. the formula *Iter populo debetur*) and explain how the *limites* of centuriation have surprisingly managed to survive.
72 IV, 1, 5.
73 STATIUS, *Silves*, IV, 23–40, already shows how roads affected the landscape. A motorway under construction is a spectacular sight from the air.
74 But care is needed. Some hollow-ways may be Roman roads robbed of material for reuse elsewhere (surface metalling suffers in particular). Flagstones may have left imprints of their presence. There are cases of roads which have deliberately been given over to arable, after the surfacing has been used perhaps for flagging yards. Other hollow-ways are more ancient still (like the Etruscan ones, in Central Italy). A hollow-road is frequently seen in a pass through a range of hills. Sometimes the depression is justified because it has found a firmer foundation.
75 For example, close to Itri, on the *Appia* (*R.E.A.*, 1960, p. 95), P. Fustier has noticed lying across the paving transverse ribs of long granite slabs in the line of an arc with concave face downhill. The slabs project 15cm above the road surface and are spaced out 25–30cm apart so as to prevent the flat top layer of flagstones from slipping down the slope and also to help the run-off of rainwater. It was also possible to cover slippery or irregular paving with soil.
76 Cf. G. GOURY, 'Observations sur une déviation de route à l'époque gallo-romaine', *C.R.A.I.*, 1941, pp. 524–30. Slight deviations may often have been connected with road decay: a traveller went alongside a section full of ruts or went round

a bramble-covered ruin, a fact which may explain the strange zigzags in the boundaries of land-holdings.

77 *R.E.A.*, 1960, p. 95.

78 MISSON (*Voyage d'Italie*, II, 11) is struck by the steepness of slopes tackled by Roman roads. In the nineteenth century, on the other hand, when gentler slopes were sought, the radius of curves was increased and zigzags were used to climb hills, while embankments became common to avoid constructional engineering and roadways were narrowed.

79 On an *agger* the road was above water in case of floods. In snowy districts these causeways have been served as guides, in the same way as the *gomphi* (cf. P. SALAMA). They also gave a position of vantage to soldiers on the march.

80 Of course, this technique has been widely used to reinforce foundations on shifting soil: 'pala-fitte' (stakes on which Spina was built).

81 J. MERTENS, in *Industrie*, no. 10, Oct. 1955, pp. 38–42, with illustrations.

82 *Nieuws Bulletin Koninkl. Nederlandse Oudheim. Bond*, 6th s. II, 1949, p. 191.

83 *Arch. hist. Gironde*, III, p. 497.

84 *Gallic War*, VII, 57–58: 'Noticing that there was a continuous marsh . . . Camulogenus made a stand there. Labienus tried at first to move up mantlets, fill in the marsh with hurdles and soil, then build a causeway' (see also VIII, 14, 4: *pontibus palude constrata*).

85 I, 63, cf. 56 and 61, 2.

86 Cf. G. MATHERAT, *R.A.*, 1936, I, pp. 53–91; 1937, I, pp. 33–62; cf. J. HARMAND, *B.S.A.F.*, 1959, p. 263.

87 R. MOUTERDE, A. POIDEBARD, *Le 'Limes' de Chalcis*, Paris, 1945, p. 43.

88 A. POIDEBARD, *La Trace de Rome dans le désert de Syrie*, 1934, p. 31. The road in question is earlier than 175 or even 162, and was later repaired by Commodus, Septimius Sevcrus and Diocletian.

89 The low-relief feature can be seen after rain as an even strip of greenery.

90 Cf. A. SIAT, A. STIEBER, R. WEIL, 'Nature pétrographique des matériaux d'empierrement d'une voie romaine à Dambach-la-Ville', *C.A.A.H.*, x, 1966, pp. 69–71.

91 *FA*, v, 4889: 6 layers; VII, 4432; XIV, 5115, 5118, 5121. *Archéologie*, 1961–62, p. 517.

92 *R.A.E.*, 1950, p. 175; 1955, p. 70; 1962, p. 124; *R.A.E.*, 1960, p. 95; 1961, p. 282.

93 Cf. a rescript from Arcadius and Honorius to Asterius, count of the East (397): materials coming from demolishing pagan temples will be used for the upkeep of bridges, highways, aqueducts and walls.

94 *Cahiers d'archéologie et d'histoire du Berry*, 1969; other examples: G. GOURY, in *C.R.A.I.*, 1941, pp. 524–30; *Gallia*, XVIII, 1960–62, p. 339, etc.

95 v, 12.

96 SYMMACHUS, *Relationes*, XXVI, 4.

97 *Gallic War*, IV, 17. The technical achievement of building this prestigious bridge was outweighed by its importance politically (it was aimed at the Barbarians' morale) and as a religious symbol (victory over the river god); it was frequently imitated, cf. TACITUS, *Annals*, I, 49: Germanicus throwing a bridge across the Rhine before a campaign.

98 LIVY, I, 33, 6.

99 Ibid., II, 10.

100 v, 40, 8.

101 *De Lingua latina*, 5, 83.

102 Cf. STATIUS, *Silves*, II, 1, 175–8.

103 DIO CASSIUS, LIII, 2; against this text can be set coins showing a bridge with arches on it that bear statues or trophies and the legend: *Quod viae munitae sunt*.

104 LIVY, XL, 51.

105 JUVENAL, *Satires*, VI, 32.

106 *Historia Augusta, Heliogabalus*, XVII.

107 HORACE, *Satires*, II-III, 31–8.

108 Cf. AMMIANUS MARCELLINUS, XXVI, 3.

109 *Panegyric of Gratian, Laudes*, III, 9.

110 This expression (which recalls Meschacébé's bison in Chateaubriand's 'Atala') is a reminder of the commonly depicted river god and reflects the actual topography of the Rhine valley, as Dion has shown (*Annuaire du Collège de France*, 1964, pp. 409 sq.).

111 Symacchus, cf. note 96.

112 SUETONIUS, *Nero*, XVI.

113 This town had several bridges, like Beneventum, Poli and Quiliano Finale.

114 Brive, Briare = defended bridge in Celtic.

115 *Gallic War*, II, 5, 6.

116 Ibid., VII, 11. Concerning the Gallic bridge at Orléans, cf. J. SOYER, 'A propos d'une variante des *Commentaires* de César', *Bull. Soc. archéol. Orléanais*, 1923). The siting of Gallic bridges differs from that of Roman ones.

117 Ibid., VII, 34.

118 Ibid., VIII, 27.

119 Criticised by P.-M. DUVAL in *R.E.A.*, 1965, p. 446.

120 Cf. *Gallic War*, I, 7.

121 Cf. TACITUS, *Annals*, IV, 73.

122 *Histories*, IV, 77.

123 Concerning the stone bridge at Lerida (Roman Ilerda), cf. CAESAR, *Gallic War*, I, 41, 2; 43, 1.

124 VIII, 4.

125 SUETONIUS, *Caligula*, 19; DIO CASSIUS, IX, 17.

[126] TACITUS, *Annals,* XIII, 7.

[127] *C.I.L.,* III, 12218.

[128] Cf. famous bridges mentioned in PLINY THE ELDER: *Historia Naturalis:* III, 101: bridge planned between Italy and Greece (Pyrrhus, Varro), IV, 1, 4: 1,000ft bridge over the Acheron; IV, 75: Xerxes' bridge of boats over the Hellespont, Darius' bridge over the Bosphorus; V, 85; Euphrates bridge; V, 86: Seleucus' bridge between Apamea and Zeugma; V, 128: bridge linking Alexandria to its pharos; VI, 13: the 120 bridges over the Phasis. In Gaul, Gregory of Tours mentions the Juvisy bridge (582).

[129] STRABO, IV, 1, 11.

[129a] No arches of Roman bridges survive in Britain, but abutments and piers may be seen at Willowford (Cumberland) and Chesters (Northumberland) on Hadrian's Wall. For a list of bridges known to have existed in Roman Britain, see the appendix to D. P. Dymond, 'Roman Bridges on Dere Street', *Archaeological Journal* CXVIII, 1961, 136–64.

[130] When looking for fords, which are always productive of small finds and coins, the course of the road will be a vital factor (at those river intersections, crossed at an angle, where a meandering waterway can have caused silting: cf. R. GAUCHAT, *Mém. Comm. Antiq. Côte-d'Or,* XXIV, 1954–58, pp. 133–9). The roadway, safeguarded on its upstream side by a bank, became narrow as it reached the ford, which was paved with flagstones or with heavy slabs held in place by tree trunks. Old maps can be as useful as air photography, vital here. Watch should be kept at periods when the water is low or dredging is taking place.

[131] Cf. PLINY THE ELDER, *Historia Naturalis,* V, 116; 142.

[132] P. 267 of the edition by Ch. Dédéyan, Paris, Les Belles Lettres, 1944.

[133] *C.I.L.,* XI, 2, 6106, cf. 6107.

[134] Cf. *C.I.L.,* XI, 1524; XII, 2555, which informs us that L. Tincius Paculus cut an exposed roadway in the rock-face along the sheer bank of the Fier.

[135] *Historia Naturalis,* XXXVI, 125.

[135a] The British reader will find more material relevant to this section in I. D. Margary, *Roman Roads in Britain* 3rd ed. 1973.

[136] Cf. L. ARMAND-CALLIAT, 'Foires et fêtes rurales dans le Chalonnais, survivances probables de l'Antiquité', *Annales de Bourgogne,* XXXIII, 1961, July–Sept., 1960.

[137] 'Le problème topographique de Litanobriga', *M.A.I.,* XIV – 2, 1951, pp. 1–16.

[138] 'Stations routières romaines de Provence', *Rev. d'Et. lig.,* 1959, p. 162.

[139] We could add the 'houses of correction' on the convicts' road to Toulon.

[140] Cf. J. AUDRY, Dr R. RIQUET, 'La basilique cémétériale de Montferrand (Aude), contribution à l'étude du peuplement des grandes invasions en Gaule', *C.R.A.I.,* April–December 1961 (962), pp. 185–204.

[141] *Manuel d'archéologie gallo-romaine,* vol. 2, Paris, Picard, 1934.

[142] The importance of these cannot be over-emphasised: they are and always have been keypoints for the guardians of law and order.

[143] Cf. *infra,* p. 127 sq.

[144] Another example of the regressive method required in studying the overall historical development of a road system can be provided by a look at the role of ancient highways in modern warfare.

[145] We should remember that the air cover for France can be examined at the photo-library of the Institut Géographique National, 2, avenue Pasteur, St-Mandé, 94. On the general method of interpretation, cf. R. CHEVALLIER, *L'Avion à la découverte du passé,* Paris, Fayard, 1964 and *La Photographie aérienne,* Paris, A. Colin, coll. 'U2', 1971.

[146] This makes it essential to watch contour lines when prospecting on maps. Contour lines swinging out and back along the line of a track may be pointers to the built-up causeway of a Roman road frequently remetalled in the past. It is useful, in this way, to compare the course of a road with a map showing hill contours and to trace how the ground evidence has evolved, as when a section of road has been given up because of flooding.

[147] All the more so since horses were not shod as in modern times and the traveller wore an open sandal, if not the *caliga* (boot).

[148] Cf. also sections below on the subject of the relays of the *cursus* and the private establishments.

[149] Cf. G. SAUTTER, *De l'Atlantique au fleuve Congo,* Paris, Mouton, 1966, and the conclusions that we have drawn from this work in *Ethnographie, archéologie et histoire,* contributed to *Mélanges A. Varagnac,* Paris, 1972.

[150] Like the example from Beire-le-Châtel, in *Gallia,* XVIII, 1960, 2, p. 339. In Gaul we may note the cult of Mars Mullo, patron of muleteers (*muliones*) or god of plenty.

[151] In many cases there are parallel roads side by side at the approach to a town (one-way system ?).

[152] Circumvallations of the kind associated with towns have also been observed around camps.

[153] Cf. *supra,* pp. 80 sq.

[154] Cf. P. LEBEL, 'Bornes, centuriation et cantonnements le long de la voie de Lyon au Rhine', *R.A.E.* I, 1950, pp. 154–61.

[155] Cf. R. FOSSIER, *La Terre et les hommes en Picardie jusqu' à la fin du XIIIe siècle*, Paris-Louvain, 1968.

[156] Cf. F. ULRIX, 'Recherches sur la méthode de traçage des routes romaines', *Latomus*, XXII, 2, 1963, pp. 157–81.

[157] Paris, ed. Technip.

[158] Good examples are provided by Nissan in *Photo-interprétation* and by Annecy, where a system of divergent roads dating from the twelfth century clashes with the Roman network (as P. BROISE shows in *Annales, 1967*, p. 859 and in a thesis on *La Cité de Genève dans l'Antiquité*). In the case of Annecy, it is strange how modern motorways have picked up the *trivium* of the past.

[159] A forthcoming paper on the problem of interpreting facts in their historical context: *Actes du Congrès international sur la cartographie archéologique et historique*, Paris, 1970 (Tours, 1972).

[160] *La Conservation de la forme circulaire dans le parcellaire français*, Paris, 1970.

[161] Cf. LIVY, XXXIX, 27. Q. Fabius Labeo had established the frontier of Philip's kingdom along the old royal road.

[162] E. de MARTONNE, in *Traité de géographie physique*, Paris, A. Colin, 1920, p. 764, pointed out how a Roman road was discovered in the Forest of Orléans thanks to the growth of calcicolous flora on the limestone flagging of the old road in an area of silica-loving plants.

[163] Generally speaking, for old roads, a forest acts as an environment favourable to conservation (there are many cases where woodland tracks follow the *margines* of Roman highways), even if the forest grew later than the road.

[164] But it may happen that a power line or a small-gauge railway follows the line of an old road (perhaps a shortcut on public land).

[165] One Roman mile = 1,480m (1,000 paces); one Roman league = 2,222m; one Gallic league = 2,415m. In Britain a good example of this phenomenon may be seen on the Roman road between Wroxeter and Whitchurch, where a datum point is provided by the discovery of two Roman milestones at Moston Pool.

[166] If a distance-measurer is used, it is worth remembering that on a scale of 1/100,000 4·5 per cent is lost on curves and on a scale of 1/200,000 some 6 per cent.

[167] J. HUBERT, in *Les Routes de France*, pp. 18 sq., has shown how Roman roads survived until the sixth, seventh, even the tenth, eleventh centuries.

[168] In using place names, coincidences will have value only if the place name has not already served to argue the line of the road.

[169] Chapels (which may have replaced pagan temples) often lay where there was an awkward or vital route to be followed: for example, the pilgrims' chapel of Notre-Dame de Beauregard on the *oppidum* of Orgon, overlooking a ford crossing the Durance, upstream from Avignon, or the sacred sites at Mont Bego and the Val Camonica along the transhumance tracks, cf. place-name series.

[170] The movement of pack animals or herds along old roads explains why there were drinking-places along them. Hence the importance of springs that never froze and of running water that could be tapped.

[171] We must be able to recognise the various changes that place names can have undergone: abbreviation, metathesis, assimilation, dissimilation, de-nasalisation, agglutination, deagglutination or aphaeresis, analogy, apocope and popular or learned etymology; not to be put off by spelling and to take care over the ways words are composed or derived and similar formations (Nogent = Neuville = Villeneuve); tautology (Estrée-Cauchy); the need to make lists for comparison between regions (chemin haussé = hohe Strasse = high street = (*via*) *levata*, following the method I suggested in my contribution in *Hommages Herescu*, 'Pour une toponymic archéologique comparée'.

[172] We must distinguish between the date when the word was created and the date when it reached the language. For the chronological interpretation of facts in folklore and legend, cf. my article in *Mélanges Saumagne*: 'Folklore, archéologie et histoire'.

Chapter 3 Roman roads in the Roman Empire: a summary

[1] On transhumance, cf. VARRO, *Res rusticae*, II, 1, 9, 10; 2, 10; and A. GRENIER, 'La transhumance des troupeaux en Italie et son rôle dans l'histoire romaine', *M.E.F.R.*, 25, 1905, pp. 293–328. Hannibal's marching and counter-marching in southern Italy can be explained in terms of these routes (supplies of fodder and availability of pasture).

[2] Cf. p. 43.

[3] It was the route 'by which the rural peasantry was subjugated' (Pl. Fraccaro). It was built in connection with the *lex de agro Piceno et Gallico viritim dividendo* (232) of Flaminius.

[4] XXXIX, 2.

[5] Cf. MARTIAL, *Epigrams*, III, 4; VI, 84, 5.

[6] Cf. LIVY, XXXIX, 2.

[7] Cf. R. CHEVALLIER, 'Le delta du Pô à l'époque romaine', *R.E.L.*, 1962 (63), pp. 141–48.

[8] V, I, 11, p. 217c.

[9] II, 9, 16 for transport of wood.

[10] *Letters*, I, 5, 2.

[11] IV, 45, the same journey in five days, and *Variae*, XII, 24, a. 537–538 on the subject of moving supplies from Istria to Ravenna.

[12] II, 16.

[13] *Historia Naturalis*, III, 17, 123.

[14] *Carmina*, 4.

[15] On the tourist trip made by Paulus-Aemilius to Greece, cf. PLUTARCH, *Parallel Lives*: Paulus-Aemilius, trans. Les Belles Lettres, Paris, 1966, 28, I (cf. LIVY, XIV, 27).

[16] Paris, Le Seuil, 7th ed., 1971.

[17] Cf. the 2,500km of the road from Susa to Sardis, normally covered in 90 days (in seven by messengers, according to Herodotus).

[18] Cf. the Egyptian hieroglyph showing a road as a highway lined on each side by papyrus.

[19] Cf. PLINY THE ELDER, *Historia Naturalis*, VI, 166.

[20] Ibid., VI, 84.

[21] Ibid., VI, 26, 101–6.

[22] Ibid., XXXVI, 94.

[23] TACITUS, *Annals*, II, 59–61.

[24] Paris, Arts et Métiers graphiques, 1949.

[25] *Les Voies romaines de l'Afrique du Nord*, Algiers, 1951.

[26] Cf. VIRGIL, *Aeneid*, I, 422 and a note by SERVIUS: *Primi enim Poeni vias lapidibus stravisse dicuntur.*

[27] Cf. *Apologia*, 72.

[28] *Historia Naturalis*, V, 38.

[29] 'Deux ans de recherches dans le Sud de la Tripolitaine', *C.R.A.I.*, April–June 1969, p. 189.

[30] PLINY THE ELDER, *Historia Naturalis*, V, 41.

[31] *Annuaire du Collège de France*, 1965, p. 475.

[32] *C.I.L.*, II, 4701, 4703, 4712, 4715, 4716.

[33] Strabo's figures represent 3,200km for roads and 2,500 for waterways.

[33a] For a full survey of Roman roads in Britain, reference should be made to I. D. Margary, *Roman Roads in Britain*, 3rd ed. 1973.

[34] We should remember that the Antonine Wall, constructed between 139 and 142, was given up as early as 181–83.

[35] LIVY, XLIV, 35.

[36] Ibid., XLV, 6.

[37] IV, 1, 2.

[38] *Bordeaux antique*, Bordeaux, 1962.

[39] The value of canalising the Moselle (a present-day problem in European context) was appreciated early in Cladius' reign by the legates for Germany, cf. TACITUS, *Annals*, XIII, 53, 3–4. It remains a vital trade route for France.

[40] *Annuaire du Collège de France*, 1963, p. 400. With respect to Spain and the North Sea, the author has emphasised (*Annuaire*, op. cit., 1965, p. 475) how the Romans were attracted by the Ocean.

[41] Note the important crossroad north of Lyons, at Ludna, close to St-Georges-de-Renains.

[42] IV, 6, 11.

[43] Up to which point came the *navicularii* of the open sea. Lake Geneva and the Swiss lakes were busy with shipping. On these problems of river navigation, cf. R. CHEVALLIER, 'Problèmes de topographie historique posés par l'étude d'un bassin fluvial dans l'Antiquité', communication au Congrès national des Sociétés savantes de Rennes, 1966.

The work by L. BONNARD: *La Navigation intérieure de la Gaule à l'époque gallo-romaine*, 1913, would be worth bringing up to date.

Water transport was preferred for all heavy materials. Cf. infra, p. 197.

[44] In his *Occident romain* (Paris, Payot, 2nd ed. 1969, chap. 14), L. HARMAND states the problem of the Atlantic seaways and gives a useful chapter summing up sea, river and land routes and the movement of men and goods in the Roman West. He points out that the entire system of roads in Belgium played a subordinate rôle to the port of Boulogne, which was the key transit station between Britain and the continent. The Claudian highway from Boulogne to Cologne via Bavai extended the sea route across the Channel as far as the Rhine. Thus the conditions were already in being for the creation of a 'natural region'.

[45] *C.I.L.*, XIII, 8877, 8909, 8929, 8908, 8920, 9055.

[46] *Annuaire du Collège de France*, 1964, p. 409.

[47] STRABO, IV, 5, 2.

[48] *Fossa Drusiana*, TACITUS, *Annals*, II, 8, 1; *fossae Drusianae*, SUETONIUS, *Claudius*, 1; the term recalls the famous *fossae Marianae* at Fos-sur-Mer on the Rhône.

[49] According to W. VOLLGRAFF, *Les Travaux de Drusus dans la Germanie inférieure*, 1940.

[50] TACITUS, *Histoires*, V, 19, 2.

[51] The organisation of *Sapaudia* (Savoy) answered the same purpose. Cf. infra, on Alpine passes.

[52] *Paris antique*, Paris, 1951.

[53] Cf. LIVY, V, 34, 8.

[54] Cf. POLYBIUS, III, 34, 4.

[55] In *De Mirabilibus auscultis*, 85–6, probably after Timeas, cf. supra, p. 13–14.

[56] *Annuaire du Collège de France*, 1959, pp. 485 sq.

[57] According to STRABO, IV, 6, 12.

[58] Information in SERVIUS, *Ad Aen.*, 10, 13.

[59] IV, 1, 3, and 12; IV, 6, 7.

[60] Cf. STRABO, IV, 6, 12.

[61] Ibid., IV, 1, 9 and IV, 6, 2.

[62] Ibid., IV, 6, 3.

[63] POLYBIUS, III, 41, 4.

[64] The stations are Cemenelum (Cimiez), the river Var. Antipolis (Antibes), Ad Horrea (Saint-Cassien), Forum Julii (Fréjus), Forum Voconii

(Les Blaïs), Ad Turrem (Tourves), Tegulata (La Grande Pugère), Aquae Sextiae (Aix), Pisavis (St-Jean-de-Brenasse), Tericiae, Glanum (St-Rémy), Ernaginum (St-Gabriel), Tarusco (Tarascon), Ugernum (Beaucaire), Nemausus (Nimes).

[65] *Historia Naturalis*, III, 20, 136.

[66] In the Late Empire, the Drôme valley was preferred.

[67] Cf. the distribution pattern of coinage from Marseilles in the Celto-Ligurian regions, H. ROLLAND in *R. Et. Lig.*, XV, 1949, pp. 139–48.

[68] SALLUST, *Histories*, II, 96, 4; cf. APPIAN, *Civil War*, I, 13, 109: Pompey did not follow the trail blazed by Hannibal, but opened up a new one, towards the sources of the Rhône and Eridan (as the Po was known).

[69] LIVY, V, 34, 8.

[70] *Gallic War*, I, 10, 4.

[71] IV, 1, 2–4.

[72] For this point see also R. DION, op. cit.

[73] STRABO, IV, 6, 7.

[74] IV, 6, 11.

[75] Cf. *Actes du Colloque international sur les cols des Alpes, Antiquité et Moyen Age*, Bourg, 1969, Orléans, 1971.

[76] Paris, 1969.

[77] TACITUS refers to this passage in *Histories*, IV, 77.

[78] Cf. H. Jürgen EGGERS, *Der römische Import im freien Germanien*, 1951.

[79] *Gallic War*, IV, 17.

[80] *Annals*, XIII, 53.

[81] Cf. SUETONIUS, XXXI.

[82] Cf. TACITUS, *Annals*, XI, 20.

[83] *Annals*, XIII, 53 and *Histories*, V, 19; cf. SUETONIUS, *Claudius*, I. This study has been resumed by R. DION in *Annuaire du Collège de France*, 1964, p. 425.

[84] For the Western Alps, cf. pp. 165 sq.

[85] Cf. TACITUS, *Annals*, I, 20, 1.

[86] Note that their nationality changed with time: Syrians tended to replace Italians.

[87] Cf. J. N. VON SADOWSKI, *Die Handelsstrassen der Griechen und Römer durch das Flussgebiet der Oder, Weichsel, der Dniepr und Niemen an die Gestade des Baltischen Meeres*, Amsterdam, 1963.

[88] *Historia Naturalis*, VI, 208.

[89] Ibid., VI, 173.

[90] Ibid., XXXVII, 45.

[91] Ibid., VI, 181 and 184.

[92] *Ibid.*, VI, 40.

[93] *Epitoma rei militaris*, III, 6.

[94] II, 5, 34.

Chapter 4   Life on the road

[1] Cf. TACITUS, *Annals*, III, 9.

[2] Their reputation varying according to their origin, cf. HORACE, *Epodes*, 4, 14: a man wearing out the Appian Way with his Gaulish ponies.

[3] Pack animals, able to use the poorest of tracks, found employment throughout protohistory (tin route). The supply train of the Roman army included even more beasts of burden than waggons.

[4] The hipposandal is a veterinary fitting intended to protect a sore foot that is unshod. In *L'Attelage et le cheval de selle* (Paris, 1931), Commandant LEFEBVRE DES NOETTES claimed that Roman horse-trappings comprised simply a saddlecloth and a bridle. More precise detail can be obtained from the panels of weapons on the arch at Orange, cf. R. AMY, P.-M. DUVAL . . ., L'Arc d'Orange, Paris, 1962, p. 87 and pp. 138 sq. It is the use of two spurs that appears to be later than the Carolingian period.

[5] And the same root as *veredus*, a Gallic steed. *Paraveredus*, of course, a supply-horse, gave *palefroi*. The word 'cheval' is also probably Gallic. All these terms are discussed in the *Dictionnaire des Antiquités*.

[6] *Georgics*, III, 536; *Aeneid*, XI, 138.

[7] Cf. JUVENAL, *Satires*, III, 254.

[8] *Annuaire du Collège de France*, 1960, p. 379.

[9] There is the opposite experience: the country road has evolved with changes in the vehicle used by the rural worker on his way to the fields (in France today a tractor or a moped): the road or lane has to be asphalted or else it vanishes between the hedges growing together.

[10] In Gaul, skill with wickerwork accompanied skill with wood.

[11] P. SALAMA, ·Considérations sur les transports routiers romains, en particulier dans la province d'Afrique', *Actes du 79e Congrès nat. Soc. sav.*, Algiers, 1957, p. 291.

[12] II, 2.

[13] X, 38.

[14] VIII, 5, 8, 17, 28, 30, 47.

[15] The heaviest loads must have been dragged on sledges or carried by water: Vitruvius mentions waggons for moving large columns or architraves. But in the quarries, special grooved tracks were needed. In other sources, ships appear to have been used for obelisks (AMMIANUS MARCELLINUS, XVII, 4, 14).

[16] Cf. *Gallia*, 1963, p. 332: relief from Jandum, showing horse and carriage. For examples from Luxemburg, cf. Ch.-M. TERNES, *Index des travaux concernant l'archéologie . . .*, Luxemburg, 1969, pl. 43 (two-wheeled chariot) and 96 (a bale being made ready).

[17] Cf. CAESAR, *Gallic War*, VII, 3.

[18] SUETONIUS, *Caesar*, 57.

[19] *Gallic War*, III, 101.

[20] According to A. M. RAMSAY (*J.R.S.*, X, 1920, p. 79 commenting on *C.I.L.*, I, 551, where the word *tabellarius*, messenger occurs), the post had been set up by the Gracchi, then abolished, to be restored by Augustus.

[21] *Life of Augustus*, 49, 5–50.

[22] *De Provinciis consularibus*, IV; *In Pisonem*, XL.

[23] *I.G.R.R.P.*, 1142.

[24] *C.I.L.*, III, 6123.

[25] *C.I.L.*, III, 7521.

[26] AURELIUS VICTOR, *Caesares*, 13, 5.

[27] *C.I.L.* VI, 8542, 8543.

[28] *Historia Augusta, Hadrian*, VII.

[29] Cf. STATIUS, *Silves*, IV, 9, 17, 19.

[30] *Severus*, 14.

[31] *Philologus*, 1968, p. 282.

[32] The paper appeared under this title ('L'Annone militaire dans l'Empire romain au IIIe siècle') in the *Mémoires* de la S.N.A.F., 1936, pp. 117–201.

[33] *Inscriptiones Graecae ad Res Romanas pertinentes*, 766.

[34] Cf. in the desert, 'Petrol-can 5' or the names given to halts on minor railway lines in France: 'Kilomètre X'.

[35] Under Louis XI, the post relays occurred every four leagues.

[36] *Secret History*, 30, 3 and 5.

[37] A settlement close by (an *oppidum*) may have fixed the site of a station. Where a station had a Celtic name in Gaul, this implies that a population centre already in existence had its position recognised when a native itinerary was brought back into service. The sites of stations may also have been established by administrative boundaries and natural routes.

[38] I, 9.

[39] Cf. PLUTARCH, *Galba*, 8.

[40] An example of a *statio* commanded by a *beneficiarius consularis*, at Sebastopolis in Cappadocia, is given in *Année épigraphique*, 1968, p. 503.

[41] *Historia Augusta, Severus Alexander*, XLV, 47.

[42] Cf. C. BOISSE, *Le Tricastin*, Valence, 1968, p. 134.

[43] Normally, night was not spent on the pass. One stopped in the valley, where the climb began, so as to go over the pass by day, taking advantage of a more pleasant temperature and better visibility.

[44] *Secret History*, 30, 4.

[45] VIII, 5, 38.

[46] Op. cit., p. 106.

[47] Op. cit., p. 197.

[48] Military posts at Marseilles already protected the Heraclean Way from Ligurian pirates, then defence was provided for the *via Domitia* by setting up citadels at Aix and Marseilles.

[49] Cf. M. LABROUSSE, in *M.E.F.R.*, LVI, 1939, pp. 151–67.

[50] *West deutsche Zeitschrift*, XIV, 99; XXI, 158. For the organisation of the road *tractus*, cf. C. JULLIAN, 'Les origines de la Savoie', *R.E.A.*, 1920, p. 273.

[51] *R.E.A.*, 1950, p. 175. A road may have changed course because of a *burgus* or a camp, cf. R. AGACHE, *Vues aériennes de la Somme et recherche du passé*, Amiens, 1962, Fig. 18.

[52] *Res rusticae*, 1, 2, 23.

[53] *C.I.L.*, XI, 5803–5804.

[54] *C.I.L.*, XI, 2031.

[55] *C.I.L.*, IV, 807.

[56] Cf. HORACE, *Satires*, I, 1, 29; I, 5, 3 and numerous proverbs.

[57] Cf. APULEIUS, *Metamorphoses*, I, 6.

[58] Cf. LIVY, XLII, 1: Magistrates went away equipped with pack mules, tents and all necessary military gear so as not to make demands on allies. They used to lodge with private citizens and made use of hospitality offered discreetly and thoughtfully; their houses in Rome were open to those who were in the habit of receiving them (cf. Caesar lodging with Catullus' father in Verona).

[59] *C.I.L.*, IX, 2689.

[60] *C.I.L.*, IV, 2146.

[61] *C.I.L.*, XIV, 4756.

[62] We have scanty information for early times, for example the 30 days of the tin route in Gaul, cf. supra, p. 14. It might be possible to establish comparisons with facts given by Greek writers: according to Herodotus, an army could normally march 150 stadia in a day (27km), a traveller could do 200, (36km). We find in Strabo (VI, 1, 4) (255), that the distance between the gulfs of Squillace and S. Eufemia in southern Italy (that is, 29km) is given as equivalent to half a day's march (cf. ARISTOTLE, *Politika*, VII, 9, 2).

[63] The ancients themselves were aware of these difficulties, cf. CICERO, *Pro Roscio Amerino*, 132: the territory of the Salentini and Bruttium, whence news may be received two or three times a year at the most; PROPERTIUS, *Elegies*, IV, 1, 36: (formerly) it was quite a journey to take the Roman highways as far as Fidenae.

[64] *Gallic War*, IV, 5.

[65] PLUTARCH, *Galba*, 7.

[66] *Historia Augusta, Maximin*, XXV.

[67] LIBANIUS, *Oratio*, 21, 15–16.

[68] *Les Routes et le trafic commercial dans l'Empire romain*, Paris, Ed. de Cluny, 1939, pp. 99–100.

[69] CICERO, *Ad Atticum*, V, 14, 1.

[70] STRABO, 569, 5.

[71] Ibid., 539, 9.

[72] Ibid., 498.

[73] XLII, 48.

74 On the speed of these movements, cf. PLU-TARCH, *Caesar*, 17, 5: one week from Rome to the Rhône.

75 PLINY THE ELDER, *Historia Naturalis*, VII, 84; VALERIUS MAXIMUS, V, 5, 3.

76 TACITUS, *Histories*, I, 56.

77 Cf. the figures quoted above, p. 192.

78 *Gallic War*, VII, 41.

79 APPIAN, *Civil War*, II, 15, 103. Twenty-seven days from Rome to Obulco 'without wetting his men's feet', it is noted in the *Iter*.

80 Cf. XLIV, 5: seven miles in the day.

81 Cf. the 20 miles (30km) per day allowed to those who had to answer a praetor's summons. Horace's journey of 13 days from Rome to Brindisi will also be recalled (supra, p. 24).

82 *Portorium, étude sur l'organisation douanière chez les Romains, surtout à l'époque du Haut-Empire*, Bruges, 1949.

83 Cf. the laws of Salpensa and Malaca.

84 *C.I.L.*, VIII, 4508.

85 *Année épigraphique*, 1914, 234.

86 *Speeches*, 359.

87 DITTENBERGER, *Orientis Graeci Inscriptiones Selectae* (Hildesheim, 1960), no. 674, 90 AD.

88 *C.I.L.*, VIII, 4508. Cf. J.-P. DARMON, 'Notes sur le tarif de Zaraï, *Les Cahiers de Tunisie*, XLVII–XLVIII, 2nd–4th quarter 1964, shows that there was a trade flow between those North African regions that lay within the Roman Empire and were well developed and a belt of pastoral farming marginal to the Empire.

89 I, 20.

90 *Historia Naturalis*, XII, 65.

91 Cf. A. PIGANIOL, 'Observations sur le tarif de Palmyre', *R.H.*, CXCV, 1945, pp. 10–23. This text (*lex vectigalis portus Hadrianae Palmyrae et fontium aquarum Aelii Caesaris*) has three sections: the general charter stating the conditions of the annual lease; a contract of 'mistosis' involving two alterations to the general tariff and method of implementing the salt tax (a monopoly); and finally the terms laid down by authority between the town of Palmyra and the tax-farmer or publican.

92 Sites can be looked for lying in corresponding positions on either side of geographical features like the two banks of a river, estuary or channel and parallel rivers (Loire–Saône, linked by numerous roads).

93 Navigation was possible even on minor water-ways, thanks to the use of bladder-floats for lightening flat-bottomed boats. One-way river-crossings will have taken place with the aid of collapsible rafts.

94 Cf. supra, pp. 93–94 – and Fig. 15.

95 IV, 1, 14.

96 *Annuaire du Collège de France*, 1963, p. 408.

97 V, 22, 38.

98 *Letters*, XVIII, 165–7; XXV, 126–7.

99 Cf. the inscription of the land survey at Orange, showing a road along each bank of the river.

100 Air photographs clearly show roads like these taking a tangential course to skirt meanders or low-lying areas (the *via Domitia* at the foot of Enseruna).

101 *Tableau de la géographie de la France*, Paris, 2nd ed. 1905, p. 379.

102 Aristides Aelius, in his *Oratio de urbe Roma* (94–95), placed emphasis on sea transport.

103 Only because of necessity, cf. RUTILIUS NAMATIANUS, *De Reditu suo*, I, 36, sq.: 'Late as it may be, we are resigned to taking the sea journey we have chosen, because, going over-land by road, the low ground is flooded by rivers and the hills are strewn with boulders.'

104 Cf. the travels of a governor of Macedonia, mentioned by TACITUS, *Annals*, V, 10.

105 *Annals*, III, 9.

106 The close connection between land and sea routes is well developed by Ptolemy in his *Geography*.

107 Cf. V. A. SIRAGO, *l.'Italia agraria sotto Traiano*, Louvain, 1958. For his part, F. BIANCOFIORE, studying the viability in ancient times of the area south-east of Bari (*Arch. Stor. Pugliese*, 1962, pp. 205–40) has the view that the emperors were concerned about main roads only.

Chapter 5   The function of Roman roads

1 Livy quotes an example of an effort to spy under the guise of tourism (XLV, 14): 'Masinissa had his son inform the Senate that he wished to come himself to Rome in order to offer sacrifice and make thanksgiving at the Capitol to Jove the Best and Greatest, and sought leave to undertake this journey, if there was no impropriety. He was persuaded not to do so.' As regards envoys from the provinces, cf. W. WILLIAMS, 'Antoninus Pius et le contrôle des ambassades provinciales', *Historia*, XVI, 1967, p. 470. For an example of a delegation from a town to Rome concerning the *immunitas*: *C.R.A.I.*, 1962, pp. 55–76.

2 *Vespasian*, 8, 5.

3 In this respect, we should bear in mind the picturesque camel caravans that the Roman world gradually came to know, cf. PLINY THE ELDER, *Historia Naturalis*, XXIV, 183.

4 *C.I.L.*, VIII, 11824: 'When groups of harvesters used to appear in the region hiring themselves out around Cirta, capital of Numidia, or on the flat country overlooked by the mountain of

Jupiter, I was always the first to garner my crop, until, leaving my home district, I went and did harvest-work for others, under a blazing sun.'

[5] SUETONIUS, *Tiberius,* 14.

[6] Cf. PROPERTIUS, *Elegies,* II, 32: Cynthia's chariot journeys to Praeneste, Tusculum and Tibur, along the *via Appia,* betray her secret feelings, cf. IV, 8, 15: Close-cropped ponies had taken my Cynthia off to Lanuvium . . . Ah! what a triumphant journey rushing over the cobbles of the Appian Way [an old Roman custom, obviously!] . . . She displayed herself to the world at large, seated close to the central shaft, with legs dangling.

[7] As in the case of Drusus the Elder, whose body Augustus accompanied from Ticinum to Rome, TACITUS, *Annals,* III, 5, 2.

[8] *Agricola,* 19.

[9] In the Republican period, the billetting of magistrates was less onerous, cf. the text from Livy quoted earlier.

[10] *Annals,* III, 9. Aurelius Victor can also be quoted concerning Trajan's roads, which allowed movement from the Black Sea to Gaul: *per feras gentes quo facile ab usque Pontico mari in Galliam permeatur* (*Trajan,* 133).

[11] PLINY THE ELDER, *Historia Naturalis,* XXIII, 95, in respect of the *via Flaminia.*

[12] P. PETIT, *La Paix romaine,* Paris, P.U.F., coll. 'Nouvelle Clio', 1967, p. 288.

[13] *Le Tibre, fleuve de Rome dans l'Antiquité,* Paris, P.U.F., 1953, p. 241.

[14] Cf. VIDAL DE LA BLACHE: 'those insubstantial things we call traffic routes'.

[15] *Historia Naturalis,* XXXVI, 5.

[16] Paris, P.U.F., 1951.

[17] Christianity reached Gaul by way of the Roman road from Milan to Arles (and also by sea).

[18] It is perhaps to be ascribed to Cicero, cf. *Pro Balbo,* 39, speaking of Rome's universal appeal: *cum ex omnibus civitatibus via sit in nostram* (in the abstract sense). The political significance of the courses taken by certain roads should be noticed. Agde, main centre of Marseilles' commerce, yet neglected by the *via Domitia;* the *Appia* passing by Tarentum. Changes of intention can be traced as the road systems evolved.

[19] *Historia Naturalis,* XIV, 2.

[20] Cf. XXVII, 3, on the majesty of the Roman Peace.

[21] Cf. ARISTIDES AELIUS, *Oratio de urbe Roma,* 108: Greeks and Barbarians alike can move around freely. Travelling meant going from one homeland to another.

[22] VIII, VII; cf. GALIAN, *De Methodo medente.*

[23] Cf. the distribution of hoards and barbarian cemeteries.

[24] CASSIODORUS, *Variae,* XII, 18.

[25] We may notice in passing old lanes that were once sheep droves, along which animals were taken to market, cf. above, discussion on place names.

[26] F. IMBERDIS, 'Les routes médiévales coïncident-elles avec les voies romaines ?', *Bull. philol. et hist. du Comité des Travaux historiques,* 1960, pp. 93–8.

[27] 'Recherches sur les routes de l'Europe médiévale . . .', ibid. 1960, pp. 99–143.

[28] *La Terre et les hommes en Picardie jusqu'à la fin du XIIIe siècle,* op. cit., p. 148.

[29] *Mélanges M. Bloch,* II, 745. On the connection between medieval hospices and old roads, cf. supra, pp. 55, 125.

[30] Quoted from a paper by J. DEPONT in a series of studies (Faculté des Lettres de Tours) on the subject of the Jacques Coeur road (*Caesarodunum,* 3, 1969, pp. 161–4).

[31] *Architettura,* III, Venice, 1581.

[32] The regulation of the Ancien Régime concerning relay oxen on the hill at Roanne appears to be a distant survival.

[33] In the north, hedges are being levelled by machine. This spells the end of the various forms of vegetational cover that have for long provided evidence of Roman roads and so ensured their survival. Sections of Roman road are being bought only to be destroyed by ploughing. However, some stretches are being better preserved because tractors throw longer and higher furrows than horses.

[34] *Revue du Nord,* April–June 1965, p. 361.

Bibliography

The subjects in the Bibliography follow the order in which they are presented in the text. To avoid repetition, there is no systematic reference to works quoted in the notes to each chapter. See p. 257 for explanation of Journal abbreviations.

The Earliest Roads

BENOIT (F.), 'La Légende d'Héraklès et la colonisation grecque dans le delta du Rhône', *Lettres d'Humanité*, VIII, 1949, pp. 104–148.

BENOIT (F.) in *Gallia*, 1968, no. 1, fig. 2, shows the Gallic track-ways around Entremont.

BIAL (P.), *Chemins, habitations et oppidums de la Gaule au temps de César*, Paris, 1874.

BORIUS (R.), 'Les monnaies gauloises d'Allonnes (Sarthe) et l'axe commercial Manche-Méditerranée', *Actes du 91ᵉ Congrès national des Sociétés savantes*, Rennes, 1966 (1968), p. 377.

BREGLIA (L.), *Le Antiche Rotte del Mediterraneo documentate da monete e pesi*, Rome, new edition 1966.

BROU (M. L. and W), *Chaussée Brunehault et monuments mégalithiques de la Gaule du Nord*, Brussels, 1970.

CAHN (H. A.), 'Le vase de bronze de Graechwill et autres importations méridionales en Suisse avant les Romains', *Actes du Colloque de Dijon*, 1958, pp. 21–30.

CARCOPINO (J.), 'Les trouvailles de Vix', *R.D.M.*, nos. 2–3–4, 5 I, 1955, p. 208; 1 II, p. 412, 15 II, 627.

CARCOPINO (J.), 'Encore la route marseillaise de l'étain', *Mélanges P. Bosch-Gimpera*, Mexico, 1963, pp. 85–93.

CIRKIN (I. B.), 'La route de l'étain et le commerce au nord de Massilia', *V.D.I.*, 1968, no. 105, pp. 96–104.

CLOS ARCEDUC (A.), 'L'organisation agraire et le réseau vicinal entre Blois et Meung-sur-Loire', *Actes du 93ᵉ Congrès national des Sociétés savantes*, Tours, 1968 (Paris, 1970), p. 245.

CLOUANT (M.), 'En suivant deux voies préromaines en Saintonge', *Revue de Saintonge et d'Aunis*, Bull. des Archives hist. de Saintonge et d'Aunis, 1928.

COQUET (M.), 'Recherches sur les voies préromaines de la Trévaresse et du plateau de Rogues vers la Durance', *P.H.*, 17, 1967, pp. 360–375.

CRAWFORD (O. G. S.), *Archaeology in the Field*, London, 1953, pp. 60–86.

CRAVAYAT (P.), 'Voies préromaines et toponymes celtiques', *Cahiers d'archéol. et d'hist. du Berry*, 1969, p. 17.

DEHN (W.), 'Die Befestigung der Heuneburg (Per. IV) und die griechische Mittelmeerwelt', *Actes du Colloque de Dijon*, 1958, pp. 55–62.

DEHN (W.), 'Les routes de l'étain, l'isthme gaulois et le carrefour de Paris', *Hommes et Mondes,* April 1952, p. 547.

DION (R.), 'Étude de la circulation transalpine avant la pacification des Alpes', *Annuaire du Collège de France*, 1959, p. 485.

DION (R.), 'Tartessos, l'Océan homérique et les travaux d'Hercule', *R.H.*, no. 224, 1960, pp. 27–44.

DION (R.), 'La voie héracléenne et l'itinéraire transalpin d'Hannibal', *Hommages A. Grenier*, 1962, pp. 527–543.

DION (R.), 'Le Danube d'Hérodote', *R.Ph.*, XLII, 1968, pp. 7–44.

DION (R.), 'Le transport de l'étain des îles britanniques à Marseille à travers la Gaule préromaine', *Annuaire du Collège de France*, 1968, p. 503.

DUCH (G. A.), 'La voie héracléenne, voie du mercure et du cinabre', *R.A.E.*, XV, 1964, 1–2, pp. 123–131.

FUSTIER (P.), 'Un itinéraire préromain jalonné et gradué', *Antiquités Nationales*, IV, 14–16, April–Dec. 1963, pp. 56–60.

GERIN-RICARD (H. de), 'Un chemin du fer préromain en Provence et en Languedoc', *B.C.T.H.*, 1932–1933, pp. 589–592.

GRESHAM (C. A.), IRVINE (H. C.), 'Prehistoric routes across North Wales', *Antiquity*, XXXVII, 1963, 145, pp. 54–58.

GRIMES (W. F.), 'The Jurassic Way', in W. F. Grimes (ed.), *Aspects of Archaeology*, London, 1951, pp. 144–171.

GUMOWSKI (M.), 'De via quae dicitur sucinea', *Meander*, 1961, pp. 44–54.

HARMAND (L.), 'César en Gaule', *I.H.*, 1970, no. 3, p. 112.

HATT (J.-J.), 'Commerce grec du VIᵉ siècle et commerce italo-grec du Vᵉ', *R.A.E.*, VI, 1955, pp. 150–152.

JACOBSTAHL (P.), 'Rhodische Bronzekannen, aus Hallstatt-Gräbern', *J.D.A.I.*, XLIV, 1929, pp. 198–200.

KIMMIG (W.), 'Kulturbeziehungen zwischen der nord-westalpinen Hallstattkultur und der mediterranen Welt', *Actes du Colloque de Dijon*, 1958, pp.

75–87.

LEBEL (P.), 'Gués et voies protohistoriques', *R.A.E.*, IV, 1953, pp. 353–358.

LERAT (L.), 'L'amphore de bronze de Conliège (Jura)', *Actes du Colloque de Dijon*, 1958, pp. 89–98.

LIÈVRE (A. F.), *Les Chemins gaulois et romains entre la Loire et la Gironde – Les limites des cités – La lieue gauloise*, Niort, 2nd edition 1893.

MARGARY (I. D.), 'The North Downs Main Trackway and the Pilgrims' Way', *Arch. J.* CIX, 1952, pp. 39–53.

MAURY (J.), 'L'association des drailles, des dolmens et des tumulus sur les Grands Causses', *B.S.P.F.*, 66, 1969, pp. 99–101.

MILLOTTE (J.-P.), 'Un type d'habitat préhistorique dans le Jura du Nord : le camp fortifié', *Annales litt. Univ. Besançon*, II, fasc. 4, Géo. 2, 1955, pp. 39–60 (32 fortified sites defending roads).

OLLIVIER (R.), 'Routes, mégalithes et peuplement', *Norois*, Jan.–March 1968, pp. 57–77.

PARIS (R.), 'Tumulus et voies romaines. Recherches faites dans le Châtillonnais', *R.A.E.*, IV, 1953, pp. 242–246, fig. 65.

PAULSEN (R.), 'Les migrations des tribus celtiques ou gauloises d'après les monnaies celtiques', *Congrès intern. de numismatique*, 1953, p. 429.

PICARD (Ch.), 'Les voies terrestres du commerce hallstattien', *Latomus*, 19, 1960, pp. 409–428.

POUYÉ (B.), 'Enquête sur un itinéraire du sel et de l'étain de l'embouchure du Rhône à celle de la Loire', *Celticum*, 9, 1964, pp. 299–302.

SAINT-DENIS (E. de), 'Les voies anciennes et les préliminaires de la bataille d'Alésia', *L.E.C.*, 1950, p. 417.

SCHWAL (H.), 'Entdeckung einer Keltischen Brücke an der Zihl . . . *Arch. Korresp. bl.* 2, 1972, 3, p. 289.

SOUTOU (A.), 'Les voies anciennes au sud de Millau (Aveyron)', *Cahiers de préhist. et d'archéol.*, 8, 1959, pp. 112–120.

SOUTOU (A.), 'Le puits funéraire de La Lagaste et le tracé préromain de la voie d'Aquitaine', *Ogam*, XII, 1960, pp. 1–15.

SOYER (J.), 'A propos d'une variante des "Commentaires" de César : de l'emplacement du pont gaulois de Genabum', *Bull. Soc. archéol. Orléanais*, XIX, 1920–1922 (23).

TERNES (Ch.-M.), 'La voirie préromaine du Luxembourg', in *Voies de communication au pays mosellan*, Luxembourg, 1968, pp. 11–28.

THÉVENOT (E.), 'La voie ancienne de Chalon à la haute vallée de la Seine', *Ann. Bourg.*, 1942, 37, p. 63. *Cf. Mém. Soc. Arch. Beaune*, 1937–40, p. 63.

VALLENTIN DU CHEYLARD (R.), 'Les routes commerciales de la Bourgogne préromaine', *Actes du 84ᵉ Congrès nat. des Soc. sav.*, Dijon, 1959 (Paris, 1961), p. 49.

VALLENTIN DU CHEYLARD (R.), 'Le commerce du bronze à travers l'*Alpis Graia*', *Actes du 85ᵉ Congrès*

nat. des Soc. sav., Chambéry-Annecy, 1960 (Paris, 1962), pp. 29–41.

VARAGNAC (A.), 'L'origine des routes', *Via*, Paris, 1950.

VINCENT (G. et A.), 'Les chemins creux en groupes de l'époque de la Tène', *R.E.A.*, XXXI, 1929, 4, pp. 327–339.

VENDRYES (J.), 'La route de l'étain en Gaule', *C.R.A.I.*, 1957, p. 204.

N.B. We should notice the *castellum* at Famars, which lies at the intersection of two pre-Roman routes: *Gallia*, XIX, 1961, pp. 159–190.

General works

There is such a wide range of books on Roman roads that any choice is liable to be subjective. The most recent publications are noted below, in particular those that have appeared since the publication of A. GRENIER's handbook. Articles have been included where they seem to be representative of a province (such as specialist studies devoted to Gaul and to the major regions of the Roman world) or informative concerning methods or results. Titles have been grouped in topics (mainly geographical for ease of reference) and within each topic in the alphabetical list of authors.

The bibliography can be brought up to date from the *Année philologique* and the *Fasti Archaeologici* (section V: The Roman West: 3 Regions and sites. Topography; cf. III, 4249, IV, 4685, IX, 4879 . . .). For Gaul, recourse should be made to the chapter 'Ponts et chaussées' in the Gallo-Roman section of the *Revue des études anciennes* (R.E.A.) for the years since 1923 and to the index of *Gallia*. For the British Isles, the annual *Archaeological Bibliography*, published by the Council for British Archaeology since 1947, is indispensable.

For maps, the following are useful:

—the *Tabula Imperii Romani* (international map of the Roman Empire at a scale of 1/1,000,000, produced under the auspices of the *Union Académique Internationale*). The following sheets have been published since the war: G36 (Coptos), 1958; HI33 (Lepcis Magna), 1954; HI34 (Cyrene), 1954; L32 (Mediolanum), 1966; L33 (Tergeste), 1961; L34 (Aquincum-Sarmizegetusa-Sirmium), 1968; L35 (Romula-Durostorum-Tomis), 1969. Further sheets are forthcoming and copies of older sheets, published before the war, may sometimes be found in libraries;

—for Italy, the series *Forma Italiae*;

—for France, the series *Carte archéologique de la Gaule romaine (Forma Orbis Romani)*. The index maps are at a scale of 1/200,000, with supporting volumes of bibliography: the *départements* so far covered are: Alpes-Maritimes (1931), Aude

(1959), Aveyron (1944), Basses-Alpes (1931), Bouches-du-Rhône (1936), Corse (1934), Drôme (1957), Gard (1941), Haute-Vienne (1964), Hérault (1946), Indre-et-Loire (1960), Var (1932), Vaucluse (1939).

—for Belgium, *Cartes archéologiques de la Belgique*, 1–2 (*La Belgique à l'époque romaine*), produced by the *Service national des fouilles*, 1968.

—for the British Isles, the *Map of Roman Britain*, Ordnance Survey, 3rd edit. 1956 (4th edit. under preparation).

A *Tabula Viarum Romani Imperii* was published by the *E.N.I.T.* on the occasion of the *IVe Congresso internationale della strada*, Milan, 1926.

AMIT (M.), 'Les moyens de communication et la défense de l'Empire romain', *P.P.*, 20, 1965, pp. 207–222.

ANGOT (A.), 'De la recherche des voies romaines d'après la délimitation des paroisses', *Rev. hist. et archéol. du Maine*, XXXVI, 1894, p. 314.

BERGIER (N.), *Histoire des grands chemins de l'Empire romain*, 1st edit. 1622; 2nd edit. 1728, 2 vol.

BERSANETTI (G. M.), 'Massimino e la rete stradale dell'impero', *Atti III Congr. di Studi Romani*, pp. 590–594.

BERTRAND (A.), 'Les voies romaines en Gaule. Voies des Itinéraires. Résumé du travail de la commission de la Topographie des Gaules', *R.A.*, 1863, II, pp. 62, 148, 342, 406 (*cf.* I, p. 344).

BESNIER (M.), 'Via', *Dictionnaire des Antiquités*, pp. 785 *sq.*

BESNIER (M.), 'Notes sur les routes de la Gaule romaine', *R.E.A.*, 1923, pp. 153–164; 1924, pp. 331–340, *cf. B.C.T.H.*, 1923, p. 75; *R.E.L.*, 1929, p. 90; *L.E.C.*, 1949, p. 251.

BOUHIER (Cl.), 'La recherche des voies antiques', *Revue du dép. de la Manche*, II, 1–8, July–Oct. 1960, pp. 201–209.

CALAIS (J.), 'Notes sur les voies romaines', *Bull. Soc. normande d'études préhist.*, XXXVII, 4, 1962, p. 99.

CAPOT-REY (R.), *Géographie de la circulation*, Paris, 1946.

CAVAILLES (H.), *La Route française, son histoire, sa fonction. Étude de géographie humaine*, Paris, 1946.

CHEVALLIER (R.), 'Les transformations d'une voie romaine', *R.A.E.*, IX, 1958, p. 247.

CHEVALLIER (R.), CLOS ARCEDUC (A.), SOYER (J.), 'Essai de reconstitution du réseau routier gallo-romain. Caractères et méthode', *R.A.*, 1962, I, pp. 1–49.

CHEVALLIER (R.), CLOS ARCEDUC (A.), SOYER (J.), *Organisation de la recherche des voies antiques*, Notice technique no. 6 du Groupe d'Archéologie antique du T.C.F., Paris.

CHOUX (J.), 'Pour la chronologie des routes antiques', *Annales de l'Est*, 5e s., I, 1950, p. 227.

CIPROTTI (P.), *Contributo allo studio della disciplina della circolazione stradale nell'antichità. Roma, Pompei.*

Rome, 1961.

CLOS ARCEDUC (A.), 'La métrique des voies gallo-romaines et ses rapports avec leur recherche', *Actes du Colloque international d'archéologie aérienne*, Paris, 1964, p. 213.

DÉCHELETTE (F.), 'Les voies de pénétration de la civilisation dans la Gaule celtique et romaine', *R.G.L.*, XXXI, 1956, pp. 109–114.

DENIS, *Itinéraire historique des grandes routes de France*, 1768.

DION (R.), reports of lectures in the *Annuaire du Collège de France*, 1959, p. 485 (traffic across the Alps); 1960, p. 376 and 1961, p. 355 (geography of traffic); 1964, p. 409 (geographical aspects of Roman commercial activity in Northern Gaul).

DUBOIS (C.), 'L'influence des chaussées romaines sur la frontière linguistique de la Belgique', *R.B.Ph.*, X, 1930, p. 441.

DUVAL (P.-M.), HUBERT (J.), LIVET (G.), TRENARD (L.), COQUAND (R.), *Les Routes de France, depuis les origines jusqu'à nos jours*, Paris, 1959.

Éducation Nationale, supp. to no. 2, Jan. 1954, pp. 17–18.

FORBES (R. J.), *Notes on the history of ancient roads and their construction*, Amsterdam, 1934 (repub. 1964) *cf. Studies in ancient technology*, 1955).

FORDHAM (G.), *Les Routes de France*, Paris, 1929.

FUSTIER (P.), *La Route. Voies antiques. Chemins anciens. Chaussées modernes*, Paris, 1968.

GALLOIS (L.), 'Les voies romaines de la Gaule', *Ann. de Géo.*, XLIII, 1934, 246, pp. 627–629.

GAUTIER (M.), 'Les enseignements des chemins ruraux', *Inform. Géo.*, May–June 1953, 3, pp. 93–97.

GERMAIN (J.), *La Route en France à travers les âges*, Paris, 1936.

GOUGENHEIM (G.), 'Routes de mots', *Annales*, 1951, 2, pp. 184–185.

GRENIER (A.), 'Les voies romaines en Gaule', *M.E.F.R.*, LIII, 1936, 5 (*cf. R.C.C.*, 1931, pp. 577–594, pp. 706–720).

GRENIER (A.), *Manuel d'archéologie gallo-romaine*, II. Field archaeology, 1. Roads, 1934 (*cf.* Navigation. Land use).

GRENIER (A.), *Le Strade romane nella Gallia*, Rome, 1937.

HAGEN (V. W. von), *Les Voies romaines*, Paris, Hachette, 1969 (the Italian edition *Roma nel Mondo, le grandi strade*, Rome, 1969, includes maps).

HARMAND (L.), *L'Occident romain*, 2nd edit. 1969, pp. 39 *sq.*, 431, chap. xv: Sea-routes, waterways and roads. Movement of men and merchandise in the Roman West).

HARMAND (L.), *L'Occident romain*, Paris, Payot, 2e éd. 1969, pp. 39 *sq.*, 431, chap. xv: Voies navales, continentales et fluviales. La circulation des hommes et des marchandises à travers l'Occident romain).

HINRICHS (F. T.), 'Der römische Strassenbau zur Zeit der Gracchen', *Historia*, XVI, 1967, no. 2, pp. 162–176.

Histoire locale: this periodical has published parts of an International Atlas of routes in prehistoric and historic times, *cf.* 1954–1955, nos. 17–24; 1957, nos. 29–32.

Journées archéologiques internationales de Compiègne, 1964. Means of communication and transport in the Roman Empire.

JULLIAN (C.), 'Routes romaines et routes de France', *Revue de Paris*, Feb. 1900, p. 565.

JULLIAN (C.), 'Routes romaines et routes de France', *Revue de Paris*, fév. 1900, p. 565.

JULLIAN (C.), *Histoire de la Gaule*, II, 1908, V, 1920.

LEBEL (P.), 'Vielles routes à travers champs et parchemins', *R.A.E.*, I, 1950, p. 31.

LEBEL (P.), 'Voies romaines d'Afrique et de Gaule', *ibid.*, II, 1951, p. 192.

LE BRETON (L.), 'De l'état de notre connaissance des itinéraires antiques', *R. Assyr. A.O.*, 52, 1958, pp. 110–116.

LECLERCQ (H.), 'Routes romaines' in *Dict. d'archéol. chrét.*, Paris, 1949.

LEFEBVRE DES NOËTTES (Cdt), 'La voie romaine et la route moderne', *R.A.*, 1925, II, pp. 105–112.

LONGUEMAR (A. de), *Étude sur les voies romaines*, 1886.

LÜDTKE (H.), 'Le vie di communicazione dell'impero romano e la formazione dei dialetti romanzi', *Actes Xe Congrès intern. linguistique*, Paris, 1965, III, p. 1103.

LUGLI (G.), 'La genesi del sistema stradale di Roma antica', *Atti III Congr. di Studi Romani*, I, 1935, p. 256.

MATTY DE LATOUR, *Les Voies romaines, système de construction et d'entretien*, 1865.

MELAYE (A.), *Itinéraires romains en Gaule*, 1905.

MUNOZ (A.), 'Le vie consolari', *Roma Nobilis*, pp. 259–261.

OOTEGHEM (J. van), 'Les routes romaines', *L.E.C.*, XVII, 1949, pp. 251–262.

PACE (B.), 'Viabilità e navigazione', *Guida allo studio della civiltà romana antica*, Naples, Rome, Milan, 1954, I, pp. 581–625.

PARIBENI (R.), 'La politica stradale degli Stati del Mondo antico', *Trasporti Pubblici*, nos. 8–9. Aug.–Sept. 1947, pp. 1–4.

RADKE (G.), *Viae Publicae Romanae*, Stuttgart, 1971 (*R.E.*, XIII, 1973, col. 1417–1686).

RADKE (G.), 'Namen und Daten: Beobachtungen zur Gesch. d. röm. Strassenbaus', *M.H.*, XXIV, 1967, pp. 221–235.

RUGGIERO (E. de), *Dizionario epigrafico*, pp. 855, 902, 924.

SAINT-VENANT (J. de), *Les Voies antiques décelées par la nature de la végétation*, 1887.

UCCELLI (A.), *La Ruota e la strada*, Milan, 1946.

VIDAL DE LA BLACHE (P.), 'Routes et chemins de l'ancienne France', *Bull. de géo. descript. et hist.*, 1902, p. 115.

Travel as a theme in literature

BENNETT (A. W.), 'The patron and poetical inspiration. Propertius, III, 9', *Hermes*, XCVI, 1968, pp. 318–340.

CASTORINA (E.), ed. of *De Reditu suo*, by Rutilius Namatianus, Florence, 1967.

CHEVALLIER (R.), 'Avec Montaigne, à la découverte de l'Italie antique', *Caesarodunum*, sup. no. 3, 1968.

DESJARDINS (E.), *Voyage d'Horace à Brindes (Sat. V, Livre I)*, geographical dissertation, Mâcon, 1855.

DOBLHOFER (E.), 'Drei spätantike Reiseschilderungen', *Festschr. K. Vrestska*, Heidelberg, 1970, pp. 1–22.

HUEBNER (W.), 'Pontem indignatus Araxes' (Vergil, Aeneid, VIII, 728), *Lemmata W. Ehlers*, pp. 103–110.

KNIGHT (W. F. J.), *Vergil: Epic and Anthropology*, London, Allen and Unwin, 1967.

MARX (F.), *C. Lucilii carminum reliquiae*, Leipzig, 1905, p. 49: Lucilius' journey from Rome to Sicily.

MATAKIEWICZ (H.), 'De itineris genere litterario', *Eos*, 1929, pp. 229–245.

PANSA (G.), 'Le 90e milliaire de la *via Valeria* et l'itinéraire d'Ovide, de Rome à Sulmona', *B.C.A.R.*, 1918, p. 189.

PERLER (O.), MAIER (J.-L.), *Les Voyages de saint Augustin*, Paris, Études augustiniennes, 1969.

Editions of the Itineraries

Editions of the *Peutinger Table*: 1st edit. 1521, 2nd edit. in *Leland's Itinerary*, edited by R. GALE for Great Britain, 1709; MORSELEY, 1732; WESELING, Amsterdam, 1735; de SCHEYB, 1753; LORIOT, 'Itinera Gordiani Augusti I: un voyage de Gordien III à Antioche en 239 ap. J.C.', *B.S.F.N.*, Feb. 1971, pp. 18–21.

MANNERT, *Tabula itineraria peutingeriana*, Leipzig, 1824.

PARTHEY (G.), PINDER (M.), *Itinerarium Antonini Augusti et Hierosolymitanum*, Berlin, 1840.

LAPIE (P.), *Recueil des itinéraires anciens comprenant l'Itinéraire d'Antonin, la Table de Peutinger et un choix des périples grecs*, Paris, 1844.

FORTIA D'URBAN, *Recueil des itinéraires anciens comprenant l'Itinéraire d'Antonin, la Table de Peutinger et un choix de périples grecs*, Paris, 1845 (*cf.* L. RENIER, *B.S.A.F.*, 1850, pp. 181–313).

DESJARDINS (E.), *La Table de Peutinger, d'après l'original conservé à Vienne*, Paris, 1869–1874 (1 vol. of text, 1 vol. of plates: the sketching has some mistakes) (*cf.* also the *Géographie de la Gaule*).

MILLER (K.), *Itineraria romana, röm. Reisewege an der Hand der T.P. dargestellt*, 1st edit. 1887, repub. with separate text, 1888; 2nd edit. Stuttgart, 1916 (plans of limited value), reprinted 1929 and 1962.

Die Peutingersche Tafel, Ravensburg, 1916, reprinted Stuttgart, 1962 (near-facsimile in colour). *Itineraria romana*, Rome, 1963.

CUNTZ (O.), *Itineraria Romana I Itineraria Antonini Augusti et Burdigalense*, Leipzig, 1929.

SCHNETZ (J.), *Itineraria Romana II. Ravennatis Anonymi Cosmographia et Guidonis Geographia*, Leipzig, 1940.

Cf. Id., *Ravenna Anonymus, Cosmographia, eine Erdbeschreibung um das Jahr 700*, trans. J. SCHNETZ, Uppsala, 1951.

A popular edition, *Les Douze Segments de la Table de Peutinger*, has been issued by the Société Gaule, 10, Paris (based on von Scheyb).

L. Dillemann has given notice of an edition of the Anonymous of Ravenna in his thesis (1962).

General works on the Itineraries

DETLEFSEN (D.), *Ursprung, Einrichtung und Bedeutung der Erdkarte von Agrippa*, Berlin, 1906.

DEPT (G. G.), 'Notes sur la Tabula Peutingeriana', *R.B.Ph.*, X, 1931, pp. 997–1011.

ELTER (A.), *Itinerarstudien*, Bonn, 1908.

FABRICIUS, 'Itineraria', *R.E.* de P.W.

GEYER (P.), *Kritische und sprachliche Erläuterungen zu Antonini Placentini Itinerarium*, Augsburg, 1891.

HEURGON (J.), 'La syntaxe des routiers romains', *B.S.A.F.*, 1950–1951, p. 145. *Cf.* 'La fixation des noms de lieux en latin d'après les itinéraires routiers', *R.Ph.*, XXVI, 1952, pp. 169–178.

KLOTZ (A.), 'Die geographischen Commentarii des Agrippa und ihre Ueberreste', *Klio*, XXIV, 1931, pp. 386–466.

KUBITSCHEK (W.), 'Eine röm. Strassenkarte', *J.O.E.A.I.*, V, 1902, pp. 20–96.

KUBITSCHEK (W.), 'Itinerarien' in *R.E.* de P.W., IX, 2, 1916, col. 2308.

KUBITSCHEK (W.), 's.v. Karten', *Ib.*, X, 2, 1919, 2600.

KUBITSCHEK (W.), 'Itinerar-Studien', *S.A.W.W.*, *Phil. hist. Kl. 61, Abh'* 3, 1919.

KUBITSCHEK (W.), 'Ein arithmetisches Gedicht und das Itinerarium Antonini', *A.C.*, 1933, pp. 167–176.

LECLERCQ (H.), 'Itinéraires', in *Dict. d'archéol. chrét.*, VII, 2, Paris, 1927, p. 1841.

LEVI (A. et M.), *Itineraria picta, Contributo allo studio della Tabula Peutingeriana*, Rome, 1967.

PALLU DE LESSERT (C.), 'La syntaxe des routiers romains et les déformations des noms de lieux dans l'Afrique romaine', *Mém. S.N.A.F.*, 7ᵉ s. V, 1904–1905, pp. 115–138.

SCHNABEL (P.), 'Der verlorene Speirer Codex des Itinerarium Antonini, der Notitia Dignitatum und anderer Schriften', *Sitzb. Preuss. Ak. d. W.*, 1926, pp. 242–257.

SCHNABEL (P.), 'Die Weltkarte des Agrippa', *Philologus*, XC, 1935, pp. 405–440.

SCHNAYDER (J.), *De Itinerariis poematis Romanorum*, Lodz, 1953.

SCHNETZ (J.), *Untersuchungen über die Quellen der Kosmographie des anonymen Geographen v. Ravenna*, Münich, 1942 (*S.B.A.W.*, Phil. hist. Abt., 1942, Heft 6).

TIERNEY (J. J.), 'The Map of Agrippa', *P.C.A.*, LIX, 1962, pp. 26–27.

UHDEN (V.), 'Zu Uberlieferung der Weltkarte des Agrippa', *Klio*, XXXVI, 1933, pp. 267–278.

UHDEN (V.), 'Die Weltkarte des Isidorus von Sevilla', *Mnemosyne*, III, 1935, pp. 1–28.

UHDEN (V.), 'Die Weltkarte des Martianus Capella', *Mnemosyne*, 3 ser. III, 1935–1936, pp. 97–124 (*cf.* also *Hermes*, LXVIII, 1937).

WEYMAN (C.), Procedere = proferre, *Archiv. f. latein, Lexikogr.*, IX, 1896, pp. 136–137 (with reference to the *Antonine Itinerary*).

Studies of the 'Peutinger Table'

CRAWFORD (O. G. S.), 'Marking where Watling Street traversed Kent: the oldest map of Roman Britain', *Ill. London News,* 29 Nov., 1924 (the best photograph of the western segment).

DEPT (G. G.), 'Notes sur la Tabula Peutingeriana', *R.B.Ph.*, X, 1931, pp. 997–1011.

DESJARDINS (E.), *Géographie de la Gaule d'après la Table de Peutinger*, Paris, 1869; *cf. Géographie historique et administrative de la Gaule romaine*, Paris, 1876 (IV, pp. 72 and 120, part of Plate IX) and, with A. LONGNON, *Géographie de la Gaule*, 1890, III, p. 480, IV, pp. 40–71.

Von FRIJTAG-DRABBE (C. A. J.), 'Die Peutinger-Karte in dem Licht der neusten Untersuchungen', *C.R. du Congrès intern. de géogr.*, Reports of Section IV, Amsterdam, 1938 (Leiden, 1938, II, p. 209).

GATTI-CROSARA (G.), 'Guardando l'Itinerarium Romanum detto Tabula Peutingeriana', *F.R.*, 22, 1957, pp. 56–64.

GROSS (H.), *Zur Entstehung der Tabula Peutingeriana*, Berlin, 1913.

HOLZ, 'Beiträge zur Erklärung und Geschichte der prutingerschen Tafel', *M.I.O.E.G.*, VI, 1886, p. 219.

JULLIAN (C.), 'La Gaule dans la Table de Peutinger', *R.E.A.* XIV, 1, 1912, pp. 60, 116, Pl. I–VIII (heliotypic fac-simile, for the section showing Gaul, of the *Peutingeriana Tabula Itineraria* of Vienna, 1888).

LEVI (A. et M.), *Itineraria picta. Contributo allo studio della Tabula Peutingeriana*, Rome, 1967.

LEVI (A. C.), TRELL (B.), 'An Ancient Tourist Map', *Archaeology*, XVII, 1964, pp. 227–236.

LEYDEN (A.), 'Eine unerklärte Inschrift auf der Peutingerschen Tafel', *B.J.*, 165, 1965, pp. 278–280.

MADDOLI (G.), 'La Tabula Peutingeriana e l'ubicazione di Temesa', *P.P.*, CXLVI, 1972, p. 331.

MILLER (K.), *Die Weltkarte des Castorius genannt die*

Peutingersche Tafel, Stuttgart, 1888 (separate text with the reprint of the 1887 edition), *cf. Mappae Mundi, die ältesten Weltkarten*, Stuttgart, 1895–1898.

MILLER (K.), *Zur Geschichte der Tabula Peutingeriana*, Freiburg in Brisgau, 1897.

PHILIPPI (F.), *Die Tabula Peutingeriana,* inaugural dissertation, Bonn, 1876.

PHILIPPI (F.), 'Zur Peutingerschen Tafel', *Rh.M.*, LXIX, 1914, pp. 40–55.

UGGERI (G.), *La Sicilia nella Tabula Peutingeriana*, Naples, 1968 (*Vichiana*, VI, 1969, pp. 127–171).

WARTENA (J. R.), *Inleiding op een uitgave der Tabula Peutingeriana*, Amsterdam, 1927.

WINKLER (A.), 'Afrique. Illustrations de la Table de Peutinger', *Rev. tunisienne*, 17, 1910, pp. 482–496.

Topographical studies using the 'Peutinger Table'

AHARONI (Y.), 'The Roman Road to Aila', *I.E.J.*, IV, 1954, pp. 9–16.

AUDIN (A.), 'Voies romaines autour de Lyon. Les trois étapes marquées du nombre XVI dans la *Table de Peutinger*', *R.A.E.*, II, 1951, p. 97.

BARRIÈRE (P. et Cl.), 'Lignes de terre et lignes d'eau d'après la *Table de Peutinger*', *R.E.A.*, XLV, 1943, pp. 91–105.

BIJVANCK (A. W.), 'De praehistorie van her Noorden', *Algemeine Geschiedenis der Nederlanden*, I, pp. 37–132.

BOSIO (L.), 'La Venetia orientale nella descrizione della Tabula Peutingeriana', *A.N.*, 1973, pp. 37–84.

CHAMPIGNEULLE (A.), 'Le problème de Ségora', *Arch. Arm.*, 1963, pp. 69–92.

DANIEL-ROPS (H.), *L'Église des apôtres et des martyrs*, Paris, Fayard, 2nd edit. 1951: Greek fac-simile of the *Peutinger Table*.

EDELMAN (T.), 'Riviermonden ten tijde vand de Romeinen', *Land en Water*, VII, 1965, pp. 240–246.

FUSTIER (P.), 'Nouvelle coupe de la voie romaine de Lyon à Roanne', *R.A.E.*, XIII, 1962, pp. 124–127.

HETTEMA (H.), 'Nog eens het Nederlandsch gedeelte der Tabula Peutingeriana', *Tidschr. Nederl. Aardryksk-genootsch*, 53, 1936, pp. 668–689.

KROON (K.), 'Het nederlandsche gedeelte van de Tabula Peutingeriana', *ibid.*, 52, 1935, pp. 319–336.

LEBEL (P.), 'La station routière de Bibe', *R.A.E.*, IV, 1953, pp. 264–267.

MIRKOVIC (M.), 'The Roman Road Naissus – Scupi and the stages Ad Fines', *Z.Ant.*, X, 1960, pp. 249–257.

MUELLER (R.), 'Die Geographie der Peutingerschen Tafel in der Rheinprovinz, in Holland und Belgien', *Geogr. Anzeiger*, 1926, Heft 9–10 (and Gotha, 1966).

TOMOWSKI (T.), 'Beitrag zu einer Rekonstruktion der Strecke Scupi-Stobi auf der T.P.', *Z.Ant.*, XI, 1961, pp. 113–125.

Examples of studies involving the 'Antonine Itinerary'

1. In Gaul

BARRIÈRE (P.), 'A propos des voies antiques des Cadurques, Organisation et circulation', *R.E.A.*, LIV, 1952, pp. 102–108.

BARRUOL (G.), MARTEL (P.), 'La voie romaine de Cavaillon à Sisteron, sous le Haut-Empire', *R.S.L.*, XXVIII, 1962, pp. 125–202.

BERCHEM (D. van), 'Les origines de l'*Itinéraire d'Antonin* et ses rapports avec les édits relatifs à la perception de l'annone', *B.S.A.F.*, 1934, pp. 212–213, *cf. Mém. S.N.A.F.*, 1937, pp. 172 *sq.*

BOUDREAU (M.), 'Voies romaines en pays boien', *Bull. Soc. archéol. Bordeaux.* LXII, 1957–62 (64), pp. 111–118.

MATHERAT (G.), 'Le problème topographique de Litanobriga', *M.A.I.*, XIV, 1951, 2, pp. 1–60.

MERLAT (P.), 'Les noms d'Ouessant', list of place names in *Annales de Bretagne,* LXII, 1955, pp. 379–391, *cf.* 'Considérations générales sur l'établissement d'une carte du réseau routier en Armorique antique et observations particulières sur une carte des voies romaines de la cité des Vénètes', *N.A.A.,* 1955, pp. 300–332.

MUELLER (R.), 'Oppidum Atuatucorum', *Gymnasium*, LXI, 1954, pp. 326–339.

OLDHAM (R. D.), 'The Antonine Itinerary of the Aurelian Road between Aix and Arles', *G.J.*, LXXII, 1928, p. 58.

REBUFFAT (R.), 'Les stations corses de l'*Itinéraire d'Antonin*', *A.F.L.A.*, XLIII, 1967 (*Études classiques*, II), pp. 217–227.

ROBLIN (M.), 'L'emplacement de Litanobriga', *B.S.A.F.*, 1943–1944, pp. 129–130.

ROBLIN (M.), 'L'habitat ancien dans la région de Pont-Sainte-Maxence', *Mélanges A. Piganiol*, Paris (1966), pp. 1087–1110.

2. For other provinces, the following are useful:

BLOCH (R.), 'Une campagne de fouilles dans la vallée du Chéliff', *M.E.F.R.*, 1941–1946, pp. 9–42.

CHATELAIN (L.), 'Carte du Maroc romain', *B.S.A.F.*, 1945–1947, p. 195.

DESJARDINS (V.), 'Note sur les martyrs de Regia', *B.S.G.A.O.*, LXV, 1944, pp. 77–81.

DERINGER (H.), 'Die römische Reichsstraße Aquileia-Lauriacum', *Carinthia*, CXXXIX, 1949, pp. 193–221.

EUZENNAT (M.), 'Les voies romaines du Maroc dans l'*Itinéraire d'Antonin*', *Hommages à A. Grenier*, pp. 595–610; *cf.* Tocolosida (last station in the *Antonine Itinerary*), *B.A.C.*, N.S. 1–2, 1965–1966 (68), pp. 160–161.

GEYER (P.), 'Orum der Rand (It. A. 20)', *Archiv. f. Latein. Lexikogr.*, IX, 1896, p. 300.

GOODCHILD (R. G.), 'The Coast Road of Phoenicia and its Roman Milestones', *Berytus*, IX, 1949, pp. 91–127 (accuracy of the *Antonine Itinerary*) (*cf. B.S.R.*, XIX, 1951 (52), pp. 43–77: identification of a station in Tripolitania).

HURTADO (V.), 'Las provincias hispano-romanas y las vias de Antonino', *El Miliario extravagante*, V, 1964, pp. 102–108.

HUSSEY (Chr.), 'Netherby Hall, Cumberland', *Country Life*, CV, 1949, pp. 142–145.

KUCHTNER (L.), 'Die Entfernungsangaben für die Römerstraß Pons Aeni ad Castra im Itinerarium Antonini', *Verhandl. d. Hist. Vereins für Niederbayern*, LXXVIII, 1952, pp. 94–98.

LA LOMIA (M. R.), 'Ricerche archeologiche a Vito Soldano', *Kôkalos*, VII, 1961, pp. 157–165.

LIGOTTI (A.), 'Identificazione di Calloniana', *A.S.S.O.*, XI–XII, 1958–1959, pp. 123–130.

LOPES PEGNA (A.), 'Itinera Etruriae', *S.E.*, XXI, 1950–1951, pp. 407–442.

MAYERSON (Ph.), 'The Desert of Southern Palestine according to Byzantine Sources', *P.A.Ph.S.*, CVII, 1963, pp. 160–172.

MELONI (P.), 'I miliari sardi e le strade romane in Sardegna', *Epigraphica*, XV, 1953 (55), pp. 20–50.

MERCATI (G.), 'S. Isicius (It. A. 27)', *R.Bi.*, N.S. IV, 1907, pp. 79–80.

MORAN (P. C.), GALLENT (G. G.), *Vias y Poblaciones romanas en el norte de Marruecos*, Madrid, 1948.

MOUTERDE (R.), 'Une dédicace d'Apamée de Syrie et l'*Itinéraire d'Antonin*', *C.R.A.I.*, 1952, pp. 355–363.

MUELLER (R.), 'Römer und röm. Poststraßen im Jülichen Land', *Heimat. Kalender des Kreises Jülich*, 1952, pp. 56–64.

OPELT (I.), 'Das Grab des Riesen Goliath (It. A. 31)', *Jb. A.C.*, III, 1960, pp. 17–23.

PASSMORE (A. D.), *The Roman Road from Caerleon to Silchester. Itinerarium Antonini Augusti. Iter Britanniarum XIII*, Swindon, 1948.

RIVET (A. L. F.), 'The British Section of the Antonine Itinerary', *Britannia*, I, 1970, pp. 34–82.

ROLDAN HERVAS (J. M.), 'Sobre los acusativos con "ad" en el Itinerario de Antonino', *Zephyrus*, XVII, 1966, pp. 109–119.

SAA (M.), *As Grandes Vias da Lusitania. O Itinerario de Antonino Pio*, I, Lisbonne, 1956 (57).

STEFAN (Gh.), 'Scythica. A propos d'un passage de l'Itinerarium Antonini, 225, 3', *Balcania*, VII, 1944, 2, pp. 344–348.

UGGERI (G.), 'La terminologia portuale romana e la documentazione dell'Itinerarium Antonini', *S.I.F.C.*, XL, 1–2, 1968, p. 225.

VELKOV (V.), *Klio*, XXXIX, 1961 (62), pp. 215–221 (a *castellum* in the *Antonine Itinerary*).

WHEELER (G. H.), 'Textual Errors in the Itinerary of Antoninus', *E.H.R.*, 35, 1920, pp. 377–382; 67, 1932, pp. 622–626.

3. For the Maritime Itinerary:

DUPRAT (E.), 'A propos de l'Itinéraire maritime: Citharista = La Ciotat', *Institut historique de Provence, Congrès . . .*, 1939, 46.

LUGAND (R.), 'Notes sur l'Itinéraire maritime de Rome à Arles', *M.E.F.R.*, XLIII, 1926, pp. 124–139.

MOUQUET (J.), 'Sur quelques ports de l'Itinéraire maritime', *R.A.*, XXXIV, 1931, 2, pp. 123–135.

UGGERI (G.), 'Sull'Itinerarium per maritima loca da Agrigento', *A. et R.*, N.S., XV, 1–3, April–Sept. 1970, p. 107.

There is a collection of papers on the *Antonine Itinerary* in the *Bulletin* 3–4, 1968, of the Société Gaule.

Topographical studies making use of several itineraries

In general, for the French sections of the itineraries, reference may be made to E. DESJARDINS, *Géographie de la Gaule romaine*; Public. des Bénédictins, *Historiens de France*; A. MOLINIER, *Les Sources de l'histoire de France*, Paris, 1901.

ALBERTINI (E.), 'Notes critiques sur l'*Itinéraire d'Antonin* et la *Table de Peutinger*', *M.E.F.R.*, XXVII, p. 463.

ALVES PEREIRA (F.), 'Consideraçôes sôbre a interpratação do Itinerarium romano na parte relativa às ligaçôes viárias de Olisipo a Emerita', *Mem. Acad. das Ciências de Lisboa*, Cl. de Letras, II, 1937, pp. 33–111.

BARADEZ (J.), 'Réseau routier de la zone arrière du limes de Numidie', *Limes-Studien*, III, Bâle, 1957 (59), pp. 19–30.

BEJARANO (V.), 'Fuentes antiguas para la historia de Salamanca', *Zephyrus*, VI, 1955, pp. 89–119.

DERINGER (H.), 'Die röm. Reichsstraße Aquileia-Lauriacum', *Carinthia*, CXXXIX, 1949, pp. 193–221.

DOERNER (F. K.), 'Dusae ad Olympum', *Studies Robinson*, I, pp. 374–379.

FAVRET (P.-M.), 'Hypothèses sur l'identification des stations des voies romaines de Reims à Verdun et de Reims à Toul', *B.C.T.H.*, 1936–1937, pp. 465–474 (*cf. id.*, Riobe, *ibid.*, pp. 461–464).

FISCHER (H.), 'Geschichte der Kartographie von Palästina', *Z.Pal.V.*, 1939, pp. 169–189.

GOODCHILD (R. G.), 'The Coast Road of Phoenicia and its Roman Milestones', *Berytus*, IX, 1949, pp. 91–127.

HENSCHELL (H.), 'Die Geographie Südwestgalliens nach den röm. Itineraria', *B.Ph.W.*, 1917, p. 47.

MARTIN (J.), 'Geminiacus vicus', *Namurcum*, 1948, pp. 47–52.

MUELLER (R.), 'Die Angaben der röm. Itinerare über die Heerstraße Köln-Eifel-Reims', *Festschrift P. Meyer*, Münstereifel, 1933; ed. *Tabula Germaniae secundae. Orte und Zeugen der Peutingerschen*

Tafel und des Antoninischen Itinerars, Köln-Lindental, 1946.

MUELLER (R.), 'Oppidum Atuatucorum', *Gymnasium*, LXI, 1954, pp. 326–339.

POLASCHEK (E.), 'Die Tabula Peutingeriana und das Itinerarium Antonini als topographische Quellen für Niederösterreich', *Jb. für Landeskunde von Niederösterreich*, XXVI, 1936, pp. 38–50.

STIGLITZ (H.), 'Röm. Lager . . . am norischen Limes', *J.O.E.A.I.*, XLVI, 1961–1963, Beibl. pp. 143–172.

STOLTE (B. H.), 'Driemaal Noviomagus', *Numaga*, XIII, 1966, pp. 233–235.

Ptolemy's 'Geography'

WILBERG (F. G.), Translation into Latin (6 parts), Essen, 1838–1845.

NOBBE (C. F. A.), 3 vol., Leipzig, 1843–1845 (index).

LANGLOIS (V.), *Géographie de Ptolémée*, a photo-lithographic reproduction of the Greek manuscript in the Vatopedi monastery on Mount Athos, Paris, 1867.

MUELLER (C.), Paris, Didot, I, 1, 1883; I, 2, 1901 (Latin translation).

CUNTZ (O.), *Die Geographie des Ptolemaeus*, Berlin, Teubner, 1923, Monumenta cartographica Africae et Aegypti.

DANGIOLO (J.), Latin translation, Paris, 1931.

STEVENSON (E. L.), English translation, New York, 1932.

YOUSSOUF KAMAL, Cairo, 1926–1951.

Studies

ALMAGIA (R.), *Monumenta Italiae Cartographica*, Florence, 1929, 1.

BERTHELOT (A.), 'Les données numériques fondamentales de la géographie antique d'Eratosthène à Ptolémée', *R.A.*, 1932, 2, pp. 1–34 (cf. *R.E.A.*, 1934, p. 51: Ptolemy's map of Gaul).

FISCHER (J.), 'Die Stadtzeichen auf den Ptolemäuskarten', *Kartographische Zeitung*, VII, 1918, p. 49.

FISCHER (J.), *Claudii Ptolemaei geographiae codex Urbinas Graecus 82. Codices e Vaticanis selecti XVIII*, Lugduni Batavorum, Lipsiae, 1932.

FISCHER (J.), *Geography of Claudius Ptolemy*, New York, 1932.

PINEAU (H.), *La Côte atlantique de la Bidassoa à Quiberon dans l'Antiquité*, Paris, 1970.

POLASCHEK (E.), 'Ptolemy's Geography in a new light', *Imago mundi*, 14, 1959, pp. 17–37.

POLASCHEK (E.), in PAULY WISSOWA, *Suppl.* X, Stuttgart, 1965, pp. 680–833.

RIVET (A. L. F.), 'Some aspects of Ptolemy's Geography of Britain', in R. Chevallier (edit.), *Littérature Gréco-Romaine et Géographie Historique* (Caesarodunum IX bis), Paris, 1974, pp. 55–81.

SCHMITT (P.), 'Recherche des regles de construction de la cartographie de Ptolémée', *Actes du Colloque international sur la cartographie archéologique et historique*, Paris, 1970 (Tours, 1972).

STAHL (W. H.), 'Ptolemy's Geography, a select bibliography', New York, 1953 (extract from *Bulletin of the New York Library*, 1951–1952).

ZIEGLER, *R.E.*, 23, 2 (1959), *Ptolemaios*, no. 66, col. 1788–1859 (cf. Sup. 10 (1965), col. 680–833; 10, 2 (1919), *Karten*, §32–58, col. 2064–2098; Sup. 4 (1924), *Geographie*, col. 654–660).

Other geographical texts

Expositio totius mundi et gentium, editor J. Rougé, Paris, 1966.

Dimensuratio provinciarum. cf. A. RIESE, *Geographi latini minores*, Heilbronn, 1878 and *R.E.*, item 5, 1 (1903), col. 647.

Studies of the Ravenna Cosmography (*Ravennati Anonymi Cosmographia*)

Editions by PARTHEY (G.), PINDER (M.) and SCHNETZ (J.), cf. supra.

FUNAIOLI (G.), *R.E.*, A, I, 1914, *Ravennas Geographus*, col. 305–310.

JACOBS (A.), *Gallia ab Anonymo Ravennate descripta*, Paris, 1858.

LEBEL (P.), 'Les noms de rivière de la Gaule chez l'Anonyme de Ravenne', *R.E.A.*, 41, 1939, pp. 121–137.

MAZZARINO (S.), 'Da "Lollianus et Arbetio" al mosaico storico di S. Apollinare in Classe', *Riv. di Studi bizantini*, N.S. 2–3 (XII–XIII), pp. 99–117.

RICHMOND (I. A.), CRAWFORD (O. G. S.), 'The British Section of the Ravenna Cosmography', *Archaeologia*, XCIII, 1949, pp. 1–50.

SALAMA (P.), 'Aïoun Sbiba. Identification de la ville romaine', *Libyca*, III, 1965, pp. 173–177.

SCHILLINGEN-HAEFELE (V.), 'Beobachtungen zum Quellen-problem der Kosmographie von Ravenna', *B.J.*, CLXIII, 1963, pp. 238–251.

SCHNETZ (J.), *Sitzungsber. Bayer. Ak.*, 1942, Heft 6 (on the sources). Cf. *Untersuchungen zum Geographen von Ravenna*, Munich, 1919; *Philologus*, LXXXVII, 101; *Zeitschrift für Namenforschung*, XV, 85; *S.B.A.W.*, 1942, Heft 6.

STOLTE (B. H.), *De Cosmographie van den Anonymus Ravennas. Een Studie over de Bronnen van Boek II–V*, Amsterdam, 1949.

SVENNUNG (J.), 'Belt und Baltisch', *Acta Univ. Upsal*, 1953, 4.

Christian itineraries

Corpus Scriptorum ecclesiasticorum latinorum, XXXVIII, Itinera Hierosolymitan saeculi III–VIII ex recensione Pauli Geyer, Prague-Vindobonae, Leipzig, 1898 (reproduction Wiesbaden, 1964).

Corpus Christianorum, Itineraria et alia geographica, Turnholti, 1965, series latina, CLXXV, CLXXVI (bibliography pp. ix *sq.*).

The following are also of use:

TOBLER (T.), *Itinera et descriptiones Terrae sanctae . . .* , Geneva, 1879; *Itineraria Hierosolymitana*, Geneva, 1877–1880.

BARTHÉLEMY (A. de), *R.A.*, 10, 1864, 2, 98, 112 (based on ms. at Verona).

STEWART (A.), WILSON (C. W.), *Library of the Palestine Pilgrims*, V, London, 1887.

And *cf. supra* the general editions by Parthey and Pinder and by Cuntz.

Examples of works using the *Itinerary from Bordeaux to Jerusalem*:

DESJARDINS (E.), *Géographie de la Gaule*, IV, pp. 31–35 for the Gallic section.

DYGGVE (E.), 'Archeologie und Statik', *J.O.E.A.I.*, XLIII, 1956, Beibl. pp. 77–86.

EDSON (Ch.), 'The Location of Cellae and the Route of the Via Egnatia in Western Macedonia', *C.Ph.*, XLVI, 1951, pp. 1–16.

GELSOMINO (R.), 'L'Itinerarium Burdigalense e la Puglia', *Vet. Chr.*, III, 1966, p. 161.

KIRSTEN (E.), in *Erdkunde*, 13, 1959, p. 414.

LORENZONI (A.), *Da Tallegatae a Beneventum nell'itinerario Burdigalese. Il corso dell'antica strada degli Italiani romani tra i fiumi Oglio e Mincio*, Brescia, 1962.

MILIK (J. T.), 'La patrie de Tobie', *R.Bi.*, LXXIII, 1966, pp. 522–530.

MOMMERT (C.), *Der Teich Bethesda zu Jerusalem und das Jerusalem des Pilgers von Bordeaux*, Leipzig, 1907.

PIECHOTTA (J.), 'Monubilis (It. Burdig., 595, 3)', *Archiv. für lateinische Lexikogr.*, 1, 1884, p. 585.

On Egeria's Itinerary

MILANI (C.), 'Studi sull'Itinerarium Egeriae. L'aspetto classico d. lingua di Egeria', *Aevum*, Sept.–Dec. 1969, p. 381.

PRINZ (O.), *Itinerarium Egeriae*, 5th edit. Heidelburg, 1960.

TRIELLITZSCH (W.), 'Aetherias Pilgerreise', *Altertum*, VII, 1961, pp. 104–111.

Also for consultation

GUNZBERG (D.), 'L'itinéraire de Theodosium', *Rev. critique d'hist.*, XVI, 1882, p. 221.

KÖTTING (B.), *Peregrinatio religiosa. Wallfahrten in der Antike und das Pilgerwesen in der alten Kirche*, Münster, 1950.

Regarding the topographical accuracy of stories about the movement of relics, *cf.* C. JULLIAN, *R.E.A.*, 1923, p. 378.

Regarding St. Ambrose's travels along Roman roads, *cf.* A. PAREDI, *Sant'Ambrogio*, Milan, 1941, pp. 275, 473.

See below the section 'Christian pilgrimage in Antiquity and the Middle Ages'.

Milestones and distance-measurement

Italian milestones are dealt with below in a separate section.

D'ANVILLE, *Éclaircissements géographiques sur l'ancienne Gaule*, preceded by a treatise on the distance-units of the Romans and the Gallic league, 1741.

D'ANVILLE, *Traité des mesures itinéraires anciennes et modernes*, 1769.

ARMAND-CALLIAT (L.), GUEY (J.), 'Un milliaire romain à Corcelle . . .', *R.A.E.*, 8, 1957, pp. 88–100.

AUBERT (G.), BOYER (R.), FÈVRIER (P. A.), TAXIL (A.), 'Un milliaire de Néron', *Hist. locale*, 9, pp. 29–32, 1957, 5. *Cf.* R. BOYER, *Cahiers ligures de préhist. et d'arch.*, no. 8, 1959, pp. 87–111.

AURES (A.), 'Note sur le système métrique des Gaulois', *R.A.*, 14, 1866, p. 183. *Cf.* a note on the dimensions of a Gallic votive altar, *ibid.*, 15, 1867, p. 108.

BEAURAIN (G.), 'Les lieues des Landes', *Revue des études rabelaisiennes*, 6, 1908, p. 666.

BERGER (F.), *Uber die Heerstraßen des röm. Reiches, II. Die Meilensteine*, Berlin, 1883.

BERTRAND (Alex.), 'Un mot sur les mesures itinéraires en Gaule à l'époque gallo-romaine', *R.A.*, 4, 1863, pp. 7, 344.

BEYER (G.), 'Die Meilen-zählung an der Römerstraße von Petra nach Bostra und ihre territorialgeschichtliche Bedeutung', *Z.Pal.V.*, 1935, pp. 129–159.

BILLORET (R.), 'Découverte de deux bornes milliaires à Soulosse', *R.A.E.*, Jan.–Dec. 1969, pp. 219–233.

BLAZQUEZ (A.), *Diversas longitudines de las milias romanas*, Madrid, 1932.

CAMPARDOU (J.), 'A propos du milliaire de Cn. Domitius Ahenobarbus imperator découvert à Treilles (Aude)', *Gallia*, VII, 1949, 2, pp. 195–205, *cf.* P.-M. DUVAL, *ibid.*, pp. 207–231.

CLOS ARCEDUC (A.), 'La métrique des voies galloromaines', *Actes Colloque intern. archéol. aérienne,* Paris, 1964, p. 213.

COLLART (P.), 'Borne milliaire à Monthey et routes romaines du Bas-Valais', *Vallesia*, XV, 1960, pp. 231–340, *cf. R.E.A.*, 1961, p. 393.

CRAVAYAT (P.), 'Un milliaire perdu de la voie de Bourges à Orléans', *Mém. Union Soc. sav. Bourges*, 1958, p. 19.

DESAYE (H.), 'Note sur un milliaire de la voie romaine de la vallée de la Drôme', *Rhodania*, 1955, Vienne, 1956, pp. 20–22.

DESCROIX (J.), 'Sur un nouveau milliaire de Claude', *Bull. Assoc. lyon. Rech. arch.*, Lyon, 1937, pp. 11–13.

DOR DE LA SOUCHÈRE, 'Milliaire d'Antibes', *Gallia*, XIV, 1956, I, pp. 89–90.

DU MESNIL (E.), 'La vraie longueur de la lieue gauloise d'après les monuments antiques de Lyon et de Vienne', *Bull. de la Diana*, 2, 1881–1884, p. 53.

DUVAL (P.-M.), 'A propos d'un milliaire de Cn. Domitius Ahenobarbus impérator découvert dans l'Aude en 1949', *C.R.A.I.*, 1951 (52), pp. 161–166;

cf. R.A.N., I, 1968, 3 (milestone of Domitius and organisation of the Narbonensis).

DUVAL (P.-M.), 'Un milliaire de Maximin Daia', *Le Vieux Nîmes*, no. 28, 1958, pp. 8–13.

DUVAL (P.-M.), 'Le milliaire de Paris', *B.S.A.F.*, 1958, p. 116.

DUVAL (P.-M.), *Paris antique*, Paris, Hermann, 1961, pp. 19, 241, 242, 280.

FANAUD (L.), 'Borne milliare des Cerrets', *Bull. Soc. d'émulation du Bourbonnais*, Moulins, t. 53, 1960, 4th quarter, p. 277.

FUSTIER (P.), 'Un itinéraire préromain jalonné et "gradué"', *Antiquités nationales et internationales*, 14–16, 1963, pp. 56–60.

Gallia, reports of the discovery of milestones::
VI, 1, 1948, p. 215; VII, 2, 1949, pp. 195–205, 207–231; VIII, 1950, pp. 111, 135; XI, 1, 1953, pp. 128–129, 141; XII, 2, 1954, p. 455; XIII, 2, 1955, p. 210; XIV, 1, 1956, pp. 89–90; XV, 2, 1957, pp. 178, 186, 190, 191, 223–224, 234–235, 239, 259, 267; XVI, 2, 1958, pp. 335–336, 366, 432; XVII, 2, 1959, pp. 420, 422–423, 428–429; etc.

GOODCHILD (R. G.), 'The Coast Road of Phoenicia and its Roman Milestones', *Berytus*, IX, 1949, pp. 91–127.

HATT (J.-J.), 'Découverte d'une borne romaine à Seltz', *Études haguenoviennes*, IV, 1962–1964, pp. 363–364.

HELENA (Ph.), 'La borne milliaire de Domitius Ahenobarbus et le trajet audois de la voie Domitienne', *Bull. Comm. archéol. de Narbonne*, XXII, 1949–1950 (51), pp. 88–105.

HIRSCHFELD (O.), 'Die römischen Meilensteine', *Kleine Schriften*, 1907, pp. 703–744 = *Sitzber. Berl. Ak.*, 1907, p. 165.

HULTSCH (F.), *Griechische und römische Metrologie*, Leipzig, 1864–1866.

INNEREBNER (G.), 'Alstraßen der Deutschgegend. Römischer Meilenstein in Laurein?', *Schlern*, XXXI, 1961, pp. 210–211.

JALMAIN (D.), 'Lieues romaines', *Bull. du groupe archéol. du Nogentais*, III, no. 4, pp. 10–11.

KÖNIG (I.), 'Zur Dedikation röm. Meilensteine, Digesta 43, 7, 2; 50, 10, 3–4, *Chiron* III, 1973, pp. 419–427.

KÖNIG (I.), *Die Meilensteine der Gallia Narbonensis*, Berne, 1970.

LANFRANCHI (G.), 'Les itinéraires à travers les anciennes unités de longueur', *Fiches A.A.A.M.*, 1971, 1, pp. 223–228.

LABROUSSE (M.), 'Un milliaire inédit de Constantin à Castelnau-Magnoac', *Pallas*, IV, 1956.

LABROUSSE (M.), 'Deux milliaires de la route romaine de Toulouse à Narbonne', *Pallas*, VI–VII, 1958, facs. 3, pp. 55–58.

LEBEL (P.), *Mém. Comm. Antiq. dépt. Côte d'Or*, XXIV, 1954–1958, pp. 22–23 (correction of *C.I.L.*, XIII, 9045).

LELONG (Ch.), 'Sarcophage taillé dans une borne milliaire du IIIᵉ siècle trouvé à Saint-Martin de Tours', *R.A.C.*, July–Sept. 1969, p. 221.

LOUIS (M.), 'Les bornes milliaires de la voie Domitienne entre le Rhône et le Vidourle', *B.C.T.H.*, 1943–1944–1945 (51), pp. 547–578, *cf.* p. 228.

NESSELHAUF (H.), 'Zu den Funden neuer Leugensteine in Obergermanien', *Germania*, 1937, pp. 173–175.

OXÉ (A.), 'Die römische Meile, eine griech. Schöpfung', *B.J.*, 131, 1926, p. 219.

Cap. de Frégate PETESCH, 'La "Belle Borne" de Cusey', *Bull. Soc. hist. et archéol. de Langres*, XIII, 174, 2nd quar. trim. 1959, p. 111 (*cf. B.C.T.H.*, 1959–1960 (62), p. 68).

PFLAUM (H. G.), 'Deux milliaires de Gaule narbonnaise', *B.S.A.F.*, 1962 (64), p. 45.

PFLAUM (H. G.), 'P. Licinius Gallienus nobilissimus Caesar et imp. M. Aurelius Numerianus nobilissimus Caesar Augustus. A la lumière de deux nouveaux milliaires d'Oum el Bouaghi', *B.A.A.*, II, 1966–1967, pp. 157–182.

The *Revue des études anciennes* (R.E.A.) gives brief details about new discoveries of milestones.

ROLLAND (H.), 'Un nouveau milliaire de l'itinéraire de Peutinger', *C.R.A.I.*, 1962, pp. 76–80.

SALAMA (P.), 'Une borne milliaire archaïque de l'Afrique romaine', *ibid.*, 1963, pp. 142–148. *Cf.* POINSSOT-MERLIN, *B.C.T.H.*, 1934–1935, p. 321.

SALAMA (P.), 'Déchiffrement d'un milliaire de Lepcis Magna', *Libya Antiqua*, II, 1965, pp. 39–45.

SALAMA (P.), 'Le milliaire archaïque de Lorbeus', *Mél. de Carthage*, 1964–1965 (66), pp. 97–115.

SANCIER (R.), 'Étude numérique d'un tronçon de voie d'Aleth à Vorgium', *Mém. Soc. d'émulation des Côtes-du-Nord*, 1963, p. 1.

SPRATER (F.), 'Römerstraßen und Meilensteine', *Festschr. Reineke*, 1950, pp. 131–132.

SUSINI (G.), 'La preparazione del corpus dei milliari' (*C.I.L.*, XVII), *Epigraphica*, XXX, 1968, pp. 180–181 (*cf.* H. H., 'Das corpus miliariorum. Stand der Arbeiten', *ibid.*, XXXII, 1970, p. 188).

TOUTAIN (J.), 'Les nouveaux milliaires de la route de Capsa à Tacape', *Mém. S.N.A.F.*, 1903, p. 153.

WALSER (G.), 'Meilen und Leugen', Epigraphica, Jan.–Dec. 1969, p. 84 (*cf. Actes du Colloque sur les cols des Alpes*, Bourg, 1969 (Orleans, 1971), pp. 55–57).

WALSER (G.), 'Zu zwei germanischen Meilensteinen', *M.H.*, XXVII–4, 1970, pp. 255–264.

WALSER (G.), 'Anepigraphe Meilensteine in der Schweiz', *Chiron* IV, 1974, pp. 457–466.

WALSER (G.), 'Die Reproduktion von Meilenstein-Inschriften', *Actes Vᵉ Congr. intern. Épigr.*, Cambridge, 1967 (Oxford, 1971), p. 437.

WUILLEUMIER (P.), *Inscriptions latines des Trois Gaules*, Paris, published by the C.N.R.S. New milestones are recorded from no. 461 onward.

New discoveries of milestones are also noted in:

Proceedings of the International Congresses on Epigraphy (indexes),
Année epigraphique,
Fasti Archaeologici.

Studies of Italian milestones

BRACCO (V.), 'L'Elogium di Polla', *R.A.A.N.*, XXIX, 1954, pp. 5–37 (*cf.* 1960, p. 149).

BRACCO (V.), 'Ancora sull'Elogium di Polla', *ibid.*, XXXV, 1960, p. 149 (*cf. N.Sc.*, 1953, p. 343).

BRUSIN (G.), 'Un nuovo miliario da Chienes e la strada della Val Pusteria', *F.A.*, III, 4249.

CARETTA (A.), 'Due frammenti di colonne miliari dell'agro Laudense', *Epigraphica*, XI, p. 44.

DEGRASSI (A.), 'Un nuovo miliario calabro della via Popillia', *Philologus*, 1955, p. 259.

DEGRASSI (A.), 'Nouveaux milliaires archaïques', *Mélanges A. Grenier*, Brussels, 1962, p. 499.

DI VITA (A.), 'Un milliarium del 252 a.C. e l'antica via Agrigento-Panormo', *Kôkalos*, I, 1955, p. 10.

DI VITA (A.), 'Una recente nota e la datazione del miliario siciliano del console C. Aurelio Cotta', *Latomus*, 1963, p. 478.

FORNI (G.), 'La strada romana da Hadria (Atri) a Pinna (Penne) (a proposito di un miliario dai pressi di Castilenti)', *Abruzzo*, I, 1963, 1–2, pp. 3–11.

LUSSANA (A.), 'Alcune osservazioni sulle pietre miliari della Transpadana, della Venezia e della Liguria', *Epigraphica*, IX, 1947 (49), pp. 68–80.

MELONI (P.), 'I miliari sardi e le strade romane in Sardegna', *Epigraphica*, XV, 1–4, p. 20.

MIRABELLA ROBERTI (M.), 'Nuovi miliari dalla Transpadana e dalla Venetia', *Atti III Congr. Intern. epigrafia*, Rome, Bretschneider, 1959, p. 353.

PITIMADA (L.), 'S. Onofrio Catanzaro, cippo miliare', *N.S.A.*, 1953, 7–12 (1954), p. 343.

SCIARRA (B.), 'Un miliario della via Herculea? nel Museo provinciale di Brindisi', *Epigraphica*, XXXII, 1970, p. 162.

SOTGIU (G.), *Studi sull'epigrafia di Aureliano*, Univ. di Cagliari, 1961.

SOTGIU (G.), 'Un miliario di Gallo e Volusiano "riscoperto" a Villanova Truschedu', *Studi Sardi*, XXII, 1971–72 (73), pp. 290–292.

STYLOW (A. U.), 'Ein neuer Meilenstein des Maximinus Thrax in Sardinien und die Strasse Karales-Olbia', *Chiron*, IV, 1974, pp. 515–532.

Roman roads: construction and course

AGACHE (R.), 'Présence de fossés parallèles à certaines voies romaines', *Bull. Soc. des Antiquaires de Picardie*, 3rd quarter, pp. 258–264 (*cf.* the special numbers 5, 6 and 7 of the *Bulletin de la Société de Préhistoire du Nord*).

BULLE (M.), 'Geleisestraßen des Altertums', *S.B.A.W.*, Phil. hist. Kl., Jahrg., 1947, Heft 2, p. 134.

CAILLEMER, 'Les voies à rainures chez les Anciens', *Congrès archéologique de France*, XLVI, 1880, pp. 277–289.

CLAES (P.), 'Les fossés-limites de la chaussée Bavai-Cologne dans la région de Liberchies', *Helinium*, IX, 1969, p. 138.

DEL PACE (Cl.), 'Sopra l'uso della pozzolana nei cementi degli antichi e specialmente nella costruzione delle strade consolari dei Romani', *Saggi di dissertaz. acad.*, Accad. Etrusca di Cortona, IX–VII.

DUVAL (P.-M.), 'La construction d'une voie romaine d'après les textes antiques', *B.S.A.F.*, 1959, pp. 176–186.

FORBES (R. J.), *Notes on the history of ancient roads and their construction*, Amsterdam, 1934, 2nd ed. 1964. *Cf. Studies in Ancient Technology* (2. Land transport and road building), II, 2, Leiden, 1955.

FOUET (G.), 'Quelques coupes de voies romaines régionales', *Actes du XXVᵉ Congrès d'Études régionales*. 'Luchon et les Pyrénées centrales', Tarbes, 1970, pp. 16–24.

FUSTIER (P.), 'Notes sur la construction des voies romaines en Italie', *R.E.A.*, 1960, pp. 95–99; 1961, pp. 276–290 (*cf.* 1958, p. 82).

FUSTIER (P.), 'Nouvelle coupe de la voie romaine de Lyon à Roanne', *R.E.A.*, Jan.–June 1962, p. 124.

FUSTIER (P.), 'Étude technique sur un texte de l'empereur Julien relatif à la constitution des voies romaines', *R.E.A.*, LXV, 1963, 1–2, pp. 114–121.

GODET (J.), 'Découvertes le long de la chaussée (romaine) Brunehaut à Petit-Enghien', *Annales du Cercle archéologique d'Enghien*, XI, 1958 (59).

HALBERTSMA (H.), 'Veenbruggen en hun Gebruik . . .', *Ber. van de rijksdienst . . . oudheidkundig Bodemonderzoek*, XII–XIII, 1962–1963, pp. 193–209 (road on a timber base).

JOUDOUX (P.), 'L'art de l'ingénieur chez les Romains', *Le mouzi*, Sept. 1961, pp. 42–48; Jan. 1962, pp. 33–37; July 1962, pp. 11–16.

LECORNEC (J.), 'Structure de la voie romaine Vannes-Angers', *Annales de Bretagne*, NAA, LXXII, 1965, pp. 175–178.

MATHERAT (G.), 'Les ponts de fascines de Jules César à Breuil-le-Sec (Oise)', *R.A.*, 1936, I, pp. 53–94; 1937, I, pp. 38–62.

MATTY DE LA TOUR, *Les Voies romaines, système de construction et d'entretien*, 1865, manuscript, Bibliothèque de l'Institut, 1866, Part 2, Vol. 3: the author carried out more than 300 sections.

MERTENS (J.), coupes in *F.A.*, V, 4889; VII, 4432, etc., *cf. R.E.A.*, 1956, p. 290.

DE RUETTE (A.), 'Hives: coupes de la chaussée romaine Arlon-Tongres', *Ardenne et Famenne*, II, 1959, pp. 120–122, 2 fig.

SIAT (A.), STIEBER (A.), WEIL (R.), 'Nature pétrographique des matériaux d'empierrement d'une voie romaine à Dambach-la-Ville', *C.A.A.H.*, X, 1966, pp. 69–71 (*cf. ibid.*, XIII, 1969, p. 39).

Susini (G. C.), 'Considerazioni sulle carregiate nelle vie urbane romane', *A. e M. d. Dep. Storia patria prov. Romagna*, XII–XIV, 1960–1963, pp. 297–300.

Ulrix (F.), 'Recherches sur la méthode de traçage des routes romaines', *Latomus*, XXII, 1963, 2, pp. 157–181.

Vasselle (F.), 'Coupe de la chaussée romaine à la sortie de Roye, de celles d'Amiens-Vermand et de Saint-Just-en-Chaussée', *B.S.A.P.*, LII, 1966, pp. 216–220.

Vasselle (F.), 'Découverte d'une chaussée romaine à Amiens', *ibid.* 1967, pp. 126–127.

Roman bridges and dykes

Alagna (E. P.), 'I ponti romani di Santa Marinella', *Boll. Informazioni associaz. archeol. Centumcellae*, IV, 1962–1963, no. 4, pp. 42–46.

Allain (Dr.), 'Pont gallo-romain et gué pavé à Argenton-sur-Creuse, Indre', *R.A.C.*, II, 1963, p. 131.

Aubin (H.), 'Die Rheinbrücken im Altertum und Mittelalter. Eine Kriegs – und wirtschaftsgeschichtliche Studie', *Rhein. Vierteljahrsbl.*, VII, 1937, pp. 111–126.

Bakalakis (G.), 'The "Classical" bridge at Amphipolis', *A.J.A.*, 74, 3, July 1970, p. 289.

Ballance (M. H.), 'The Roman Bridges of the Via Flaminia', *P.B.S.R.*, XIX, 1951, pp. 78–117.

Barcacila (A.), in *Stud. Cerc. Istor. Veche*, XVII, 4, 1966, p. 645 (on scene CI of Trajan's Column).

Barruol (G.), 'Le pont romain de Ganagobie', *Gallia*, XXI, 1963, 2, pp. 314–323.

Bedeschi (V.), 'Una strada e un ponte in Brescia antica', *Commentari dell'Ateneo di Brescia*, 1946–1947, pp. 69–76.

Blanc (A.), 'Ponts gallo-romains et très anciens de l'Ardèche et de la Drôme', *Gallia*, XXV, 1, 1966, pp. 77–99.

Blanchet (A.), 'Découvertes faites récemment dans le lit de la Loire, à Ancenis', *B.S.A.F.*, 1950–1951, p. 28.

Blondel (L.), 'Le pont romain de Genève', *Bull. Soc. hist. et archéol. Genève*, V, 1925–1934, pp. 128–140.

Blondel (L.), 'L'emplacement du pont de César sur le Rhône', *Genava*, 1938, pp. 105–115.

Blondel (L.), 'Pont romain de Genève', *ibid.*, 1954, p. 205.

Bundgård (J. A.), 'Caesar's Bridges over the Rhine', *A.Arch.*, XXXVI, 1965 (66), pp. 87–103.

Colomb (J.), *Ponts du Moyen Age*, Cannes, 1967.

Cüppers (H.), 'Vorröm. und röm. Brücken über die Mosel', *Germania*, 45, 1967, 1–3, pp. 60–69.

Cüppers (H.), *Die Trierer Römerbrücken*, Mainz, Philipp von Zabern, coll. du Rheinisches Landesmuseum, Trierer Grabungen u. Forsch. V, 1969.

Degrassi (N.), 'Il ponte romano di Olginate e la Strada da Bergamo a Como', *Riv. archeol. d. antica prov. e diocesi di Como*, f. 127, 1946, pp. 5–23.

Donini (A.), *Ponti su monete e medaglie*, Rome, 1959, Pontif. Univ. Gregoriana.

Dubois (J.), 'La chaussée des Césars et le pont de Saint-Avertin', *B.S.A.T.*, XXXVI, 1970, pp. 109–141, 13 fig.

Dymond (D. P.), 'Roman Bridges on Dere Street, County Durham: with a General Appendix on the Evidence for Bridges in Roman Britain', *Arch.J.* CXVIII, 1961, pp. 136–164.

Eršovič (N. I.), 'Au sujet du passage du Rhin par Jules César', *V.D.I.*, 1968, 140, pp. 120–130.

Fugier (H.), 'Le latin *pontifex* et les faiseurs de chemins latins et indiens', *R.E.L.*, 1961 (62), p. 68.

Gallia, bridges or piers at: Baudven (XII, 2, 1954, 439); Besançon, XI, 1, 1953, 134; Champagne (timber), XIX, 2, 1961, 424, fig. 46–51; Kembs, VIII, 1950, 166; Metz (piles), XVI, 2, 1958, 328; Pont d'Areuilhes, XVII, 2, 1959, 416; Pont des Arches, XX, 2, 1962, 529; Substantion, XIX, 1, 1961, 12; Vaison, XII, 2, 1954, 460; Villeperdrix, XVIII, 2, 1960, 372, fig. 16.

Galliazo (V.), *I Ponti di Padova romana*, Padua, 1971.

Gazzola (P.), *Ponti romani*, Contributo ad un indice sistematico con studio critico bibliografico, Florence, Olschki, 1963.

Gose (E.), 'Neue Beobachtungen an der Römerbrücke', *T.Z.*, XXVII, 1964, p. 153.

Harmand (J.), 'Sur les "ponts de fascines" de Breuille-Sec', *B.S.A.F.*, 1959, p. 271.

Hatt (J.-J.), 'Découverte des vestiges d'un pont romain à Kembs', *C.A.A.H.*, 1952, p. 83.

Kraus (O.), 'Die römische Rheinbrücke bei Köln', *B.J.*, CXXX, 1935, p. 232.

Labrousse (M.), *Toulouse antique*, Paris, 1968 (on bridges, pp. 303–309).

Lamboglia (N.), 'Restauri e ricerche sui ponti romani (Vado Ligure)', *Riv. Ingauna*, 1952, 1, p. 24.

Lamboglia (N.), 'Restauri e ricerche sui ponti romani di Val Ponci (Finale Ligure)', *Riv. Ingauna*, Jan.–March 1954, pp. 9–14.

Laur-Belart (R.), 'Die Römerbrücken von Augst im hochrheinischen Strassennetz', *Festschrift E. Vogt*, Zürich, 1966, pp. 241–246.

Leaning (J. B.), 'The Date of the Repair of the Bridge over the River Chabina', *Latomus*, XXX, 2, Apr.–June 1971, p. 386.

Manière (G.), 'Voies et ponts antiques dans la commune de Saint-Martory (Haute-Garonne)', *Gallia*, XXVII, 1969, 2, p. 163.

Matherat (G.), 'Les ponts de fascines de J. César à Breuil-le-Sec (Oise)', *R.A.*, VII, 1936, pp. 53–94. (Cf. *B.S.A.F.*, 1935, p. 89.)

Schetter (W.), von Uslar (R.), 'Zu den pontes longi' (Tac., *A.*, I, 63, 3), *Gymnasium*, LXXXVII, 1971, pp. 201–224.

Schwab (H.), 'Keltische Brücke zw. Cornaux (Neuenburg) und Gals (Bern)', *S.P.*, XXX, 1966, pp. 9–10.

TUDOR (D.), 'Un pont romain ignoré dans la région du Bas-Danube', *Latomus*, 1961, p. 501.

Roman roads and the study of place-names (toponymy)

The majority of works on the ancient roads touch on the question. The list given below concentrates mainly on published material dealing with road-names (hodonymy). While the examples quoted are principally French, studies are also quoted for other countries to help in the compilation of series for comparative purposes, as recommended by the author in 'Pour une toponymie archéologique comparée', *Hommages Herescu*, 1964, pp. 93–96.

AEBISCHER (P.), 'L'étymologie du français "chaussée" et un passage du "Roman du Brut"', *Onomastica*, V, 1953, pp. 1–7.

ANDRÉ (J.), 'Les noms latins du chemin et de la rue', *R.E.L.*, 1950, pp. 104–134.

ARMAND-CALLIAT (L.), 'Lieux consacrés à Mercure dans la montagne chalonnaise', *B.C.T.H.*, 1943–1945, p. 167.

BLANCHET (A.), 'Hypothèse à propos de la voie Régordane', *C.R.A.I.*, 1945, pp. 458–463.

BONFANTE (G.), 'Tracce di terminologia palafitticola nel vocabolario latino?', *A.I.V.*, XCVI, 1937–1938, p. 62 (this hypothesis, accepted by G. DUMEZIL, *Jupiter, Mars, Quirinus*, p. 126, is rejected by G. PATRONI, *R.I.L.*, LXXII, 1938–1939, pp. 16–24).

BRUNEL (Cl.), 'Le nom de la voie Régordane', *Romania*, 1958, pp. 289–313.

BRUNOT (F.), *Histoire de la langue française*, Vol. VII, Paris, A. Colin, 1926, pp. 202–227 (new edit. 1967).

BUCQUET (H.), 'Quelques précisions sur les "chaussées" anciennes et modernes', *R.I.O.*, V, 1953, pp. 129–130.

CARNOY (A.), 'Toponymie des chaussées romaines en Belgique et dans les régions avoisinantes. Essai d'hodonymie.', *A.C.*, XXIII, 1954, Part I, pp. 5–28.

CHENON (E.), 'Les termes "grand chemin", "chemin royal" et les anciennes voies romaines au Moyen Age', *B.S.A.F.*, 1925, pp. 300–301.

CHEVALLIER (R.), *La Toponymie des voies antiques*, Notice technique no. 5, Groupe d'Archéologie antique du T.C.F., Paris.

CHRISTMANN (E.), '"Kem, Kim, Kümmel", als Benennungen für Römerstraßen von Luxemburg-Metz bis Speyer-Lauterburg', *Germania*, Anzeiger, 27, 1943, pp. 72–79.

CHRISTMANN (E.), KAISER (K. W.), 'Beiträge der Flurnamenforschung zur Römerstraßenforschung in der Pfalz', *B.N.*, N.S., I, 1966, pp. 179–213.

CONNEAU (J.), 'La Pouyade, La Poujade, La Pouge, noms de voies antiques', *Bull. archéol. du Vexin français*, 4, 1968 (69), p. 119.

CONNEAU (J.), *Les Appellatifs de voies antiques et leurs dérivés en toponymie française*, duplicated typescript, 1969.

DU CANGE, sections: 'calceia', 'caminus', 'leuga', 'ru(t)a'.

ESCALLIER (E.), 'Un itinéraire alpin de Gargantua', *Bull. Soc. Et. H.A.*, 1954, p. 42; 1956, p. 94.

FOUCAULT (J. A. de), 'La route dans la toponymie du Pas-de-Calais', *R.I.O.*, June 1968, pp. 101–105.

FOURNIER (P.-F.), 'L'origine du mot chaussée', *Bull. philol. et hist. du C.T.H.*, 1960 (61), pp. 41–53.

GILLES-GUIBERT (M.), 'Le chemin dans la toponymie du Midi de la France', *École nat. des Chartes. Positions des thèses*, 1952, pp. 63–67.

GILLES-GUIBERT (M.), 'Noms des routes et des chemins dans le Midi de la France au Moyen Age', *Bull. philol. et hist. du Comité des T.H.*, 1960 (61), pp. 1–39.

GRENIER (A.), 'La toponymie des voies gallo-romaines', *R.C.C.*, 15–30 March 1930.

GRIERA (A.), 'Algunas designaciones del concepto via en catalan, *via Domitia*, I. Études de linguistique consacrées au Sud de la France et au Nord de l'Espagne', *Annales Fac. Lettres Toulouse*, 1954.

GYSSELING, *Mededelingen van d. Veren. van Naamkunde te Leuwen*, 1957, 24 (names related to roads in Northern Gaul).

HARSH (P. W.), 'Angiportum, platea and vicus', *C.Ph.*, XXXII, 1937–1950.

HERBILLON (J.), 'Routes et chemins en toponymie gallo-romaine', *R.B.Ph.*, XLVI, 1968, 1, pp. 81–86.

HEURGON (J.), 'La fixation des noms de lieux en latin d'après les itinéraires routiers', *ibid.*, XXVI, 1952, pp. 169–178.

HOCHULI (E.), *Einige Bezeichnungen für den Begriff Straße, Weg und Kreuzweg in Romanischen*, Zurich-Aarau, 1926.

HOYOUX (J.), 'Figure et destinée de la chaussée Brunehaut au Moyen Age et à l'époque moderne', *Bull. Inst. archéol. liégois*, LXV, 1945, pp. 71–94.

IRIGOIN (P.), 'Montjoies et oratoires', *B.M.*, XCIV, 1935, pp. 145–170.

LANG (L.), 'Les lieuxdits "Spiegelberg" et leur intérêt archéologique', *Soc. d'hist. et d'archéol. de Saverne*, LIII–LIV, 1966, pp. 44–45.

LAUR-BELART (R.), 'Zwei alte Straßen über den Bözberg'. *S.P.*, Oct. 1968, p. 30; *cf.* XXXII, 4, 1968, p. 72.

LEBEL (P.), 'Voies romaines d'Afrique et de Gaule', *R.A.E.*, II, 1951, p. 192 (comparison of names of road-stations and inns) (*cf. ibid.*, 1950, p. 31; 1953, p. 353).

LOUIS (R.), 'A propos des Montjoies autour de Vézelay. Sens successif et étymologie du nom "Montjoie"', *Pub. annuelles Soc. des fouilles . . . Yonne*, place-name series, I, Auxerre, 1939.

MATHERAT (G.), 'Les chaussées Brunehaut et les anciennes voies romaines en Bourgogne et en

Picardie', *Annales de Bourgogne*, XI, 1939, pp. 121–126.

MURET (E.), 'Noms de lieux, vestiges archéologiques et vieux chemins', *Revue d'hist. suisse*, II, 1931, pp. 409–420.

NIEDEREHE (H. J.), *Strasse und Weg in der gallo-romanischen Toponomastik*, Geneva-Paris, 1967.

OLIVIERI (O.), 'Di alcune tracce di vie romane nella toponomastica italiana', *A.G.I.*, 1934, pp. 200–201.

PALLU DE LESSERT (C.), 'La syntaxe des routiers romains et les déformations des noms de lieux dans l'Afrique romaine', *Mém. Ant. Fr.*, LXV, 1906, pp. 115–138.

QUENTEL (P.), 'Un nom des anciennes routes, Carhaix', *R.I.O.*, XVIII, 1966, pp. 255–270.

ROBLIN (M.), 'Enquêtes pour l'hagiotoponymie française', *Annales*, 1934, p. 342.

ROBLIN (M.), 'Les Montjoies', *B.S.A.F.*, 1945, pp. 45–47 (*cf. ibid.*, 1938, p. 165).

RUBAUD (R.), 'Les voies romaines de Bar-sur-Aube et les lieux de Courcelange, Traucosange et Preverengeval', *Bull. Soc. archéol. dép. Aube*, 2, 1968, p. 46.

SMITH (A. H.), *English Place-name Elements*, Cambridge, 2 vol., 1956 (II, p. 162) (other publications: The Place-names of Gloucestershire, 1964–1965; . . . of Westmorland, . . . of the West Riding of Yorkshire . . .).

SOENENS (F.), 'Le patronage de saint Martin et les voies de pénétration dans l'arrondissement de Lille', *Bull. Soc. d'ét. de la prov. de Cambrai*, XXXIX, 1942–1943, pp. 125–140.

SOUTOU (A.), 'Un toponyme des mauvais chemins, la Vitaterne', *R.I.O.*, 1963, p. 264; *cf. R.I.O.*, 1956, pp. 1–10.

THEVENOT (E.), 'Le toponyme "Maison-Rouge" en pays éduen. Dans quelle mesure il est en rapport avec les voies romaines', *R.A.E.*, XIX, 1968, pp. 312–320.

VANNERUS (J.), 'La reine Brunehaut dans la toponymie et dans la légende', *Bull. Cl. Lettres*, Royal Acad. of Belgium, 5th series, XXIV, 1938, pp. 301–420.

ZELLER (J.), 'Vicus, platea . . .', *A.L.L.G.*, XIV, 1905, p. 301.

Entries and articles in Dictionaries and Encyclopaedias should also be consulted:

Dictionnaire des Antiquités,

Real-Encyclopädie: sections: *decumanus, limes, via*, . . .

The Ancient Roads of Italy

Etruria will be dealt with separately below.

In general, references should be sought in the volumes of the *Forma Italiae*.

ADAMESTEANU (D.), 'Note su alcune vie siceliote di penetrazione', *Kôkalos*, VIII, 1962, pp. 199–209.

ADAMESTEANU (D.), 'La fotografia aerea e le vie di Magna Grecia', *Atti Convegno Taranto*, 1962–1963, pp. 39–58.

ALFIERI (N.), 'Problemi della rete stradale attorno a Ravenna', *C.C.A.R.*, Ravenna, 1967, pp. 7–20.

ALPAGO-NOVELLO (A.), 'Appunti sulla via Claudia Augusta Altinate', *A.I.V.*, 1944–1945, pp. 723–744.

ALPAGO-NOVELLO (A.), *Da Altino a Maia sulla via Claudia Augusta*, Milan, 1972.

ALVISI (G.), 'Problemi di viabilità nell'Apulia settentrionale', *Arch. Clas.*, XIV, 1962, pp. 148–161.

ALVISI (G.), 'Nuove individuazioni di preesistenze archeologiche', *Urbanistica*, 46–47.

ALVISI (G.), *La Viabilità romana della Daunia*, Bari, 1970.

The *Appia antica*: several articles in the periodical *Capitolium*, 10–12, XLIV, Oct.–Dec. 1969; see also 1968, 2, p. 72; 7–8, pp. 251, 255; 9–10, pp. 307, 328; 1969, 3, pp. 47–75.

ASHBY (Th.), FELL (R. A. L.), 'The via Flaminia', *J.R.S.*, XI, 1921, pp. 125–190.

BALDACCI (O.), 'La Sardegna nella Tabula Peutingeriana', *S.S.*, XIV–XV, 1955–1957 (58), pp. 219–338.

BANTI (L.), 'Via Placentia-Lucam, contributo allo studio della guerra annibalica', *A. et R.*, N.S., XIII, 1932, pp. 1–11, pp. 98–120.

BAROCELLI (P.), 'Piccolo S. Bernardo', *N.S.A.*, 1924, pp. 385–392.

BIANCOFIORE (B.), 'La viabilità antica nel tratto a Sud-Est di Bari e di suoi centri culturali', *A.S.P.*, 1962, pp. 205–240.

BOSIO (L.), 'La via Postumia da Oderzo ad Aquileia in relazione alla rete viaria romana della Venetia', *A.I.V.*, CXXIII, 1964–1965, pp. 279–338.

BOSIO (L.), 'La via romana dalla Pannonia alla X Regio e il cammino dei Longobardi', *Convegno Studi Longobardi*, Udine, 1970, pp. 155–164.

BOSIO (L.), *Itinerari e strade della Venetia romana*, Padua, 1970.

BRACCO (V.), 'L'elogium di Polla', *R.A.A.N.*, XXIX, 1954, pp. 5–37.

BRACCO (V.), 'Ancora sull'elogium di Polla', *ibid.*, XXXV, 1960, p. 149.

BRACCO (V.), 'Il luogo di Forum Anni', *A.S.C.L.*, XXXVI, 1965–1966, pp. 151–163.

BRUSIN (G.), 'La via Annia da Altino ad Aquileia', *Atti Convegno retroterra Veneziano*, Mestre-Marghera, 1955, pp. 27–34.

BUCK (R. J.), 'The Via Herculia', *P.B.S.R.*, XXXIX, 1971, pp. 66–87.

Capitolium, *cf. supra*, l'*Appia* (les revues *Italia nostra* et *Le Vie d'Italia* consacrent régulièrement des articles aux voies romaines).

CASTAGNOLI, *Via Appia*, Milan, 1956.

CORRADI (G.), *Le Strade romane dell'Italia occidentale*, Turin, 1939.

DE BON, 'La via Postumia da Verona a Vicenza', *Ateneo Veneto*, 128, 1941.

DEGRASSI (A.), 'La via seguita da Traiano del 105 per

recarsi nella Dacia', *R.P.A.A.*, XXII, 1946–1947, p. 167.

DEGRASSI (A.), 'La via Annia e la data della sua costruzione', *Atti Convegno retroterra veneziano*, Mestre, 1955, pp. 35–46.

DEGRASSI (A.), 'Un nuovo miliario calabrese della via Popillia', *Philologus*, 1955, p. 259.

DEGRASSI (A.), 'Nouveaux milliaires archaïques', *Hommages A. Grenier*, Brussels, 1962, p. 499.

DI VITA (A.), 'Un milliarium del 252 a.C. e l'antica via Agrigento-Panormo', *Kôkalos*, I, 1955, pp. 10–21.

DUVAL (Y.-M), 'Sur la via Latina', *Caesarodunum*, 1969, 3, p. 197.

ESSEN (C. C. van), 'The via Valeria from Tivoli to Callarmelle', *P.B.S.R.*, XXV, 1957, pp. 22–38.

ESSEN (C. C. van), 'A propos de la via Ardeatina et de la via Laurentina', *M.N.I.R.*, 9, 1957, pp. 131–147.

ESSEN (C. C. van), 'A propos du plan de la ville d'Ostie', *Hommages W. Déonna*, coll. Latomus, XXVIII, 1957, p. 509 (course of the Salaria).

FATUCCHI (A.), *Le strade romane del Casentino*, Arezzo, 1974.

FORNI (G.), 'La strada romana da Hadria a Pinna', *Abruzzo*, I, 1963, 1–2, pp. 3–11.

FRACCARO (Pl.), 'La via Claudia Augusta', *R.I.L.*, LXXII, 1938, 39, p. 141.

FRACCARO (Pl.), 'Strade romane nell'agro pavese', *Boll. Soc. Pavese di Storia patria*, XLVI, 1946 (47), pp. 7–27 (N.S.I.).

FRACCARO (Pl.), 'La via Postumia nella Venezia', *Festschrift R. Egger*, I, 1952, pp. 251–275.

FRACCARO (Pl.), 'La via romana da Milano a Piacenza', *Miscellanea G. Galbiati*, Milan, 1961, I, pp. 203–211.

FREDERIKSEN (M. W.), WARD-PERKINS (J. B.), 'The ancient road systems of the central and northern Agar Faliscus (Notes on Southern Etruria, 2)', *P.B.S.R.*, XXV (XII N.S.), 1957, pp. 67–203

GARDNER (R.), 'The via Claudia Valeria', *P.B.S.R.*, IX, 1920, pp. 75–106.

GASTALDI FOIS (P.), 'La rete viaria romana nel territorio del municipium di Bergamo', *R.I.L.*, CV, 1971.1, pp. 211–222.

GELSOMINO (R.), 'L'Itinerarium Burdigalense e la Puglia', *Vet. Chr.*, 3, 1966, pp. 161–208.

GRENIER (A.), 'La transhumance des troupeaux en Italie et son rôle dans l'histoire romaine', *M.E.F.R.*, 25, 1905, pp. 293–328.

HARRIS (W.), 'The via Cassia and the via Traiana Nova between Bolsena and Chiusi', *P.B.S.R.*, XXXIII, 1965, pp. 113–133.

HERZIG (H. E.), *Le reseau routier des régions VI et VIII d'Italie*, 1970.

HERZIG (H. E.), 'Namen und Daten der Via Aurelia', *Epigraphica*, XXXII, 1970, pp. 50–65.

HERZIG (H. E.), 'A propos de l'administration routière dans la Vénétie', Regio X, *Il territorio veronese in età romana*, Vérone, 1973, pp. 87–95.

HINRICHS (F. T.), 'Der röm. Strassenbau zur Zeit der Gracchen', *Historia*, XVI, 1967, pp. 162–176.

HOMO (L.), *Rome impériale et l'urbanisme dans l'Antiquité*, Paris, Albin Michel, 1971 (pp. 357 sq. on town-streets).

KAHANE (A.) and WARD-PERKINS (J. B.), 'The Via Gabina', *P.B.S.R.*, XL, 1972, pp. 91–126.

KIRSTEN (E.), 'Viaggiatori e vie in epoca greca e romana', in *Vie di Magna Grecia, Atti II Convegno Magna Grecia*, Taranto, 1962, pp. 137–158.

LAMBOGLIA (N.), 'La via Aemilia Scauri', *Athenaeum*, 1937, pp. 57–68.

LORENZONI (A.), *Da Tallegatae a Beneventum nell'itinerario Burdigalese*, Brescia, 1962.

LUGLI (G.), 'Strade romane', *Encicl. Ital.*, XXXII.

LUGLI (G.), 'La genesi del sistema stradale di Roma antica', *Atti III Congr. Studi romani*, I, Rome, 1935, p. 256.

LUGLI (G.), 'Osservazioni sulle stazioni della via Appia Antica da Roma ad Otranto', *Festschrift R. Egger*, 1952, pp. 276–293.

LUGLI (G.), 'La via Appia attraverso l'Apulia ed un singolare gruppo di strade orientate', *Atti III Congr. Storico Pugliese*, Brindisi, 1954, p. 12. (*Cf. Atti IX Congr. Storia Architettura*, Bari, 1955 (59), p. 33.)

LUGLI (G.), 'Il sistema stradale della Magna Grecia', *Atti II Convegno Magna Grecia*, Taranto, 1962, pp. 23–27.

LUGLI (G.), 'Il sistema stradale della Magna Grecia', *Études étrusco-italiques*, Louvain, pp. 111–118.

MANSUELLI (G. A.), 'Il commercio delle pietre Veronesi nella regione VIII e la viabilità emiliano veneta nell'età romana', *Il territorio veronese . . .* , Verona, 1973, pp. 77–85.

MANSUELLI (G. A.), 'La rete stradale e i cippi miliari nella regione ottava', *A. e. M.d. Dep. di Storia patria per le prov. di Romagna*, VII, 1941–1942, pp. 33–69.

MARCELLO (J.), *La Via Annia alle porte di Altino*, 1956, p. 121.

MARTINORI (E.), *Le Vie maestre d'Italia*, I, Via Flaminia ; II, Via Cassia, Rome, 1930.

MARTINORI (E.), *Via Nomentana, Via Patinaria, Via Tiburtina*, Rome, 1932.

MARZULLO (A.), 'L'elogium di Polla, la via Popilia e l'applicazione della lex Sempronia agraria del 133 a.C.', *Rassegna storica salernitana*, I, 1947, pp. 25–57.

MATTHEWS (K.), 'The embattled driver in ancient Rome Expedition', *Bull. of the Univ. Mus. of the Univ. of Pennsylvania*, III, 1960, pp. 22–27.

MAZZARINO (S.), 'Aspetti di storia dell'Appia antica', *Helikon*, 1968, pp. 174–196.

MELONI (P.), 'I miliari sardi e le strade romane in Sardegna', *Epigraphica*, XV, I–II, Jan.–Dec. 1953 (55), pp. 20–50.

MIRABELLA-ROBERTI (M.), 'Nuovi miliari dalla Transpadana e dalla Venetia', *Actes du IIIᵉ Congrès d'épigraphie*, p. 353.

MIRABELLA-ROBERTI (M.), 'Les routes romaines du Val Camonica', *Actes du Colloque sur les cols des Alpes*, Bourg, 1969 (Orléans, 1971), p. 53.

Mostra della via Appia Antica, Rome, 1956 (Palazzo Venezia).

Mostra: la via Praenestina. I suoi monumenti, i suoi paesaggi, Rome, 1967, Palazzo Venezia (Italia Nostra, a cura di L. Quilici) (1969).

NISSEN (H.), *Italische Landeskunde*, Berlin, 1883 (*passim*).

OLIVIERI (D.), 'Di alcune tracce di vie romane nella toponomastica italiana', *A.G.I.*, XXVI, 1934, p. 191.

OLIVIERI (D.), 'Die Erschliessung Italiens durch die römischen Straßen', *Gymnasium*, LXXII, 1964, p. 228.

PERNIGO (M. G.), 'Le strade romane nel territorio di Verona: La Via Gallica', *Vita Veronese*, XXIII, 1-2, 1970, 2-6.

PERNIGO (M. G.), 'Le vie minori', *Ib.*, XXIII, 3-4, 1970, pp. 82-84.

PFIFFIG (A.), 'Via Thorrena', *Annali Fac. Lett. Perugia*, VI, 1968-1969 (70), p. 323.

QUARINA (L.), *Le vie romane del Friuli*, Udine, 1970.

RADKE (G.), 'Die Straße des Konsuls P. Popillius in Oberitalien', *Latomus*, XXIV, 1965, 4, pp. 815-823.

Saggi di Foto-interpretazione, Rome, 1964 (L. Quilici, la Via Caere-Pyrgi, pp. 5-15; P. Sommella, La Via Ardeatina, pp. 17-32).

SCHMEIDT (G.), 'Contributo della foto-interpretazione alla conoscenza della rete stradale dell' Umbria nell'alto Medioevo', *Atti III Convegno Studi Umbri*, Gubbio, 1965, pp. 171-210.

SERRA (G.), 'Appunti onomastici sulla storia antica e medioevale di Asti', *R. St. lig.*, XVIII, 1952, pp. 72-102.

SORDI (M.), 'La via Aurelia da Vada a Pisa nell' antichità', *Athenaeum*, XLIX, 1971, 3-4, pp. 302-312.

STERPOS (D.), *Communicazioni stradali attraverso i tempi*, Rome, Soc. Autostrade, 1959-1966: 1. Milano-Piacenza-Bologna, 1959; 2. Bologna-Firenze, 1961; 3. Firenze-Roma, 1961; 4. Roma-Capua, 1966; 5. Capua-Napoli, 1959.

STERPOS (D.), 'La strada romana in Italia, Società Autostrade', *Quad. 17*, Rome, 1969.

'(La) via Aurelia da Roma a Forum Aureli', *Quaderni dell'Ist. di Topografia antica della Università di Roma*, IV, Rome, 1968.

TIBILETTI (G.), Problemi gromatici e storici, *R.S.A.*, II, 1972, pp. 87-96.

TOZZI (P.), *Saggi di Topografia storica*, Florence, 1974, p. 61: viabilità di età romana fra Cremona e Brexia.

TOZZI (P.), 'Una nuova via romana fra Milano e Cremona', *Athenaeum*, LII, 3-4, 1974, pp. 320-325.

VENEZIANO (L.), 'La strada romana da Bolzano a Ponte Gardena', *R.I.L.*, CVI, 1972, pp. 116-121.

VENEZIANO (L.), 'La via Claudia Augusta nell'alta Val Venosta', *Contributi dell'Istituto di Storia antica I*, Milan, 1972, pp. 212-219.

'Vie di Magna Grecia', *Atti II Convegno Magna Grecia*, Taranto, 1962.

VINSON (P.), 'Ancient roads between Venosa and Gravina', *P.B.S.R.*, XL, 1972, pp. 58-90.

WALSER (G.), 'Fortleben röm. Strassen in Italien. Zur Geschichte der via Aemilia Scauri', *A.A.*, 1960, p. 207.

WISEMAN (T. P.), 'Roman Republican road building', *P.B.S.R.*, XXXVIII, 1970, 122-135.

WISEMAN (T. P.), 'Viae Anniae', *P.B.S.R.*, XXXII, 1964, pp. 21-37 and XXXVII, 1969, pp. 82-91.

Etruria

ANZIANI (D.), 'Les voies romaines de l'Étrurie méridionale', *M.E.F.R.*, XXIII, 1913, pp. 169-244.

ASHBY, (T.), 'La rete stradale romana nell'Etruria meridionale in relazione a quella del periodo etrusco', *S.E.*, III, 1929, pp. 171-185. Cf. 'Das röm. Straßennetz in Südetrurien in seiner Beziehung zu dem der etruskischen Periode', *Klio*, XXV, 1932, pp. 114-117.

COLONNA (G.), 'L'ingresso del santuario. La via Caere-Pyrgi ed altri problemi', *Arch. Clas.*, XIX, 1967, 2, pp. 342-348.

DUNCAN (G.), 'Notes on Southern Etruria, III Sutri (Sutrium)', *P.B.S.R.*, XXVI, 1958, pp. 63-134.

HEURGON (J.), 'La Vie quotidienne chez les Étrusques', Paris, Hachette, 1961 (p. 18 on travel).

LOPES PEGNA (M.), 'Itinera Etruriae', *S.E.*, XXI, 1950-1951 (52), pp. 407-442; XXII, 1952-1953 (54), pp. 382-410 (II. I percorsi tirreni).

LOSACCO (U.), 'Le cave: arcane strade d'Etruria', *L'Universo*, Nov.-Dec. 1969, p. 937.

RITTARO (R.), 'Contributi per la carta archeologica dell'Etruria: strade romane nel Chianti settentrionale', *S.E.*, XI, 1937, p. 353.

TRACCHI (A.), 'Di alcune antiche strade dell'Etruria settentrionale . . .', *L'Universo*, March-Apr. 1971, p. 337.

WARD-PERKINS (J. B.), 'Etruscan and Roman Roads in Southern Etruria', *J.R.S.*, XLVII, 1957, 1-2, pp. 139-143.

WARD-PERKINS (J. B.), 'Etruscan Engineering, Road-Building, Water-Supply and Drainage', *Hommages A. Grenier*, Brussels, 1962, pp. 1636-1643.

For roads in the *ager veientanus et faliscus*: *P.B.S.R.*, XXIII, 1955, p. 44; XXV, 1957, p. 67; XXVI, 1958, p. 63; XXIX, 1961, p. 1; XXX, 1962, p. 116; XXXI, 1963, p. 100; XXXVI, 1968, pp. 18, 73.

For the Caere-Pyrgi road, cf. R. MENGARELLI, *S.E.*, XI, 1937, Pl. V (archaeological map of the territory of Caere), p. 94.

Gaul (detailed studies)

For an overall view, *cf. supra*: General Works.
For full details of roads across the Alps, *cf.* the bibliography given by the author in the *Actes du Colloque international sur les cols des Alpes occidentales et centrales, Antiquité et Moyen Âge*, Bourg, 1969 (Orleans, 1971).

ALLIX (A.), *L'Installation de l'homme, la route romaine et la possession du sol en Oisans*, Grenoble, 1929.

AMY (R.), 'Découverte d'une portion de voie romaine à Aix-en-Provence', *R.A.N.*, I, 1968, p. 251.

ANDRÉ (J.), 'Voies terrestres et fluviales entre l'Armorique et le Centre de la Gaule romaine', *R.A.C.*, I, 1961, p. 58.

ARMAND-CAILLAT (L.), 'Les voies romaines du Chalonnais', *XIᵉ Congrès Assoc. bourguignonne des Soc. sav.*, Chalon-sur-Saône, 1934.

AUBERT (G.), BOYER (R.), FÉVRIER (P.-A.), 'Étude partielle de la voie romaine de Forum Voconii à Riez', *Histoire locale*, no. 9-12, 1952, pp. 2-4.

AUBERT (G.), BOYER (R.), FÉVRIER (P.-A.), 'Évolution de la grande voie transversale des Alpes Maritimes au Rhône', *Histoire locale*, nos. 17-24, 1954 (55), pp. 2-12; nos. 29-33, 1957, pp. 3-14; nos. 35-36, 1959, pp. 2-4; nos. 37-38, 1960, pp. 2-8.

AUDIN (A.), 'Les voies axiales de la ville romaine de Fourvières', *C.R.A.I.*, 1943, pp. 11-14.

AUDIN (A.), 'Le confluent de Lyon', *Les Études rhodaniennes*, 1947, pp. 99-118.

AUDIN (A.), 'Le carrefour de Lyon', *Histoire locale*, no. 1, 1949, pp. 10-11.

AUDIN (A.), 'Voies romaines autour de Lyon', *R.A.E.*, II, 1951, pp. 97-104 (*cf. Rev. de Géo. de Lyon*, XXVII, 1952).

BARRIÈRE (P.), 'A propos des voies antiques des Cadurques; organisation et circulation', *R.E.A.*, LIV, 1952, pp. 102-108.

BARRUOL (G.), *Les Peuples préromains du Sud-Est de la Gaule, Études de géographie historique*, Paris, de Boccard, 1969.

BARRUOL (G.), MARTEL (P.), 'La voie romaine de Cavaillon à Sisteron sous le Haut-Empire, étude topographique', *R.S.L.*, XXVIII, 1-4, 1962, pp. 125-202.

BARTHE (Mᵍʳ E.), 'La voie Domitienne et son trajet de Narbonne à Portel', *Bull. Comm. archéol. Narbonne*, XXVIII, 1964-1965, pp. 36-50.

BENOIT (F.), 'La voie d'Italie en Espagne à l'époque d'Auguste sur le territoire d'Arles', *R.E.A.*, XL, 1938, pp. 133-148.

BENOIT (F.), 'Les itinéraires commerciaux en Provence dans l'Antiquité', *Assoc. G. Budé, VIIᵉ Congrès, Aix, 1963, Actes*, Paris, 1964, pp. 362-385.

BIÉVELET (H.), 'L'exploration archéologique de Bavai: note sur le premier mille de la Bavai-Reims', *Revue du Nord*, 1969, pp. 457-472.

BLONDEL (L.), 'Genève nœud de circulations routières. La route romaine d'Annecy à Genève', *Mélanges A. Babel*, 1963, pp. 61-68.

BOISSE (Cl.), *Le Logis de Berre. Essai d'étude économique d'un carrefour routier*, Paris, 1968 (thesis).

BOUSSARD (J.), 'Les voies romaines de la civitas Turonum', *B.C.T.H.*, 1945-1947 (50), pp. 191-192, 194, 235-237.

BOUTON (A.), *Les Voies antiques, les grands chemins médiévaux et les routes royales du Haut-Maine*, Le Mans, 1947.

BOUTON (A.), 'Les voies antiques du Maine et leur transformation au haut Moyen Age', *Revue hist. de droit fr. et étr.*, 1956, p. 308.

BRAUN (J.), 'Les voies romaines du canton d'Obernai', *Revue d'Alsace*, 96, 1957, pp. 7-31.

BRAUN (J.), 'Les voies romaines de l'arrondissement d'Erstein', *Revue d'Alsace*, 98, 1959, pp. 30-48.

BRAUN (J.), 'Les voies romaines de l'arrondissement de Sélestat', *Revue d'Alsace*, 100, 1961, pp. 7-29.

BROISE (P.), 'Les voies romaines en Savoie', *Caesarodunum*, 5, 1970, pp. 273-279.

BROISE (P.), 'Le cadastre sarde, auxiliaire des recherches de topographie antique en Savoie', *Acte. du Colloque international sur la cartographie archéologique et historique*, Paris, 1970 (Tours, 1972).

BRUNEL (Cl.), 'La voie Régordane', *Romania*, LXXIX, 1958, p. 289.

CALAIS (J.), 'Étude sur les voies romaines du département de la Seine-Maritime', *Bull. Comm. Ant. S.-M.*, XXIV, Fécamp, 1962-1963, pp. 179-198.

CHAMPIGNEULLE (A.), 'Voies antiques entre Nantes, Angers et Poitiers', *Actes 91ᵉ Congrès nat. Soc. sav.*, Rennes, 1966 (68), p. 241.

CHAMPIGNEULLE (A.), 'Vues nouvelles sur la topographie du Nord de l'Aquitaine antique', *Société des sciences de Cholet*, 1969, pp. 121-129.

CHAPOTAT (G.), *La Croisée de Vienne*, Bourgoin, 1959 (= *Évocations*, 1956, pp. 1550-1551; 1957, pp. 1806-1812; pp. 1838-1843).

CHAUME (M.), 'Voies anciennes de Beaune à Fleurey', *M.C.A.C.*, XXII, 1942-1946 (51), pp. 265-271.

CHAUMEIL (L.), 'Les chemins creux de Bretagne', *Ann. de Géo.*, LVIII, 1949, 309, pp. 55-58.

CLOS ARCEDUC (A.), 'L'organisation agraire et le réseau vicinal entre Blois et Meung-sur-Loire', *Actes 93ᵉ Congrès nat. Soc. sav.*, Tours, 1968 (70), Geographical Section, p. 245.

Colloque international sur les cols des Alpes, Antiquité et Moyen Age, Bourg, 1969 (Orléans, 1971).

COULOUMA (K.), 'Les voies Domitiennes de l'Hérault à l'Orb', *Rhodania*, XX-XXII, 1938-1946, pp. 33-40.

COURAUD (R.), 'Voies romaines de la Haute-Vienne: la voie de Limoges à Poitiers', *Bull. Soc. archéol. et hist. du Limousin*, 88, 1961, pp. 25-48; 89, 1962, pp. 10-28; 90, 1963, pp. 3-62.

COURAUD (R.), 'Observations sur les voies romaines', *ibid.*, 93, 1966, pp. 11-16.

DAYET (M.), LEBEL (P.), 'Le passage de la Loue à

Cramant (Jura) par la voie de Lyon à Strasbourg', _R.A.E._, 1952, p. 251.

DELÉAGE (A.), 'Le réseau des chemins ruraux dans la plaine chalonnaise et la centuriation romaine', _Mém. Soc. d'Hist. et d'arch. de Chalon-sur-Saône_, XXIX, 1940, pp. 144–151.

DENIZOT (G.), 'La voie Domitienne entre Narbonne et le Rhône', _Actes 81e Congrès nat. Soc. sav._, Rouen-Caen, 1956, 58, pp. 91–102.

DEPONT (J.), 'Le chemin de Jacques Cœur', _Caesarodunum_, 3, 1969, pp. 161–164.

DERNIER (A.), 'Les pavelots de Vouillé et la voie romaine Poitiers-Nantes jusqu'à Gourgé', _Bull. Soc. Antiq. W._, 1971, p. 67.

DEROLEZ (A.), 'La cité des Atrébates à l'époque romaine', _Revue du Nord_, 1958, 160, pp. 505–533.

DION (R.), 'Les voies romaines du Nord de la France étudiées sur les cartes', _Publications de la Soc. de Géogr. de Lille_, 1944–1945, pp. 5–35.

DION (R.), 'Robrica ou Rubrica', _Caesarodunum_, IX, 1974, pp. 158–161.

DION (R.), 'La circulation transalpine', _Annuaire du Collège de France_, 1959, p. 485.

DUFOURNET (P.), 'Deux trouvailles archéologiques inédites à Seyssel, Haute-Savoie, et le problème de Condate', _Actes 85e Congrès nat. Soc. sav._, Chambéry-Annecy, 1960 (62), pp. 83–101.

DUFOURNET (P.), 'Le réseau routier gallo-romain de Vienne à Genève et la position des stations d'Etanna et de Condate', _Actes Congrès nat. Soc. sav._, Lyon, 1964 (65), pp. 35–71.

DUFOURNET (P.), 'Organisation du territoire dans l'Antiquité . . .', _Actes 91e Congrès nat. Soc. sav._, Rennes, 1966 (Paris, 1968), p. 99.

DUFOURNET (P.), 'Voie romaine de Condate (près de Seyssel) à Aquae (Aix-les-Bains). Vestiges dans le Val de Fier, Seyssel (Haute-Savoie)', _Revue savoisienne_, 1970, pp. 21–32.

DUVAL (P.-M.), _Paris antique_, Paris, Hermann, 1961.

ÉTIENNE (R.), 'Les passages transpyrénéens dans l'Antiquité. Leur histoire jusqu'en 25 av. J.-C.', _A.M._, 67, 1955, 32, pp. 295–311.

ÉTIENNE (R.), _Bordeaux antique_, Bordeaux, 1962.

FANAUD (L.), _Voies romaines et vieux chemins en Bourbonnais_, Moulins, 1960.

FÉVRIER (P.-A.), _Le Développement urbain en Provence_, Paris, 1964 (pp. 189 sq.: road network, 199: roads and towns).

FOUET (G.), 'La villa d'Es Cabiros à Larroque et la voie romaine de Montmaurin à Saint-Bertrand de Comminges', _Pallas_, 15, 1968, pp. 127–136.

FOURNIER (P.-F.), 'Augustonemetum, nœud de routes', _Revue d'Auvergne_, 83, 1969, p. 291.

FOURNIER (P.-F.), 'Anciennes routes de Clermont au Gévaudan dans la région de Brioude', _Almanach de Brioude_, 1970.

FUSTIER (P.), 'Contribution à l'étude des voies romaines de Lyon à la Loire', _Histoire locale_, 2, 3–4,

1950, pp. 2–3 (cf. _R.A.E._, I, 1950, p. 179).

FUSTIER (P.), 'Repérage et coupes de la voie romaine de Lyon à Roanne', _R.A.E._, VI, 1955, pp. 70–76.

FUSTIER (P.), 'Nouvelle coupe de la voie romaine de Lyon à Roanne', _ibid._, Jan.–June 1962, pp. 124–127.

FUSTIER (P.), 'Étude sur les liaisons antiques entre Loire et Saône', _Archéocivilisation_, N.S., 1967, pp. 3–4, 43–51.

FUSTIER (P. et A.), 'Communications antiques entre Loire et Saône', _Actes Congrès Budé_, Lyon, 1958, p. 320.

GRAS (P.), 'Le nœud routier de Chalon. Les routes d'Autun, Chalon et Beaune', _B.S.H.A.C._, XXXIV, 2nd p., 1956–1957, pp. 41–67.

GRAS (P.), 'La voie romaine de Chalon à Langres est-elle une voie d'Agrippa?', _Annales de Bourgogne_, 30, 1958, pp. 160–167.

GRÉGOIRE (L.), 'Les voies romaines bourbonnaises', _Les Cahiers haut-marnais_, 1954, 37, pp. 51–61.

GREMAUD (G.), 'Le carrefour dijonnais à la fin de l'époque romaine', _B.C.T.H._, 1951–1952, pp. 375–377.

GREMAUD (G.), 'Les vestiges de la voie d'Agrippa de Lyon à Trèves au parc de Dijon', _Actes 81e Congrès nat. Soc. sav._, Rouen-Caen, 1956, pp. 105–111.

GREMAUD (G.), 'Les origines de Dijon', _Actes 84e Congrès nat. Soc. sav._, 1961, p. 87.

GRIVAULT (J.), 'Observations sur le tracé de la voie romaine de Rouen à Dieppe', _Bull. Soc. normande d'études préhist._, 1962, p. 87.

HATT (J.-J.), 'Les découvertes de l'archéologie antique en Alsace de 1926 à 1946', _Revue d'Alsace_, 1946, pp. 85–100 (cf. _C.A.A.H._, 1948, p. 201).

HENAULT (M.), 'La voie romaine de Bavay à Reims (dite chaussée de Brunehaut). Essai de reconstitution de son tracé antique. Les stations, les colonnes milliaires', _B.C.T.H._, 1941–1942, pp. 451–469.

HUBERT (G.), 'Voies antiques. Les relations entre Jublains et Vieux', _Annales de Normandie_, 10, 1960, pp. 3–24.

JALMAIN (D.), _Archéologie aérienne en Ile-de France, Beauce, Brie, Champagne_, Paris, 1970.

JALMAIN (D.), 'Étude des voies romaines entre Seine et Loire', _Actes du Colloque international sur la cartographie archéologique et historique_, Paris, 1970 (Tours, 1972).

JANICOT (G.), 'Le pays creusois à l'époque gallo-romaine. Les voies', _Mém. Soc. Sc. nat. et archéol. de la Creuse_, XXIX, 1946, pp. 578–621.

LABROUSSE (M.), _Toulouse antique_, Paris, de Boccard, 1968 (on highways, pp. 291–303; on old roads around Toulouse, pp. 334–371; for milestones, cf. index).

LAMBERT (E.), 'Les routes des Pyrénées Atlantiques et leur emploi au cours des âges', _Publ. del Inst. de Estudios Pirenaicos_, Zaragoza, 1951, p. 62 (cf. _Mélanges D. Faucher_, Toulouse, 1948, p. 319).

LEBEL (P.), 'Toponymie et histoire. La pénétration

d'une forêt . . .', *Annales de Bourgogne*, XV, 1943, pp. 255–259.

LEBEL (P.), 'La route. Examen d'un tronçon de voie', *ibid.*, XXII, 1950, pp. 287–290.

LEBEL (P.), 'Enquêtes. Vieilles routes à travers champs et parchemins', *R.A.E.*, I, 1950, p. 31.

LEBEL (P.), 'Bornes, centuriation et cantonnements le long de la voie de Lyon au Rhin', *ibid.*, pp. 154–161.

LEDUQUE (A.), *Étude sur l'ancien réseau routier du Boulonnais*, Lille, 1957.

LEDUQUE (A.), *Recherches topo-historiques sur l'Atrébatie*, Lille, 1966.

LEDUQUE (A.), *Essai de topographie historique sur la Morinie*, Lille, 1968.

LEMAN (P.), *Les Voies romaines de Bouvines*, Carvin, 1960.

LEVIS-TRAFFORD (A. de), 'Italicus clivus d'Ammien Marcellin', *Travaux de la Soc. d'Hist. et d'Archéol. de la Maurienne*, XII, 1955, pp. 50–57.

MARIE (Cdt), 'La viographie romantique du Nord de l'Aquitaine romaine', *B.S.A.O.*, VIII, 1966, pp. 419–453.

MARILIER (J.-M.), 'Le pays bas-dijonnais et ses voies anciennes', *M.C.A.C.*, XXII, 1942–1946, pp. 274–280.

MARQUION (P.), 'L'itinéraire d'Hannibal . . .', *Cahiers d'hist.* XVII.2, 1972, p. 105.

MATTY DE LATOUR, *Voie romaine de la capitale des Andes à celle des Rhedones*, Rennes, 1871.

MERLAT (P.), 'Considérations générales sur l'établissement d'une carte du réseau routier en Armorique ancienne et observations particulières sur une carte des voies romaines de la cité des Vénètes', *N.A.A., Annales de Bretagne*, LXII, 1955, pp. 300–332; 1956, p. 19.

MERTENS (J.), 'La chaussée romaine de Reims à Trèves', *Le Pays Gaumais*, La Terre et les Hommes, 17, 1956, pp. 91–115.

MEYNIER (A.), 'Le mystère des chemins creux de Bretagne', *Geographia*, July 1957, 2.

MONCHO (R.), 'Notes sur les voies romaines dans les Alpes méridionales', *Les Alpes Unies*, 4, 1963, pp. 3–20.

PIVETEAU (J.), 'Voies antiques de la Charente', *Bull. et Mém. Soc. archéol. et hist. Charente*, 1954, pp. 33–56, 57–69.

RADKE (G.), 'Röm. Straßen in der Gallia Cisalpina und der Narbonensis', *Klio*, IC II 1964, pp. 299–317.

ROBLIN (M.), 'Les voies antiques du terroir de Paris au 1/25,000. Atlas international des routes protohistoriques et historiques', *Histoire locale*, 1951, 5–8, pp. 2–3.

ROBLIN (M.), *Le Terroir de Paris aux époques galloromaine et franque*, Paris, 1951 (pp. 92–150).

ROBLIN (M.), 'De Fontenay-aux-Roses à Issy-les-Moulineaux. Les chemins antiques des domaines suburbains de Lutèce', *Hommages A. Grenier*, III,

1962, pp. 1327–1338.

ROBLIN (M.), 'Habitats disparus de la région de Senlis', *Actes 90ᵉ Congrès nat. Soc. sav.*, 1965 (66), pp. 222–257.

ROBLIN (M.), 'L'Oise et ses affluents . . .', *Actes 91ᵉ Congrès nat. Soc. sav.*, Rennes, 1966, pp. 203–238.

ROBLIN (M.), 'Histoire du peuplement et de l'habitat en France aux époques anciennes', *Annuaire de l'École des Hautes Études* (IVᵉ Section), 1967–1968, pp. 239–248, *cf.* 1968–1969, pp. 229–236.

SANCIER (R.), 'Étude numérique d'un tronçon de voie d'Aleth à Vorgium', *Mém. Soc. d'émulation Côtesdu-Nord*, 1963.

SERVAN (P.), 'Voies antiques de la moyenne vallée de l'Huveaune', *P.H.*, X, 1960, pp. 189–221.

SIAT (A.), STIEBER (A.), WEIL (R.), 'Nature pétrographique des matériaux d'empierrement d'une voie romaine à Dambach-la-Ville', *C.A.A.H.*, X, 1966, pp. 69–71.

SOUTOU (A.), 'Les voies anciennes au sud de Millau (Aveyron)', *Cahiers de préhist. et d'archéol.*, 8, 1959, pp. 112–120.

SOUTOU (A.), 'Une voie ancienne de Toulouse à Rodez', *Annales Fac. Lettres Toulouse*, Pallas, X, 1961, pp. 97–107.

SOUTOU (A.), 'Via Domitia', *Annales Fac. Lettres Toulouse*, XII, 1963, 5.

SOUTOU (A.), 'Les vestiges gallo-romains d'Arzens et le tracé de la voie d'Aquitaine entre Bram et Carcassonne', *Cahiers lig. préhist. archéol.*, 1963, no. 12, pp. 150–158.

SOYER (J.), 'Les voies antiques de l'Orléanais', *Mém. Soc. archéol. et hist. de l'Orléanais*, XXXVII, 1936.

SOYER (Mˡˡᵉ J.), 'Présentation d'une carte des voies anciennes de la région est et sud-est de Poitiers, établie d'après la couverture aérienne de l'I.G.N.', *Actes 87ᵉ Congrès nat. Soc. sav.*, Poitiers, 1962 (63), pp. 187–195.

THÉVENOT (E.), 'Y eut-il une grande voie romaine entre Avallon et Troyes?', *R.A.E.*, III, 1952, pp. 181–185.

THÉVENOT (E.), *Les Voies romaines de la cité des Eduens*, Brussels, 1969.

THÉVENOT (E.), 'La voie d'Autun vers la Séquanie', *Latomus*, XXX, Oct.–Dec. 1971, p. 1124.

TOUTAIN (J.), 'Note sur la voie romaine de Lutèce à Rotomagus (Rouen), dans le Parisis et le Vexin français, de Paris à Saint-Clair-sur-Epte', *B.C.T.H.*, 1943–1945 (51), pp. 267–279.

VASSELLE (F.), 'Découverte d'une chaussée romaine à Voyennes (Somme)', *B.S.A.P.*, 1969, p. 27.

WERNER (L. G.), 'La voie romaine d'Epomanduodurum à Cambete et à Augusta Rauracorum', *B.C.T.H.*, 1934–1935, p. 581.

WILL (E.), in *Gallia*, XX, 1962, 1, p. 97: a sketch of the road-network in Roman times around Saint-Quentin-Vermand.

WUILLEUMIER (P.), 'De Lyon à Mâcon', *R.E.A.*, XLI,

1939, p. 247.

WUILLEUMIER (P.), AUDIN (A.), 'Les voies axiales de Lugdunum', *Gallia*, 1–2, 1943, p. 125.

Benelux countries

In the case of Belgium, discoveries connected with roads receive regular publication in *Archéologie*, the half-yearly review of the *Centre national de recherches archéologiques en Belgique*.

AMAND (M.), 'Contribution à l'étude de la voirie antique au sud-ouest de Tournai', *Hommages à W. Deonna*, Brussels, 1957, pp. 49–58.

BREUER (J.), *Le Strade romane nel Belgio*, Rome, 1938.

BYVANCK (A. W.), *Le Strade romane nei Paesi Bassi*, Rome, 1938.

BYVANCK (A. W.), 'De Tabula Peutingeriana en de romeinsche Wegen in Nederland', *Geschiedkundige Atlas van Nederland*.

DESSEL (C. van), *Topographie des voies romaines de la Belgique*, Brussels, 1877.

GANSBEKE (P. van), 'La voie commerciale de la Bretagne au Rhin à l'époque romaine', *R.B.Ph.*, XXXV, 1957, p. 746.

GAUCHEZ (V.), 'Topographie des voies romaines de la Gaule Belgique', *Annales de l'Acad. d'archéol. de Belgique*, XXXVIII, 3ᵉ, s. VIII, 1882.

JACQUES (F.), 'Saint Martin, titulaire d'églises et de chapelles dans le Luxembourg et au Grand-Duché. Son patronage est-il un gage certain d'antiquité?', *Ann. de l'Inst. arch. du Luxembourg*, 92, 1961, p. 253.

MARIËN (M. E.), *Par la chaussée Brunehaut de Bavai à Cologne*, Brussels, 1963.

MERTENS (J.), 'La chaussée romaine de Reims à Trèves', *Le Pays Gaumais*, 1956, 3–4, pp. 91–115.

MERTENS (J.), *Archaeologica Belgica*, no. 33.

MERTENS (J.), 'Les routes romaines de la Belgique', *Industrie*, IX, 1955, no. 10, pp. 673–683. (*Cf. F.A.*, V, no. 4889; VII, no. 4432; IX, no. 6160; X, no. 5539, 5731, 5757; XI, no. 5412 *sq.*; XII, no. 6111; and numerous notes in the half-yearly review *Archéologie*.

MODDERMAN (P. J. R.), in *Nieuwsbulletin van de Koninklijhe Nederlandse Oudheidkundige Bond*, 6th s. II, 1949, p. 191.

MOREL (Dr.), PEYRE (P.), 'Une voie à ornières dans les Cévennes', *Mél. Benoît*, Bordighera, 1972, IV, p. 183.

STOLTE (P. M.), 'De zuidelijkeweg van de Tabula Peutingeriana door het land der Bataven', *Berichten van de rijksdienst voor het oudheidkundig bodemonderzoek*, IX, 1959, pp. 57–67.

TERNES (Ch.-M.), 'Les routes romaines de la Moselle luxembourgeoise', in *Voies de communication au pays mosellan*, Luxembourg, 1968, pp. 33–67.

TERNES (Ch.-M.), 'Le réseau routier du Luxembourg antique', *Ogam*, 19, 1967, pp. 169–180.

TERNES (Ch.-M.), 'Les voies romaines du Grand-Duché de Luxembourg vues par A. Wiltheim', *Hémecht*, 1, 1968, p. 99.

TERNES (Ch.-M.), *Répertoire archéologique du Grand-Duché de Luxembourg*, Brussels, 1970, map V, p. 189.

VANNERUS (J.), 'Voies antiques . . .', *Ac. Roy. Belg.*, *Mém.*, XI, 2, 1943.

Voies de communication et réseau routier de la Gaule Belgique, Journées archéol. de Compiègne, May 1964.

Great Britain

AMODIO (E.), 'Una strada romana in Britannia', *Romana*, 1939, pp. 644–648.

The Annual Register 1771 (1794, 5th ed.), Observations on the Roman Roads from Whitaker's History of Manchester.

BERRY (B.), *A Lost Roman Road. A Reconnaissance in the West Country*, London, Allen, 1963.

BONSER (W.), *A Romano-British Bibliography, 55 B.C.–A.D. 449*, Oxford, 1964, pp. 108–142.

BOUMPHREY (G. M.), *Along the Roman Roads*, London, 1935.

CRAWFORD (O. G. S.), *Topography of Roman Scotland*, 1949.

'Field Archaeology in Great Britain', Ordnance Survey, 5th edit., 1973.

GIBSON (J.), *The Road of the Roman*, York. Unit. Automob. Serv., 1933–1934.

GOODYEAR (F. H.), CHARLTON (J. M. T.), 'A Roman Road in North Staffordshire', *N.S.J.F.S.*, VII, 1967, pp. 27–33.

GRAHAM (A.), 'The Roman Road to Raeburnfoot', *Proceedings of the Society of Antiquaries of Scotland*, 1947–1948, vol. 82, 7th s., vol. X, pp. 231–234.

GREEN (Ch.), RAHTZ (P. A.), 'Excavations of Ermine Street in Lincolnshire', *Ant. J.*, XXXIX, 1959, pp. 1–2, 77–86.

HARDEN (D. B.), *Guide to an Exhibition of Air-Photographs of Archaeological Sites*, Ashmolean Museum, Oxford, Nov. 1948–Feb. 1949, section XI: Roman Roads.

HOUGHTON (A. W. J.), 'The Roman Road from Wroxeter to Whitchurch (Salop)', *N.S.J.F.S.*, I, 1961, pp. 51–55.

HOUGHTON (A. W. J.), 'The Roman Road from Greenforge through the Central Welsh March', *Trans. Shrops. Archaeol. Soc.*, 56, 1960, pp. 223–243.

HOUGHTON (A. W. J.), 'A Roman Road from Ashton, N. Herefordshire to Marshbrook, Salop.', *Trans. Shrops. Archaeol. Soc.*, 57, 1966, pp. 185–190.

HUGHES (G. M.), *Roman Roads in South-East Britain*, Londres, 1936.

MARGARY (I. D.), 'Roman Road from London to Sussex', *Antiquity*, VI, 1932, 23, pp. 350–356.

MARGARY (I. D.), *Roman Ways in the Weald*, London, 2nd edit., 1956.

MARGARY (I. D.), *Roman Roads in Britain*, London, 3rd edit., 1973.

MILLER S. N. (ed.), *The Roman Occupation of South-West Scotland*, Glasgow, 1952.

PEEL (J. H. B.), *Along the Roman Roads of Britain*, London, 1971.

PHILLIPS (Ch. W.), 'A New Roman Road in South Lincolnshire', *Antiquity*, V, 1931, 19, pp. 355–359.

STRONG (E.), *Viaggio attraverso le strade della Britannia romana*, Rome, 1938.

The Viatores, *Roman Roads in the S.E. Midlands*, London, 1964.

Switzerland

ALFÖLDI (A.), 'La corporation des Transalpini et Cisalpini à Avenches', *S.P.*, 16, 1952, pp. 3–9.

BERCHEM (D. van), 'Bâle et Augst. Réflexions sur le site d'une ville', *Publications du Centre européen d'études burgondomédianes*, 3, 1961.

BERGER (L.), 'Die Gründung der colonia Raurica und die Bedeutung det Mittelland-Hauenstein Straße', *Provincialia, Festschrift Laur-Belart*, 1968, pp. 15–24.

BLONDEL (L.), 'Fortifications préhistoriques et marché romain au Bourg-de-Four (Genève)', *Genava*, 1934, pp. 39–63.

BLONDEL (L.), 'La route romaine de Genève à Nyon', *Genava*, 1937, pp. 64–74.

BLONDEL (L.), 'Carouge . . .', *Genava*, XVIII, 1940, pp. 54–68.

BLONDEL (L.), 'Milliaire de Vollèges dans le Val de Bagnes', *J.S.G.U.*, 1944, pp. 144–146.

BLONDEL (L.), 'La route romaine du Mont-Joux. Étude topographique', *Hommages à A. Grenier*, Brussels, 1962, 1, pp. 308–315.

COLLART (P.), 'Borne milliaire à Monthey et routes romaines du Bas-Valais', *Vallesia*, XV, 1960, pp. 231–240.

EXCHAQUET (H.), *Dictionnaire des Ponts et Chaussées*, containing a list of highways built by the Romans in Helvetia, 1789.

GILLIARD (F.), 'Par les voies romaines: l'héritage romain de l'Helvétie', *Vie, art et cité*, Lausanne, 1938.

LAUR-BELLART (R.), 'Zwei alte Straßen über den Bözberg', *S.P.*, XXXII, 1968, pp. 30–52.

LAUR-BELLART (R.), 'Nachlese zu den Bözberg-straßen', *S.P.*, XXXII, 4, 1968, p. 72.

MOOSBRUGGER-LEU (R.), 'Ein unbekanntes Stück Römerstraße im Jura', *Provincialia*, 1968, pp. 406–409.

PELICHET (Ed.), 'Contribution à l'étude de l'occupation du sol de la colonie Julia Equestris', *Festschrift für R. Bosch*, Aarau, 1947, pp. 117–136.

POGET (S. W.), 'Voies romaines de la contrée Orbe-Yverdon-Sainte-Croix', *S.P.*, XIV, 1950, pp. 11–15.

RADKE (G.), 'Namen und Daten. Beobachtungen zur

Gesch. des röm. Straßenbaus', *M.H.*, 24, 1967, pp. 221–235.

STAEHELIN (F.), *Die Schweiz in römischer Zeit*, Bâle, 1948.

VIOLLIER (D.), *Le Strade romane della Svizzera*, Rome, 1937.

WALSER (G.), Itinera romana. I. Die römischen Strassen in der Schweiz. I. Die Meilensteine, Berne, 1967 (Vol. II will deal with the *Alpis Poenina*, the Great St. Bernard).

WIEDEMER (H. R.), 'Die Walenseeroute in frühröm. Zeit', *Helvetia Antiqua, Festschrift E. Vogt*, Zürich, 1966, pp. 162–172.

From the Rhine to the Danube

ALFÖLDY (G.), *Noricum*, London, 1974.

DANZER (J.), 'Die Entwege-Rätselhafte Altstraßen zw. Pitten und Schwarza', *J.O.E.A.I.*, XLVII, 1964–1965, Beibl., pp. 220–290.

DERINGER (H.), 'Die römische Reichsstraße Aquileia-Lauriacum', *Carinthia*, CXXXIX, 1949, pp. 193–221.

DERINGER (H.), 'Die römischen Meilensteine der Provinz Noricum', *Festschrift Egger* 2, 286–314; *Carinthia*, 1953, pp. 736–764.

DIETZ (J.), 'Flur- und Straßennamen im Norden und Westen Bonns', *Rh. V.J.*, 1940, pp. 307–323.

EGGER (R.), 'Neues aus Kärntens Römerzeit', *Carinthia*, CXXXVIII, 1948, p. 266.

EGGER (R.), 'Oberösterreich in römischer Zeit', *Jahrb. der oberösterreich. Musealvereines*, XCV, 1950, pp. 133–168.

FINK (W.), 'Auf den Spuren einer alten Römerstraßen', *Jber. Hist. Ver. Straubing*, XXXIV, 1931, pp. 26–28.

FITZ (J.), 'Roman road-repairs between Aquincum and Mursa', *A. Ert.*, LXXXIII, 1956, pp. 197–205.

FROHN (W.), 'Siechenhäuser und Verkehrstraßen im Rheiland', *Rheinische Vierteljahrsblätter*, I, 1932, p. 143.

GOESSLER (R.), *Le Strade romane in Germania*, Rome, 1938.

GÖRLICH (W.), 'Der antike Straßenzug Aquileia-Virunum-Lauriacum und die Brücke in Villach', *Festschrift R. Egger*, 1954, pp. 132–134.

HAGEN (H.), *Römerstraßen der Rheinprovinz*, Bonn, 1931.

HELL (M.), 'Spuren von Altstrassen am Pass Lueg in Salzburg', *Archaeologia Austriaca*, 5, 1972, p. 97.

HEYDENDORF (W.), 'Carnuntum im röm. Straßennetz', *Mitt. d. Vereins der Freunde Carnuntums*, V, 1952, pp. 6–8.

JANDAUREK (H.), *Oberösterreichische Altstrassen. Die Strassen der Römer, Schriftenreihe der Oberösterr. Landesbaudirektion X*. Wels Oberösterr. Landesverlag, 1951.

JIRECEK (C. J.), *Die Heerstrasse von Belgrad nach Con-*

stantinopel und die Balkanpässe. *Eine historisch-geographische Studie*, 1877, repub. 1967 (Nachträge, Arch. Epigr. Mitt. 10, 1886, 85–104, 205–208).

KOBAN (H.), 'Die alten Straßen auf der Südseite der Plöckenpasses', *Festschrift R. Egger*, 1954, III, pp. 126–131.

LEBER (P. S.), *Die römische Staatsstrasse von Villach zum Zollfeld*, Klagenfurt, 1971.

LINDENMAIER (H. M.), *Römersiedlungen und Römerstraßen in Mitteleuropa . . .*, Naturwiss. Diss. Halle, 1941.

MACHATSCHEK (A.), 'Die alten Poststationen an der Straße zw. Wien und Linz', *Wiener Jahrbuch für Kunstgesch.*, XX, 1965, pp. 137–158.

MARIĆ (R.), 'Civitas Confluentes', *Bull. Fac. Philos. Novi Sad*, I, 1956, pp. 5–12.

MAYER (O. E.), 'Das röm. Straßendorf bei Schloß Rimburg und die röm. Wurmbrücke', *Heimatbl. d. Landkr. Aachen*, I, 1931, pp. 10–14.

MEYSSELS (Th. F.), *Auf Römerstrassen durch Osterreich, von Aguntum nach Carnuntum*, Vienna, 1960.

MIRKOVIĆ (M.), 'The Roman Road Naissus-Scupi and the Stages Ad Fines', *Z. Ant.*, X, 1960, pp. 249–257.

MÓCSY (A.), 'Zu Rekonstruktion des Straßensystems von Savaria', *A. Ert.*, XCII, 1965, pp. 27–35.

MÓCSY (A.), *Pannonia and Upper Moesia*, London, 1974.

MOSER (E.), 'Zum Hahdel um Christi Geburt über Brenner und Reschen', *Kleeman Festschrift*, Bonn, 1972, pp. 83–98.

NAGY (L.), *Le Grandi Strade romane in Ungheria*, Rome, 1938.

NIERHAUS (R.), 'Die Westgrenze von Noricum und die Routenführung der Via Claudia Augusta', *Ur- und Frühgesch. als histor. Wissenschaft, Ernst Wahle Festschrift*, Heidelberg, 1950.

NIERHAUS (R.), 'Röm. Strassenverbindungen durch den Schwarzwald', *Bad. Fundber.*, XXIII, 1967, pp. 117–157.

NOLL (R.), 'Römische Siedlungen und Straßen im Limes-gebiet zw. Inn und Enns (Oberösterreich)', *Der röm. Limes in Österreich*, XXI, 1958.

OHLENROTH (L.), 'Röm. Burgi an der Straße Augsburg-Kempten-Bregenz', *29. Ber. d. R.G.K.*, 1940, pp. 122–156.

PARET (O.), 'Die "Straßendämme" am Rand des Federseebeckens', *Germania*, 1951, pp. 1–5.

PASCHER (G.), *Der röm. Limes in Österreich*, 19. Röm. Siedlungen und Straßen im Limesgebiet zw. Enns und Leitha, Vienna, 1949.

PETRI (H.), 'Römerstraßen und german. Landnahme', *Zeitschr. f. Ortsnamen-Forschung*, XVII, 1941, pp. 21–32.

PRASCHNIKER (G.), *Le Grandi Strade romane nell'Austria*, Rome, 1938.

REINHARDT (W.), 'Moorwege im Meerhuser Moor', *Germania*, 43, 1965, 2, p. 413.

ROSSI (L.), 'The Representation on Trajan's Column of Trajan's Rock-Cut Road in Upper Moesia', *Ant.J.*, XLVIII, 1968, 1, pp. 41–46.

SCHICKER (J.), 'Die heidnischen Friedhöfen und die Limesstraße bei Lauriacum', *R.L.O.E.*, XVII, 1933, pp. 85–116.

SCHLEIERMACHER (W.), 'A. B(rigantio)', *Germania*, XLIII, 1965, 2, pp. 320–321.

SCHUMACHER (K.), 'Erforschung des röm. u. vorrömischen Strassennetzes in Westdeutschland', *Ber. R.G.K.*, 1906, p. 11.

SCHUMACHER (K.), 'Ortsnamen und Römerstraßen in Westdeutschland', *M.Z.*, p. 10, 1915, 65.

SPRATER (F.), 'Römerstraßen bei Kaiserslautern', *Beitr. zur Kunst und Gesch. des Mainzer Lebensraumes Mainz*, 1936, pp. 21–27.

SPRATER (F.), 'Von den ältesten Straßen der Pfalz', *Abh. zur Saarpfälz. Landes und Volksforsch.*, 1, 1937, pp. 18–22.

SPRATER (F.), 'Funde von Leugensteinen in der Pfalz', *Germania*, 1937, pp. 28–33.

SPRATER (F.), 'Römersstraßen im Haardtgebirge', *Festschrift d. Röm. Germ. Zentralmuseums in Mainz*, 1952, 1, pp. 1–4.

TERNES (Ch.-M.), 'Le réseau routier de la Rhénanie romaine', in *La Vie quotidienne en Rhénanie romaine*, Paris, Hachette, 1972.

TERNES (Ch.-M.), 'Les moyens de transport de l'époque romaine au pays de Trèves', *B.A.L.*, 2, 1971, pp. 15–18.

VOIGT (L.), *Raetia Latina*, Düsseldorf, 1959.

VULPE (R.), *Histoire ancienne de la Dobroudja*, 1938.

WEISHAUPT (C.), *Beiträge zur Kenntnis Römerstraßenzuges von Augusta Vindelicorum bis Juravo*, Munich, 1841.

WELLS (C. M.), *The German Policy of Augustus*, Oxford, 1972.

WINSAUER (G.), 'Auf den Spuren der Römerstraße', *Almannia*, IX, 1935, pp. 29–31.

WOLFF (K. F.), 'Uber alte Wege und Brücken, Betrachtungen und Vermutungen', *Schlern*, XVIII, 1937, pp. 38, 83, 194.

Greece and the Balkans

ALFÖLDI (G.), 'Eine röm. Straßenbauinschrift aus Salona', *A. Arch.*, XVI, 1964, fasc. 3–4, pp. 247–256.

ALFÖLDI (G.), 'Eine Straßenbauinschrift aus Salona', *Klio*, XLVI, 1965, pp. 323–327.

BEŠEVLIEV (V.), 'Bermerkungen über die antiken Heerstrassen im Ostteil der Balkanhalbinsel', *Klio*, LI, 1969, p. 483.

CEKE (H.), 'La branche Sud de la via Egnatia', *Monumentet* 2, 1971, pp. 33–36.

COLLART (P.), 'Une réfection de la via Egnatia sous Trajan', *B.C.H.*, LIX, 1935, pp. 394 *sq.*

COURBIN (P.), 'Une rue d'Argos', *B.C.H.*, 80, 1956,

pp. 183–218.

DEGRASSI (A.), 'La via seguita da Traiano del 105 per recarsi nella Dacia', *R.P.A.A.*, XX, 1943–1944, p. 167.

DOBIAS (J.), *Le Strade romane nel territorio cecoslovaco*, Rome, 1937.

HAMMOND (N. G. L.), 'The Main Road from Beotia to the Peloponnese through the Northern Megarid', *A.B.S.A.*, XLIX, 1954, pp. 103–122.

HAMMOND (N. G. L.), 'The Western Part of the Via Egnatia', *J.R.S.*, LXIV, 1974, pp. 185–194.

MCDONALD (A. W.), 'Overland communications in Greece during L. H. III, with special reference to Southwest Peloponnese', *III Intern. Colloquium on Mycenaean Studies*, 1961 (64), pp. 217–240.

MAKARONAS (Ch. J.), 'Via Egnatia and Thessalonike', *Studies Robinson*, 1951, pp. 380–388.

PANAITESCU (E.), *Le Grandi strade romane in Romania*, Rome, 1938.

PAŠALIĆ (E.), 'Röm. Straßen in Bosnien und Herzegowina', *Archaeologia iugoslavica*, III, 1959, pp. 61–73.

PIRKOVIC (I.), 'Crucium, die röm. Poststation zwischen Emona u. Neviodunum', *Situla* 10, Ljubljana, 1968.

SERGEJEVSKI (D.), 'La voie romaine sur le Nevesinjsko polje', *Glasnik zemoljskoy Muzejan Sarajem, N.S.* III, 1948, pp. 43–62 (Erzegovine).

STADTMUELLER (G.), 'Das röm. Straßennetz der Provinzen Epirus', *Historia*, III, 1954, pp. 236–251.

TODOROV (Y.), *Le Grandi strade romane in Bulgaria*, Rome, 1937.

TRÉHEUX (J.), 'Une nouvelle voie thasienne', *B.C.H.*, LXXIX, 1955, 2, p. 427.

TSONTCHEV (D.), 'La voie romaine Philippopolis-Carassura et sa bifurcation près de Ranilum', *Annuaire de la Bibl. nat. et du Musée nat. de Plovdiv*, 1940–1941.

TSONTCHEV (D.), 'La voie romaine Philippopolis-Sub Radice', *Latomus*, XVIII, 1959, 1, pp. 154–170.

UGOLINI (L. M.), 'La via da Roma a Buthrotum. Note di topografia illirica', *B.C.A.R.*, LXI, 1933 (1934), 1–2, pp. 18–32.

VERDELIS (N. M.), 'Der Diolkos am Isthmus von Korinth', *M.D.A.I.(A)*, 71, 1956, pp. 51–59.

VLADIMIROV (V.), 'Nouvelles données sur la voie romaine Oescus-Serdica au ive siècle', *Archeologija*, VI, 1963, 1, pp. 33–34.

VULIC (N.), *Le Strade romane in Jugoslavia*, Rome, 1938.

WILKES (J. J.), *Dalmatia*, London, 1969.

YOUNG (J. H.), 'Greek Roads in South Attica', *Antiquity*, XXX, 1956, 118, pp. 94–98.

The Middle East

AVI-YONAH (M.), 'A New Dating of the Roman Road from Scythopolis to Neapolis', *I.E.J.*, XVI,

1966, pp. 75–76.

BALLANCE (M. H.), 'Roman Roads in Lycaonia', *A.S.*, VIII, 1958, pp. 223–234.

BALLANCE (M. H.), 'Derbe and Faustinopolis', *A.S.*, XIV, 1964, pp. 139–145.

BEAUVERY (R.), 'La route romaine de Jérusalem à Jéricho', *R.Bi.*, 64, 1957, pp. 72–101.

DE ROSSI (G. M.), 'Le vie carovaniere dell'antica Siria', *Boll. d. Unione Storia ed Arte*, X, 1967, 4, pp. 69–76.

DILLEMANN (L.), *Haute-Mésopotamie orientale et pays adjacents*, Beyrouth, 1962, pp. 129 *sq.*

DUNAND (H.), 'La voie romaine du Ledja', *M.A.I.*, 1933, p. 521.

FOUCHER (A.), 'La vieille route de l'Inde de Bactres à Taxila', *Mém. D.A.F.A.*, I, 1942–1947.

FURLANI (G.), 'Sul significato delle strade processionali dell'Asia occidentale antica', *Aegyptus*, 1942, pp. 1–2.

GOODCHILD (R. G.), 'The Coast Road of Phoenicia and its Roman Milestones', *Berytus*, IX, 1949, pp. 91–127.

HAREL (M.), 'Israelite and Roman Roads in the Judean Desert', *I.E.J.*, XVII, 1967, pp. 18–26.

KALLAI (Z.), 'Remains of the Roman Road along the Mevo-Beitar Highway', *I.E.J.*, XV, 1965 (66), pp. 195–203.

LEVI (D.), *Le Grandi strade romane in Asia*, Rome, 1938.

MACPHERSON (I. W.), 'Roman Roads and Milestones of Galatia', *A.S.*, IV, 1954, pp. 111–120.

MITTMANN (S.), 'The Roman Road from Gerasa to Adraa', *Annual of the Department of Antiquities of Jordan*, XI, 1966, pp. 65–87.

POIDEBARD (A.), *La Trace de Rome dans le désert de Syrie, du 'limes' de Trajan à la conquête arabe*, Paris, 1934.

POIDEBARD (A.) and MOUTERDE (R.), *Le Limes de Chalcis*, Paris, 1945.

SCHMIDT (J.), 'Straßen in altorientalischen Wohngebieten', *Baghdader Mitteil.*, 3, 1964, pp. 125–147.

STARR (S. F.), 'Mapping Ancient Roads in Anatolia', *Archaeology*, XVI, 1963, 3, pp. 162–169. *Cf.* 'In the tracks of conquerors, rulers, pilgrims and merchants: first findings of an expedition to map the ancient roads of Anatolia', *I.L.N.*, 243, 1963, n. 6486, pp. 859–861.

TALIP (S.), *Le Strade romane in Anatolia*, Rome, 1938.

North Africa

BARADEZ (J.), *Fossatum Africae*, Paris, 1949.

BARADEZ (J.), 'Réseau routier de commandement, d'administration et d'exploitation de la zone arrière du *limes* de Numidie', *Limesstudien*, Vorträge des 3 intern. Limeskongr., Bâle, 1959, pp. 19–33.

CAGNAT (R.), *L'Armée romaine d'Afrique*, Paris, 2e éd. 1912, p. 695.

CHEVALLIER (R.), 'Essai de chronologie des centuriations romaines de Tunisie', *M.E.F.R.*, 1958, pp. 61–128 (sur les rapports des voies et des centuriations, voir l'*Atlas des centuriations romaines de Tunisie*, Paris, I.G.N., 1954).

CORÒ (F.), 'Le antiche strade romane della Tripolitania occidentale', *R.C.I.*, 1931, pp. 1–20, 103–116.

COSNEAU (E.), *De Romanis viis in Numidia*, Paris, 1886–1887.

CRAWFORD (O. G. S.), 'Causeway, Tarik el Jemil', *Antiquity*, XII, 1938, 48, pp. 479–480.

DAVIN (P.), 'Note au sujet de la voie romaine d'Ammaedara à Thélepte', *B.C.T.H.*, 1928, p. 400.

EUZENNAT (M.), 'Les voies romaines du Maroc dans l'Itinéraire d'Antonin', Hommages à A. Grenier, II, Brussels, 1962, pp. 595–610.

FERRON (J.), 'Borne indicatrice à Lixus', *Latomus*, XXVI, Oct.–Dec. 1967, p. 945.

GALLAND (L.), 'Mons, Mopth . . . et Mopti, fouilles et topographie africaines', *M.E.F.R.*, LXI, 1949, p. 73.

GOODCHILD (R. G.), *The Roman Roads and Milestones of Tripolitania*, Tripoli, 1948.

HAGEN (V. W. von), 'Strade romane in Libia', *Esso rivista*, XXI, 1969, 3, pp. 12–15.

HAMMOND (N.), 'The Lost Roman Road of Tunis and Libya', *I.L.N.*, July 1965, 6571, pp. 27–29.

LECLANT (J.), 'Per Africae sitientia. Témoignages des sources classiques sur les pistes menant à l'oasis d'Ammon', *B.I.A.O.*, 1950, pp. 193–253.

MORAN (C.), GUSTAVINO GALLENT (G.), *Vias y poblaciones romanas en el Norte de Marruecos*, Madrid, 1948.

REYNIERS (F.), 'Signalisation et topographie en Tunisie et Tripolitaine', *R.I.O.*, XIII, 1961, pp. 41–53, 100–102.

ROMANELLI (P.), *Le Grandi strade romane nell'Africa settentrionale*, Rome, 1938.

ROSSI (E.), 'Le relazioni del Fezzàn con Tripoli e la costa del Mediterraneo', *Boll. d. Soc. Geogr. Italiana*, fasc. 5–6, 1948.

SALAMA (P.), 'Le réseau routier de l'Afrique romaine, *C.R.A.I.*, 1948, pp. 395–399.

SALAMA (P.), *Les Voies romaines de l'Afrique du Nord*, Algiers, 1951.

SALAMA (P.), 'La via hadrumetina en Byzacène', *C.T.*, XII, 1964, t. 45–56, pp. 73–86.

SALAMA (P.), 'La voie romaine de la vallée de la Tafna', *B.A.A.*, II, 1966–1967, pp. 183–217.

SCHMITT (P.), *Le Maroc de Ptolémée*, Tours, 1973.

THOMAS (B. E.), *Trade Routes of Algeria and the Sahara*, Berkeley-Los Angeles, 1957.

THOUVENOT (R.), 'La route romaine de Salé à l'Oued Beth', *C.R.A.I.*, Jan.–March 1956, pp. 120–125.

THOUVENOT (R.), 'Les vestiges de la route romaine de Salé à l'Oued Beth', *Hesperia*, XLIV, 1957, 1–2, pp. 73–84.

TISSOT (Ch.), 'Le bassin du Bagrada et la voie romaine de Carthage à Hippone par Bulla Regia', *Mém. Acad. Inscr.*, Paris, 1881.

TOUTAIN (J.), *Les Cités romaines de la Tunisie*, Paris, 1896, pp. 133–143.

Iberian Peninsula

For general purposes, see the *Noticiario* of the Archivo español de arqueología.

ALARCÂO (J.), 'On the Westernmost Road of the Roman Empire', *Archaeology*, 20–3, June 1967, p. 174.

ALVAREZ (E.), 'Vias romanas de Galicia', *Zephyrus*, XI, 1960, pp. 5–103.

BESNIER (M.), 'Itinéraires épigraphiques d'Espagne', *Bull. hispanique*, XXVI, 1924, pp. 5–26.

BLASQUEZ Y DELGADO AGUILERA (A.), SANCHEZ ALBORNOZ (Cl.), 'Vias romanas del Valle del Duero y Castilla la Nueva', *Junta Superior de excavaciones y antiguedades, Memorias*, 1915, no. 6.

BONSOR (G.), 'Les villes antiques du détroit de Gibraltar', *Bull. hispanique*, XX, 1918, pp. 77–127.

BUSTAMANTE BRICIO (J.), 'La calzada romana Pisori-Flaviobriga en el valle de Mena', *Boletin de la Institución Fernan Gonzales*, XLVIII, 1964, 163, pp. 272–276.

CALLEJO SERRANO (C.), 'El puente romano de Alcantara', *A.E.A.*, XLIII, 1970, nos. 121–122, pp. 213–218.

CARRILLO (P.), 'Via romana del Summo Pyrineo a Cesaraugusta', *Seminario de Arte Aragonés*, Institución Fernando el Católico de Zaragoza, III, 1951, p. 31.

ÉTIENNE (R.), 'Les passages transpyrénéens dans l'Antiquité. Leur histoire jusqu'en 25 av. J.-C.', *A.M.*, 67, 1955, pp. 295–311.

FERNANDEZ ARENA (A.) and HUARTE ARANA (P.), *Los Caminos de Santiago*, Barcelona, 1965.

GALLARDO (A.), 'Una via romana al Coll d'Ager', *B. Centre excursionista de Catalunya*, XLIV, 1934, pp. 26–27.

GOLABARDES (M.), 'Las vias romanas en el Ampurdan', *Ampurias*, IX–X, 1947–1948, pp. 35–41.

HERNANDEZ (F.), 'El cruce del Odiel por la via romana de Ayamonte a Merida', *A.E.A.*, XXXI, 1958, 97–98, pp. 126–152.

JALHAY (E.), *Broteria*, I, 1950, p. 560 (the road from Emerita Augusta to Bracara Augusta).

LAMBERT (E.), 'Les routes des Pyrénées atlantiques et leur emploi au cours des âges', First International Congress on the Pyrenees, Institute of Pyrenean Studies, Saragossa, 1952.

LOEWINSOHN (E.), 'Una calzada y dos campamentos romanos del Conventus Astrum', *A.E.A.*, XXXVIII, 1965, 111–112, pp. 26–49.

MONTEAGUDO (L.), 'Via romana entre Betanzos y Guitiriz (Coruña)', *A.E.A.*, XXVIII, 1955, 92, pp. 300–305.

NICTO (G.), 'Los hallazgos de Recilla de Valdaraduey y el trazado de la via romana de Asturica a Clunia',

Revista de Archivos, LXIII, 1957, 2, pp. 671–701.

PEMAN (C.), 'Nuevas precisiones sobre vias romanas en la provincia de Cadiz', *A.E.A.*, XXI, 1948, pp. 255–268.

RIBASI BERTRAN (M.), 'Les communications romaines d'Illuro', *Museu*, I, 1948, pp. 67–70.

ROLDAN HERVAS (J. M.), *Iter ab Emerita Asturicam. El camino de la Plata*, Salamanca, 1971.

TARACENA AGUIRRE (B.), 'Las vias romanas en España', *Crónica del III Congreso Arqueológico del Sudeste Español*, Murcia, 1947, pp. 249–255.

The 'Limes'

ALFÖLDI (G.), 'Die ethische Grenzscheide am römischen Limes', *Schweizer. Beitr. z. allgem. Gesch.*, 1950, pp. 37–50.

BARADEZ (J.), *Fossatum Africae*, Paris, 1949.

BARADEZ (J.), *Vue aérienne de l'organisation romaine dans le Sud algérien*, Paris, 1949.

BARADEZ (J.), 'Réseau routier de la zone arrière du limes de Numidie', *Limes-Studien*, III, 1957 (1959), Bâle.

BIRLEY (E.), *Research on Hadrian's Wall*, Kendal, 1961.

BIRLEY (E.), (ed.) *The Congress of Roman Frontiers Studies 1949*, Durham, 1952.

COLLINGWOOD (R. G.), 'The British Frontier in the Age of Severus', *J.R.S.*, 1923, p. 69.

DEMAN (A.), 'L'identification des stations occidentales du Mur d'Hadrien', *Latomus*, XIII 1954, pp. 577–589.

FABRICIUS (E.), section 'limes' in *R.E.*

GEBERT (W.), 'Limes-untersuchungen zur Erklärung des Wortes und zu seiner Anwendung', *B.J.*, CXIX, 1910, pp. 200–205.

HAMMOND (N.), 'The Limes Tripolitanus. A Roman Road in North Africa', *J.B.A.A.*, XXX, 1967, pp. 1–18.

PASSERINI (A.), section 'limes' in *Dizionario epigrafico De Ruggiero*, IV, 1957, col. 1074–1280.

VON PETRIKOWITZ (H.), SCHLEIERMACHER (W.), *Limes-Forschungen*, Studien zur Organisation der röm. Reichsgrenze am Rhein und Donau, Berlin, 1959.

PIGANIOL (A.), 'La notion de limes', 5th International Congress on the Limes, Yugosl. Acad. Arch. Proceedings, III, Zagreb, pp. 119–122.

POIDEBARD (A.), *La Trace de Rome dans le désert de Syrie, du limes de Trajan à la conquête arabe*, Paris, 1934.

POIDEBARD (A.), and MOUTERDE (R.), *Le Limes de Chalcis*, Paris, 1945.

Quintus Congressus internationalis limitis romani studiosorum, Zagreb, 1963.

Roman Frontier Studies 1969, Cardiff, 1974.

SCHLEIERMACHER (W.), *Der römische Limes in Deutschland*, Berlin, 1959.

Studien zu den Militärgrenzen Roms, Vorträge des 6. internation. Limeskongresses in Sud-deutschland, *B.J.*

Beih. XIX, Köln, 1967.

Vorträge des III intern. Limeskongresses, Bâle, 1959.

Vehicles, travellers and road-users. Economic problems.

ANDRÉ (J.), 'Introduction à l'étude des relations commerciales des Vénètes d'Armorique avec le centre de la Gaule romaine', *R.A.C.*, 1962, pp. 58–63.

ARMAND-CALLIAT (L.), 'La ferrure à clous et ses origines', *M.S.H.A.C.*, XXXIII, 1952, p. 14.

ARMAND-CALLIAT (L.), 'Foires et fêtes rurales du Chalonnais, survivances probables de l'Antiquité', *Annales de Bourgogne*, XXXIII, 1961, p. 160.

AUBERT (X.), 'Évolution des hipposandales', *Revue des Musées*, 1929.

BERCHEM (D. van), 'L'annone militaire dans l'Empire romain au IIIe siècle', *Mém. S.N.A.F.*, 8th, X, 1937, pp. 117–201.

BOULNOIS (L.), *La Route de la soie*, Paris, 1963.

CALDERINI (A.), 'Viaggi e avventure di viaggio dei tempi di Orazio', *Le Vie d'Italia*, July, 1935, pp. 498–508.

CHARLESWORTH (M.), *Trade-Routes and Commerce of the Roman Empire*, 2nd edit. 1926; trans. P. GRIMAL, *Les routes et le trafic commercial dans l'Empire romain*, Paris, 1938.

COARELLI (F.), 'Su alcuni vetri dipinti scoperti nella Germania indipendente e sul commercio alessandrino in Occidente nei primi secoli dell'impero', *Arch. Class.*, Ist. Univ. Rome, 1963, pp. 61–85.

COROT (H.), 'Essai de classification typologique et de statistique des hipposandales', *Pro Nervia*, 4, 1928.

Dictionnaire des Antiquités, fig. 5123.

ESPÉRANDIEU, LANTIER (R.), *Recueil des bas-reliefs*, cf. index.

FILLIOZAT (J.), 'Les échanges de l'Inde et de l'Empire romain aux premiers siècles de l'ère chrétienne', *R.H.*, 201, 1949, pp. 1–29.

FRIEDLÄNDER (I.), *Darstellungen aus der Sittengesch. Roms in der Zeit von Augustus bis zum Ausgang der Antonine*, 10th edit., Leipzig, 1922, I, p. 318.

Gallia: horse-shoe: V, 1947, 2, pp. 441–442; XII, 1954, 2, p. 523; XIV, 1956, 2, pp. 212, 215; XVIII, 1960, 2, p. 246.

hipposandal: VII, 1949, 1, p. 137; VIII, 1950, pp. 165, 178; X, 1952, pp. 28–30; XII, 1954, 2, p. 514; XVI, 1958, 2, p. 278; XVII, 1959, 2, p. 355.

GARELLI (P.), CASSIN (E.), GERNET (J.), DETIENNE (M.), 'Recherches comparatives sur le problème du char', *Problèmes de la guerre en Grèce*, Paris, 1968 (pp. 289–318).

GONZENBACH (V. von), 'Die Verbreitung der gestempelten Ziegel der im I. Jahrh. n. Chr. in Vindonissa liegenden röm. Truppe', *B.J.*, 163, 1963, pp. 76–100.

GORCE (D.), *Les Voyages, l'hospitalité et le port des lettres dans le monde chrétien des IVe et Ve siècles*,

Paris, 1925.

GRAND (R.), in B.S.A.F., 1940, p. 246 (on the origins of modern vehicle-harness).

HABEREY (W.), 'Gravierte Glaßschale und sogenannte Mithrassymbole aus einem spätrömischen Grabe von Rodenkirchen bei Köln', *B.J.*, 149, 1949, pp. 94–104 (a bronze waggon with four wheels on parallel axles and drawn by two oxen).

HUGONIOT (E.), 'Hipposandale de Jarrioles . . .', *Mém. Union Soc. sav. Bourges*, IX, 1961–1962, p. 13.

JULLIAN (C.), 'Voyageurs de Gaule', in *Histoire de la Gaule*, V, 1920, pp. 148–151.

KIRSTEN (E.), 'Viaggiatori e vie in epoca greca e romana', *Atti II Convegno Magna Grecia*, 1962, pp. 137–158.

LAFAURIE (J.), 'Les routes commerciales indiquées par les trésors et trouvailles monétaires mérovingiens', in *Moneta e scambi nell'alto medioevo*, Spoleto, 1961, pp. 231–278.

LEFEBVRE DES NOËTTES (Cdt), *L'Attelage, le cheval de selle à travers les âges. Contribution à l'histoire de l'esclavage*, Paris, 1931 (cf. *B.S.A.F.*, 1924, pp. 85–90, 253–261).

LEJEUNE (M.), 'Chars et roues à Cnossos. Structure d'un inventaire', *Minos*, IX, 1968, pp. 9–61.

MERTENS (J.), 'Nouvelles sculptures romaines d'Arlon', *Mélanges W. Peremans*, 1968, pp. 147–160.

MÓCSY (A.), 'Latrones Dardaniae', *A. Ant. Hung.*, XVI, 1968, pp. 351–354.

MUSSANO (G.), *Il turismo nell'antica Roma*, Rome, 1933.

PERLER (O.), MAIER (J. L.), *Les Voyages de saint Augustin*, Paris, 1969.

POLGE (H.), 'L'amélioration de l'attelage a-t-elle réellement fait reculer le servage?', *J.S.*, 1967, pp. 5–42.

POLGE (H.), 'Perspectives sur la paléohistoire de l'attelage en Eurasie', *Actes 92ᵉ Congrès nat. Soc. sav.*, Strasbourg, 1967 (70), p. 183.

REINACH (A. J.), 'Les Gaulois en Égypte', *R.E.A.*, 1911, p. 33.

REINACH (A. J.), 'Voyageurs et pèlerins dans l'Égypte gréco-romaine', *B.S.A.A.*, 13, 1910, pp. 111–150.

SALAMA (P.), 'Considérations sur les transports routiers romains, en particulier dans la province d'Afrique', *Actes 79ᵉ Congrès nat. Soc. sav.*, 1954 (57), p. 291.

SCHWARZ (J.), 'L'Empire romain, l'Egypte et le commerce oriental', *Annales*, 1960, 1, pp. 18–44.

SKEEL (C. A. J.), *Travel in the First Century after Christ*, Cambridge, 1901.

TUDOR (D.), 'Interfecti a latronibus', *Ac. Rep. Pop. Rom. Stud. Cerch. Ist. veche*, 1953, pp. 583–595.

VIGNERON (P.), *Le Cheval dans l'Antiquité gréco-romaine*, Nancy, 1968.

WILL (E.), 'Marchands et chefs de caravanes à Palmyre', *Syria*, 1957, pp. 262–277.

The 'Cursus Publicus'. The Imperial Post.

BECKER (H. J.), *Röm. Verkehrsstraßen und cursus publicus*, Saarbrücken, 1933.

BELLINO (S.), 'Cursus publicus', in De Ruggiero, *Dizionario epigrafico*, II, 2, Spoleto, 1910.

BONCHAUD, *Recherches historiques sur la police des Romains concernant les grands chemins, les rues et les marchés*, Paris, 1800.

CARY (M.), 'Direction Posts on Roman Roads', *C.R.*, L, 1936, p. 166.

CIPROTTI (P.), 'Contributo allo studio della disciplina della circolazione stradale nell'antichità: Roma e Pompei', *Rivista Giuridica d. circolazione e dei Trasporti*, 15, 1961, 3.

DEGRASSI (A.), *I.L.L.R.P.*, I², 1965, 454, n. 3 on the *tabellarii*.

DESJARDINS (E.), *Les Tabellarii, courriers, porteurs de dépêches chez les Romains*, Bibl., *E.P.H.E.*, fasc. 35, 1878, pp. 51–81.

DIESNER (H. J.), 'Zum vandalischen Post und Verkehrswesen', *Philologus*, CXII, 1968, pp. 252–287.

DOMASZEWSKI (von), 'Die Beneficiarposten und die römische Straßennetze', *Westdeutsche Zeitschrift*, XIV, 99, XXI, 1902, pp. 158–211.

FUSTIER (P.), 'Un poste de la police des routes à Lay (Loire)?', *R.A.E.*, 1950, p. 175.

GORCE (D.), *Les Voyages, l'hospitalité et le port des lettres dans le monde chrétien des IVᵉ et Vᵉ siècles*, Paris, 1925.

HOLMBERG (E. J.), *Zur Geschichte des Cursus publicus*, Diss. Uppsala, 1933.

HUDEMANN (E. E.), *Geschichte des Postwesens zur röm. Kaiserzeit*, Berlin, 2nd ed., 1878 = *Storia del servizio postale romano durante l'epoca imperiale* in *Biblioteca di storia economica* V. Pareti, VI, Milan, 1929, p. 437.

HUMBERT (G.), section 'Cursus publicus' in *Dictionnaire des Antiquités*, I, 2, p. 1645.

KORNEMANN (E.), section *Postwesen* in *R.E.*, XXII, 1, 1953, p. 988.

LABROUSSE (M.), 'Les burgarii', *M.E.F.R.*, LVI, 1939, pp. 151–167.

LECLERCQ (M.), 'Poste publique et privée', in *Dict. archéol. et chrét.*, XIV, 1948, 2, p. 1631.

NAUDET (J.), 'De l'administration des postes chez les Romains', *Mém. de l'Inst. impérial de Fr.*, Acad. des Inscr. et B.L., Paris, XIII, 1858, 2, pp. 166–240.

OHLENROTH (L.), 'Römische Burgi an der Straße Augsburg-Kempten-Bregenz', *B.R.G.K.*, XXIX, 1939, pp. 122–156. Cf. *Bayerische Vorgeschichtsblätter*, XVII, 1948, pp. 36–44.

OOTEGHEM (J. van), 'Le service postal à Rome', *L.E.C.*, XXVII, 1959, pp. 187–197.

PEKÁRY (Th.), *Untersuchungen zu den römischen Reichsstraßen*, Bonn, 1968.

PFLAUM (H. G.), 'Essai sur le "cursus publicus" sous le Haut-Empire romain', *M.A.I.*, XIV, 1940, pp. 189–240.

PFLAUM (H. G.), 'La monnaie de Trèves à l'époque des empereurs gallo-romains', *Congrès intern. de numism.*, Paris, 1953 (57), pp. 273–280 (the 'cursus' of a prefect of vehicles).

RAMILLI (G.), 'Un iscrizione veronese sul "cursus publicus"', *Archivio veneto*, LXXXVIII, 1969, 5.

RAMSAY (A. M.), 'A Roman Postal Service under the Republic', *J.R.S.*, X, 1920, pp. 79–86.

RAMSAY (A. M.), 'The Speed of the Roman Imperial Post', *ibid.*, XV, 1925.

R.E., sections: 'agentes in rebus', 'beneficiarius', 'cursus publicus', 'fiscus', 'frumentarius', 'manceps', 'Nachrichtenwesen', 'Postwesen', 'tabellarii'.

RIEPL (W.), *Das Nachrichtenwesen des Altertums mit besonderer Rücksicht auf die Römer*, Leipzig, 1913.

ROSTOVTZEFF (M.), 'Ein Speculator auf der Reise', *R.M.*, XVI, 1926.

SCHMIDT (W.), 'Die röm. Poststation in Noreia', *J.O.E.A.I.*, XXVII, 1932, 2, pp. 194–222.

SEECK (O.), 'Cursus publicus', *R.E.*, IV, 1901, p. 1846.

ZAWADZKI (T.), 'Sur une inscription de Phrygie relative au "cursus publicus"', *R.E.A.*, LXII, 1960, 1–2, pp. 80–94.

Road-stages. Roads and human settlement

ANDRÉ (J.), 'Densité et répartition de la population en Vénétie romaine', *Annales de Bretagne*, LXVII, 1960, pp. 103–106 (population-growth along Roman roads).

ARMAND-CALLIAT (L.), 'Foires et fêtes rurales dans le Chalonnais, survivances probables de l'antiquité', *Annales de Bourgogne*, XXXIII, 1961, 3, p. 160.

ARNAUD (R.), CANDIE (E.), 'Des voies romaines de la ville de Mèze et du site de Frontiana', *Atti Ier Congr. intern. Studi Liguri*, Bordighera, 1952, p. 218.

AUDIN (A.), 'Le problème de Ludna', *Bull. hist. et archéol. de Lyon*, 1931, pp. 41–50.

AUDY (J.), and RIQUET (R.), 'La basilique cémétériale de Montferrand (Aude). Contribution à l'étude du peuplement des grandes invasions en Gaule', *C.R.A.I.*, April–Dec. 1961 (62), pp. 185–204, 8 ill.

BERCHEM (D. van), 'Le développement des voies de communication et son influence sur l'habitat', *Actes du Colloque international 'Les sources de la civilisation européenne'*, Bucarest, 1970, p. 135.

BOYER (R.), 'Le problème de la *mutatio* d'Anteae', *P.H.*, IV, 1954, 15, pp. 3–10.

BOYER (R.), FÉVRIER (P. A.), 'Stations routières romaines de Provence', *R.S.L.*, XXV, 1959, pp. 162–185.

CHAMPIGNEULLE (A.), 'Le problème de Ségora', Cholet, 1962, *Annales de Bretagne*, LXX, 1963, I, pp. 69–92 (*cf. Actes 87e Congrès nat. Soc. sav.*, Poitiers, 1962, pp. 121–147.

CRANE (T.), 'Caveat viator. Roman country inns', *C.B.*, XLVI, 1969, pp. 6–7.

CRAVAYAT (P.), 'Une station frontière des Bituriges', *Mém. Union Soc. sav. Bourges*, 1957 (*cf.* 1958).

DAIN (Ph.), 'L'*oppidum* de Chênehutte-les-Tuffeaux représente-t-il Robrica?', *Actes 93e Congrès nat. Soc. sav.*, Tours, 1968 (Paris, 1970), pp. 281–293.

DUPUICH (J.-J.), 'Martigny-les-Bains, ville d'eau de la cité des Leuques', *Latomus*, XXVII, 1968, pp. 635–649.

DURVIN (P.), 'Les fouilles de Litanobriga', *B.S.A.F.*, 1959, p. 92.

FABRICIUS (E.), section 'mansio' in *R.E.*

FAVRET (P.), 'La station gallo-romaine de Bibe, en Champagne', *B.S.A.F.*, 1935, pp. 96–101.

FAVRET (P.), 'Riobe', *B.C.T.H.*, 1936–1937, pp. 461–464.

FAVRET (P.), 'Hypothèses sur l'identification des stations des voies romaines de Reims à Verdun et de Reims à Toul', *ibid.*, 1936–1937, pp. 465–474.

FLEISCHER (R.) and WEBER (E.), 'Immurium, Moosham', *J.O.A.E.I.*, XLVII, 1964–1965, Beibl. pp. 105–208 (a Julio-Claudian *mansio* that survived until the third century).

FOGLIATO (D.), 'La "mansio" al Ponte di Romagnano sul Sesia', *Soc. Piemontese di Archeol. e B.A., A. e M.*, III Convegno di Varallo Sesia, 1960, pp. 235–242.

FOUET (G.), 'La villa d'Es Cabiros à Larroque et la voie romaine de Montmaurin à Saint-Bertrand-de-Comminges', *Pallas, Annales . . .* Toulouse, XV, Oct. 1968, pp. 127–136 (a villa visible from a busy road).

FUSTIER (P.), 'Un poste de la "police des routes" à Lay', *R.A.E.*, I, 1950, pp. 175–180.

GERSTER (W.), 'Beitrag zur Gesch. einiger Bezeichnungen für Gasthaus . . .', *Vox Romanica*, IX, 1946–1947, p. 57.

GIRRI (G.), *La Taberna nel quadro urbanistico e sociale di Ostia*, Rome, 1956.

GODET (J.), 'Des fouilles à Warelles', *Annales du Cercle archéologique d'Enghien*, XI, 1958 (59): a small station on the Roman road from Bavai towards the North, with a cemetery of the second century.

GRAFF (Y.), 'L'établissement romain des Bons Villers (Liberchies)', *C. Arch.*, II–III, 1959: a station on the Bavai-Tongres-Cologne road, soon a military site, perhaps a frontier post.

GUIGUE, *Les Voies antiques . . . déterminées par les hôpitaux du Moyen Age*, Lyon, 1877.

GUITER (R.), 'La station Combusta de la voie Domitienne', *Société agricole, scientifique et littéraire des Pyrénées orientales*, LXVIII, 1953, pp. 29–37.

HATT (J.-J.), 'Tres Tabernae (Saverne)', *Gallia*, 1950 (51), p. 166, *cf.* 1953, I, p. 153.

HATT (J.-J.), 'Une station romaine près du col de Saverne', *R.A.E.*, II, 1951, p. 121.

HATT (J.-J.), 'La station romaine de Mackwiller', *Revue d'Alsace*, 1955, pp. 158–162.

JANNORAY (J.), 'Fabrègues (Hérault)', information in *Gallia*, XI, 1953, I, pp. 99–100, possibly a *mansio* on the *via Domitia*.

KAHRSTEDT (U.), *Kulturgeschichte der röm. Kaiserzeit*, Berne, 2nd edit. 1958, p. 132: road-settlements.

KLEBERG (T.), *Hôtels, restaurants et cabarets dans l'antiquité romaine. Études historiques et philologiques*, Uppsala, 1957.

KLEBERG (T.), 'Röm. Wirtshäuser und Weinstuben', *Das Altertum*, Bd. 15, 1969, Heft 3, p. 146.

KUBITSCHEK (W.), section 'mansio', in *R.E.*, XIV, 1930, pp. 1231–1251.

LEBEL (P.), 'La station routière de Bibe', *R.A.E.*, IV, 1953, p. 264.

LEBEL (P.), 'Andesina et Solimariaca, stations routières gallo-romaines', *ibid.*, VI, 1955, pp. 379–392.

MARILIER (J.-M.), 'Chemins, finages et habitat de plaine, origine et évolution', *Mém. Comm. Antiq. dép. Côte-d'Or*, XXII, 2, 1942–1946 (51), pp. 275–284.

MATHERAT (M.), 'La "mutatio" (relais de poste) de Rousseloy (Oise)', *B.S.A.F.*, 1936, pp. 169–175.

MATHERAT (M.), 'Le problème topographique de Litanobriga', *M.A.I.*, XIV, 1951, 2, pp. 1–16.

MATTY DE LA TOUR, 'La voie romaine de Caesarodunum à Juliomagus et l'emplacement de la station Robrica', *B.M.*, 1874, pp. 742–767; 1875, pp. 205–224.

MERTENS (J.), 'Le "vicus" d'Amay', *F.A.*, XIV, no. 5382 (controlled the crossing over the river Meuse made by the Roman highway from Arlon to Tongres. This was a well constructed road, built in the later second century and remetalled several times); *ibid.*, 5423, Blicquy ('vicus' where the road from Bavai forks to go towards the North Sea and towards Ghent).

MERTENS (J.), Le Relais romain de Chameleux, Brussels, 1968.

NIMAL (P.), 'Remarques sur les origines antiques de Bapaume', *Revue du Nord*, 187, Oct.–Dec. 1965, p. 635 (relationship to Roman roads).

OURSEL (P.), 'La station romaine d'Ad Silanum (route de Lyon à Rodez). Essai de localisation', *Revue du Gévaudan*, N.S., no. 7, a. 61, pp. 39–48.

PERROUD (M.), 'La station romaine de Labiscone-Lépin), *Mém. et Doc. Soc. savois. d'Hist.*, LXXIII, 1938.

PÉTREQUIN (P.), ODOUZE (J.-L.), 'Habitat romain à Moulin-Rouge, commune de Lavans-lès-Dôle (Jura)', *R.A.E.*, XIX, 1968, pp. 255–266.

PICK (K.), SCHMID (W.), 'Frühgeschicht. Befestigungsanlangen im Bereiche der Isonzofront', *Jahreshefte des österreich. arch. Instituts*, XXI–XXII, Beiblatt. col. pp. 277–308 (mutatio ad Pirum).

REICHART (J.), in *Sammelblatt des. hist. Vereins Ingolstadt*, 1950, pp. 39–49 (relationship of Roman roads and villas).

ROBLIN (M.), 'Influence de la route antique sur l'habitat', *Annuaire, E.P.H.E.*, 4th cent., 1970, p. 311.

ROUCHON (M. U.), 'La station gallo-romaine des Souils (Haute-Loire)', *B.C.T.H.*, 1932–1933, pp. 621–623.

ROUCHON (M. U.), 'Découvertes archéologiques en Haute-Loire', *ibid.*, 1957 (59), p. 147 (*Sanssae*, a station on the Agrippa road).

SICARD (O.), 'Recherches sur la station romaine de Calcaria-la-Chapelle-Saint-Hermès, à Marignane', *P.H.*, XVIII, 1968, pp. 248–252.

SOUTOU (A.), 'Les vestiges gallo-romains d'Arzens et le tracé de la voie d'Aquitaine entre Bram et Carcassonne', *Cahiers ligures de préhistoire et d'archéologie*, 1963, p. 150 (the 'mutatio' at Cedros).

STIEBER (A.), 'La station romaine de Kuttolsheim', *C.A.A.H.*, 130, 1949, pp. 253–256.

STIEBER (A.), 'Stations romaines à Kalhausen', *Annuaire de la Soc. d'Hist. et d'Archéol. de la Lorraine*, 1967–1968, pp. 33–37.

THÉDENAT, in particular 'horrea', in the *Dictionnaire des Antiquités*.

THÉVENOT (E.), 'La station routière de Fines le long de la route romaine de l'Oisans et les limites du pays des Ucenni', *R.E.A.*, 1941, p. 234.

THÉVENOT (E.), 'La station antique des Bolards à Nuits-Saint-Georges, Côte-d'Or', *Gallia*, VI-II, 1948, pp. 289–316.

VETTERS (H.), 'Magdalensburg', *J.O.E.A.I.*, XLVII, 1964–1965, p. 28; XLVIII, 1966–1967, p. 20: a forum for Roman traders, alongside the road.

WIEDENHOFF (J.-P.), 'La station romaine de l'Usspann au col de Saverne', *B.S.H.A.S.*, I, 1952, pp. 3–4, 16–17 (*cf.* J.-J. HATT, *C.A.A.H.*, 1954, pp. 35–51).

WOLFF (Ph.), 'L'hôtellerie, auxiliaire de la route. Notes sur les hôtelleries toulousaines au Moyen Age', *B.C.T.H.*, I, 1960 (61), p. 189.

WUILLEUMIER (P.), 'De Lyon à Mâcon', *B.A.L.A.*, 1938, pp. 13–14 (the problem of Ludna).

See *D.A.* (Dictionnaire des Antiquités), section 'mulomedicus'.

See the section 'mansio' in the index of *Gallia*:

Pluviers, II, 1944, p. 243.

Pouillé-Thésée, 1963, p. 416.

Rieutor, X, 1, 1953, p. 99.

Soulosse, 1959, p. 361.

Tarrare, XII, 2, 1954, p. 413.

Uspann, XIII, 1950, p. 166.

For the station on the Little St Bernard, *cf.* *N.S.A.*, 1924, pp. 385–392.

Public Finance, Law, Administration, Customs

BERCHEM (D. van), 'L'annone militaire dans l'Empire romain au IIIe siècle', *Mém. S.N.A.F.*, 1936, p. 117.

CAGNAT (R.), *Étude historique sur les impôts indirects chez les Romains*, Paris, 1882.

CAGNAT (R.), 'L'annone d'Afrique', *M.A.I.*, XL, 1915, p. 247.

CAGNAT (R.), 'L. Antistius Rusticus, légat de Cappadoce', *C.R.A.I.*, 1925, p. 227 (concerning a 'curator viarum').

DARMON (J.-P.), 'Notes sur le tarif de Zarai', *C.T.*, XLVII–XLVIII, 3rd–4th quarter 1964, pp. 7–23.

DE LAET (S. J.), *Portorium, étude sur l'organisation douanière chez les Romains, surtout à l'époque du Haut-Empire*, Bruges, 1949.

GRIFFE (E.), 'La Narbonnaise occidentale au temps du préteur Fonteius', *A.M.*, 69, 1957, pp. 59–64 (identification of toll-posts).

HATT (J.-J.), 'Nouvelles fouilles . . . à Strasbourg . . . Découverte d'un poste de douane ou de péage', *C.A.A.H.*, CXXXII, 1952 (53), pp. 63–82.

PFLAUM (H. G.), *Essai sur les procurateurs équestres sous le Haut-Empire romain*, Paris, 1950.

PFLAUM (H. G.), *Les Carrières procuratoriennes équestres sous le Haut-Empire romain*, Paris, 1960–1961, 4 vol.

PIGANIOL (A.), 'Observations sur le tarif de Palmyre', *R.H.*, CXCV, 1945, pp. 10–23.

SAUMAGNE (Ch.), 'Iter populo debetur', *R. Ph.*, LIV, 1928, p. 320.

SAUMAGNE (Ch.), 'Un tarif fiscal au IVᵉ siècle de notre ère d'après des fragments épigraphiques découverts à Carthage', *Karthago*, I, 1950, p. 109.

Land-routes and waterways

ANDRÉ (J.), 'Voies terrestres et fluviales entre l'Armorique et le Centre de la Gaule romaine', *R.A.C.*, I, 1961, p. 58.

ARMAND-CALLIAT (L.), 'La batellerie de la Saône dans un passé proche et lointain', *Arts et trad. popul.*, VIII, 1960, pp. 22–46.

BENOIT (F.), 'La voie rhodanienne et le problème des courants d'influence dans le Midi de la Gaule', *Cahiers rhodaniens*, XI, 1964, p. 55.

CHEVALLIER (R.), 'Problèmes de topographie historique posés par l'étude d'un bassin fluvial dans l'Antiquité', *Actes Congrès nat. Soc. sav. Rennes*, 1966 (68), pp. 71–98.

CHEVALLIER (R.), 'Navigations et ports antiques. Esquisse d'une problématique', *Atti del Convegno intern. di Studi sulle Antichità di Classe*, Ravenna, 1967 (68), pp. 219–247.

DEMOUGEOT (E.), 'L'inscription de Lattes (Hérault)', *R.E.A.*, LXVIII, 1966, 1–2, pp. 86–100 (on the subject of *utricularii*).

DUFOURNET (P.), 'Organisation du territoire dans l'Antiquité . . . Liaisons voies d'eau – voies de terre dans le bassin de Seyssel . . .', *Actes 91ᵉ Congrès des Soc. sav.*, Rennes, 1966 (Paris, 1968), p. 99.

DUPRAT (E.), 'A propos de l'Itinéraire maritime: Citharista=La Ciotat', *Mém. Inst. hist. de Provence*, 1932.

FREZOULS-FASCIATO (M.), 'Note sur Vérone, Brescia et la batellerie du lac de Garde aux trois premiers siècles de notre ère', *Hommages à A. Grenier*, II, Brussels, 1962, pp. 689–706.

GAGÉ (J.), 'Gadès, l'Inde et les navigations atlantiques dans l'Antiquité', *R.H.*, 205, 1951, pp. 189–216.

LE GALL (J.), *Le Tibre, fleuve de Rome dans l'Antiquité*, Paris, 1953.

LÉVÊQUE (P.), 'La date du Périple de la mer Erythrée', *R.E.G.*, LXXVI, 1963, pp. 428–429.

LÉVÊQUE (P.), 'Nouvelles constatations sur le Périple de la mer Erythrée', *ibid.*, LXXIX, 1966, pp. 730–732.

LUGAND (R.), 'Note sur l'itinéraire maritime de Rome à Arles', *M.E.F.R.*, XLIII, 1926, pp. 124–139.

PALMER (J. A. B.), 'Periplus Maris Erythraei. The Indian Evidence as to the date', *C.Q.*, 1947, pp. 137–140 (the Periplus of the Red Sea).

ROUGÉ (J.), 'Utricularii', *C.H.*, IV, 1959, pp. 285–306.

ROUGÉ (J.), *Recherches sur l'organisation du commerce maritime en Méditerranée sous l'Empire romain*, Paris, S.E.V.P.E.N., 1966.

SCHOFF (W. H.), *The Periplus of the Erythraean Sea*, travel and trade in the Indian Ocean by a merchant of the first century, New York–London, 1912.

UGGERI (G.), 'Sull'Itinerarium per Maritima loca da Agrigento a Siracusa', *A. e R.*, XV, 1970, 2–3, pp. 107–117.

Travel by Christians in Antiquity and the Middle Ages

ARENAS (F.), ARANA (H.), *Les Chemins de Saint-Jacques*, Barcelona, Paris, 1968.

BAUTIER (R. H.), 'Recherches sur les routes de l'Europe médiévale. De Paris et des foires de Champagne à la Méditerranée par le Massif Central', *Bull. philol. et hist. du C.T.H.*, 1960 (61), pp. 99–143.

BÉRAUD SUDREAU (J.), 'Le culte de saint Jacques de Compostelle et la recherche des chemins suivis par les pèlerins', *Actes 93ᵉ Congrès nat. Soc. sav.*, Tours, 1968, Paris, 1970, pp. 509–518.

BLIN (L.), 'Le grand chemin de Paris à Lyon par la vallée de la Loire, au bas Moyen Age', *Bull. philol. et hist. du C.T.H.*, 1958 (59), pp. 237–266.

BURG (A. M.), 'Le christianisme dans l'Est de la Gaule: ses voies de pénétration en Alsace', *Trois provinces de l'Est*, Pub. Soc. sav. d'Alsace, Strasbourg, 1957, pp. 193–203.

CUOZZO (E.), 'Riflessioni in margine all'itinerario di Roberto il Guiscardo nella spedizione contro Salerno del 1076', *R.S.I.*, LXXXI, 4, 1969, p. 706.

DONNET (A.), *Saint Bernard et les origines de l'hospice du Mont-Joux (Grand-Saint-Bernard)*, Geneva, 1942.

DUPARC (P.), 'Un péage savoyard sur la route du Mont-Cenis aux XIIIᵉ et XIVᵉ siècles: Montmélian', *Bull. philol. et hist. du C.T.H.*, I, 1960 (61), p. 145.

FOURNIAL (E.), 'La route de Paris à Lyon et l'importance commerciale de Charlieu au bas Moyen Age', *Bull. de la Diana*, XXIX, 1944, pp. 210–243.

GANSHOF (F. L.), *Le Moyen Age*, Paris, Hachette, 1953.

GRAS (P.), 'Un itinéraire bourguignon au Vᵉ siècle', *Annales de Bourgogne*, XXVI, 1954, p. 185.

GUIGUE, *Les Voies antiques . . . déterminées par les hôpitaux du Moyen Age*, Lyon, 1877.

HUBERT (J.), 'Les grandes voies de circulation à l'intérieur de la Gaule mérovingienne d'après l'archéologie', *Actes VIᵉ Congrès intern. d'études byzant.*, II, Paris, 1948, p. 183.

HUBERT (J.), 'Méthode pour reconstituer les voies de la Gaule au VIIᵉ siècle ap. J.-C. d'après les cartes de répartition des découvertes archéologiques', *B.S.A.F.*, 1948–1949 (52), pp. 169–170.

HUBERT (J.), 'Les grandes voies de circulation à l'intérieur de la Gaule mérovingienne d'après l'archéologie', *Actes VIᵉ Congrès intern. d'études byzant.*, II, Paris, 1952, pp. 183–190.

HUBERT (J.), 'Les routes du Moyen Age', in *Les Routes de France*, Paris, Association pour la diffusion de la pensée française, 1959, p. 54.

IMBERDIS (Fr.), 'Les routes médiévales coincident-elles avec les voies romaines?', *Bull. philol. et hist.*, 1960, pp. 93–98 (*cf. Annales*, I, 1939, p. 410).

IRIGOIN (P.), 'Origines des Montjoies oratoires', *Découvertes*, XVIII, July 1970, p. 19.

LA COSTE-MESSELIÈRE (R. de), 'Chemins médiévaux en Poitou', *Bull. philol. et hist. du C.T.H.*, 1960 (61), pp. 207–223.

LAFAURIE (J.), 'Les routes commerciales indiquées par les trésors et trouvailles monétaires mérovingiens', in *Moneta e scambi nell'alto medioevo*, Spoleto, 1961, pp. 231–278.

LAMBERT (E.), 'Ordres et confréries dans l'histoire du pèlerinage de Compostelle', *A.M.*, Jan.–April 1943, pp. 217–218.

LAMBERT (E.), 'Le livre de Saint-Jacques et les routes du pèlerinage de Compostelle', *Revue géog. des Pyrénées et du S.-O.*, XIV, 1943, 1, pp. 1–33.

LAMBERT (E.), 'Les relations entre la France et l'Espagne par les routes des Pyrénées occidentales au Moyen Age', *Mélanges D. Faucher*, Toulouse, 1948, pp. 319–328.

LAMBERT (E.), 'Le monastère de Roncevaux, la légende de Roland et le pèlerinage de Compostelle', *Mél. Soc. toulous. d'études classiques*, 2, 1948.

LAMBERT (E.), 'Le pèlerinage de Saint-Jacques de Compostelle', *Études d'histoire médiévale*, Paris, 1959.

LANTIER (R.), 'Une translation de reliques sur un bas-relief de Vienne (Isère)', *C.R.A.I.*, 1955, p. 146.

LATOUCHE (R.), *Les Origines de l'économie occidentale*, Paris, Albin Michel, 1956.

LEMAN (M.), 'Le passage de la voirie antique à la voirie médiévale: exemple de Beauvais', *Actes Congrès nat. Soc. sav.*, Reims, 1970.

LOUIS (R.), 'Sanctuaires primitifs et récits hagiographiques. A propos des fouilles de Saint-Maurice-en-Valais (Suisse)', *R.A.E.*, V, 1954 (55), pp. 380–387.

PESCI (B.), 'L'itinerario romano di Sigerico, arcivescovo di Canterbury', *R.A.C.*, XIII, 1936, pp. 43–60.

RENOUARD (Y.), 'Les voies de communication entre pays de la Méditerranée et pays de l'Atlantique au Moyen Age', *Mélanges Halphen*, Paris, 1951, p. 587.

RENOUARD (Y.), 'Le pèlerinage à Saint-Jacques de Compostelle', *R.H.*, 1951–1952, p. 254.

RICAU (O.), 'Pour débroussailler les chemins de Saint-Jacques', *Actes 94ᵉ Congrès nat. Soc. sav.*, Pau, 1969 (Paris, 1971), pp. 367–374.

RICHARD (J.), 'Passages de la Saône aux XIIᵉ et XIIIᵉ siècles', *Annales de Bourgogne*, 1950, p. 245.

ROBLIN (M.), 'Le culte de saint Martin dans la région de Senlis. Contribution à l'histoire du peuplement dans la "civitas" des Silvanectes', *J.S.*, 1965, pp. 943–963.

ROUSSEL (P.), *Les Pèlerinages à travers les siècles*, Paris, Payot, 1954.

SAENENS (F.), 'Le patronage de saint Martin et les voies de pénétration dans l'arrondissement de Lille', *Bull. Soc. d'études prov. de Cambrai*, XXXIX, 1942, pp. 125–140.

VIELLIARD (J.), *Le Guide du pèlerin de Saint-Jacques de Compostelle*, Mâcon, 2nd ed., 1950.

WOLFF (Ph.), 'L'hôtellerie, auxiliaire de la route. Notes sur les hôtelleries toulousaines au Moyen Age', *Bull. philol. et hist. du C. T.H.*, 1960 (61), p. 189.

ZUNDEL (A.), *Les Routes en Alsace à la fin du Moyen Age*, thesis at the École des Chartes, 1960.

Roads in recent times

BLANCHARD (M.), *Bibliographie critique de l'histoire des routes des Alpes occidentales à l'époque napoléonienne, 1796–1815*, Grenoble, 1920.

BOISSONNADE (P.), 'Les voies de communication sous le règne de Henri IV et l'œuvre du gouvernement royal', *Revue Henri IV*, 1909.

BONNEROT (J.), *Les Routes de France*, Paris, P. Laurens, 1921.

BONNEROT (J.), 'Esquisse de la vie des routes au XVIᵉ siècle. État des routes et leur entretien avant les Valois, le sel et les chemins sauniers', *Rev. des Questions hist.*, CXV, 1931, pp. 5–88.

BONNEROT (J.), *La Guide des chemins de France de 1553 par Ch. Estienne*, Paris, H. Champion, 1936 (Bibl. E.P.H.E., fasc. 265).

CHOMEL (V.), EBERSOLT (J.), *Cinq Siècles de circulation internationale . . . Un péage jurassien du XIIᵉ au XVIIIᵉ siècle*, Paris, 1951.

EECKMAN (A.), 'Un voyage en Flandre, Artois et Picardie en 1714 publié d'après le manuscrit du sieur Nomis', *Annales du Comité flamand de France*, XXII, 1895, pp. 337–572.

ESTIENNE (Ch.), *La Guide des chemins de France*, 1553. *Cf.* J. BONNEROT.

EXPILLY (J.-J.), *Le Géographe manuel*, 'containing the description of all the countries in the world . . . their capital cities, with their distances from Paris and the roads leading there by land as well as by sea', Paris, 1757, 2nd edit. 1771.

FORDHAM (H. G.), 'Catalogue des guides routiers et des itinéraires français, 1552–1850', *Bull. de Géo. hist. et descriptive*, XXXIX, 1919, pp. 213–256.

FORDHAM (H. G.), 'La cartographie des routes de France', *ibid.*, XL, 1925, pp. 69–86.

FORDHAM (H. G.), *Les Guides-routiers. Itinéraires et cartes routières de l'Europe. 1500–1850*, 1926.

FORDHAM (H. G.), *Les Routes de France*. A bibliographical study of the road-maps, -itineraries and -guides of France, followed by a catalogue of road-itineraries and -guides, 1552–1850, Paris, 1929.

GAUTIER (H.), *Traité de la construction des chemins*, 1693.

HAMY (E. T.), *Recueil de voyages et de documents pour servir à l'histoire de la géographie depuis le XIIIᵉ siècle jusqu'à la fin du XVIᵉ siècle*, Paris, 1908.

IMBERDIS (F.), 'La route de Paris au Languedoc à travers l'Auvergne', *Bull. Assoc. Géo. fr.*, no. 35, July 1929, pp. 69–71.

IMBERDIS (F.), 'Comment on écrit l'histoire. De La Fontaine aux voies romaines', *Bull. hist et sc. de l'Auvergne*, LXIV, 1944, p. 287.

IMBERDIS (F.), *Le Réseau routier de l'Auvergne au XVIIIᵉ siècle*, Paris, P.U.F., 1967.

KARL (M.), 'Un itinéraire de la France et de l'Italie imprimé á la fin du XVᵉ siècle', *Revue des langues romanes*, LI, Vol. I, fourth century, 1908, p. 551.

LECREULX, *Mémoire sur la construction des chemins publics et les moyens de les exécuter*, 1782.

LEGRAND (L.), 'Itinéraire de Wissant à Lyon', *B.E.Ch.*, XLVII, 1886, p. 197.

MILLIN, *Voyage dans les départements du Midi de la France*, 1807.

NOLIN (J.-B.), *France*, avec les grandes routes et l'indication des bureaux de messageries, Paris, 1761.

PAGEAULT (F.), 'Les routes dans la généralité de Bourges au XVIIIᵉ siècle', *École des Chartes, Position des thèses*, 1942, pp. 95–105.

PIÉTRESSON DE SAINT-AUBIN (P.), 'Le Mémoire sur les grands chemins militaires partant de Bavai par Dom Ch. J. BEVY, historiographe de France, 1781', *Revue du Nord*, XXXVIII, 1956, pp. 257–271.

PIGANIOL DE LA FORCE (J.-A.), *Nouveau voyage de France*, with an itinerary and special maps, Paris, 1724.

POUJOL (Ch.), *Ébauche d'histoire régionale de la Poste aux Lettres*, 'Département de l'Oise', Méru, 1954.

ROSSI (G. M. de), *Sulla distrazione delle vie romane nei dintorni di Roma durante il secolo XIX*, *Strenna dei Romanisti*, Rome, 1974, pp. 172–191.

VAILLÉ (E.), 'Les maîtres de poste et les routes postales sous l'Ancien Régime', *Bull. d'inf.*, June 1937, p. 39.

VAILLÉ (E.), *Histoire générale des postes françaises*, Paris, P.U.F., 1947.

VIGNON (E. J. M.), *Études historiques sur l'administration des voies publiques en France aux XVIIᵉ et XVIIIᵉ siècles*, Paris, 1862–1880 (*Cf. id., Notions sommaires sur les voies publiques de la France et leur administration antérieurement au XVIIᵉ siècle*).

With these aims in mind, use can be made of:

—general schedules issued by the postal services,

—early surveyors' manuals, *cf.* DANFRIE, *Déclaration de l'usage du graphomètre*, Paris, 1597.

—depositions made by stewards and land-agents,

—statistical evidence for the various departments,

—all tales told by early travellers; references will be found in:

—d'ANCONA's edition of the *Journal de Voyage de Montaigne*,

—the *Catalogue* of the Fossati-Bellani collection (Ambrosienne, Milan),

—L. SCHUDT, *Italienreisen im 17 und 18 Jahrh.*, Vienna, 1959,

—the catalogue of the TURSI collection (Marciana, Venice),

—the card-indexes at the Hertziana Library (Rome) and at the German Institute of the History of Art (Florence),

—the *Bibliographie universelle des voyages* (Boucher de la Richarderie, 1808).

Abbreviations

A.A.	Arch Anz Berlin	A.C.	Arch. Classica
A.A.A.M.	Ass. Amis Arch Mosellans	A. Ert	Arch Estisito Hung
A.A.H.	Acton Ant Hung	A.E.A.	Archivo Esp Arg.
A. Arch	Acta Arch Copenhagen	A. et R.	Atena e Roma
A.B.S.A.	Annok Brit School Athens	A.F.L.A.	Ann Fac Lettres Aix
A.C.	l'Antig Class	A.G.I.	Arch Glott Italia

A.I.V.	Atti del Ist Veneto	L.E.C.	Les Etudes Class
A.J.A.	Amer. Jour. Arch.		
A.M.	Ann du Midi	M.A.I.	Metra Div Sar Aeml Ins
Ant. J.	Antig Journal	M.C.A.C.	Mem Comm Arch. Cote d'Or
A.N.	Aguileice Nostra	M.E.F.R.	Mel L'Ecolé Fr de Rome
Arch. J.	Arch Journal	M.H.	Mus. Helveticum
A.S.P.	Arch Stor Pugliese	M.I.O.E.G.	MiH Inst Ost Ges Wien
A.S.C.L.	Archir Storico Calabrio	M.S.H.A.C.	Mem Soc Hist de Chalon
A.S.	Anatolian Studies	M.Z.	Mainzer Zeits
A.S.S.O.	Arcl Stor Sciclia Or		
		N.A.A.	Not of Arch Armoricaine
B.A.A.	Bull. Arch Algerem	N.S.J.F.S.	North Staffs Journal Fld Study
B.A.C., N.S.	Bull. Arch. Com Trav Hist		
B.A.L.	Bull. des Antig Luxembourg	P.A.Ph.S	Proc Amer. Phil Soc
B.C.T.H.	Bull. Com Trav Hist	P.B.S.R.	Proc Brit Sch at Rome
B.C.A.R.	Bull. Comm Arch Com Roma	P.P.	Parola del Passato
B.C.H.	Bull. Corr Hell	P.H.	Provence Hist
B.E. Ch.	Bib L'Ecule des Chartes		
B.I.A.O.	Bull. I'Inst Arch Orientale	R.A.	Rev. Arch
B.J.	Bonner Jahr	R.A.A.M.	Rendi Aocael. Aretu Nap
B.M.	Bull. Monumental	R.A.C.	Rev. Arch Centre
B.N., N.S.	Bull Soc Arch Touraine	R.A.E.	Rev. Arch d L'Estestl
B.S.H.A.C.	Bull. Arch Com Trav Hist	R.A.N.	Rev.
B.S.A.O.	Bull. Soc des Ant Ouest	R.B.Ph.	Rev. Belge Phil
B.S.A.A.	Bull. Soc. Arch D'Alex	R.Bi.	Rev. Biblique
		R.E.A.	Rev. Etude Arch
C.A.A.H.	Cah. Alsaciens Arch Hist	R.G.K.	Rom Germ Komm
C.B.	Class. Bull.	R.G.L.	Rev. Geo. Lyon
C.C.A.R.	Corsi Cult Art Ravennate	R.H.	Rev. Hist
C.N.R.S.	Centre Nat. Research Scient	R.I.L.	Rend Ist Lomberdo
C.P.H.	Class Phil. Chicago	R.I.O.V.	Rev. Int. d'Onomastique
C.R.	Class Rev	R.M.	Rheinioch Mus
C.R.A.I.	C.R. Acad des Incript	R.P.A.A.	Rendi Pont Acc Arch.
C.T.	Cahier de Tunisia	R.S.L.	Riv Studi Liguri
C.T.H.	Com Trav. Hist.	R.S.I.	Riv Storica Ital Naples
D.A.	Derembrig and Selaglio	S.B.A.W.	Sitz Bayer Aks Wiss
		S.E.	Studi Etruschi
E.P.H.E.	Ecole Prat Houte Etudes	S.I.F.C.	Studi Ital di Fil. Class
		S.N.A.F.	Soc Nat Ant France
F.A.	Fastc Arch	S.P.	La Suisse Primitive
F.R.	Felix Ravenna	S.S.	Studi Sardi
I.E.J.	Israel Expl Jour	T.C.F.	Tourist Club France
I.H.	L'Inf Hist	T.Z.	Titer Zeits
I.L.N.	Illustrated London News		
		V.D.I.	Vestnik Dreung Istora Moscow
J.D.A.I.	Jahr Deubch Arch Inst	Vet. Chr	Vetera Christ
J.O.E.A.I.	Jahr Ost Arch Inst Wien		
J.R.S.	Jour Roman Soc.	Z. Ant	Ziva Antika
J.S.	Journal des Savants	Z Pal V	Zats Deutschen Palesting Ver

Geographical Index

General Index

Ancient authors and selected sources

Medieval and modern authors